Prospects for the 70's

English Departments
and
Multidisciplinary Study

Edited by

Harry Finestone
and
Michael F. Shugrue

New York

The Modern Language Association of America

1973

Contents

Introduction

SINCE 1962 the Association of Departments of English has sponsored workshops, seminars, and publications on major issues in the field of English. The essays, reports, and resolutions which follow (all originally printed in either the *ADE Bulletin* or *PMLA*) document the Association's intensive recent effort to examine the hypothesis that participation in the development of inter- or multidisciplinary studies could enhance and regenerate the teaching and learning of language and literature.

With modest support from the United States Office of Education during 1971–72, ADE sponsored sixteen regional and national seminars to investigate ways in which the traditional field of English might participate in the design, conduct, and evaluation of interdisciplinary courses and programs.

The first major seminar, held at Northwestern University in November 1971 with the joint sponsorship of the Curriculum Center in English and the Center for the Teaching Professions, invited graduate students, classroom teachers, English department chairpersons, and specialists in a dozen other fields to discuss expanded definitions of literacy needed to develop courses and programs for students whose backgrounds, abilities, and interests testify to the cultural and linguistic pluralism of American society.

The seminar sponsored by the University of South Florida in February 1972 examined administrative problems faced by departments establishing interdisciplinary courses and attempted to define the kinds of interrelationships that exist between English and such other fields as the social sciences and the rapidly developing world of leisure studies.

At the City College of New York in April 1972, participants addressed themselves particularly to urban education and to minority education. The seminar was predicated on the assumption that graduate education in the usual research-trained, Ph.D.-producing sense must be expanded to include other alternatives—in part on the assumption that societal needs require a reordering of priorities and a reallocation of resources to improve teaching at every level.

The final national seminar, jointly sponsored by California State University, San Francisco, in June 1972, developed model undergraduate and graduate interdisciplinary programs; demonstrated through exemplifications how interdisciplinary approaches to a text can enrich classroom situations; and attempted to provide a rationale for interdisciplinary studies that would stimulate scholarly research, justify administrative support for innovative programs, and lead to the establishment of nontraditional courses and programs for undergraduate and graduate students alike.

In all, more than five hundred chairpersons of departments, representatives of professional associations, and leaders in English and related disciplines engaged in the discussions. The present collection suggests the sources for the interest in interdisciplinary studies, major issues debated during the seminars, and points of agreement.

The interest and involvement of English departments in such programs arises for many reasons. The most ominous, perhaps, is voiced by Alan Hollingsworth of Michigan State University: "We must become interdisciplinary first of all for the reason of self-preservation. The social sciences, especially sociology and behavioral psychology, are writing the humanities out of the future of education. For fifteen or twenty years, sociology has been assuming a role something like the role of literary culture in [Matthew] Arnold's time."

Barry Marks of American University sounds a more positive note: "English faculties have come increasingly to recognize—and what is more important, to acknowledge openly—that they are interested, deeply interested, in matters which are ordinarily thought to be the special preserve of other academic departments. As professional students of literature we speak on the one hand about love and the social order, alienation and identity, and the presence or absence of God from the natural world, while we hide behind such self-protective labels as 'American Literature to the Civil War.' On the other hand, we have with massive false humility failed to explore and develop the knowledge which imaginative writers have to contribute both to our academic colleagues in the social sciences, the natural sciences, and the other arts, and to society at large."

Indeed, in his moving Presidential address to the Modern Language Association in 1970, Maynard Mack of Yale University had urged the profession to "reach out to the schools"; "to the disadvantaged, whether black, brown, yellow, or white"; "to the general community of educated men and women"; "to the media"; "to each other"; "to new arrangements of literary study"; and "to wider significances than those we have been in the habit of attempting."

Henry Winthrop, Professor of Interdisciplinary Social Sciences at the University of South Florida, offers another compelling reason for the participation of departments of English in interdisciplinary work: "If we wish to be realistic, we should recognize that most of our contemporary issues are, in fact, interdisciplinary. They are interdisciplinary in the sense that the findings, methods, and occasionally the values . . . of several of our traditional academic disciplines have a significant, though partial, contribution to make toward the understanding and resolution of these same issues."

Interest in interdisciplinary work also comes about because of changes in student interests and needs; demands from non-majors that their educational needs, as well as those of majors, be met; and criticisms of the heavily vocational or professional training given by most English departments. As

John H. Fisher, former Executive Secretary of MLA, observes, "Our students are much more ready for interdisciplinary work than most of us. They do not see the difficulties, only the imaginative sweep."

Interest is sparked, too, by the expansion and fragmentation of knowledge and by the importance to contemporary society of cultural pluralism, not only native but international; and of media pluralism, including especially film, radio, television, and theater.

Speakers and participants in the ADE seminars readily agreed, however, that interdisciplinary study cannot be seen as a panacea for the ills besetting many English departments. They recognized the dangers of dilettantism, faddishness, and change for its own sake. And they acknowledged the intellectual and administrative problems involved in making a commitment to interdisciplinary work. Professor Marks warned, "If we are going to be interdisciplinary, I don't think we should merely play at it. We should subject ourselves to the highest standards of both or all of the disciplines in which we propose to work."

Noting that an interdisciplinary program is not "antidisciplinary or nondisciplinary," Daniel Bernd, Dean of Cultural Studies at Governors State University in Illinois, reminds us that the aim of interdisciplinary study is not to produce generalists with "Leonardesque aspirations." Such work does not solve "the teaching versus research problem, although it inevitably demands enormous attention to teaching. Moreover, it cannot be a program "with an unequal relationship among disciplines; that is, where one or several disciplines are instrumental to another's purposes." Any interdisciplinary course or program depends upon the identity and integrity of individual disciplines brought together under the rubric of a problem or issue that allows of and, indeed, requires a multiple-discipline approach. Each discipline contributes its special insights to a problem or topic while acting at the same time as a validity check and guide to other disciplines.

For Professor Marks, "the only really sound basis for interdisciplinary studies" is to be found in men and women "seriously formulating questions and seeking answers which cannot be dealt with satisfactorily within the confines of a single field, and who therefore need contact with colleagues and students from other fields as well as their own."

The papers that follow attempt to provide a rationale for the involvement of English departments in interdisciplinary work. They discuss frankly the difficulties surrounding the introduction of interdisciplinary courses and programs that make special demands on the time and energy of individual faculty members and on limited departmental resources. They outline model programs that have been established, and they suggest administrative strategies for experimenting with interdisciplinary study.

The collection argues for a careful review of existing English programs, for discussion of the potential and limitations of interdisciplinary work, and for careful experimentation with nontraditional approaches to the teaching and learning of language and literature. If the collection stimulates debate in departments and among faculty members, it will have served the profession well.

We should like to thank the California State University, Northridge, and the University Foundation; Wallace Douglas and the Curriculum Center in English at Northwestern University; Theodore Gross and the Department of English at the City College of New York; Parker Ladd and the Association of American Publishers; John Margolis and the Department of English at Northwestern University; Claude Mathis and the Center for the Teaching Professions at Northwestern University; James Parrish and the Department of English at the University of South Florida; Caroline Shrodes and the Department of English at the California State University, San Francisco; and Donald Tuttle and the United States Office of Education.

For their hard work in making the regional seminars successful, we owe a special debt of gratitude to Nell Almquist, Jeanne Coulter, Olive Piper, Elizabeth Roath, and Edith Smith.

HARRY FINESTONE
MICHAEL F. SHUGRUE

Public Hostility to the Academy: What Can Chairmen of Departments of English Do?*

John C. Gerber

University of Iowa

IT IS the misfortune of those of us now in higher education to have at least three threats to our well-being converging upon us simultaneously. Any one of them can disrupt our work; the three together can destroy our professional life as we have known and enjoyed it.

The first of these threats is the public hostility toward us created by the new life style of our students. Though fewer confrontations with police and administrations have occurred this fall, fewer windows been broken and buildings burned, in the minds of most adult Americans the campus hippie continues as a threat to their moral and social stability. They bitterly resent what to them is our unwillingness or inability to put down campus disorders and enforce traditional patterns of decorum. As they see the situation, instead of endowing their wholesome, well-scrubbed, and loving sons and daughters with practical wisdom, we turn them into impractical, profane, long-haired, pot-smoking, drug-using semi-strangers who look as though they have just rolled out of a sleeping bag—and probably have. It is no use arguing that we have not been—and indeed could not have been—responsible for so fundamental a cultural change as the one the young people in our country have undergone in the past five years. The public identifies hippie culture with the college campus, and they hold us largely responsible for it. In retaliation many of them strongly support politicians who promise to put us down.

The second threat to our well-being is the new wave of anti-intellectualism that started during the Johnson administration and that has gained great strength during the Nixon-Agnew administration. As Richard Hofstadter has pointed out, anti-intellectualism in this country is older than our national identity (*Anti-Intellectualism in American Life*, p. 6). Although it surfaces only periodically, it is always latent in the suspicion and distrust of those who pretend to be creative, critical, or contemplative. Now that it is surfacing again, the academy, as usual, is its special target. This time,

* An address to the ADE meeting at MMLA in Detroit, 6 Nov. 1971. Reprinted from *ADE Bulletin*, No. 32 (Feb. 1972), pp. 17–21.

however, there is unusual virulence in the attack, because we seem better off than previously, more powerful, and hence more of a threat to the majority of citizens. Those of us in the humanities must bear the brunt of this attack. For although the academy as a whole is a target for anti-intellectuals, they make a gross kind of distinction between those who, in Max Weber's words, live *off* ideas rather than *for* ideas. They seldom criticize professors of, say, agronomy, accounting, dentistry, and medicine, whose efforts seem to them to result in practical public benefit, but there is no such toleration for the efforts of those of us in the humanities. Our ideas seem much too impractical and often much too subversive. As one of our Iowa state senators engagingly put it recently, "We need more Ph.D.'s in history like we need a hole in the head." If state legislatures ever insist on examining and approving line budgets, we are the ones most likely to suffer.

The third threat, of course, is the current economic recession. Were this a period of prosperity, the public might be more understanding about campus unrest and not so resentful of faculty intellectuals. So long as pay envelopes are full and regular, other threats can be borne with some equanimity. But in a recession such as the one we are now experiencing, otherwise tolerable threats to public stability become intolerable. Hurt by inflation and unemployment, and shaken by the growing disrespect for law and order, the average man wants to get even. Since, like Ahab, he can't strike at the system itself, he settles for harpooning a symbol in the system toward which he already bears a grudge. In this instance, we, seemingly well paid, secure, aloof—and possibly dangerous—become the average man's Moby Dick. Politicians, as you well know, vie with one another to cast the most telling harpoons; papers play up our weaknesses and play down our accomplishments; ministers of the fundamentalist variety accuse us of being atheists and communists; and legislatures not only reduce appropriations but hint at direct control of our budgets and even of our curricula. For those of us in higher education, then, the times are truly out of joint.

Within such an unhappy context, let us look at some of the specific points of difference between the public and ourselves.

Our system of academic tenure is certainly one such point. We believe academic tenure to be essential if we are to teach and write conscientiously and honestly. The public, however, looks upon it as a shield for self-indulgence. No other group, they contend, enjoys such extraordinary immunity from accountability. The farmer, the independent businessman, or the professional person, if he slacks off, suffers an immediate loss of income. The industrialist is responsible to his board of directors and stockholders, the white-collar worker to his boss, the blue-collar worker to his foreman and union, and the politician to the electorate. But we, so the story goes, because of academic tenure, are accountable to no one but ourselves.

We believe, of course, that we are an extraordinarily industrious lot. The public, however, convinced that we work only when we are in the classroom, thinks we are idlers. They catch us frequently in our homes between eight and five on weekdays. (Recall for yourself the look you got from a carpenter or meter-reader who caught you in your house at eleven o'clock in the morning.) They contemplate with indignation the fact that our Christmas, spring, and summer vacations add up to four months, and that some of us receive time off with pay to visit libraries or even go abroad. They look upon our research, at least research in the humanities, not as work but as some arcane and impractical pastime. Of what possible use to society, they ask, is an article on Traherne's prosody, a book on John Donne's conceits (whatever they may be), or a costly new edition of *The Scarlet Letter* that results in only thirty minuscule changes in the text?

Generally speaking, we see ourselves as vigorous, alert, and competent. The public sees us as dreamy, absent-minded characters who would be lost in class without our dog-eared and yellowed notes. In other fields, they argue, an incompetent gets fired; in higher education, the longer he lives the higher his pay, the lighter his load, and the fewer his students.

We believe that we are useful and responsible citizens. Our bitterest critics see us using academic tenure as a cloak for nothing less than subversion. They are quick to note that academic freedom to a great extent rests upon the tenure system. And since they view academic freedom as freedom to advocate the overthrow of the establishment, they can conclude that the tenure system is little less than a threat to the republic. To the far rightists, it is in the same category with communism, fluoridation, the United Nations, and the memory of Eleanor Roosevelt.

We in English hold that our main function is to teach literature; the public, including in this instance some of our colleagues in other departments, believes that our main function is to teach writing, by which they mean correct spelling and prescriptive grammar. Recall what a stranger says to you immediately when you are introduced as a professor of English. It is not, "Oh, I wish I had had a chance to take more Victorian literature." It is invariably, "Oh, I'll have to watch my grammar," or "I've always had trouble with spelling," or "I never did learn how to write," or even "My course in freshman composition was the most useful course I ever had in college." What we consider to be our main function, in short, is to many others a frivolous activity, and what we increasingly neglect is what others think to be our real and maybe our total excuse for being. Even the editor of one of our own English journals recently wrote, "Our profession came from society's need for people who can write and speak. Literary study is a parasite, merely an adjunct to the necessary study of rhetoric."

When we *do* indulge in the teaching of grammar, the public thinks us even more captious and irresponsible. Whereas they accept the results of scientific study in other fields without question, they become enraged when we apply the scientific process to the study of language. They want no nonsense about relativity in grammatical usage. They are paying us, they contend, to defend usages that are right in an absolute sense, and *that* is what they want their sons and daughters taught. I was once told that I was a disgrace as an English professor because I admitted that I don't find the locution "it's me" offensive. In short, if we were fully and directly accountable to the general public, you and I would be teaching freshman composition.

In talking thus briefly about the broad forces that converge upon us and certain specific points of difference between the public and ourselves, I hope that I have conveyed the impression that the present situation is serious—more serious even than the one some of us lived through in the 1930's. Then only money was scarce, not confidence in higher education. Now both money and confidence are in low supply.

Given this situation, then, what should chairmen of departments of English do to improve these vital relations with the general public?

One answer, of course, is to do nothing. With varying intensity we all share the belief that we are successfully playing crucial roles in the human drama and that if the public doesn't think so, so much the worse for the public. It is tempting, therefore, to argue that the present situation is not really serious, that the public has no real grounds for its criticism, that higher education has weathered other storms and has always come through stronger than ever. Or, if we admit that some small action is indicated, it is tempting to load the whole business on the shoulders of the administration. After all, they're the ones paid to worry over these big public issues. We're too busy with catalog copy, schedules, budgets, work-study forms, our classes, and a hundred other things that fill our days from morning to night. Besides—and this is the most seductive thought of all—most of us aren't going to be chairmen much longer. Let our replacements worry about what the public thinks of us.

As I say, it is tempting to do nothing. But such a response, as we all really know, would be nothing but a cop-out. It is the response, to paraphrase Emerson, of a department chairman, not of Man as department chairman. It is responding to the lure of the woods though we manifestly have miles to go before we sleep. The public may have only limited grounds for its criticism of us, but its criticisms have an emotional validity that we can ill afford to neglect. It is perfectly clear to anyone except the complete dreamer that the academic life we have known and enjoyed is going to change profoundly unless we can justify its existence more effectively than we are currently doing.

Many of those who do recognize that the academy is in deep trouble recommend that we organize as soon as possible and let a professors' union assume responsibility for our relations with the public. Already, according to Myron Liebermann in the October 1971 *Harper's*, 50,000, or six percent, of the country's 836,000 college and university faculty members are employed under terms of a union contract. Collective bargaining is on the rise, especially in state and municipal institutions in New York, Pennsylvania, California, and Hawaii. And now that the National Labor Relations Board has affirmed that faculty members at private universities are "entitled to all the benefits of collective bargaining they so desire," we may expect to see the movement spread to private schools too. Should the economic recession continue for any length of time, more than half of the faculties represented by persons in this room are likely to be unionized by 1980.

Unionization may well take care of some of our problems with the public. Those who argue for it maintain that a union contract will provide protection against political interference, and provide the pressure necessary for higher education to obtain its fair share in the competition for public and private funds—as has been dramatized by the spectacular rise in salaries in the branches of the City University of New York after those faculties were organized. Proponents of unionization argue, also, that education will improve because unions will make us all more accountable for what we do. To bargain successfully with management, faculties through their unions will have to be able to prove their effectiveness in carrying out their assignments, particularly their teaching assignments.

But however successful a union may be in representing us in the process of collective bargaining on economic matters, it cannot possibly represent us on intellectual matters and should not be expected to do so. Whether we unionize or not, we English teachers are the only persons who can adequately set forth our deep concern with esthetic and moral values, with matters generally of the mind and spirit. And we shall have to do it with great skill—greater skill, obviously, than we have mustered heretofore. Wayne Booth put it most succinctly in conversation after his Thursday night talk: "We have to sell ourselves without selling out."

Maybe we have been so fearful of selling out to our critics that we have failed to make legitimate attempts to win them over. Be this as it may, we seem almost to *invite* criticism. Our statements of purpose are vague and misleading, and the premises on which we base our operations, many of them, are questionable.

Let me try to document these assertions briefly. For a study of our objectives I have gone to the material published in a variety of college and university catalogs. These, presumably, are the official public descriptions of our work and not the ideals or exhortations of a few individuals.

Many departments of English make *no* statement of objectives. Such omissions may be due, of course, to restrictions imposed by registrars. If so, the rulings of these registrars should be fiercely opposed, because the lack of published aims suggests aimlessness and lays a department open to uninformed criticism.

Many of the statements of objectives that *do* appear in our catalogs are pieties that offer no indication of what is really being done and no usable criteria for assessing the department's work. Let me cite a few examples: "To provide a solid liberal education," "to cultivate mental and physical poise," "to give emphasis to traditional values," "to inculcate humane values," "to instill Christian values through writing and the study of literature," "to provide a mastery of great literary works written in English," "to provide a thorough foundation for graduate work in English." None of us, I'm sure, objects to these splendid purposes, but they are hopes rather than realizable aims. One chairman cheerfully admitted to me that his statement of objectives is window-dressing. "We can't possibly tell," he admitted, "whether we're making our students more humane."

What is just as disturbing about these printed objectives, especially at the undergraduate level, is that they seem to bear so little relation to the courses offered. Despite the wide diversity in objectives, the courses listed in our catalogs seem remarkably similar. It is quite possible, needless to say, that courses with the same titles may be taught quite differently in two schools, but it does seem that an investigation would disclose *some* significant difference between the undergraduate courses of a department that promises a thorough foundation for graduate study and those of a department that promises a broad humanistic education. There are other curiosities too. A department that makes a big to-do in its statement of objectives about training students to write clearly offers one advanced course in writing. A department that promises its students extensive training in critical reading lists courses that are almost all historically oriented. A department that promises its students broad familiarity with the literature written in our language offers only one or two courses a semester in American literature. A department that promises a broad acquaintance with Western literature offers nothing above the sophomore level in any literature other than English and American. And departments that promise an understanding of our culture through literature offer nothing in Afro-American literature— though most are now trying to rectify this omission.

The best that can be said for our catalog copy is that it is poor public-relations material. But I fear the basic trouble is not with our composition but with our failure to ask ourselves seriously what we're about. During the past ten years, like some of you, I have occasionally been asked to evaluate the work of departments of English other than my own. The most awkward moments on these visits occur when we talk about goals. On a few occasions it is good talk: it deals with the needs of their particular students, the needs of the special regions, the needs of society as a whole. But with most staffs the talk turns on the old clichés. Occasionally someone becomes belligerent and makes it clear that I am impertinent for asking about objectives. One person told me that I was being paid to *provide* objectives. Another said I had been around long enough to *know* what the objectives of English departments are. And a third in a small liberal-arts college started on a long list of aims headed by good spelling. Only once in these visits have I encountered a staff that had seriously attempted to identify its specific and realizable aims.

At the risk of sounding a bit like a behaviorist, I would suggest that our most pressing obligation at the moment is to redefine our goals in reasonably precise terms; that these goals be realizable ones that can be used as criteria for measuring the success or failure of our programs; and that they clearly relate to the needs of students and of society, as well as reflecting our own deepest convictions. What I have in mind is a series of what might be called intermediate goals—not vague pieties on the one hand or the excessively narrow goals of the behaviorists on the other. For example, a department, it seems to me, contributes more to the general understanding and common good when it asserts that one of its purposes is to train the student to read a literary work in a variety of ways—as form, autobiography, myth, psychology, metaphysics, and so on—than it does when it claims to turn out liberally educated men and women. The latter might properly be termed a "hope" or an "ultimate objective," but it illuminates no one when listed as an immediate goal.

As I have already indicated, we need, too, to assess the premises upon which the activities of our departments are based. I am speaking here of our *real* premises, the ones which are implied in our operations.

> 1. *Premise*: That English majors need no formal practice in writing after the freshman course and that graduate students need none at all. Few departments offer more than one or two courses in advanced composition and creative writing. What evidence do we have that directed practice is unnecessary to perfect the art of writing, though it is necessary for all other arts? Or that those who will teach writing need no instruction in it?

2. *Premise*: That only belletristic works are appropriate for study in our classes. Thus most professors of English have their students study Addison and Steele but not Locke or Hume; Fanny Burney but not Darwin or Huxley. What evidence do we have that we are best serving our students by defining literature so narrowly?

3. *Premise*: That coverage is an indispensable principle in organizing courses and degree programs. We feature surveys of periods, of genres, and, God help us, of English literature from the eighth century to this morning. We expect undergraduate majors to have had courses in all periods in English and American literature, and Ph.D. candidates to have a working knowledge of all periods and genres, as well as concentrations in two or three. What evidence do we have that coverage creates dedicated and discerning readers or even critics and scholars?

4. *Premise*: That students learn most and enjoy literature best by moving from large contexts to small ones. We recommend the large surveys to sophomores; period and genre surveys to upperclassmen and beginning graduate students; and the highly focused seminars to the advanced graduate students. What evidence do we have that this is sound psychology rather than simply neatness? Our Director of Undergraduate Study at Iowa points out that the typical sophomore who wants to be an English major is primarily interested in ideas, issues, great names, a few great works. The big survey simply dampens his interest. In fact, I've heard it plausibly argued that only the advanced Ph.D. candidate is ready for a survey course.

5. *Premise*: That literature is best taught when divided sharply along national lines. What evidence is there for this? The fact is that Emerson, for example, was more profoundly influenced by Coleridge and Carlyle than by Franklin, Edwards, Crèvecoeur, and Bryant; and that the American naturalists owed more to the French and the Russians than to their American antecedents.

6. *Premise*: That our subject matter can best be taught by meeting students three times a week. The vast majority of undergraduate and graduate courses in English are three-credit-hour courses. What evidence do we have that this is the best way to handle our material? Common sense suggests that not all of it can be cut up into such tidy little bits, and some persons feel that students dedicate themselves more strongly to learning in six- and even twelve-hour courses.

7. *Premise*: That the best way to prepare a Ph.D. candidate to teach basic undergraduate courses is to have him specialize in one field or even one author. Evidence? The next is a corollary.

8. *Premise*: That the best way to determine whether an applicant for a position is likely to be an effective teacher of undergraduates is to ask him questions about his dissertation. Evidence?

The list of such premises could be continued almost indefinitely, especially if I included the premises undergirding our teaching of freshman composition. I hope these eight are enough, however, to indicate the need for a reassessment of our means as well as our ends.

In conclusion, let me state my major propositions:

1. That a serious division has developed between the public and us.

2. That while the public is often prejudiced and ill-informed, we are also responsible for this division.

3. That if we are to undertake to improve the situation we must first put our own houses in order.

In 1959, when the profession was on dead center, the MLA under the leadership of Geo. Winchester Stone, Jr., called a Basic Issues Conference. The result of this conference, widely publicized in our journals and at other conferences, had a unifying effect that helped us enormously during the growth years of the 1960's. We need another such shot in the arm. If this were a national convention I would suggest another national conference, maybe a Basic Obligations Conference this time.

But a large conference is not necessary if you and I begin—like next Monday—to reassess the aims of our departments and the premises on which our operations are based. No matter what we do, of course, there are segments of the public that we shall never please. But there are other segments, large and important ones, whose support we can win back if we can convince them of the high usefulness of our purposes, and if we can demonstrate the validity of our methods. We have invested our lives—you and I—in the teaching of English because we believe in it; it is inconceivable that we should not make every attempt possible in times like these to persuade the public to share this belief.

Maynard Mack

Yale University

We have met the enemy and he is us.

Pogo

Never did eye see the sun unless
it had first become sunlike.

Plotinus

I

I BEGIN this address with three quotations. The first is from the *Pampaedia* of John Comenius, written in the 1650's, though not published till modern times:

Our first wish is that all men should be educated fully to full humanity; not only one individual, nor a few, nor even many, but all men together and single, young and old, rich and poor, of high and low birth, men and women—in a word, all whose fate is to be born human beings. . . . Our second wish is that every man should be wholly educated, rightly formed not only in one single matter, or in a few, or even in many, but in all things which perfect human nature.[1]

My second quotation is from Arnold's *Culture and Anarchy*, 1869, a passage most of us are familiar with, though it is not apparent that we have been much influenced by it:

The great men of culture are those who have had a passion for diffusing, for making prevail, for carrying from one end of society to the other, the best knowledge, the best ideas of their time, who have labored to divest knowledge of all that was harsh, uncouth, difficult, abstract, professional, exclusive; to humanize it, to make it efficient outside the clique of the cultivated and learned, yet still remaining the best knowledge and thought of the time. . . .[2]

My last is from one of our contemporaries, Harold Taylor, writing just a year ago:

Liberal education in its true sense is not an education which you get over with in order to go on to an adult preoccupation with professional academic studies. It is the source of the ideas and attitudes which infuse the professional studies with their meaning for society and mankind. It turns the doctor toward the healing arts in a spirit of humanity, the lawyer toward the protection of human rights, the architect toward the beauty and function of form in creating the human environment, the teacher toward his students, and defines the uses to which knowledge should be put.[3]

° The Presidential address, a compressed version of which was delivered at the 85th Annual Meeting of the MLA in New York, 27 Dec. 1970. Reprinted from *PMLA*, 86 (1971), 363–74.

Though cavils can be raised against details in any of these statements, I cite them for a spaciousness of outlook that is appropriate, here on the threshold of the 1970's, to a company of teachers and scholars whose subject is the modern languages and literatures. A spaciousness, I think, that is appropriate also to our problems. For what is very clear in December 1970 is that we who teach the oncoming generations have arrived at some sort of watershed beyond which the familiar landmarks look different, or even begin to fade away. I am not referring when I say this to the matters that may be foremost in our minds at this instant—such matters as the flight of students in several prominent universities from literature to the social sciences, which may or may not be an omen for us all, or the continuing shrinkage of federal, state, and private funds, with everything that this implies in the way of fewer jobs, fewer fellowships, and fewer opportunities for educational innovation just when such innovation is most required. Nor do I refer, *primarily*, to the looming threat—and already sometimes the serious fact—of interference from outside the university, or to the current student mood, which, though quiet at the moment, is not, I think, serene, and simmers on in a highly unstable mix of battle fatigue, self-exploration, and what my president at Yale has lately called "monumental scorn" for things as they are.[4]

These are all concerns of importance for our future both as individuals and as a profession; but the problems that affect us most profoundly have obviously longer roots than these and are fed by a more general malaise. Part of this malaise is expressed, as we are all aware, in a fundamental questioning of authority, not, as in most former times, in the simple conviction that it is being exercised badly or by the wrong class or group, but in the anarchical conviction that the principle of authority is itself the Antichrist. "The most dangerous intellectual aspect of the contemporary scene," says a notable sociologist in a recent essay, is that a fair portion of our youth today no longer "distinguish between authority and power. They see the one as being as much a threat to liberty as the other," forgetting that "there can be no possible freedom in society apart from authority."[5] To this may be added what Charles Silberman says in his remarkable study of American education for the Carnegie Corporation, published only a few months ago and based on three and one-half years of firsthand research and observation:

The most rebellious among the young . . . do not recognize the authority of knowledge, of skill, of simple truth; to a frightening degree they do not even understand the concept. When they question the college administration's authority, say, to make parietal rules or take disciplinary action for infractions of other rules, they are challenging the legitimacy of there being any rules at all. . . . When they question the administration's or the faculty's right to make or enforce academic regulations, they frequently are denying that there are, or can be, standards of learning or of scholarship.[6]

There is food for sobering reflection here, and the reflection does not brighten appreciably when we weigh into this account Professor Martin Trow's report before the American Sociological Association of September last. He points first to what he describes as "the break-down of consensus among faculty and students about the basic nature and functions" both of their common enterprise (education) and their common home (the university). "The multiversity was," he says, speaking of that institution as if it were already in the past,

tied together by a complex set of procedures both collegial and bureaucratic which managed to effect the necessary degree of coordination of a very wide range of diverse activities and people, maintained necessary control over expenditures and personal records, while preserving for the teaching and research units a very high degree of freedom and autonomy. These procedures, while often irritating and cumbersome and slow, and faulty in other respects, nevertheless gained the acquiescence of most participants in the institution; and indeed the basic assumption was that the procedures themselves could be modified through other regular procedures.[7]

This consensus is badly eroded, Professor Trow concludes, and he goes on to suggest that it is improbable it can be speedily restored, if indeed it can ever be, drawing on the findings of a survey of "representative samples of faculty, graduate students, and undergraduates in some 300 colleges and universities across the country" carried out in the spring of 1969 for the Carnegie Commission on Higher Education. What these samples divulge is a most impressive difference in attitude between younger and older teachers, not only on issues where the difference is hardly surprising, e.g., on whether graduate students should have a "formal consultative role" in the appointment and promotion of faculty, but on issues where the difference is both surprising and, I think, disturbing.

To the proposition that "In the United States today there can be no justification for using violence to achieve political goals," two-thirds of the older academics gave strong assent, as compared with about one-third of the teachers under 30. (Among graduate students in the leading universities, the proportion . . . falls to a quarter.)

When asked whether "campus disruptions are a threat to academic freedom?" about two-thirds of the older academics expressed strong agreement as compared with only about one-third of the faculty under 30. Differences by age were about the same with respect to the statement "students who disrupt the function of a college should be expelled or suspended."

At the difficult intersection of academic norms and freedom of speech, the question was asked whether "faculty members should be free on campus to advocate violent resistance to public authority." Two-thirds to three-quarters of the older academics expressed their strong disagreement with that idea, as compared with only about a third of the college and university teachers under 30.

I shall not linger over other questions asked in the survey, for I think these three excerpts make the point. Whether controlled for status (i.e., teaching assistant or regular faculty), rank (i.e., the very young full professor), type of institution, or subject area, Professor Trow points out, "differences by age persist strongly" on all matters that concern the purposes, conduct, and governance of the educational process, rising in the social sciences to a discrepancy as wide as seventy to ninety percent of younger faculty favoring radical student activism as against thirty to forty percent of their elders.

The implications of such figures and the validity of the samplings on which they are based are, of course, always open to question, as Professor Trow willingly concedes. Even if validated, moreover, the figures are capable of several alternative explanations. It is conceivable that Time, which qualifies the spark and fire of all things, will bring in his familiar whirligig of change. It is conceivable that a wider experience of the sickening ease with which trains of circumstances, once set in motion, can proceed to destinations past all human guessing will cause some drawing back from the brink. But it is equally conceivable that the value differences between young faculty and old are here to stay, either because there has been a decisive change in the kind of young person to whom the academic life now appeals, or because the whole of the younger generation, for whatever reason, has experienced, or is experiencing in varying degrees and with varying consequences, an alienation that will not easily be overcome. Professor Trow's own cautious conclusion is by no means reassuring, the less so since it accords so well with personal observations that everyone in this room will have already made:

When we look at these and other attitudes I have not reported, we see delineated two quite different conceptions of the university associated with age. . . . On the one hand, we see a traditional view of the liberal university, committed to teaching, research, and a variety of "services" to other institutions, but with sharp limits on its permissible intervention *as an institution* into the political life of the environing society; on the other, a profound hostility to that society and a passionate belief that the university is, or ought to be, a major instrument for its reform and transformation.

I tend to believe that the differences that we are finding are not going to disappear over time, but are likely to persist and perhaps become sharper. And if they do, this would have two sets of consequences: first, it will place in positions of responsibility increasingly large numbers of academic men who are quite fundamentally opposed to the present organization and structure of the colleges and universities and to the politics of consensus by which they have been governed. Secondly, the same trend will widen the gulf between the colleges and universities and the environing society. These developments would . . . further increase the strains in the governance of our present institutions, thus further increasing the difficulties that the colleges and universities are having with those groups which furnish their resources and support. I suspect that these developments will be decisive for the future of many of these institutions.

Thus far Professor Trow. If he is even partly right, there *could* be a crisis of authority in the offing beside which all current manifestations would look pale. I cannot think this a happy prospect for either our profession or the nation.

II

Here, then, are some of the symptoms, as we all see them around us, of the general unease. What are its roots? Over the past year or so, new explanations, new theories, have been offered to us almost weekly, including—this past fall—those of the alliterative Mr. Agnew! But the one that has struck me personally as having most interest is Paul Goodman's. We are confronting, Goodman thinks, something like a geological shift in our concept of the nature of things, "a religious crisis," as he puts it, "of the magnitude of the Reformation in the fifteen hundreds."[8] He tells of a conversation he had with a young man on a campus in Massachusetts:

He was dressed like an American Indian—buckskin fringe and a headband, red paint on his face. All his life, he said, he had tried to escape the encompassing evil of our society that was trying to destroy his soul. "But if you are always escaping," I said, "how can you make a wise judgment about society or act effectively to change it." "You see, you don't dig," he cried. "It's just ideas like 'wise' and 'acting effectively' that we can't stand." He was right. He was in the religious dilemma of Faith vs. Works: Where I sat, Works had some reality; but in the reign of the Devil as he felt it, all Works are corrupted. They are part of the System: only Faith can avail.

To which Goodman wryly adds: "But he didn't have Faith either."

In times as confused as ours today, we may be grateful, I think, for even such light on our situation as a rather loose analogy like this affords. Certainly a general Reformational iconoclasm has lately been showing its head among us. Certainly, too, a Puritanism of sorts is abroad in the land, as others than Goodman have pointed out; and while its differences from the sixteenth- and seventeenth-century variety are many and crucial, some of the surface resemblances are striking. The new dispensation insists, like its predecessor, on a distinctive life style that affects dress, deportment, and speech; it shows a marked hospitality to visionary experience and a warm concern for extending the vocabulary and intimacies of family life to larger units or communes, in the vein of such seventeenth-century sects as the Family of Love; it often adheres (except in sexual matters, stereo systems, and motorcycles) to a very high standard of frugality and self-denial despite the affluence that surrounds it; it exhibits a striking inner assurance of rectitude, or what used to be called "election," so pronounced sometimes that its simultaneous claims to egalitarianism and anti-elitism become comical (as on Orwell's Animal Farm, it is a society where some are plainly more equal than others); and finally—to come to the attitude that the new dispensation in its extreme forms perhaps shares most fully with an earlier Puritanism—it sees itself as necessarily divided from the nonelect, which is to say, from the old and the more moderate young and from the secular authorities, by an impassable gulf. Once Satan is held to be ubiquitous, as by Paul Goodman's interlocutor, what solution can there be short of Armageddon?

All these resemblances, if one wished, might be built into a coherent fantasy, but I think it would be dangerous on several counts. For one thing, as I am sure Mr. Goodman would remind us were he here, the generation about which we are thus generalizing is anything but monolithic in its attitudes and practices, as we all know from our classrooms. Furthermore, as a theory of behavior the comparison with Puritanism leaves out more than it includes: Bunyan, for instance, would not have been happy at Woodstock—though it may well be that the only reasonable response to that is: so much the worse for him. It is precisely on such symbolic occasions as Woodstock that today's pressures on our traditional concepts of what is appropriate for human nature stand out dramatically. Finally, and this is the point I want to stress most, it does not become those of us who have grown old in the profession and have held its reins to root the perplexities of our present situation in causes or changes that simply exculpate ourselves. I know of no particular evidence that requires us to manufacture guilt fantasies like the Stalinist victims of the thirties—to do so would in itself be an act of hubris claiming a degree of influence we know we do not have; but conversely I see no ground on which we can or should dissociate ourselves from what has taken, is taking, and may yet take place on the academic scene, whether in the long run it evolves into a better scene or a worse. We are and must remain parts of a single continent with those we teach, and the bell that tolls so loudly in their ears has a message for us as well.

My own version of its message varies a little from Mr. Goodman's, for the analogy that leaps to mind in my case is not from history but myth and is perhaps most clearly to be glimpsed if we consider for just a moment a theme that haunted Greek poetry almost from its beginnings and afterward haunted Virgil's imagination, too. The *Aeneid*, as everybody knows, is Virgil's tale of three cities: Troy, Carthage, and Rome. The price of the founding of Rome is that Troy and Carthage must be left behind: Troy in flames, Carthage unfinished with the body of Dido its queen on her funeral pyre also in flames. "The processes of history," runs a recent brilliant essay on this Virgilian situation, "are presented as inevitable, as indeed they are, but the value of what they achieve is cast into doubt. Virgil continually insists on the public glory of the Roman achievement, the establishment of peace and order and civilization. . . . But he insists equally on the terrible price. . . . More than blood, sweat, and tears, something more precious is continually being lost by the necessary process; human freedom, love, personal loyalty, all the qualities which the heroes of Homer represent, are lost in the service of what is grand, monumental, and impersonal."

The *Aeneid* enforces the . . . paradox that all the wonders of the most powerful institution the world has ever known are not necessarily of greater importance than the emptiness of human suffering.[9]

Do we not see here as in a mirror a clear image of some of our own national tensions and dilemmas?

The image becomes yet more striking if we look directly at those heroes of Homer just cited, particularly as the Greek playwrights viewed and reviewed them in the years of the Peloponnesian wars, years like our own when the ceremony of innocence, in Yeats's phrase, was indeed drowned, and Athens, which had once saved all Greece, was beset by doubts within and a Spartan enemy without. Again and again in these plays one theme stands out, the cost of the Greek achievement; and this is so most luminously of all in the *Iphigeneia at Aulis* of Euripides. Iphigeneia, Agamemnon's own daughter, comes rejoicing to what she supposes to be her wedding to Achilles, but suffers instead the altar and the knife as the sacrifice that Artemis insists on before the Greek fleet can sail for Troy. Let me quote again from an exceptionally fine essay on the play:

The Greeks are caught in the trap formed by two inescapable forces [i.e., on the one hand, Artemis, who feels that the Greeks have deprived her of something and demands compensation, and, on the other, Aphrodite, whose symbol is Helen, the cause of the war]. . . . Since "Helen" is "over there," in the East, there is no way by which the Greeks can see that the problem lies closer home, within themselves. It appears as something coming from without, a necessity imposed upon them (none of the male characters . . . questions the presupposition that the war is justified) and so when the excessive concentration on the one side [Helen] arouses a compensating demand from the other [Artemis], the resulting conflict is felt as a battle of opposing absolutes, in which the individual is crushed. "Individual" perhaps begs the question; it is fairer to say, "something represented by Iphigeneia is crushed." It has happened before, in other Greek dramas—*Alcestis, Antigone, Hecuba,* to name only a few; a young girl has gone through the travesty of a marriage in which the true bridegroom is Death. . . . The question raised is always, How shall Greece be regenerated after this price has been paid? Are the values on which Greece has prided itself for generations and which have made Greece what she is, setting her apart as a culture and a consciousness from the older dominant power of Persia, worth the price they have extracted from the Greek spirit?[10]

I do not believe it is altogether fanciful to see here in the Greek situation at least a shadowing of our own. Greece was undergoing at the time an agonizing reconsideration and reinterpretation of her central myths of concern, to borrow Northrop Frye's useful phrase; and is not something similar happening to us? Our myth for a very long time has been made up in considerable part of an accommodating worldly Puritanism expressing itself in energy, tenacity, resourcefulness, generosity, and moral force, together with a vision of salvation that calls on others who want to be saved to be like us. With this myth we broke a continent—broke it all too well, we realize today, and problems now arise around us that, almost for the first time in our history, certainly for the first time in the popular consciousness, require tragic choices. Beauty and what we have always called "progress," we begin to see, are beyond a certain point incompatibles. So, it may be, are prosperity and a tolerable purity of air and water. So likewise, it begins to seem, are power and compassion: we who have put a man on the moon cannot or will not open up our ghettos, pay the price in pride and probably in affluence that it takes to be rid of an offensive war. This is not because we are a nation of villains, but because in tragic life, where, as Meredith pointed out long ago, "no villain need be," our passions *do* spin the plot. And it is just here, it seems to me, that our Puritan energy crosses the other part of our national myth, which has always been a belief in our radical innocence. We have thought of ourselves, and in certain times and places we have been thought of by many outside our borders, as the New Covenant, the American Adam, the melting pot of gold at the end of the western rainbow, the one far-off divine event to which creation moved. We have been Henry James's ingenues encountering Old World corruption, the fresh young Lochinvars with know-how who rode to the rescue of an ailing Europe, the nation of organizational and mechanical genius where every small-town kid could take his jalopy apart Saturday and put it back together on Sunday—and where, alas, in 1970, it is a rare piece of good luck to find a competent garageman, let alone a well-run railroad.

The intent of these remarks is not to belittle what we are. I do not belong to the scoffers at our best achievements. Beside the debit and credit sheet of the other great nations of this or any other age ours can hold its own, and its best entries are glowing. But is that not precisely the source of our malaise? Our central myths of concern, including our sense of who we are and what we thought was our mission in the world, are caving in. We mean well, at least we believe we mean well, yet we do evil. We possess unprecedented wealth, yet our own poor are always with us, to say nothing of the poor of the world. We aspire to the American Dream, but what we have got is the American Way, a society where the things that are not for sale grow fewer every year. Are not these the disquieting facts that all thoughtful Americans are brooding on today, and the young perhaps more keenly than any? Even in our unconscious minds I suspect these grinding readjustments may be taking place, dislocating in a profound way that necessary systole and diastole, that simultaneous growth of identification with the group and individualization apart from it and against it, which psychologists tell us is the norm of wholesome personality development. It is as though—to choose a different and in my view more searching metaphor—the play we are acting in on the stage of the world, which we had supposed to be a melodrama complete with hissable villain and happy rewards for the brave and the free as they exit to strains of "From the Halls of Montezuma," had turned by some nightmare into a tragedy where we struggle with forces beyond our control and are consumed by our very virtues.

III

I have so far, I hope, been pointing to a state of mind, a state of affairs, that is recognizable by us all, however badly I may have described it. The crucial question remains: what response as teachers and scholars are we to make to it? And here of course I can give only one man's view.

The first and easiest response is retreat. This is a response we have seen some of our students and former students making—Goodman's noble savage in the red paint is only an especially dramatic case—and it has of course a long and honorable tradition behind it, stretching back even to the *first* Academy. "One who has joined this small company," says Socrates in a famous passage of the *Republic*, referring to the company of those who have renounced the life of politics for private satisfactions:

One who has joined this small company and tasted the happiness that is their portion; who has watched the frenzy of the multitude and seen that there is no soundness in the conduct of public life, nowhere an ally at whose side a champion of justice could hope to escape destruction; but that, like a man fallen among wild beasts, if he should refuse to take part in their misdeeds and could not hold out alone against the fury of all, he would be destined, before he could be of any service to his country and his friends, to perish, having done no good to himself or to anyone else—one who has weighed all this keeps quiet and goes his own way, like the traveler who takes shelter under a wall from a driving storm of dust and hail; and seeing lawlessness spreading on all sides, is content if he can keep his hands clean from iniquity while this life lasts, and when the end comes takes his departure, with good hope, in serenity and peace.[11]

What Goodman's Indian has in mind, it will speedily be objected, is certainly not *this*. True enough; but neither, if we are honest, is a good deal of our scholarship; and I am not entirely sure in my own mind that a diet of pot and rock is much more irrelevant to our own spiritual needs and those of the nation and the world at this moment than a diet of unabashed professionalism. As Arnold says in one of the passages with which I began, the *great* men of culture are those who have a passion for diffusing it, for making it prevail, for carrying it from one end of society to the other. We can understand and respect a decision to do otherwise, but it is not the sort of decision we need just now in our colleges and universities, where that immortal garland is still to be run for, not without dust and heat.

An alternative response is to destroy. Destroy the authority of scholarship, discipline, mastery, truth. Destroy the authority of the profession—and of its professional organizations—and of its very subject, language and literature—by making it instrumental, either intentionally or blindly, to parochial wars. There are two ways of doing this. One is to accept the doctrine that we often hear today to the effect that the great literature of the human past has no relevance for a world in turmoil, cannot any longer speak to blacks in the ghetto, or to Chicanos, Indians, Orientals—or even to a certain group of our own writers, if we may believe a series of interviews that appeared not long ago in the *New York Times*. "No. I don't read. I don't have the patience," one was quoted as saying. "It's just easier to go to a movie and let it all wash over you." Another: "We are a generation raised on rock 'n' roll. You read Hemingway or 'Death in Venice' in college, and there was no meaning for us." And a third: "I find I'm reading less and less . . . I really don't know why. My friends don't read much either. Everything seems boring. It's ironic, I guess; here we are, writers who don't read. That's life, I suppose."[12]

Well—to each his own. Small wonder that one of the writers interviewed was "convinced that some of the writers under thirty aren't as good as some of the writers over thirty when they were our age." How could they be? A great writer is the cutting edge of a craft and concern that stretch back to Homer, and to cut himself off from their accumulated force is like shutting off the current to a power tool:

> All around his black hair
> Was spread; in the dust his whole head lay,
> That once charming head: now Zeus had let his enemies
> Defile it on his native soil.

Irrelevant? How many times in Belleau Wood, at Okinawa, or in the rice paddies even as I speak . . . ? And place beside that the lines that Homer immediately placed beside it:

> She ordered her bright-haired maids in the palace
> To place on the fire a large tripod, preparing
> A hot bath for Hector, returning from battle.
> Foolish woman! Already he lay far from hot baths,
> Slain by grey-eyed Athena, who guided Achilles' arm.

Irrelevant? Boring? In Tuscaloosa, New Harmony, and Medicine Hat they do not think so. They have lived through that moment too many times. Translate it into the language of the ghettos and Cambodia, and they do not think so either. "Far from hot baths, he was indeed, poor man," runs a poignant comment on this passage, which I have never known any student to read without pausing before he spoke again:

And not he alone. Nearly all the *Iliad* takes place far from hot baths. Nearly all of human life, then and now, takes place far from hot baths.[13]

Nevertheless—though I think the young writers I have cited are wrong in their estimate of our literary inheritance—I do not feel that we who teach what they neglect have cause to lay much flattering unction to our souls. All too often we too treat it as if it were boring and irrelevant—*our* Iphigeneia to be offered up on the altar of professional success.

The other way in which we can destroy the subject we profess and with it our own calling is to entertain the notion that the world's great literature is all part of some sort of ghastly conspiracy to support the status quo: I believe the current term is the military-industrial complex. This, in my opinion, is to misread altogether the nature of our subject. Doubtless literature can be put to that use or any other if we work at it hard enough, but it will resist us every step of the way and defeat us in the end when we least expect it. "Men who burn books," one of the outstanding men of letters of our times has reminded us, "know what they are doing":

Reading is a mode of action. We engage the presence, the voice of the book. . . . A great poem, a classic novel, presses in upon us; they assail and occupy the strong places of our consciousness. They exercise upon our ambitions and most covert dreams, a strange bruising mastery. . . . The artist is the uncontrollable force; no western eye, since Van Gogh, looks on a cypress without observing in it the start of flame.[14]

Yes. And the pictures of society, our own or any other, that look back at us from the mirrors that the great artists hold up to us are not likely to predispose anyone in favor of what *is*. In Dante's hell, potentates and popes keep company with traitors, gluttons, and politicians, and even one of his own former teachers—a warning to us all. Rabelais, long before our time, writes over the archway of his Thélème, Do what you will. Montaigne reminds kings and all others who would pull rank on us that no matter how high you build the throne, all the man sits on is his own behind. Pope, born dying, keeps enough breath in his little body for fifty-six years to go down in flames with the fourth book of the *Dunciad* taking the whole Hanoverian Establishment with him; Byron cuts down to size Castlereagh and the Peace of Vienna; and Shelley, as if he were simply announcing the state of the weather, tells the world calmly that poets are the true legislators of mankind. What a scruffy, conceited, unreconstructed, biologically non-degradable collection of frail human beings they all are! What a mess they would make of it if *they* had to rule. Yet how precious their vision is precisely because it is loyal to something that lies beyond the capacity of any Establishment except the human heart to provide: compassion, justice, peace, love.

As for the greatest of them all, what is the vision of society that his King Lear wins through to in the madness that tells us he is beginning to be sane?

Thou has seen a farmer's dog bark at a beggar?
. . . And the creature run from the cur? There
thou might'st behold the great image of authority:
a dog's obeyed in office.
Thou rascal beadle, hold thy bloody hand!
Why dost thou lash that whore? Strip thine own back;
Thou hotly lust'st to use her in that kind
For which thou whipp'st her. The usurer hangs the cozener.
Through tatter'd clothes small vices do appear.
Robes and furr'd gowns hide all. Plate sin with gold,

And the strong lance of justice hurtless breaks;
Arm it in rags, a pygmy's straw does pierce it.
None does offend, none, I say, none.

But this is an image—no more—you will say. The world rolled on in its course after this was listened to in the Globe, much as it always has. Very true, and the reasons why are plain. Literature is a treacherous weapon at the barricades. For that, you need tracts, manifestoes, *Uncle Tom's Cabins*, and the speech I just read apart from the rest of the play; you need what Brecht thought he was doing in *Mother Courage*, not what he actually did; you need Hotspur and Fortinbras, not Falstaff and Hamlet; a claque, not a literary critic. The virtue of a tract is that you know precisely what party it serves. The greatest literature is different; it serves no party save that of our common humanity. It spreads before us, in the words of one of the early presidents of this Association, "the unconscious autobiography of mankind";[15] "a superb library of human situations," to quote a more contemporary voice, "an endless repertory of encounters";[16] and so, bringing us face to face with all that we have been, much that we might be, stands as a perpetual challenge to whatever we become. This is why neither our subject nor our profession, still less our professional Association, disposes of any power worth talking about when applied in a provincial war to capture some particular secular city, be it Marxist, Maoist, Guevarist, Freudian, Jungian, or even Charles Reich's Consciousness III. What we guard and must always guard is not my city or your city but the freedom of the visionary faculty itself.

IV

If, then, we reject the temptation to escape from our calling and the equal temptation to misuse it, what is our proper course? I think it can be described in one word: outreach—as John Comenius urged.

I will not try to supply details for the procedures I am about to suggest, for time runs out, and even if it did not, what one mind could muster would make a pitiful showing beside the innovations that are already germinating on some campuses and should be germinating on all. Let me instead simply enumerate the areas of outreach that I think all of us who teach in colleges and universities must make our particular concern during the coming decade.

1. *We must reach out to the schools.* We must do everything in our power to establish a mutually informative and forbearing relationship with those who teach there and those who learn there—and the place to start is at home in our own communities, now. Snobbism is the generic disease of which racism is one species, and we have all of us been carriers of it, as the attitudes show that we have taken, and apparently helped inculcate in our students, toward the schools and community colleges and even the good-but-not-quite-so-"distinguished"-university-as-our-own just down the road.

2. *We must reach out to the disadvantaged, whether black, brown, yellow, or white.* How this is best done, experimentation will have to show, but we are not without models. One of this Association's ablest Elizabethan scholars has been Project Director lately, in his spare time, for a "Coopera-

tive English Project" carried on in collaboration between Case Western Reserve University and Cleveland East Technical High, a ghetto school. There is a mimeographed report on this Project by its Director, whose last paragraph ends as follows:

In spite of repeated frustrations and defeats, and in spite of the long odds against them, the students we have worked with have remained in school year after year, although the temptation to drop out must have been great. For every one who has completely given up hope and merely goes through the motions of studying "to beat the system," there are several more whose hopes, however wounded, are still alive. Their cynicism is superficial and protective, and despite it they have a freshness, a capacity for enthusiasm, and even an innocence rarely found. . . . To give these students the chance they deserve, the University faculty must recognize high school teachers as their colleagues and be willing to make their contribution day after day in the city schools.[17]

We who have ears to hear, let us make a supreme effort to hear.

3. *We must reach out to the general community of educated men and women.* We must learn to talk to those who follow "mysteries" other than ours about *our* subject in the normal language of men. Plans are afoot for this Association to publish a more general journal than *PMLA*, beginning in 1975, as many of you know; but this must be simply an earnest of our full intention, and again the place to begin is in our own communities. If we do not think we know how to interest the members of the local Kiwanis, what makes us sure that we can interest their daughters and sons?

But there is more at stake than this. All over the civilized world today, the humanist disciplines are in serious trouble because they have neglected to speak either with or to the "humanity" that gives them their name. Philosophy, we are warned in a recent symposium, is largely "withdrawn into an arid desert of linguistic conundrums, as remote from life as the absurder forms of scholasticism"; the Fine Arts show alarming signs of getting lost "in jargon or recondite iconography when, for the first time, they are capable of reaching out to millions"; History has become an exercise in competing historiographies. As for the so-called Classics, we all know what has happened to *them*—despite the fact that their audience has in fact grown:

Homer sells by millions; Thucydides hundreds of thousands; even Tacitus tens of thousands. The hunger to know about the ancient world is insatiable. The professional classicists, however, rarely provide the diet; indeed more often than not the providers live on the fringe of the profession.[18]

Is this not uncomfortably like our own case? We must, of course, often write for each other, as the doctors must, the lawyers, the theologians. But this activity does not release us from the obligation to reach, in addition, a much wider public than the one at which we usually aim.

4. *We must reach out to the media.* We must show a resourceful and energetic hospitality toward the educative contributions of the other symbol-using forms such as television, film, photography, and the visual arts generally. We and our books are no longer the sole or even the chief transmitters of attitudes, values, vicarious experience, and we must learn to live with this situation. But our hospitality should by no means be uncritical or spineless. The communities and states, the colleges and universities of this

country have established the most complicated licensing system the world has ever seen in an effort to guarantee the qualifications of those who teach; yet television, the most powerful because the most dramatic and ubiquitous teacher of them all, is free to enter every home at all hours of the day and night, the sole qualification demanded of it in most instances being that it sell products. As students of verbal imagery, should we not show some concern for the visual-verbal? as believers in the value of poetry, some interest in advertising, which is one of its meretricious forms? as linguists, some responsibility for the decay of our common language, to which the media along with many other agencies in these times massively contribute?

While I am on this subject, one of the initiatives our Association has taken that I am proudest to report to you is a proposal that in cooperation with the National Council of Teachers of English we have lately placed in the hands of the National Endowment for the Arts and Humanities. The funds, if granted, will support a pioneering two-year effort to consider how language and literature may best make their contribution in a society where other forms of imaginative expression have become through technology equally (or far more) "accessible," in all senses of that term. The title of the proposal—"Language, Literature, and the Responsible Human Being: A New Approach to the Humanities"—perhaps gives a sufficient indication of its direction and scope.

5. *We must reach out to each other.* I have in mind here, first, the collaboration and mutual assistance that ought to go on between those of us who teach the English language and its literature and those of us who teach the other modern languages and their literatures. We must inaugurate and engage in shared courses and interdepartmental majors more generously than we now do. We must strive to create a common major in "Literature" that will be at once solid and exciting. And we must insist that our graduate students receive at least an elementary grounding in a literature other than their own—if need be through translations.

I have in mind here, too, the collaboration that ought to go on among our home institutions. We should create reciprocal opportunities for qualified students, undergraduate as well as graduate, to transfer for a semester or a year to another institution, if their work will be benefited. There is no reason why all junior-year programs, for instance, must be located abroad. Furthermore—and here we come to a form of circulation that we could bring into being quite easily—colleges and universities of roughly the same orientation and composition should arrange regular year-long exchanges of members of their faculties, either on a one-to-one or round-robin basis. What most of us know least about in our professional life are the organizations and procedures current in English and foreign language departments other than our own. The short-run as well as the long-run advantages of having a continuous inflow of new ideas and perspectives supplied by one or more staff members returning from Universities X, Y, or Z and by one or more visitors arriving from Universities A, B, or C would be immense.

Finally, I have in mind the kind of collaboration that will enable us to speak with a more united and penetrating voice on the national scene. It is not beyond our ingenuity, I feel sure, to devise an assembly of humanists (perhaps the Delegate Assembly, if approved, will evolve in this direction) that can represent us with some authority before the public and before the

Congress. We *have* a National Endowment for the Humanities, under-funded though it is; where is the corresponding body to advise that should have been supplied by us?

6. *We must reach out to new arrangements of literary study.* For our undergraduate students, we must be able to accommodate the accelerated three-year B.A. and also the five-year B.A. that includes a year for work and self-testing in the society at large—options that will surely continue to grow in popularity. We must also be able to accommodate the many variants of the four-year program that are nowadays evolving, from those that set the student largely free of course work for sustained reading or writing during one of his college years to those that combine formal study with opportuni-ties to learn-by-doing in the community nearby. To this I must add that we have yet to give serious thought to creating a scheme of things that will extend to undergraduates the teaching responsibilities they deserve to have, not for our sake but theirs. If our favorite truism is true—namely, that the surest way to master a subject is to teach it—it strikes me that we have been derelict in this regard or at the least unimaginative.

For our graduate students, we must also reach out to a new pluralism of programs and goals. We must take the stress off the "D" for Doctor and affix it to the "Ph" for Philosophia, the love of wisdom—or to the "A" for Arts. In other words, we must reaffirm ends, not means. We must also encourage our students to reach out by initiating programs that enable them to do so, programs more intensive, probably more protracted, and certainly more liberal than the usual two years of course work, which will carry them toward literature and sociology, literature and anthropology, literature and psychology, literature and the other arts, or any one of a number of other fruitful combinations, including learning theory, thus mak-ing them not only better teachers but more perceptive scholars and more comprehensive human beings. As there are many mansions in the house of learning, there should be many paths leading into it, and we should not forget either at the rising or the setting of the sun what a house is meant for: to be lived in, by living men and women.

7. *Finally, we must reach out to wider significances than those we have been in the habit of attempting.* I have sometimes used the word *calling* in this address, because I believe we *have* a calling. Though our profession asks no Hippocratic oath, I think we are committed by the nature of our subject, which is, after all, the lifeblood of all the world's singers and seers, and by the very special bond that the teaching of literature almost inevi-tably engenders between teacher and student—a bond that at its best re-quires putting the whole self on the line, naked and frail, with all its embarrassing inadequacies—to three unevadable trusts.

One trust is language. Language is the human city—"a city to the building of which," says Emerson, "every human being brought a stone,"[19] though nowadays, not guessing what it cost, many seem blindly to want to bulldoze it down. Like other cities, language is susceptible of pollution, becomes murky, noisome, suffocating. That is the condition we face now. Never, I suspect, has our common tongue been so debased and vulgarized as it is today in commerce, so pretentious, overblown, and empty as it is in the babble of the learned and bureaucratic jargons, not excepting ours, so tired, mechanical, and unimaginative as it is in the obscenities of the young.

And when this happens, whether we believe with Ben Jonson that behavior contaminates language ("Wheresoever manners and fashions are corrupted, Language is. It imitates the publicke riot")[20] or with Ashley Montagu and the moderns that language contaminates behavior (". . . the world we perceive is the world we see through words. . . . Hence . . . the importance of teaching language not so much as grammar but as behavior."),[21] the possibility of community recedes. Manners deteriorate, language deceives; our lines of communication to each other choke up with misread signals, false alarms, and unnecessary terrors, till all that can finally get through to us will be the insinuating suave voice of Big Brother, urging us to feed and grow fat. These things we cannot change single-handedly. But we can help others to become more aware of them, and we can vow for ourselves and our own intraprofessional disagreements that we will put away language that inflames and divides and cleave to language that reaches out and unites—"language designed," to borrow a phrase of Ashley Montagu's that I particularly like, "to put man *into touch* with his fellow man."

Our second trust is the world's great literature, all of it, or as much of it as each of us can master, Classical, European, Oriental, Third World, American. But of that I have been speaking all along, and I will only add here that the student whom we have failed to bring close to Oedipus discovering that he himself is the plague; or to Aeneas leaving Troy with his father on his back and leading his small son by the hand, an unforgettable rendering of the human trinity of courage, memory, and hope; or to Ivan Karamazov's dreaming of the Grand Inquisitor; or to Captain Ahab losing his humanity "in the very act of vindicating it," yet confronting without flinching the principle of chaos that is both within him and without; or to Molly Bloom remembering it like it was and telling it like it is—that student we shall have disadvantaged indeed. There is a stanza about this in Auden's fine poem on "The Shield of Achilles." On the old shield in Homer, a dancing space and athletes at their games; on the new shield of the 1970's, "a weed-choked field":

> A ragged urchin, aimless and alone,
> Loitered about that vacancy, a bird
> Flew up to safety from his well-aimed stone:
> That girls are raped, that two boys knife a third,
> Were axioms, to him, who'd never heard
> Of any world where promises were kept.
> Or one could weep because another wept.

And that, precisely, is our third trust. The world where promises are kept must be rebuilt, and the only power on earth with which we can hope to build it is the moral imagination—what Wordsworth calls in that famous passage at the *Prelude*'s close "reason in her most exalted mood," what Shelley describes in his *Defence* when he says that "A man, to be greatly good, must imagine intensely and comprehensively; he must put himself in the place of another and of many others. The pains and pleasures of his species must become his own." A world where promises are kept will be as easy—and as hard—to build as that.

A poet of our own time who has meditated deeply on this problem has also written eloquently about it; and since the passage is extremely pertinent to the themes I have been touching on tonight, and is not widely known, I shall close by quoting part of it. One way of accounting for our present sense of nightmare, this poet suggests, "is to say that the *knowledge* of the fact has somehow or other come loose from the *feel* of the fact, and that it is now possible, for the first time in human history, to *know* as a mind what you cannot *comprehend* as a man":

What I think of is the "good Germans" who *knew* the gas ovens in the concentration camps but were able to live with that knowledge in easy conscience and comparative tranquility until they began to troop, in huge, shamed crowds, to performances of *The Diary of Anne Frank*. What I think of is the Americans and the Russians and the Chinese of our own generation—shall we call them the "good" Americans and Russians and Chinese—who *know* Hiroshima (the walking dead who could not die stumbling through the dark that first day with "great sheets of skin peeled from their tissues to hang like rags") but who, in spite of that knowledge, are still able to talk about the repetition of those horrors (and horrors even worse) as conceivable, as possible.

This divorce between the knowledge of the fact and the feel of the fact exists in our world whether we like its existence or not and it is because it exists that the word, art—or, better, the word, poetry (which stands, in their essential likeness, for all the arts)—belongs beside the word, science, in these grave discussions. Not until mankind is again able to *see feelingly*, as blind Gloucester says to Lear upon the heath, will the crucial flaw at the heart of our civilization be healed. And to see feelingly only poetry can teach us.

No man who comes to knowledge through a poem leaves the feel of what he knows behind, for the knowledge he comes to is the knowledge of that *feeling life* of the mind which comprehends by putting itself in the place where its thought goes—by realizing its thought in that only human realizer, the imagination. It is for this reason that the teaching of poetry . . . is as important to the university in crisis as the teaching of science. . . . For only when poetry itself—which means all the powers of all the arts—regains its place in the consciousness of mankind will the triumphant civilization the sciences have prepared for us become a civilization in which men can live alive.[22]

Ladies and gentlemen, it is painfully clear that we have a faith to keep. Let us keep it.

Notes

1 *John Amos Comenius, 1592–1670: Selections* (Paris: UNESCO, 1957), p. 97.

2 London: Smith, Elder, 1869, p. 49.

3 *Students without Teachers: The Crisis in the University* (New York: McGraw-Hill, 1969), p. 14.

4 Kingman Brewster, "The Deeper Unrest," an address delivered before the Ford Hall Forum in Boston, 6 Dec. 1970.

5 Robert A. Nisbet, "The Twilight of Authority," *The Public Interest*, 4, No. 15 (1969), 5.

6 C. E. Silberman, *Crisis in the Classroom: The Remaking of American Education* (New York: Random, 1970), p. 26.

7 Martin Trow, "Expansion and Transformation of Higher Education," a revised and expanded version of a paper read before the American Sociological Association in Washington, 1 Sept. 1970. I am grateful to Professor Trow for allowing me to see a copy of this unpublished manuscript.

8 Paul Goodman, "The New Reformation," in the *New York Times Magazine*, 14 Sept. 1969, p. 14.

9 Adam Parry, "The Two Voices of Virgil's *Aeneid*," *Arion*, 2 (1963), 78.

[10] Introduction to Euripides, *Iphigeneia at Aulis*, trans. Kenneth Cavander (Englewood Cliffs, N.J.: Prentice-Hall, 1972).

[11] Plato, *Republic*, vi, 496.

[12] "Young Writers Say They Don't Read," *New York Times*, 23 May 1969.

[13] Simone Weil, "The *Iliad*, or The Poem of Force," trans. Mary McCarthy, in *The Mint*, ed. Geoffrey Grigson, No. 2 (1948), p. 85.

[14] George Steiner, *Language and Silence: Essays 1958–1966* (Harmondsworth, Middlesex: Penguin, 1969), p. 29.

[15] James Russell Lowell, in his Presidential address before this Association, *PMLA*, 5 (1890), 22.

[16] Letter from Benjamin DeMott to Michael F. Shugrue, 29 Aug. 1970.

[17] Robert Ornstein, "The East Technical High School—Case Western Reserve University Cooperative English Project, 1969–1970" (unpubl. report).

[18] *Crisis in the Humanities*, ed. J. H. Plumb (Harmondsworth, Middlesex: Penguin, 1964), p. 8.

[19] "Quotation and Originality," in *Letters and Social Aims* (Boston: Osgood, 1876), p. 177.

[20] *Works*, ed. Hereford and Simpson, viii (1949), 593.

[21] "The Language of Self-Deception," in *Language in America*, ed. Neil Postman, Charles Weingartner, and Terence Moran (New York: Pegasus, 1969), pp. 82, 95.

[22] Archibald MacLeish, "Crisis and Poetry," an address before the Yale Alumni Convocation in the Arts and Sciences, 7 Oct. 1960.

The American Scholar Reconsidered*

Theodore L. Gross

City College of New York

THE ENGLISH DEPARTMENT is the metaphor of a university. Its preoccupations form the image that the university casts upon society, that mirror held up to human nature which reflects the persistent, vexing, moral questions of education: Is the department concerned with the best that has been thought and said, or is it concerned—because it must be concerned— with the most basic form of basic writing? Is it struggling to persuade students that "a good book is the precious life-blood of a master spirit," or is it becoming increasingly preoccupied with television, movies, radio, journalism, public relations—the mass media that largely shape the sensibilities of students? Is it basing its assumptions on a white, Christian, Anglo-Saxon tradition, or is it looking outward, where English isn't the only language spoken by literate men and women and foreign customs are more than the exotica of a Puritan culture? Is it responding to the text alone, or is it shifting its curriculum so as to engage the problems of the world outside? Is it only historical? Antihistorical? Cultural? Countercultural? Self-consciously literary? Vocationally expedient? The questions return, and return again, demanding answers from us as we acknowledge more readily than ever before that we are in the eye of the moral storm, that almost every student of every college sits in the classroom of an English department, and that the responsibility to make a society literate and more humane begins and often ends in that room, with questions that cluster, like Kierkegaard's finger in the night, to point toward us.

Like you, I am a chairman. My department has 19 full professors, 21 associate professors, and 10 assistant professors on the tenured staff; 27 assistant professors, 44 instructors, 14 part-time lecturers, 11 evening session lecturers, and 1 research assistant on the nontenured staff. This department of 148 people offers fifty percent of its courses in writing, fifteen percent in introductory literature, and thirty-five percent in electives. These cold figures indicate the scope of a large department in an urban-centered college which has committed itself to Open Admissions—that is, a department in which the great problems of the seventies are reflected and where they must be solved if we are to survive as a profession. From the perspective of

* An address to the ADE Seminar in New York, 13 April 1972. Reprinted from *ADE Bulletin*, No. 34 (Sept. 1972), pp. 30–36.

this department in a college that is fittingly called the "city college," I would like to suggest some guidelines for an English department of the future that will do more than dress up students for their performance in other departments and be more than a way station on the high road to sociology or anthropology or history; more than a polarized unit in which the grammarians face the poets or the critics in varying degrees of distrust; more even than a metaphor of a university. And I would like to address my remarks to what I consider to be two societal conditions that will control the curriculum, the hiring, and the structure of any English department— whether it is four-year, two-year, rural, or urban—in the last quarter of the twentieth century: the great degree of leisure time that will be available to all of us and the shift in vocational opportunities that await the student of language and literature.

I

Let us begin with our name and our structure.

The designation of our departments as "English" departments is inorganic to their purposes. The political revolution of 1776 had its literary revolution sixty-one years later in 1837, when Emerson published *The American Scholar*, but it has only begun to enter upon its educational revolution. In the events at Berkeley and Columbia universities we witnessed a student revolution, but not the educational revolution that should have followed: students are now involved in campus governance, but they are not sufficiently involved in a campus education that gives strength and meaning to their political roles or to the careers they will soon enter. The gods of our pantheon are still Chaucer, Shakespeare, Milton, and a host of other English authors; our grammar is still largely an English grammar; our style of thinking, English. We have been educated in this tradition—a deeply civilized, highly urbane tradition—but we know that our everyday, mundane lives run counter to that heritage.

The paradoxes of our professional lives are legion and not accidental. We have been trained for an elitist profession, but we are asked to perform democratic tasks; we have written dissertations on Spenser, but we are teaching remedial writing; we are committed to the book, but the students have been culturally shaped by television and film; we have studied a body of culture that is fundamentally Anglo-Saxon, but we teach many students who are black and Asian and Hispanic; we pay homage to the history of English literature, but we are surrounded by the consequences of American history and the political presence of America; we are in an English department, but our work is involved with the literature of the world and with the language that is spoken by Americans. I list all of these paradoxes collectively because they form a background against which we seek to accomplish our central desire: the humanistic training of a new generation of students. The word *humanistic* seems to me essential. We are clearly no longer an English department but a humanities department—or, at the very least, a department of language and literature. "Hidden name and complex fate," Ralph Ellison called one of his autobiographical essays—our true name has been hidden, and it is time we acknowledged it so as to signify the proper direction of our work. Our complex fate is perhaps less easily discovered and defined; but one way of beginning to understand it is by examining the traditional structure which we assume and which has so great an effect on our curriculum.

II

At the City College we have had a rather conventional structural arrangement. The English department belongs to a Humanities division which, together with the Social Science and Science divisions, compose the College of Liberal Arts and Sciences. In this Humanities division, the following departments are represented: Classics, Germanic and Slavic Languages, Romance Languages, Art, Music, Speech and Theater, Library, and English. I need not rehearse the traditional competition for promotions, sabbaticals, and course programs with which you are already familiar—it is a competition which can be healthy, as each department challenges the other from the point of view of its own discipline and its own needs; more often it leads to a departmental rivalry that is not only demoralizing and petty but inhibits the growth of the university. It is, too often, *only* political and leads to an unnecessary waste of resources and a lack of clarity in the curriculum.

In the courses offered by these departments, the two societal patterns that I have suggested—leisure and work—already find themselves reflected. We have departments that are concerned with esthetics, literature, thought —the intellectual life, which obviously needs no justification in this forum and which should lead finally to the fruitful use of leisure time. Within the same departments we have service components—basic writing, speech therapy, language training—that bear directly upon the vocation of the students. These divisions within departments, particularly language and literature, should not be separated: the student who is learning to write should be learning to read, from the same person, if possible, so that he knows that writing can be converted from a skill into an art, and reading from a duty to a labor of love. The departments themselves should remain intact, not only because they are a convenient political arrangement within a university, not only because they perpetuate a cultural tradition that is worth offering our students, but because they will be crucial in an education that becomes more and more interdisciplinary. It takes a long time to become a literary critic or scholar, a historian, economist, linguist, or physicist; we can argue so forcefully for interdisciplinary education because we ourselves have been solidly trained in a particular discipline. In looking to the future, we should not delude our students into thinking they will confront this highly specialized technological age by absorbing a homogenized education we call interdisciplinary. I am traditionalist enough to believe that a student must understand one professional discipline before he can appreciate another, which is another way of saying that the departmental structure is sensible; but I am sufficiently aware of the world which this student will enter to realize that his life will be sterile unless he can fill the huge mass of time that will be available to him once he has finished his ever-decreasing workaday week—and this is another way of urging interdisciplinary education, of bringing together classics, German, Romance languages, art, music, and English, not to speak of the social and physical sciences, so that he may fill his leisure time more meaningfully. I see the primary purpose of a humanities department of the future, apart from its traditional functions, as twofold: it should offer students a more imaginative preparation for the use of leisure time and provide them with a broadly conceived training for many different types of professions which faculties of "English" departments have not yet considered.

III

Once literature was read by the elite, who sent their children to Harvard, Yale, and Columbia; now it is read by captive masses in state and city colleges who—as some have argued—have no taste or desire for it and upon whom it appears to be wasted. At one time this division between the culturally well groomed and the culturally unwashed functioned without particular difficulty—in a democratic society we maintained a class-oriented higher education that has only recently been challenged by blacks, by women, and by students of all races. In a nation which has always divided the serious worker from the poet, in a nation of immigrants who scarcely paused to "enjoy" themselves, the arts have always seemed peripheral and the artist, to use Faulkner's term, a nice pet to have around the house. Only the wealthy could appreciate art. When the working people earned enough money to rest, they saw cheap Hollywood movies or Broadway shows or television; they had no fundamental respect for leisure time. Some of the immigrant groups, it is true, had an attitude toward American education that can be characterized only as religious, and the brilliant and tenacious few did break the barriers of the private colleges and sit with the sons of the leisure class. But, as Alfred Kazin points out in *The Walker in the City*, "It was never learning I associated with that school: only the necessity to succeed"—the school prepared the child for success, which meant work, and which gave a clarity to the student's goals and to the college curricula.

We still train people for services, for success, and the English departments of large city colleges will continue to attract highly motivated students who happen to be disadvantaged; it is no accident that at the City College of New York, for example, we are contemplating the creation of a medical school that will stand beside our Schools of Nursing, Education, Architecture, Oceanography, and Engineering; that part of our curriculum which is preprofessional will continue to be clearly defined and extremely important. But at the same time—and this seems to me particularly significant in a college that has been called the proletarian Harvard—we are establishing the first Center for Performing Arts in the history of the college, a center which will train professionals but which will also act as a catalyst for arts programs throughout the curriculum and help to create an atmosphere in which the arts will be valued and become a part of the students' education.

Within the traditional curriculum, a significant way of enhancing respect for leisure time is by exposing the student and the teacher to a truly interdisciplinary education before he discovers his field of concentration and decides upon his occupation. This means drawing upon all of the humanistic disciplines, presenting them organically, and implementing the ideas that have been suggested by many of the participants in these ADE seminars. I list only a few that have seemed to me most fruitful and that we are translating into our own needs at the City College.

1. At the Northwestern conference, John Gerber recommended a course that has been successful at the University of Iowa. Three instructors from three different disciplines and departments meet with advanced students for long blocks of time—perhaps for seven hours on two separate days. The course composes the entire program of both students and faculty members and might involve, for example, a literary critic, a historian, and a sociologist discussing different aspects of American civilization; or it might include a drama critic, director, and sociologist discussing Genet's *The Screens* and culminate with a production of the play.

2. At the City College we are currently requiring of English majors a historical survey of English and American literature, modeled upon the Kenneth Clark civilization lectures, which involves three instructors and three times the usual number of students: on Mondays there is a large lecture, and on Wednesdays and Fridays discussions of the lectures. The three instructors are specialists in their periods so that when, for example, the lectures on the Middle Ages occur, the medievalist delivers them. Art, music, and film augment this course.

3. In our Basic Writing division, we have introduced a course in which writing instructors sit with teachers from psychology, sociology, and history so that the freshmen submit themes on the work that they and their instructors have discussed together. We are also experimenting with a lecture series that will be attended by freshmen in three sections of basic writing so that, once again, the students will have substantive material for the papers they write.

These are only several ideas that have captured my imagination; there are already many others that have been suggested in the workshops of these seminars, in the position papers prepared by participants, and in the addresses that will finally be assembled by Michael Shugrue and Harry Finestone. Indeed, the large body of materials on interdisciplinary education will reflect some of the most creative thought in higher education today. Curriculum changes of the sort we are projecting have compelling advantages: they bring faculty and students together in a mutual learning experience; they break the arbitrary scheduling pattern of most universities—instead of interrupting the learning experience after fifty minutes and having the students fly from one class to another, like a television observer whose commercial has come, learning proceeds according to its natural length of time, with consequent improved attendance; they permit instructors to know one another so that the strong may help the weak, so that people in different departments—and this point is especially important in a college as large as ours—can learn from each other; finally—in an era when judgment of nontenured personnel is increasingly important—observations can be made most naturally.

All of this is familiar and involves modifications that do not seem unrealistic—the interaction of traditional disciplines and of media will relate students to the world they experience so that they are prepared to concentrate in a particular field and to make more meaningful use of their leisure time. After the student has married, chosen a profession, and created a family, he or she should be prepared—if the education has been persuasive enough—to continue educating himself for the rest of his life. I do not mean merely demanding a higher quality of television entertainment but maintaining an active involvement in what we now call (somewhat disparagingly) adult education. Adult centers should appear in every community—not only in affluent areas—so that people can study languages or medieval poetry at their leisure. The federal, state, and city governments should float bond issues that will support these centers, but—let me move quickly, like an agile chairman, from the ideal to the practical—since this aid will probably not be forthcoming, the university itself will have to begin thinking in terms of carrying on its education for alumni, not only at night or on the weekend, but during regular class hours, perhaps even in classes with undergraduates. At the City College, we are considering Saturday classes in film, television, women's studies, and black studies: students will enroll as usual, and alumni and interested people from the community will be invited into the classroom. In our creative writing program we are planning lectures for students on all aspects of publishing, to which representatives from the publishing world will be invited. Like many of you, we are considering the use of radio and television in terms of expanding our curriculum. At the Tampa conference in February, educators from Florida spoke of courses for retired people which would provide a real service for individuals with a great deal of free time.

These ideas reflect early attempts to make leisure more meaningful for those who are no longer in college, to make education an ongoing pleasure, not just a form of work against which evenings and weekends and vacations are measured. For it is becoming increasingly apparent that the great problem of the last quarter of the twentieth century, which is intimately linked with leisure time, is the problem of boredom, the inability of the individual to respond to things and people around him with real interest. The injustices of this country that produce the anger and bitterness which result in sporadic violence conceal deep feelings of boredom and apathy. Boredom is at the root of our social and educational problems, the reason for aggression and destructiveness and a host of other sins that seem so confusing. Whether they are committed in the cities or in the universities, it is the national disease that lies encrusted in the fatty layers of that archetypal T.V. viewer who sits with his beer and pretzels, watching an endless array of superstars and falling asleep as the news flickers over him; bordeom is the disease that causes us to murder easily and to create instant corrective measures; to gain weight and join the Weight Watchers; to drink or take drugs or have encounter sessions or show X-rated movies until we embarrass ourselves and tremble with the thought that indeed the center will not hold, mere anarchy is loosed upon the world. Erich Fromm puts this idea most cogently in his study of aggression.

The increase of boredom is brought about by the structure and functioning of contemporary industrial society. It is by now widely recognized that most manual work is boring because of the monotony and repetitiveness; much white-collar work is boring because of its bureaucratic character, which leaves little responsibility and initiative to the individual. But leisure, meant to be the reward for boring work, has become boring too; it follows by and large the consumption pattern, and is in fact managed by industry, which sells boredom-compensating commodities. The difference is that boredom in work is usually conscious, while leisure boredom is unconscious. Among the answers to the question of how violence—and drug consumption—can be reduced it seems to me that perhaps one of the most important ones is to reduce boredom in work and in leisure. This requires drastic changes in our social and economic moral structure.

Man is a passionate being, in need of stimulation; he tolerates boredom and monotony badly, and if he cannot take a genuine interest in life, his boredom will force him to seek it in the perverted way of destruction and violence. I believe that the further study of what has become the illness of the age—boredom— could make an important contribution to the understanding of aggression.

I do not want to be more programmatic and design a curriculum at this time; but I do want to stress that we are speaking of extremely significant matters. In an era when urban public education is available for everyone, the American scholar must be a person whose education is an organic element in his life and not merely a preparation for life, like all the other preparations that prevent the American student from living and becoming the American scholar. With a wider sense of how he can use his leisure time, the college graduate will have a healthier attitude toward his work.

"The mass of men lead lives of quiet desperation," run Thoreau's famous words in *Walden*. "There is no play in them, for this comes after work." The boredom that stretches across the faces of some of our students is at least partially due to the lack of connection between their studies and the routine work which they see reflected in their parents' lives and foresee desperately in their own lives. Their leisure, it is clear, will be satisfying to them only if their work is satisfying: one will not exist without the other.

IV

In America, an individual's profession is a critical index to his character. We ask a casual acquaintance, "What do you do for a living?" and we mean, Who are you, What are you, What is your morality—literally, What do you do for a living? This significance that we attach to work is obviously not only American. Lionel Trilling reminds us of the great pathos in Othello's haunting cry, "Othello's occupation gone," and we know of Freud's insistence that the proper balance between *arbeit und leibe*, work and love, is essential for the happy life. But America has always been particularly a work-oriented society; in the world of New England Calvinism, the Gilded Age, and especially twentieth-century technocracy, work has defined the quality of people's lives.

Our problem in the City College English department is probably not untypical and will bring my thoughts about work into specific and sharp focus. Our elective offerings have gone from seventy-one to sixty-one in a matter of two years; our students have drifted into the fields of psychology, sociology, and anthropology to discover the answers to life in modern America. We have lost some of our majors for this reason, and the recovery of them must clearly come from interdisciplinary work. Some of the thinkers who have stirred our common imagination—Norman O. Brown, Buckminster Fuller, Marshall McLuhan, B. F. Skinner, Levi-Strauss, Sartre, and Reisman—cannot be, and obviously won't be, ignored by any sensitive faculty of humanities; we will broaden our perspective more than ever before to include these thinkers. In the process we will probably destroy the concept of individual majors altogether on an undergraduate level—Yale and other universities have already contemplated doing so.

But, more directly, we have lost our majors because we have misled our students. We have created the feeling that they can *only* enter teaching, publishing, journalism, and related fields; the job opportunities seem limited, and to ask them to study our subject for love of our subject alone is asking a little too much in an America whose morality is money and where jobs have become scarcer in teaching than at any time since the economic depression of the 1930's. One of our immediate answers to this very pragmatic problem is the creation of a manual, inspired by Linwood Orange's article, "English: The Pre-Professional Major," in the February 1972 issue of the *ADE Bulletin*, that will be distributed to freshmen so that they will realize how English can prepare them more suitably than any other subject for careers in law, medicine, editing, programming, banking, sales, marketing, insurance, public relations. The list, as we know and as our students ought to know, is almost endless in this era of communications.

The companies our students join will have to be more responsive to the problems that result from a leisure society. If schools can reward their teachers for continuing education, why shouldn't companies have a similar merit system, particularly when advanced work in English can only improve their ability to write and speak? Corporations like Chase Manhattan and Consolidated Edison already have skills courses for employees. There is no reason why a public utility like Con Ed cannot offer a course in ecology for workers—good for Con Ed's public image, good for its worker's training. In a day when these companies, as an executive of Con Ed recently told me, are conducting "social audits" meant to prevent a Ralph Nader or a Jack Anderson from exposing them to the public, this idea should be met with enthusiasm. Once students know that a wide range of corporations and companies have a real interest in humanistic education; once their older brothers and sisters tell them that their practical future is linked to their educational present, our subject must be more compelling— to the students and to us.

It is not especially difficult to advise undergraduates of job opportunities. I am simply codifying what we do informally anyway; nevertheless, it will help greatly to have future employers advise freshmen, in a handbook such as I have suggested, that studying language and literature is the preparation they think most desirable. But this suggestion does not penetrate to the heart of the problem. To do this we need to examine the preparation of those who enter our own profession and who pass on the values that they themselves have struggled to achieve. When we talk of the American

Scholar reconsidered, we turn quite naturally to the cathedral where scholarship ought to live in its purest form and where the American Scholar should be found as a leader and a guide—the graduate school.

One of the conflicts a graduate student faces in an urban-centered department is the great distance between what he is studying and what he is teaching; and if graduate schools do not make some sort of accommodation, they will find themselves addressing fewer and fewer students in an age when young people are questioning the validity of a higher degree for what they need to do in their everyday working lives. Students will continue to pursue the Ph.D. out of habit, although it is no accident that the D.A. has challenged its authority; but the time has arrived when a chairman like myself will simply not hire a candidate with a Ph.D. from an institution —Harvard, Yale, Princeton, or any institution—if he is unprepared for the realities of our teaching. We simply cannot afford to conduct an apprenticeship for people whose work will be partially devoted to making a society literate.

Recently I was one of those involved in a dialogue with an eminent critic who teaches the graduate students of our university—the students who become, in certain cases, the instructors in our college department. I suggested the great difficulty these graduate students have in bridging their two worlds. From the critic's point of view, these students should continue to pass on the best that has been thought and said (here we agreed absolutely), and they should not, as he claimed some of them did, teach "Mickey Mouse" courses, cheating the Open Admissions students of the best that the culture could make available to them (once again we agreed). He saw the difficulties inherent in this educational world we both inhabited, suggesting that perhaps mass education, carried on in the tradition each of us knew so well, might be impossible, that all students should have college available to them but not all students should be educated; and we agreed that the city and state and federal governments, after boasting of Open Admissions, will threaten to restrict funds so that this promising program might become simply another betrayal of the common man in America. The audience of which we were members included those who write for and edit journals like the *New York Review of Books, Partisan Review, Commentary,* the *New York Times Book Review,* and *Dissent*—all who came to the meeting thought of themselves as liberals in education as well as in politics. When some of us suggested that the contemporary student is bored, we were met with howls of execration, and the dialogue that ensued was, it seems to me, an echo of the dialogue one has heard over the years, a sort of litany of liberalism, but a little tired, like the responses between minister and congregation of another time when abstract faith was still possible:

"Bored? Why, there are problems of pollution and poverty in this country."

But he's bored, we answered.

"Why, you must impress upon him the intrinsic significance of the Western tradition."

But he's bored. He works well now that his revolutionary fires have been banked and jobs are scarce, but there is a veneer of boredom difficult for even the finest teachers to penetrate.

"All students are bored. That is the condition of their being. *I* was bored when I was a student—it wasn't until afterwards that the meaning of my education made sense to me."

> The hot water at ten.
> And if it rains, a closed car at four.
> And we shall play a game of chess.
> Pressing lidless eyes and waiting for a knock upon the door.

The dialogue rambled and never became a conversation. We insisted that the quality of this boredom is different, objects oppress us as never before; bureaucracy, T.V., mass media are ever present in our lives. It is more than a matter of just the "hot water at ten"; it is different, we argued, it will be different, and the interesting question is, after all, why is this student bored?

The world of culture and the world of action—a bloody crossroads, and I for one am too inured to a life of thought, too *comfortable* in a life of thought, to legislate strictly for action. But one loses patience. Berkeley and San Francisco, Columbia and City College and Cornell underwent convulsive revolutions in 1968 and 1969, and these same people who wrote the essays we revered as graduate students were appalled. Now that many of the students' younger brothers or sisters are bored, these same intellectuals tell us they shouldn't be bored. But you can't tell a student not to protest and you can't tell a student not to be bored. The attempt to do so is to confirm the age-old divisions between the elite and the masses that have constituted the ongoing dialectic of our culture. Magazines and movements will come and go; we will write books for each other—which will come and go —and probably continue to promote each other on that basis; but when children and adults are watching the same programs, the quantity of boredom surely becomes qualitative and is different from the boredom of the past.

Perhaps it is of little difference to our intellectual leaders. Perhaps they should not be centrally concerned with the question of the reconsideration of the American Scholar, although the distance between the intellectual and the pragmatic world within which he functions seems to me unnatural and inorganic, to return to Emerson's language, as though the concerns of ADE, NCTE, and CCCC are in a sense plebeian. Shouldn't the graduate schools be providing leadership in higher education? If not, what is the purpose of the graduate school? Shouldn't the graduate schools be relating their education to this culture? If not, why do they exist? Why should department chairmen compel those who teach graduate students to reconsider their own scholarship so that graduate students can find jobs? Must economics determine the quality of scholarship? Don't these graduate instructors become, to paraphrase Emerson's language, "bookworms" rather than Man Thinking? One need not be apocalyptic to see that the distinctions between culture and politics can scarcely be made any longer and that we have indeed come to the crossroads we would all like to avoid: the professor with the two-course load or the research professor—look at them, there they go, no teaching at all—who write about the liberal tradition do seem a little like the Puritan minister filled with exquisite torment, preaching to his congregation about salvation: unless the researcher emerges with work that warrants this luxury, he will not be met with sympathetic eyes.

But the luxurious way of life enjoyed by the researcher or the two-course-load teacher is already eccentric—one knows that, in some vital sense, it is eccentric and no longer concerned with the education that is carried on everywhere in our society, so that few people look to this way of life for guidance. It has severed itself from its roots and divided itself from its original unit and fountain of power; these professors have tacitly conspired with the society in which, to recall Emerson's language in *The American Scholar*, "The members have suffered amputation from the trunk, and strut about like so many walking monsters—a good finger, a neck, a stomach, an elbow, but never a man"—they are the delegated intellect but not Man Thinking, "the victim of society, . . . a mere thinker, or still worse a parrot of other men's thinking." It has been for many of us a great disappointment, this unwillingness to reconsider the American Scholar; and behind the immediate squabbles between teachers and scholars, between novelists and scholars, between researchers and activists, protesters and resisters, culturists and counterculturists, lies a deep failure of the imagination. "For what would we really know the meaning of?" Emerson asks. "The meal in the firkin; the milk in the pan; the ballad in the street; the news of the boat; the glance of the eye; the form and the gait of the body;—show me the ultimate reason of these matters . . . and the world lies no longer a dull miscellany and lumberroom, but has form and order."

Surely these ideas are American, for they attempt to make education organic to the society it serves. We must prepare our students far more broadly than we have by alerting them to the many different vocations for which the study of literature and language can prepare them; we must concern ourselves with these same students—and those in our communities —once they leave our institutions, offering them different ways in which they may use their leisure time more meaningfully. Interdisciplinary work will be the foundation upon which the American Scholar constructs his education, and—since graduate schools will not assume the leadership—we must be the architects of a scholarship that is pertinent to students. As higher education comes to be increasingly dominated by the city, state, and federal governments; as private colleges continue to diminish in social significance and more colleges provide open admissions to students; as junior colleges flourish and educate more and more students who enter service occupations and have greater amounts of leisure time; as the walls of our institutions—four-year, two-year, urban, and rural—begin to crumble and the outside world becomes inextricably linked with our academic lives; as all of these cultural forces converge, the questions of our society will become the direct questions of the universities. The English department, converted by then, one hopes, to a humanities department and assuming the responsibility of making a society literate and more humane, will remain at the center, providing a moral axis upon which form and order in education and the society turn in a meaningful way. By 1984 more people will be in a process of education than in the entire labor force of this country, and if current projections prove to be correct, that figure will be eighty percent of the population. For the first time in our national history, humanism may become more than an eccentric word of the elite. It may be made truly American, by you and me. For in these years ahead, we are the ones who will have to reconsider the image of the scholar and make it, as Emerson wished it to be, uniquely American.

The Scholars and the Anti-Self*

Caroline Shrodes

California State University, San Francisco

ON THE first of those tragic days in early May, before some of our classes had been "reconstituted," the emergency alarm shattered the peace of the Humanities building as we were discussing the influence of Blake on Yeats in English 186.

In disciplined silence we filed out into the quad. At a reasonably safe distance from the cold, gray walls, we re-formed in clusters—instructors with instructors, blacks with blacks, hippies with their bearded brothers and gypsy-clad sisters, the "squares" with their own kind, all speculating in subdued tones. Rumor had it that this time a bomb had been planted, not in the despised headquarters of ROTC, but in the heretofore inviolable citadel of humanities, language and literature. In twenty minutes the safe-return bell sounded. As if nothing had happened, we tried to resume our academic discussion. But the reverberations of the strident alarm continued, echoing the warning cries from the campuses of Kent, Jackson, and Augusta. We were no longer in the world of Blake and Yeats. Even a reference to the students' culture hero, R. D. Laing, whose analysis of the divided self might conceivably arrest their interest in the oppositions that recur in Yeats's poetry, failed to evoke response.

If the bomb threat had been authentic, why? Humanities students and faculty are the "good guys," under constant attack from the academic Right. However, long before this latest crisis, it should have been apparent to us that in most of the nation's colleges, students in the humanities have not found us adequately responsive to their needs, that we have often seemed to them like Yeats's "old, learned, respectable bald heads," smugly insulated from the real world, denying its passions. Might not we too recoil at the appearance among us of a Catullus in the flesh, as righteously as some of our colleagues reacted over the rumored participation of a few students in a recent Haight-Ashbury "nude-in"? Was a Blakean marriage of Heaven and Hell only a metaphor that enables us to discuss polarities with safe academic detachment? Indeed, what might our cultivation of the anti-self do to our style of teaching or to our personal value system? Was it even possible that many of our students in their search for "relevance" have taken the poets too literally? Perhaps they have assimilated better than we

---

* The keynote address at the California State University, Northridge ADE Seminar, 29 June 1970. Reprinted from *ADE Bulletin*, No. 26 (Sept. 1970), pp. 4–11.

the revolutionary implications of Blake's poetry or of Conrad's "in the destructive element immerse." If so, must we not assume some responsibility for the chaos of our world and the attacks on the towers of Academia?

Some of our critics have in fact made this accusation, after noting that many of the student dissidents and "revolutionaries" *are* students of the humanities. Indeed, at my own college we have been indicted by our president for teaching alienation because we are ourselves alienated, bitter because we are not teaching in Ivy League colleges. The assumption of some of our critics seems to be that American society is healthy if only we will all desist from reading the *New York Review of Books* and the *New Republic*, trust in law and order, and deny the sick voices of our divided selves.

We must reject this analysis and listen to our students, who perceive the roots of their alienation in a relentlessly escalating war to whose immorality and brutality we are being systematically desensitized; in an economic and political system that places material above human values and ignores the realities of racism, poverty, and environmental pollution; and in an educational system whose adherence to dead formulae and structures makes it seem an accomplice of the forces of destruction. We should remember that these same students, ill-mannered and exhibitionist, who give violent expression to their hostility and rage, have participated in the civil-rights movement, have been beaten by the police, jailed, reviled by the public, and lived under the constant threat of being drafted and killed in a war they repudiate. Our despair over their lack of discipline, their demands for instant gratification and understanding, must be countered by our appreciation of their generous giving of themselves to causes in which they believe. It is apparent that opposed forces in our students are contending for mastery: defiance and rage at the enormity of society's hypocrisy and injustice and a need to assert their humanity; experimentation in encounter groups with the feelings we have largely asked them to suppress; and imaginative efforts to reach out for human contact. Only by giving adequate recognition to them can we help them resolve these polarities in life-affirming rather than destructive action.

What images, then, can we draw upon from our vast literary tradition that will engage students accustomed to the mind-blowing sounds of the Grateful Dead, the Jefferson Airplane, or the emotions; students who have been stimulated by the psychedelic, pyrotechnical, and stroboscopic worlds which they inhabit; who have experimented with a variety of drugs and perhaps, like Blake, have been transported to strange places and experienced celestial visions; who know, in the words of one chronicle, "what it is to be burned by salt fire, to smell colors, to see sounds, and much more frequently, to see feelings"? This is the same generation of students who in the Port Huron statement make the commitment, "Our work is guided by the sense that we may be the last generation in the experiment with living." When we recall that their lives have been shadowed by this fear, we can hardly be shocked by the intensity of their demands. Nor dare we arrogantly dismiss such students, as did the Dean of Columbia who belittled their concern over the university's involvement with the Institute for Defense Analysis as "having about as much significance as telling me they like or dislike strawberries."

These students whose imaginations have been nourished by the subcultures they have helped to create, whose life styles reflect their sense of urgency in maintaining a precarious balance between pleasure and reality, who are capable of total commitment of their lives to making a better world, have a great deal to teach us, albeit a different order of learning. Perhaps our success in the classroom even bears a reciprocal relationship to what we are able to learn from them, for if we have failed to hear their voices, there is slight probability that they have reverently listened to ours.

But, we may ask defensively, have we not for some time been confronting our failures and making concessions to external pressures and to student demands for relevance? Look, for instance, at our revised doctoral programs. Instead of emphasizing the sterile minutiae of scholarship and putting a premium on our candidate's memory, we now permit him to demonstrate the quality of his mind by selecting only three or four areas for examination. Instead of limiting to the distant past the possible subjects for research, we may now accept dissertations on Allen Ginsberg and Le Roi Jones or even on the annotated edition of *Lolita*; we now approve of studies which draw upon related disciplines as a means of illuminating the work of art. We can now regard as an anachronism George Stewart's satirical account in *Doctor's Oral* of the system in which the fate of the trembling graduate student depends on whether his inquisitors will succeed in confusing his memory of the number of lilies in the hand of the Blessed Damozel.

We have listened patiently to students, reorganized our undergraduate curriculum, and increased the number of electives; we have supported innovations in method and technique; we have offered experimental courses in The Contemporary Consciousness and The New Grotesque. But we must acknowledge that thus far such experiments have proceeded largely from motives of expediency or even out of fear for our own survival. In this sense, but at an opposite pole from our critics, we *are* alienated from our best selves, from the selves that dare, with the vision of a Blake or Yeats, to push beyond the boundaries of the given, the safe, the respectable. We have accepted a diminished view of our students, of ourselves, of the revolutionary nature of our subject matter, and of human possibility.

If we are concerned with helping our students satisfy their need for *becoming* rather than *doing*, for extending the range of choice open to them, for finding meaning and value in the flux of sensations that bombard them—needs, according to the existentialists, as compelling as "the need for sunlight, calcium, or love"—we must frankly acknowledge that to a large extent we have failed. We have failed because we are haunted by ghosts, phantoms of the hoary academic halls in which we had our training as transmitters of sacred tradition: the fading spirits of neo-humanism and the Puritanism of the twenties; the ghosts of the New Critics, many of them as detached as the dead from the realities of the seventies; the shadows of Germanic philology, which decreed that literary study must be a rigorously scientific discipline; the remnants of an elitism that defensively asserts our superiority over the gods of the marketplace at the same time that we pander to its competitive spirit.

It is a truism that the dominant influence on the teaching of literature for the past three decades has been that of the New Criticism, an impact that admittedly has enriched literary study by freeing it from the sterility of its former emphasis on the historical approach and secondary materials.

However, in the process it has propelled us into an intellectual vacuum that has its correlative in the isolation of teacher from taught as well as poem from poet.

The syndromes of scientism and elitism among scholars in our profession must share responsibility for the dissent directed against the university. In the supercilious insistence that the literary work must be studied in isolation, they have fostered the kind of classroom practice which Aldous Huxley describes in *Point Counter Point*: "The substitution of simple intellectual schemata for the living complexities of reality; of still and formal death for the bewildering movements of life."

Distinguished scholars continue to regard the response of the audience as outside the purview of literary study and dismiss it as extrinsic. Still less would they accept the insights of depth psychology, anticipated by Lascelles Abercrombie almost half a century ago in his penetrating statement that reading poetry involves "the transmission of energy rather than substance." In spite of the irrefutable evidence that art is rooted in prelogical processes of the mind which are not penetrable by the application of reason alone, many of us would still reduce literature to a "stratified system of norms." Although Wellek concedes there is no need for reification of these norms, the New Critics developed their own metapsychology. Blackmur speaks of "direct apprehension," sustained contact with the work which puts us in direct possession of principles whereby works *move* without injury or disintegration; Tate declares that "the poem is its own *knower*" (my italics). In endowing literature with these anthropomorphic powers, they thus magically exorcise any errant or uncomfortable impulses that might be latent within them. They provide additional strictures which would render the experience of literature "anesthetic" (Frederick Crews's adjective to characterize much of their criticism). Ransom would withhold the "absolute name of art" from works of literature rendered "impure" by the intrusion of ideas. Warren and Wellek admonish the student of literature that if his study is not precisely a science, his task is to "translate his experience . . . into intellectual terms, assimilate it to a coherent scheme which must be rational if it is to be knowledge." Should the critic or the reader unwittingly lapse into attaching some significance to the way he is affected by the work of art, he is guilty of the Affective Fallacy. Should he speak of emotion, Wimsatt and Beardsley decree, it must be dependent on a precise object. And, finally, they would remove from our consideration the possibility of enjoyment: "It may well be that the contemplation of this object, or pattern of emotive knowledge, which is the poem, is the ground for some ultimate emotional state which may be termed the aesthetic (some empathy, some synaesthesis, some objectified feeling of pleasure). It may well be. The belief is attractive; it may exalt our view of poetry. But it is no concern of criticism, no part of criteria."

Perhaps the attitude that most alienates our students is best summed up in Wimsatt's attack on the Chicago neoclassical school, which is guilty of "latent affectivism" and strong tendencies toward pluralism! These charges epitomize the concerns of the critic for whom psychologism (sic) is an intrusive violation of the purity of art. With great indignation Wimsatt states that two of the most important terms of the Chicago critics are pleasure and purpose! Accordingly, even Coleridge must be repudiated for having so departed from his venerated system as to state that the poem proposes, for its immediate object, pleasure, not truth. The inviolability of "the mode of existence of a literary work of art" must not be threatened by such extraneous concerns. In a tone of incredulity, Wellek alludes to those who cherish the idea that poetry is supposed to order our impulses and that its value lies in some sort of psychical therapy, a heresy, he reminds us, which led Richards finally to the admission that "this goal may be accomplished by a bad as well as a good poem, by a carpet, a pot, a gesture as well as by a sonata." To make sure that the villainy of psychology is emphasized, he concludes by saying that anarchy, skepticism, and "complete confusion of values is the result of every psychological theory, as it must be unrelated either to the structure or the quality of a poem." In their repudiation of "insidious psychological relativism," the New Critics are thus casually dismissing the Aristotelian theory of catharsis, whose reverberations from Milton to Kenneth Burke and Lionel Trilling lend support to the mithridatic function of art.

Is this righteous rejection of possible therapeutic value an effort to avert the threat of being surprised or made anxious by feelings not contained in our systems of classification? Have we invented some of our more esoteric literary puzzles as a means of insulating ourselves from the world our students see as wantonly destructive? Are our ingenious solutions to them a form of undoing whereby wrestling with the paradox in the work conceals from us the contradictions within ourselves? Such isolation of the work from the responder, however well-meaning and idealistic, evokes just accusations of irrelevance and nihilism. In Benjamin DeMott's words, "The poem became a set of relations within itself, a fascinating clockworks that told no time."

What, then, are the alternatives to limiting our goals to transmitting the genteel tradition and enjoining our students to assimilate their experience of the work to a rational and austere theory of literature? What might be the consequences were we to change our emphasis in an attempt to give fresh meaning to their literary experience; were we to encourage them to become active participants as well as spectators in their reading of imaginative literature; were we, instead of imposing a structure into which they must accommodate their experience, to accommodate our structure to their needs and experience? It is scarcely necessary to "reconstitute" a class whose texts are The New Grotesque or *Coriolanus*. Our classes may also be transformed by asking more of ourselves than we are accustomed to give, although not more of our subject matter than it insistently invites. But we *shall* be required to initiate a different order of questions: Does the greatness of art lie in its tension, its texture, and its paradox, or does its transcendent power lie in the human response? Is the folio in an encrusted vault a testament of great art if there is not a single reader? Does erosion of the work of art take place through extending the number of its responders and enlarging the range of its satisfactions, or would a classic be more likely to suffer erosion if, through a narrow and elitist approach, we sacrificed the human connection? Has our teaching been designed to liberate our students from parochialism, to extend their consciousness and accordingly the possibilities for choice? Have we helped them to make reason and intellect the conscious allies of their emotions? In our imposition of external standards, have we also encouraged them to internalize their experience? Have we helped them to discover the anti-self which, Yeats reminds us, "comes but to those . . . whose passion is reality"; to summon the "energy to assume the mask of some other life," a mask "whose lineaments permit the expression of all" they most lack? Remembering also with Yeats that the man who is capable of letting his imagination fuse with the corporate imagination has available for his use all the images ever wrought by men as well as the power to create new ones, are we willing to reject the customary formula which freezes our teaching style, limits our vision, and contracts our subject matter? Such a commitment would require that we sacrifice our often indulgent enclaves of privacy; that we attempt to recapture the sense of immediacy and excitement that we felt in our own initial experience of literature.

Instead of lamenting the passing of the old order in which a silent generation (which many of us deplored) was content to strive solely for security and comfort, we should welcome the contemporary student whose flamboyance reflects the prodigality of his feelings. Instead of resenting his demand for relevance, we should be glad that he is not asking us to reduce our study of literature but rather to extend it. He does not want merely to be entertained, but he is rejecting the passive role to which we have assigned him and asking to be recognized as an active participant in his own learning. He wants to be acknowledged as a unique individual with an identity of his own, which, although still unformed, is seeking to become more fully realized. At the same time he is asking our help in creating a community, a community which gives recognition to the importance of each individual voice in a process of mutual discovery and exploration. He is seeking to build a world in which the teacher, as well as the students, having shared the experience of reading a work of literature, responds with the fullness of his being; who affirms his authenticity, in Harold Taylor's words, by taking the radical risk of "disclosure of himself in the fullness of his certainties and ambiguities. . . ." Recognizing like Auden that "since life does not exist in a series of autonomous departments, aesthetic values do not nourish themselves . . . ," the modern student is not content to respond to a work of literature and then see it fragmented and apportioned into arcane categories. He is asking to be free to organize his experience of literature in his own way before being forced to accommodate it to structures we have defined for him. He is reminding us that if he is encouraged to discover the reverberations that literature has for him, his understanding will be deepened. He knows intuitively that there is no meaningful instruction without delight.

Were we to accede to these requests, many of us would be venturing into an unknown and uncomfortable world. Since we have been effectively enjoined to regard response to literature as extrinsic to its proper study, there is much that we would need to learn. However, it is possible that only such a radical change in emphasis may enable us to help to create the conditions necessary for sustained and significant literary study.

Such a shift in our hierarchy of values will require the development of an organic theory of response to literature, which will draw upon pertinent theories from such disciplines as philosophy, cultural anthropology, and depth psychology, as well as from studies of archetype and myth and literary criticism. We may perceive that our former atomistic view of the world has been replaced by a holistic conception of man and a dynamic view of the universe in which "there is a constant interchange of energy between living beings and their environment," including the books we read.

Simon Lesser in *Fiction and the Unconscious* and Norman Holland in *The Dynamics of Literary Response* have broken ground in extending our awareness of the role the unconscious plays in our response to literature. The pioneer work of Ernst Kris on "aesthetic ambiguity" and Lawrence Kubie's study of the creative process throw light upon the reader's transformations of the secondary elaborations of the writer. The processes by which the writer consciously shapes his dreams, the means by which he "gives to aery nothings/A local habitation and a name," provide a paradigm for the way in which the reader imposes order upon the writer's vision. In Sartre's words, reading is the "dialectical correlative" of writing and an exercise in generosity: "What the writer requires of the reader is not the application of an abstract freedom but the gift of his whole person, with his passions, his prepossessions, his sympathies, his sexual temperament, and his scale of values." Accordingly, Sartre continues, "the literary object has no other substance than the reader's subjectivity; Raskolnikov's waiting is *my* waiting which I lend him. . . . Raskolnikov . . . would only be a shadow, without the mixture of repulsion and friendship which I feel for him and which makes him live. But, by a reversal which is the characteristic of the imaginary object, it is not his behavior which excites my indignation or esteem, but my indignation and esteem which give consistency and objectivity to his behavior."

An organic theory of response will enable us to understand the relationship between the sources and energies of art and the transmutations that take place in the reader's imaginative re-creation of it; it will suggest how art may serve as a catalyst to bind or free the energy of the reader and thus account for the vast differences in response not only among bright, untutored students, but among their highly trained instructors and the professional critics. It may persuade the teacher of literature that by permitting, even encouraging, a private response to the work of art, far from violating its integrity, he may help his students to distinguish between what is in the self and what is in the work as well as to refine their judgment and enrich their understanding.

A comprehensive theory should clarify the relationship between the personality of the reader and his response to imaginative literature. It will remind us that his capacity to enter fully and imaginatively into the world the writer has created is determined not only by the formal and affective properties of literature but also by the dynamics of his personality. We shall need to ask whether it is meaningful to say that tension is inherent in the poem; or whether tension resides in the reader who projects it upon the work when, to paraphrase Christopher Caudwell, there is a disparity between his being and his consciousness. And we might question whether it is possible to have a "direct apprehension" of a poem; whether revelation can be so pure that it is not filtered through the fallible perceptions and the viscera.

A theory of response will help us to understand why literature in its representation of experience which differs only in degree from that of the reader may lead to a confusion of symbol with reality, a confusion in which a harrowing episode in a novel or the anguished feelings of a character may become interchanged with the circumstances of his life. The affective power of literature may be so compelling that he may attribute to a character his own anxieties and thus thrust them outward; he may project upon a character the hate or fear he finds intolerable in himself. When this happens, the reader is reacting to the work in the same repetitive pattern with which he responds to his own experience. For an occasional reader the identification may be so complete that it precipitates an acting out of his own destructive impulses. With another equilibrium of forces the same images may provide a substitute release from tension or, in Kenneth Burke's phrase, "a strategy for encompassing a situation." For such a reader the shock of recognition may reveal facets of his personality formerly inaccessible to him. He may be sufficiently flexible to move freely from the role of participant to that of detached spectator. As participant he too may relive his own experience; but as spectator he will be able critically to appraise the character's fantasies or fears at the same time that he recognizes them as his own; in so doing, he may become able to reduce to life-size and endow with a reasonable share of human fraility even the seemingly omnipotent and magical figures of his childhood. When the reader can view his own image in the mirror with both feeling and detachment, vicarious experience may serve as a catalyst to extend the range of his consciousness.

An organic theory of response will need to ask questions about the ways in which involvement in the work may impair literary judgment and expose critical bias. What kinds of response betray deep involvement, detachment, or a simulated detachment which may mask intensity of feeling? Why do some readers respond with underdistance and others with overdistance? How valid is the hypothesis that a surplus of libidinal energy invested in the work determines the former, and inability to experience the work emotionally, the latter; that ambivalence in the personality may elicit self-contradictory responses in the same reader? Is there a positive correlation between the capacity of the reader to move freely on more than one psychic level and his ability to make sophisticated literary judgments? We may recall Freud's comment that "every genuine poetical creation must have proceeded from more than one motive, more than one impulse in the mind of the poet and must admit of more than one interpretation."

A theory of response should clarify the means by which the formal elements of the work may counteract the reader's failure to distinguish the organized sequence of events the writer has portrayed from the unorganized events of his own life. Why does a highly allusive work replete with myth and archetype—for example, Joyce's *Ulysses*—evoke a more personal response and greater distortion than a highly structured naturalistic novel? Responses to projective techniques may provide a paradigm for response to literature. A protocol from a semistructured Thematic Apperception Test in which the respondent reflects confusion concerning his sexual identification should enable one to predict a similar confusion in his interpretation of a work of fiction in which sexual ambiguities are implicit. Understanding of a respondent's obsessive and repetitive response to differing forms and his inability to unite into an organic whole the disparate, unstructured images of a Rorschach blot should enable one to predict that he will make stereotyped and peripheral responses to a work of literature; bizarre responses to form, resistance to the color cards, or inability to perceive human beings in motion would suggest that his isolation is too deeply rooted to permit him to enter imaginatively into the work. At the same time such a comparative study should illuminate the ways in which form, imagery, texture, and movement in literature may disarm the reader and lead to a "transmission of energy rather than substance." Recognition of the nature of the projective process may enable us to interrupt the circular processes which impede understanding of both the self and the work of art.

Such interdisciplinary studies should illuminate the complex processes by which the storyteller, in Freud's words, "is able to guide the current of our emotions, dam it up in one direction and make it flow in another"; by which literature may at once minister to the pleasure principle and to the reality principle; by which it may elicit symbolic responses, whereby man, as Cassirer suggests, "projects his reality and comes to know it." Exploration of these heuristic theories should encourage experimental study and influence classroom practice. At the same time a more imaginative and daring approach to the teaching of literature should contribute to the development of an organic theory of response.

If we tenaciously hold to the conviction that literature, however deeply felt and skillfully taught, is incapable of changing man's attitudes, of moving his heart—much less of altering his behavior—we shall reinvoke a self-fulfilling prophecy. If our exposure to "the best that has been thought and said in the world" does not permit us to transform our accretions of knowledge into being and act, we have failed to apprehend fully the literature we profess to love, to suspend willingly our disbelief and surrender to its eloquence. If we are willing, however, to explore with our students the full resources of our subject, the energy inherent in art may serve as a catalyst to set their energy free, and the work of art may be transformed by their energy. When this happens, it may become for all of us a bridge to reality, an enhancement of being, a vision of order, and a celebration of life.

The Management of English*

Paul Olson

University of Nebraska

I AM TOLD by some of my friends that management has to do with looking at systemic relations, examining the goals of a community of people and trying to relate what these people say they want to do and what they really do. Management may be used to develop a strategy that will allow the community of people to say to itself that it does not really want to do what it says it wants to do; management may also be used to create a sufficient change in the community—in its responsibility system—so that it can, in some measure, achieve the goals that it says it wants to accomplish. Management has to do, then, with the relationship between our stated goals and what we get done.

Let me try to set forth what I think would be a management problem for a department of English. Let us say that we have a number of young professors who read some works written after 1500; some of the works are what Victorian gentlemen would call "excessively baudy." When they come into the classroom, they are moved by the spirit of the work; there comes a point at which the professorial diction disappears and another kind of diction pervades the classroom. The department has a discussion on the decorum of diction and teaching. The decorum of diction in literature is something that we have talked about since the time of Donatus' commentary on *Terence*.

Renaissance culture and most subsequent English literary cultures assumed that the decorum of diction in literature had something to do with the decorum of diction in life—with class structures, with contexts, with the intention of the speaker. On the other hand, the assumption of many modern literature teachers and of those who administer their programs has been that the decorum of diction in the classroom ought to be something approximating Martin Joost's "frozen level." It has also been regarded as quite appropriate for literary critics in English departments to talk about the decorum of diction in literary works, but not appropriate for these same critics to ask questions with respect to the decorum of diction employed in the classroom. Yet one could imagine a department saying to itself, "Are these standards which we carry only into the literary works which we teach—into our analysis of those literary works—are they also the standards

* An address to the Northwestern ADE Seminar, 11 Nov. 1971. Reprinted from *ADE Bulletin*, No. 33 (May 1972), pp. 20–29.

that we carry into the analysis of our own behavior and the behavior of our students in the classroom? If not, why not?"

Let us suppose that this English department is under a great deal of public pressure to be "less radical"; like all centers in the humanities, it is supposed to have done bad things at times of crisis in our country's recent history. Thus, let us say, there is a further division of spirit—now one not within the department but between the department and the larger community which "surrounds" and "supports" it. Let us say that the department had to make some decisions about what it is as an educating agent, about how it can best serve the public it claims to serve. Both radical and conservative in the department are concerned about serving the public. Can the department serve the cause of the public education best by adopting the mores of the public? Or by "educating the public to whatever solution the department arrives at"? If the department "consolidates its mores," does it consolidate those mores on public terms? On the terms of the literary-criticism and literature-and-life canons which it proclaims? Does it decide on a decorum according to some professional terms separate from either of these? To what extent can a department constitute its own culture, separate from the whole culture of the region? These are not, I think, simply academic questions. They are fundamental to the process of evaluation.

Our tendency is to regard ourselves as bound to the folk when we think of such things as economic policy, policy with respect to the distribution of wealth; we tend not to think of ourselves as bound to the folk when it comes to such questions as decorum.

The problem I have tried to set forth is fundamentally a management problem. It seems to be cause for an analysis of customary rules, of risks in the situation, of the educational opportunities; it seems to require some sort of elaboration of group strategy.

I will not "solve" the problem I have posed. I wish simply to display it to suggest that what management does may not be a trivial issue in the humane disciplines. I wish to look at other like management problems which have come to the profession of "English," what we have stated as goals, what we have arrayed as possible resources for reaching the goals, and what we have gotten. Perhaps if we look at some of the goals we have stated for ourselves, what we've done, what risks we have taken, and what opportunities we have, we will be clearer about how we have managed ourselves and how we ought to. Certainly, English is managed. It constitutes a series of large corporate investments, and perhaps the largest departmental teaching investment that American higher education makes. That this much money should be put into what people have defined as English is a bit anachronistic, given the predominant pragmatism of American state legislatures and the American public. The investment involves a large number of employees; the creation of systematic evaluation procedures according to which employees are salaried and promoted; the creation of other evaluation procedures according to which members of the American public are allowed to pursue or not pursue an "education" and obtain scarce, high-salaried jobs. Enormous power is vested in a department of English. Failure in the first year of college tends to come more often from freshman English than any other subject.

If English is managed effectively, it is managed unobtrusively, and primarily by the development of an *ethos*: what Kuhn calls a "paradigm community." You can find out how English is managed by looking at the promotion policies of departments, at the tests which they develop and which, through encouragement or acquiescence, they allow major testing agencies to develop. You can discover how English is managed by looking at the systemic evaluation procedures, the curricular requirements and grading procedures, the stop-and-go signals of all kinds which are set up within English departments. You can discover a good deal about the management of English by looking at the publication policies of the journals used in deciding who gets the cookies and who doesn't at the university; about the ethos, culture, and value system of the editors and readers of those journals.

Whereas you can tease out a management ideology by looking at the relationships among these various systems, you can also detect what it is by looking at the profession's justifying documents. At times the profession pulls together its public rhetoric in a kind of central credo designed to affect other systems. I'd like to look at two central justifying documents that the profession has created in the last forty years—look at them in relationship to the decision-making practices and allocation of resources which are advocated in them. There is a relationship between what these documents say and what happens within departments. (Justifying documents are important in the way that the Declaration of Independence is important, constituting, as they do, an appeal to the outside community: a statement or *raison d'être* for services rendered or about to be rendered. They are efforts to rationalize the present and to create a new kind of a future, simultaneously.) The one document is the 1961 *National Interest and the Teaching of English*; the other is the 1943 *Literature in American Education*. What is most interesting about the documents is the lack of consonance between the general goals described in the documents and the mechanisms described as appropriate to achieving the goals.[1]

The first document, *National Interest and the Teaching of English*, bears, to the decade of the sixties, something of the sort of relationship that the documents which the Study Commission will put out will bear to the decade of the seventies. The document was MLA and NCTE sponsored and carried to thousands of people across the country, but particularly to the Congress as an appeal for the extending of federal funding to Title XI English institutes and for the granting of further federal funding (Bureau of Research funds) for curriculum development centers. Many of us profited enormously from the effectiveness of the document in that it gave to us better salaries and to our departments more money for research, for fellowships, for institutes, and the like.

In the middle of the document appears a statement which suggests that Sputnik is not very far from the consciousness; it is right on the horizon, sitting there like a flying saucer:

In the fields of science and mathematics . . . the spectacular appearance of Sputnik provided the impetus for a re-examination and for developments in the re-education of leading high school teachers. In English the disparity between what the specialist knows and what the schools teach is even greater. But no dramatic orbiting of the linguistic satellite draws public attention to this disparity.

Given the impediment to parity of rhetorical effectiveness posed by the Russian Orb, the English profession rather bravely begins its efforts to persuade the Congress that English deserves significant funding, comparable to that given to science and mathematics.

The title of the book is interesting: *The National Interest and the Teaching of English.* The "national interest" semantically plays subtly into the notion of national defense; it is, after all, the National Defense Education Act that people are endeavoring to amend. Title XI of that act is to be extended. It is difficult at first for those of us who think of ourselves as innocents, as sort of Milly Theales in a world of Kate Croys, to conceive exactly how the national interest and the national defense are going to be served by the teaching of English. But there it is: English will strengthen the state within while mathematics and science will ward off the enemy whose little capsules float overhead.

The ideology of the document—the tall ideas that are stated as "what English will do for the nation," the managerial goals—are interesting and exciting. First, English is said to preserve humane values in a society: "The teaching of English plays a vital role in preserving human values in a technological society." It is the humanizing process that begins in English departments. The second thing that English does is to assist communication, also necessary to the democratic process. "Democratic institutions require informed communication, or more specifically, democratic institutions depend on intelligent, informed communication." Those are the goals: to create humane men and to create effective communication, i.e., democratic men.

Now, what are the mechanisms for reaching the goals? The central section of the book is entirely dedicated to the study of those mechanisms; here the real proposals with respect to the management of money and management of behavior come out. What is seen as assisting democracy and assisting communication in democracy is interesting. The first chapter deals with the standards of preparation of English teachers; the second chapter deals with state certification. A further section deals with what constitutes the "disciplines of English": what is inside the discipline and what is outside it. In short, what the book addresses itself to in its early sections are power mechanisms; it does not address itself to the substance of those power mechanisms in relation to the announced goals: that is, to the question of whether through credentialing legislation and definitions of a discipline you can "humanize" a person, or assist him in developing intelligent, informed communication (or assist his teachers to assist him).

There is a list of college courses that are popular for teachers-to-be, popular courses which are good for teachers. The courses are English and American literature, Shakespeare, Chaucer, nineteenth-century lit, seventeenth-century lit, eighteenth-century, and "Masterpieces." The book suggests that to this list of required or highly encouraged courses should be added other courses perhaps not always currently taught which would assist teachers to be more in touch with the discipline: world literature, contemporary literature, and critical analysis. It is the day of Brooks and Warren in the freshman and sophomore college courses, and one can see a procession of little Brookses and Warrens extending at least into junior high school and flowing from these suggestions of courses for teachers.

Another chapter deals with factors that make for success in high schools as defined by a survey conducted by the National Council of Teachers of English. A variety of factors make high-school programs "successful": special attention to able students; the influences of "superior" homes and backgrounds on students who possess them; school emphasis on academic achievement; community interest in education; community interest in cultural offerings (apparently opera and "legitimate theater"); school insistence on high standards; emphasis on fundamentals of English (included here are grammar, usage, punctuation, and drill). There are other factors that are said to be important, some that wouldn't produce a chuckle now. I have given you those which most reflect the times, a high percentage of the total number of factors listed.

If we chuckle now at the naïveté and snobbishness of the factors listed, that is an indication of historical perspective that has come to us across a decade of civil-rights struggle and a developing consciousness of the extent to which America, like other nations, has made the notion of "quality education" bear the burden of agendas which have little to do either with intellectual excellence ("quality") or with real learning ("education").

After the book deals with the mechanisms, it comes home to the tall ideals again:

The teaching of English will only become effective if the conditions under which it is taught improve. Present programs for preparing English teachers must be reassessed and new programs be developed to assist many practicing teachers. School libraries must be expanded, teaching loads reduced. Research must supply better answers for some of the English teacher's urgent questions. A national reawakening of interest and activity in English is long overdue. Our political democracy can provide our youth with the conditions of liberty: abundance, freedom of action, an accessible system of schools. But the ability to think and write and read, an intimate contact with ideals, beauty and morality, all central in English studies, are needed to equip our citizens to use their freedom wisely. America is now a major world power. As never before our country must think about its responsibilities to mankind and about its need for citizens to meet these awesome responsibilities. Tomorrow's leaders must learn today whatever truth, and beauty, and wisdom our culture can provide. Only a quality education will prepare our youth for the test. Only a balanced education will insure the quality needed. The national interest demands vigorous leadership to improve all educational programs.

In 1961, what English would do was to further democratic goals; to develop some sense of world responsibility in citizens whose empire extended to Asia, Africa, and South America; to provide for that efficient communication which will make man who is *capax rationis* into democratic man.

But when *efficient communication* is defined, it is defined primarily in terms suggested by the business community or the respectable successful community; usage, spelling, the decorum of language of the successful is held up far more often than are any skills profoundly needed in the thinking of responsible democratic man: i.e., thinking about a system from a perspective outside the system, thinking using a variety of coherent ("elegant," in physicists' language) ways of explaining events; thinking about what knowledge means for action.

The statement that the society already provides abundance, freedom of action, and an accessible system of schools was written during the first days of the Kennedy regime: the poverty program was just getting under way; the civil-rights movement had hardly begun. Vietnam was still Ngo Dinh Diem. Accessibility, freedom, and abundance are posited as prior to what English does, i.e., to provide ideals, beauty, and morality; but one wonders if they are themselves supported by the English programs suggested or by the decision-making systems implicitly offered. Are accessibility, freedom, and abundance supported by the success factors which make good high-school English programs: "Anglo" and elitist forms of cultural expression (opera, etc.)?

What troubles one is that the book never questions whether successful programs depend upon elitist conditions or whether elite groups define success in American education. The book does not tell how the exclusions of a new credentialing system for teachers which includes more courses in English like those encouraged in graduate school will make for that accessibility, freedom, and abundance in education which will support whatever is true and beautiful and wise in our culture. It does not tell how institutes will make good men; yet it suggests that they will.

If you look at the literature courses listed in their order of preferences, you will notice that, though "literature" is part of a subject described as encouraging a sense of world citizenship and democratic values, the literature which is read primarily comes out of strongly "hierarchical" or "imperial" societies rather than village societies, tribal societies, or tribal democratic societies (such as the Hopi). When world literature is mentioned, no literature that comes from oppressed parts of the world is listed. In the main, the literary study implied for classroom teachers, in the book's listings of courses, is the study of work which comes from rather triumphant countries.

When the book discusses the study of language (this discussion was seen as a considerable breakthrough and probably was just that), it argues for a much more intensive study of linguistic science and suggests that English teachers need to know, among other things, the descriptive approaches to usage by such "democratic" voices as that of the late C. C. Fries. It is interesting, however, that when one comes to the composition section, the section that deals with those courses where people are "started" and "stopped," the issue of usage is not raised in Friesian terms. There are sections on marking papers, on the need for remedial English, and on the fact that 150,000 students failed college English tests. What is assumed is that English departments will further the same linguistic norms that they have always furthered, that any "new rhetoric" developed will assist people to meet those norms better; it is never suggested, implicitly or explicitly, that the composition norms which created remedial English and brought 150,000 students to fail college English tests might themselves be norms which spoke less to democracy and clear thought than to class and clear syntax as defined by Donald Davidson.

Who has to learn new tricks in the world of democracy, ideals, beauty, and morality? The teachers learn new tricks in learning a new linguistic science, but insofar as language patterns are to be altered, the people who are expected to alter are Shaw's "undeserving poor." It is clear that no challenge is intended to the notion that a mastery of "standard usage" is necessary to a man who wishes to make it through the decision-making system. A linguistic revolution is described in the book and the rise of linguistic science described, but no suggestion is made that this ought to have any effect on the power structures that exist within the university; that English departments, perhaps, ought to go out of existence to make way for the new science or that new departments ought to be created on the basis of the coming into existence of new knowledge.

The National Interest and the Teaching of English had the desired effect. Thanks to the book and some good political footwork in Washington, English came to be a priority Office of Education subject. Millions were spent on new curricula and institutes; new credentialing systems requiring the desired courses were created by state Departments of Education. That was a revolution. And yet few people would argue that we reached the humane and democratic goals, or even the communicative goals, which the document sets forth, let alone the goals having to do with "truth," "beauty," "wisdom," and sense of world responsibility. One could argue that the failure—if there was one—had to do with Congress' failure to provide enough money. One might alternatively argue that there was no failure— that the kind of education and the kind of "humane culture" we got in the sixties were of a piece with the mechanisms which we described as good and the courses which we described as desirable. Congress may have supported us less for the world we said we wanted than for the mechanisms we said we would keep alive.

One of the reasons for our receiving the sort of public support that we have received may be that we have constituted a useful sorting system, a system providing the country with some of the means for reaching goals which constitute polar opposites of the goals stated at the beginning and the end of our document. Congress funded us because we made no threat to "liberal education's" sorting system in the document we provided to Congress. To look at the rhetoric at the beginning and the end and then to look at the mechanisms is to reassure oneself that "mechanisms" have nothing to do with "rhetoric." This may not have been willful on our part; but, to put it in another way, no congressman seeing the book could have possibly worried that the world would become the least bit more democratic, that it would change in any fundamental way, should all of the changes advocated in the book be enacted.

The structures addressed are not the structures that English professors control. What is suggested is that *Congress* do new things. What is not suggested is that departments of English or professional societies alter present power mechanisms. No suggestion is made that there be a fundamental reexamination of, say, how people are hired in English departments; no questions are asked about which literatures of what nations are to be admitted to the curriculum. No new, or old, nation builders thrive here. No one asks what the functions of freshman English are in sorting people; no questions are asked of testing standards. One of the sad things about the documents we have written is that the enemy has always been out there, the enemy has always been someone other than ourselves; the enemy has almost never been the system which we control.

The second document is called *Literature in American Education*. It is an older document. It was put out in 1943 by the MLA Commission on

Trends in Education. The authors of this document are some of our most distinguished people in the study of the humanities: Tom Pollock, William McVane, Edward Zeydel, Marjorie Nicolson, Howard Lowry, and others. The document is not written by the fools who are our enemies, nor is it a deliberately journalistic or superficial document. It represents the best thought of the time: the threat is fascism in 1943; and the MLA Commission on Trends in Education knows where fascism comes from. Fascism in 1943 comes from the educationists. The enemies are fascists; enemies of required foreign-language studies; enemies of required literature; enemies of required Greek and Latin.

Many are the things that the educationists do that German and Italian fascists also do: first of all, they repudiate "traditional broadening subjects: literature, language, philosophy, and mathematics." Secondly, they "insist on a substitution of practical contemporary knowledge and skills." Thirdly, they deny "the value of intellectual education"; and, fourth, they support "the rise of the social sciences." A quotation from *Mein Kampf* gives capsule expression to the anti-intellectualism of the educators: a Hitler who could say "what was wrong with German education in the nineteenth century was that too many people got interested in too many books" anticipates those "educators" who are destroying the life of the mind.

Literature in American Education is not addressed to the Congress (federal funding is not in sight). The document's function is to develop public support for the continuation of required courses in the foreign languages and in English, and, further, to suggest that required courses in Latin and Greek (or at least in the Latin and Greek classics) would not be a bad idea. Our document says that it will not deign to address itself to pedagogy or teaching (Was it Horace who spoke of literature as the "teaching" or "delighting"?) but rather to more fundamental things: i.e., why literary studies should continue. The significance of the study of literature is all bounced off the crisis in Europe, the fact of concentration camps, Hitler and Mussolini, and the bombings in London. We are on a darkling plain where ignorant armies clash by night. What English does is keep us human ("antifascist"). Literature sees man as a man; fascism sees man "as an integer":

Literature enlarges the understanding. More powerful in its effect than reports on slums and poverty is the recollection of Lear in the storm seeing the bond between himself and the poor naked wretches who "bide the pelting of the pitiless storm." Literature places one in touch with other countries. Our government, seeking to cement our alliances with other countries, grows hopeful when more Americans will know the literature of our good neighbors. [One hears the echo of the Good Neighbor Policy.]

Literature also gives one an understanding of democracy; it makes one understand a "truly democratic man" like "Jefferson." Literature relates man to his past; to see how it relates man to his past may be helpful.

The value one places on an older literature depends, of course, on the acceptance of some general principles about liberal education that it is not the province of this report to discuss at length. The knowledge of the past, the very act of memory itself, is one of the marks distinguishing men from the brutes. Man without learning, and the remembrance of things past, falls into a brutish sottishness, and his life is no better to be accounted of than to be buried alive. Little good the decisions of freemen, if men are actually not free, but are slaves to the provincial bounds of their own day, unable to pass in their imagination through other ages than their own. Their problems have no point of reference. They decide upon the issues of private and public life from no long and time-enlightened view. The inevitable result is a thinning of the individual, and a thinning of the whole working of democracy. It is the individual who loses most. Here man must turn at last upon himself. After society has done its best for him, the political and economic sphere leaves him finally in his own company, the highest function of a democracy being to ensure the sacred rights of personality. The final act of such a government is to restore man to himself, to give him back the privacy that is rightfully his. In practice this return is made anyhow, under freedom or under slavery. You educate man for the society in which he lives, but you educate him ultimately for his inevitable solitude.

The picture of the contemplative slave restoring himself to himself and invulnerable in his own solitude is a picture conceived somewhere on the campuses of New York University or Columbia University, not from observing the mean streets between, even in 1943.

Finally, there is an attractive statement of what literature does:

Human liberty depends not on charters and institutions alone; it depends on memory—on the ancient heritage of men—on the voice of that human confederation scattered through many lands and many ages which it is the business of literature to make known. We have been progressively forgetting that heritage, and trying to live as children without parents or teachers to guide them. In a recent statement of his faith in a liberal education, Mr. Wendell Willkie, in an issue of *The American Scholar*, put the challenge squarely before us. "When you range back and forth through the centuries, when you weigh the utterance of some great thinker, absorb the meaning of some great composition in painting, or music or poetry, when you live these things within yourself and weigh yourself against them, only then do you become an initiate in the world of the free." This is the true freedom that we covet for our children here.

Some of the goals, then, of literary study are the understanding of the world of poverty and pain, the understanding of world culture, and the creation of a truly democratic sense. Yet, though the world is mentioned in the document, there is no non-European writer ever mentioned, no writer who comes out of a tradition other than that of Europe or the United States. No postmedieval writer who writes out of an oppressed tradition is mentioned: neither traditional nor modern African writers writing in English; not Senghor writing in French; not W. E. B. DuBois, not Richard Wright, not Ghandi or Tagore; and not Black Elk. None of the literatures of non-European, English-speaking peoples who spoke English after they were colonized are mentioned.

The picture of Lear and the servant awakens a kind of tenderness; sympathy for the slave is mentioned throughout the book. But no one is asked to see W. E. B. DuBois, in his old age speaking in a high rage much in the mood of Lear, as Lear; no one is asked to look at Garvey—recently dead, broken, and, Lear-like, jailed, exiled from his "native land"—as fixed upon a "wheel of fire." The real slave in America is never mentioned; Jefferson, on his plantation, is truly a democratic man.

The actuality of the document is that men of good faith and civilized sensibility, men of breeding and taste in the eighteenth-century sense (the phrase still echoes in the MLA at times), out of neither malice nor cruelty but out of a failure of seriousness—out of a failure to carry out in their "management practices" the principles they profess—are blinded to the existence even of those phenomena to which the works they are mentioning and the perceptions they are advocating could most appropriately have been brought home. Class interest may have something to do with that, but it is surely not all. The blindness is more than a class blindness; it is human and sentimental.

At no point is one asked to carry his perceptions into action. At no point is it suggested that one should test whether this rhetoric has substance. If the function of literature is to protect human liberty, cosmopolitanism, sympathy, then the test of the effectiveness of literary teaching ought to be whether the society in which the work is taught becomes more civil, somehow, by virtue of the process. One can say, "We cannot show this in the case of any individual student"; yet, with departments of English in that day carrying the enormous power which they carried (from four to twelve years of English in school, and one or two years in college), one should have been able to look at this question in the large.

The document cites Matthew Arnold's contention that a work of literature is a "truly social work":

It does not try to teach down to the level of inferior classes; it does not try to win them for this or that sect with ready made judgments and watch words; it seeks the harmonious goodness of all men, by administering to all the powers that make up men's lives. It calls out their being at more points and thus makes them live more.

The document never asks why America has not become a more largely classless society if literature can do these good things.

The document is sad in some ways; it is a neurotic document in the clinical sense, in that the failure of civility in the United States is never seen as the responsibility of the men who speak; it is always projected on someone "out there."

One may ask what the function of such documents is. First of all, they are consensual documents; their function is to justify power mechanisms and funding decisions such as required courses or NDEA Institutes. There is nothing wrong with seeking funds or power so long as one conceptualizes clearly the relationship between *what* one obtains the funds (and/or power) to accomplish and what the mechanisms one employs to accomplish one's goals will actually accomplish. The two ought to be of a piece. There may be something wrong with laying claim to creating a future which one cannot create, with bringing a plague in the name of liberation and placing one's nails only on other people's eyes, with failing to root out all partial claims and intermediate mechanisms, all the rituals of "profession" and "craft" that are not at one with the ends we claim to seek. Having done all, we will yet create enough that is plaguey and tragic.

We ought not to despair altogether. Some interesting things are being written about the effect of the humanities on this country. A recent essay by Kenneth Keniston on cost accounting in American education suggests that the effect of undergraduate training in the humanities has been to make students a little more humane, a little more tolerant, and a little more insightful into the conditions which create both tragedy and the sense of identity.

The Greening of America and *Revolution Without Marx or Jesus* suggest that there have been significant shifts in value systems in the country, perhaps partly because of the sorts of training in the humanities people have had. What people put on the best-seller lists are not only sado-masochistic fantasies of sexual power; *Bury My Heart at Wounded Knee* spent many weeks at the top of the nonfiction list. Many of our students know who they are and have made their reading-writing lives and their community lives more coherent than would seem possible, given my descriptions of what we are vis-à-vis what we proclaim we are.

Yet we live in a hideously inhumane world. What I would like to do in the work of the Undergraduate Study Commission[2] and also in my own teaching is to say, "If such and such is what we want, then this is what we have to do," and to pursue that doing into the mechanisms of activeness. If we are endeavoring to preserve liberty with literature in 1943, then we have to hold the mirror up to nature as that nature exists, perhaps, in the streets of New York between N.Y.U. and Columbia. If the English department is predicated on the notion that the schools can provide abundance, freedom, accessibility, then the classroom formats, the tests, the exams, etc., have to be set up precisely to encourage abundance, freedom, accessibility. If the notion is that literature holds the mirror up to nature, then literature must be brought home to nature. Literature as a metaphor for life is first of all a metaphor for the educational formats we provide. I recall studying Joseph Copek's *R.U.R.* in a class which was as close to the conditions of *R.U.R.* as any I have known. We ought to look on novels as metaphors for our classes: some of our classes have a Horatio Alger plot (that is the most common one, I think); some of them have a sort of Henry Miller plot; and many of them have a kind of *Pamela, or, Virtue Rewarded* plot.

Kierkegaard said somewhere, "Purity of heart is to will one thing"; management, effective management, is also to will one thing. If we are to be effective as agents of the humane values we profess, we have to do what we say we wish to do.

Let me make some suggestions about what we might be doing. If the study of literature is to be genuinely democratic, then I think it has to be the study of the total fantasy life of people (or peoples)—that is, of their games, their rituals, their myths, their daydreams, their nightdreams; the structure of those fantasies, their iconology and the ways in which they function to rehearse the future and to summarize the past in a specific culture. You cannot separate the "formal-literary" from the "ongoing" life of a people.

If we say we care about the slave and his freedom, we will have to read the literature of the slave in a context which permits us to sense what it is like to struggle with the master.

If we say that we care about "world responsibility," about the "white peace" and its destructive effects on cultures which do not emulate our technology, then we will learn the visions of those cultures and open ourselves to learning from their values.

At present I am teaching a course in Indian literature; now we are reading Scott Momaday, Black Elk, and some Navaho and Pueblo chants. There are both Indian and Anglo students in the course. The course is not entirely what I want it to be—the Indian students feel somewhat oppressed by the format of the course and by the presence in it of so many Anglos (perhaps particularly by the presence of an Anglo teacher). For them to feel like wrestling with their tradition and the traditions of other Native American peoples in this context requires a cultural leap on my part and on theirs. Conversely, it is very hard to get white students to the point where they are doing anything but delineating their own guilt, to get them to the point where they can begin to delineate their own responsibilities. The Sioux, the Winnebago, and to some degree the Omaha in our area are engaged in the great struggle of nation-building now—endeavoring to reconstruct a past in the way in which Renaissance Florence endeavored to reconstruct its past using a Roman republican idiom. The reconstruction has two movements: an effort to recover legal and land rights stolen by the white community and an effort to construct political and psychological identity around the great rituals, stories, types, and symbols of eternity of those nations prior to the white incursion. My class is endeavoring to relate to this effort: the white students to the legal-land aspect of it, the Indian students to the other side of it. Some of the students are writing school materials on the basis of the kind of insight into the relationship between two cultures that we together are trying to develop. The State Department of the state of Nebraska said that it would publish these. The question then becomes, "When we have written the materials, who judges them? Does the State Department judge them as appropriate, or does the Winnebago Tribal Council?" We have been studying the iconology of Sioux literature by laying, side by side, *Black Elk Speaks* (a set of visions), *The Sacred Pipe* (a collection of Sioux rituals), *Lakota Stories* (a collection of sacred stories), and commentary given to the class by a group of Sioux medicine men: John Fire, Richard Full Bull, and Henry Crow Dog. Some of the students may be going to the Brule reservation to make some movies; one of the things that they may be looking at is the extent to which the fantasy structures that appear in Sioux literature have been internalized and kept alive to reappear in the broken architecture, the tribal council formats, the storytelling that the Brule Sioux presently use. The movie may look at the interaction between the architectural, kinetic cultural formats of the Sioux, and those of the townspeople who live around the reservation. Another student is working on questions of alcoholism and Indian people in Lincoln: why no culture-oriented treatment centers, why hundreds of arrests and no provision of legal counsel? Do you have therapy sessions with all Indian people in it, or persons of only one tribe? Do you have therapy sessions with Indians and Anglos mixed? What are the resources that lie in traditional Indian culture for overcoming, as opposed to encouraging, alcoholism? The student and the psychiatrist may, together, have to begin a study of Indian religious literature, particularly the literature of the Native American Church. What the students are trying to do is to carry their understanding of how literary structures rehearse a civic life back to the civic life around them in such a way as to make it a more understanding and democratic civic life.

If we care about civility, if we care about the tall ideals that we've talked about—and I think we do—we ought to look at how we manage our departments; we ought to cease our eternal haranguing of "the educators," cease giving our exclusive attention to vocational-education-for-graduate-school. That is not even sound economic policy for the future of studies in either language or literature. We ought to be looking to see where the arenas are in which the kinds of skills that we have can be brought into play. What kinds of civic imagination are expressed by a school; what's the "literary plot" of the schools within a mile of our department's teaching building? (Jules Henry, I think, has a very nice analysis of that sort of thing in *Culture Against Man.*)

We ought to start looking at children's fantasies: what kinds of generic structures appear in the fantasies of children down the street, and what kinds of futures are they rehearsing? To what extent can we use our knowledge of the fantasies of our own people and of others the better to understand where we begin in educating the imagination? And whose imagination is educated, the children's or ours? That of Henry James or that of his contemporary, Black Elk? I have come to understand myself and my own children better by virtue of using my training as a literary scholar in watching the kinds of imaginative structures that they create in free fantasy situations.

We ought also to be looking at newspapers as expressions of a sort of literary life; we probably ought to buy some newspapers ourselves.

We ought to be looking at the materials that are close at hand: e.g., the Winnebago tribe has had a tremendously rich literature. Paul Radin did some research on that literature and wrote his accounts of *The Trickster* and *The Journey to Life and Death.* Carl Jung read those books; Northrop Frye read Jung's books. But we are likely to teach Frye without Radin and without the Winnebago.

There are enough arenas in which we can express our sense of what it is to understand other people's language and another man's imaginative life. We have enough to do so that we can abandon the mechanistic power games having to do with credentialing, certification, graduate empires, the preservation of the departmental domain, which we have played. We have enough to do in helping ourselves really to discover America. English departments could go out of existence or reorganize; and we might be the more creative and useful to the culture as college teachers. We have enough to do so that we ought not be desperate in the face of a declining market. The public will buy our services if we offer them and if they are, indeed, services. We have enough to do.

Amos Tutuola has written a book called *Ajaiya and His Inherited Poverty.* Tutuola is an interesting man. He was a RAF pilot from Nigeria, is a Christian who makes use of traditional Yoruba mythic patterns as a way of expressing his own Afro-Christian intuitions, a novelist redoing Augustine's "stealing the gold of the Egyptians," and making use of it "in the new temple." As a medievalist, I find Tutuola facing exactly the issues that medieval writers faced as they endeavored to work out a relationship to the sacred story of a classical past. Tutuola's book begins with the issue of inherited poverty: what do we do with our inherited poverty? That's really what I have been trying to talk about. Ina and her brother are talking about their mother and father, who have been poor all their lives; all of their ancestors have been poor, and they wonder what will ever happen to them if they can't escape their inherited poverty:

Of course Ina and I do not hear these sorrowful discussions between my father and mother about their inherited poverty at all, but we were still singing loudly and with melodious voices, and laughter to the hearing of our mother and father, "how poor we are, how poor we are, how poor we are, etc." After a few minutes that we had been singing this song, both of us stood up, and we continued to sing this song loudly as we were entering the sitting room, which our mother and father sat, and when we met both of them as they dropped down their heads, which showed us that they were thinking about our poverty with sorrow at that moment. Then Ina and I stopped singing at the same time. So as both of us stood before them, and then they lifted up their heads and were looking at us, I asked from my father loudly, "Father, are we going to die in this poverty? But, of course I believe you have inherited it from your fore-father." As Ina and our mother were still looking on, my father replied with grief, "Of course my fore-father might have died in poverty, and as well as I'm going to die in poverty soon, but now I will make it clear to you that if father and mother die in poverty it does not mean that their children will die in poverty as well, if they can work hard." Then I asked again from my father with a clear voice, "But father, I wonder? You are working more and more farms and crops, and you are getting more farms and crops than the other farmers in this village. You know my father, this village contains about 4,000 people, but we are the poorest among them all." Then my father shook his head up and down, and he replied with sorrow, "Well, of course, maybe all the other farmers in this village are not poor. But I believe one thing, that is you or your own sons may be free of this, our poverty, provided you or your own sons continue to work hard." But as my father wanted to continue his explanations about the poverty, Ina interrupted suddenly with a loud voice as she faced our mother, and she said, "But I do not agree to our father's explanations, that you should continue to work hard, because I notice that you, as our mother, is very industrious, and you work more than any of the other women in this village, but as you are growing old, it is so that our poverty is growing worse along with you. Why is that so our mother?" Then our mother breathed in and out heavily, and she replied sorrowfully, "Although I am very industrious, and I am still in poverty, that does not mean that I am destined with poverty. Anything can happen to a person who is born under this sun. But I advise you now, that you and Ajaiya should not be discouraged by our continuous poverty. We are not destined with poverty at all, as the rest of the people in this village had thought us to be."

Well then a figure called the joker comes in, and mother dies. As she dies Ajaiya says, "After a few minutes she became a very little conscious, and after awhile she began to talk, but with a very faint voice. It was very hard to understand the words that which she was speaking out this time, but when she wanted to stop the last breath, then she began to advise Ina and I, as she was dying. 'I am dying, and leaving both of you in your poverty. But do not be discouraged to continue to work hard. You will be all right in the near future, if you work hard.' Then she died."

Notes

[1] I read one of the documents prior to publication and I probably could have changed it had I the prescience. I am not attacking other people's faults. Men whom I respected and continue to respect were involved in a basic way in the creation of the document. The ethos that I'm trying to develop is not an ethos directed toward hunting out some nasty bastards who have done bad things in the past; seeing, we all bear

Oedipus' blindness in confronting the present; we aren't very often capable of redeeming the past by paying blind eyes for sibylline insight. The tragic burden of lack of perception which all of us bear tempts us simultaneously to declare ourselves overly responsible, and therefore capable of acting only if we can take on everything, or as not responsible at all, and therefore not obligated to our pasts.

[2] A federally supported program to investigate innovative programs in the undergraduate education of teachers.

Thawing the Frozen Curriculum*

Wallace W. Douglas

Northwestern University

I

> Let us not be so involved in present efforts to improve the intellectual level of American schools that we overlook preparations for dealing with our success in doing so. The peril of success under the conditions sketched is the growth of what had been called "meritocracy."
>
> Jerome Bruner

"IN SEPTEMBER 1959 there gathered at Woods Hole on Cape Cod thirty-five scientists, scholars, and educators to discuss how education in science might be improved in our primary and secondary schools." The meeting was prompted by "a conviction that we were at the beginning of a period of new progress in, and concern for, creating curricula and ways of teaching science, and that a general appraisal of this progress and concern was in order, so as to better guide developments in the future."[1] Jerome Bruner, in *The Process of Education*, thus describes the origin and intent of the Woods Hole Conference, to which for more than a decade all curriculum designers in the United States have looked for authority.

In the years just before Woods Hole, Bruner says,

Various learned societies were searching for and finding ways of establishing contact between their leading scholars and educators in the schools. For their part, educators and psychologists were examining anew the nature of teaching methods and curricula and were becoming increasingly ready to examine fresh approaches. (p. viii)

The scientists and others who came together at Woods Hole also did so, Bruner says, "to consider anew the nature of the learning process"; they intended to discuss the "new questions about our conceptions of learning and teaching" that they had begun to raise as a result of noticing and trying to correct the fact that "school programs [had] often dealt inadequately or incorrectly with contemporary knowledge" (p. 2, cf. pp. 69–70). The specific questions that Bruner reports as having been asked during the Conference were:

---

* An address to the Tampa ADE Seminar, 12 Feb. 1972. Reprinted from *ADE Bulletin*, No. 34 (Sept. 1972), pp. 7–17.

61

What shall be taught, when, and how? What kinds of research and inquiry might further the growing efforts [toward reform?] in the design of curricula? What are the implications of emphasizing the structure of a subject, be it mathematics or history—emphasizing it in a way that seeks to give a student as quickly as possible a sense of the fundamental ideas of a discipline? (pp. 2–3)

The basis for answering such questions was the "bold" hypothesis that "any subject can be taught effectively in some intellectually honest form to any child at any stage of development." Expanded for the purposes of linear schooling, this became the notion of the spiral curriculum:

If one respects the ways of thought of the growing child, if one is courteous enough to translate material into his logical forms and [make it] challenging enough to tempt him to advance, then it is possible to introduce him at an early age to the ideas and styles [of thought, perhaps] that in later life make an educated man. We might ask, as a criterion for any subject taught in primary school, whether, when fully developed, it is worth an adult's knowing, and whether having known it as a child makes a person a better adult. (pp. 33, 52)

Realized or exemplified, the spiral curriculum became, in the teaching of literature (among other things, no doubt), giving children "an awareness of the meaning of human tragedy and a sense of compassion for it." So Bruner asked whether it is not "possible at the earliest appropriate age to teach the literature of tragedy in a manner that illuminates but does not threaten." Evidently assuming a universal agreement on at least what is "the tragic," if not on what are tragedies, Bruner found his answer readily enough. First, and (he says) proceeding in the manner of Piaget, we must "ask about the child's conception of the tragic." It is only, he goes on,

when we are equipped with such knowledge, that we will be in a position to know how the child will translate whatever we present to him into his own subjective terms. So equipped, we can then find many possible ways to begin: through the use of children's classics, through presentation of a commentary on selected films that have proved themselves.[2]

I suppose it is only hindsight—the result of a decade of mere anarchy and innocence drowned, of great murder in the earth and moons radiant with terror in the infuriated air—that makes us today feel the insufficiency of Woods Hole. Now we are likely to think, or at least to feel, that the "scientists, scholars, and educators," the men who gathered in September 1959 at Woods Hole on the Cape under the benign stewardship of a retired rear admiral,[3] were a somewhat overly selected sample of society. They were, all of them, people who had succeeded in the school system they were discussing. Indeed most of them had attained to its very highest reaches. Eight of the participants were from Ivy League schools, to whom certainly could be added the two from M.I.T. and perhaps the one from Teachers College. Two others were from Swarthmore and Chicago, two from Andover and Exeter, and two from the Rockefeller Foundation and ETS. Perhaps the four participants from Illinois should—or may—be included in this group, and the two from Hopkins and Michigan.[4]

I do not mean to say simply that the backgrounds of the participants at Woods Hole made them unwilling to change the system that had prepared them to give the rewards they themselves had once desired and, no doubt, had quite early come to believe they deserved. The case is rather that, having made it in the schools, the participants (Acceptable Ethnics, Ideal

Americans, and a foreigner) did not, as it were, recognize the rewards. If not quite a fact of nature, the system embodied in the schools must have been pretty close to a fact of consciousness for those who gathered at Woods Hole. Perhaps they would have called themselves pragmatists—though the hour for that word had not yet come round—and would have seen themselves as technicians looking for the bugs in a system that had, for some reason or other, ceased to turn out the well-machined parts necessary for the final assembly job.

Today we would also find much to daunt us in the very problem that was formulated at Woods Hole. Probably the participants were influenced not only by the launching of Sputnik but also by a decade or more of conservative criticism of the schools, in which it was alleged that the schools had been subjected to the principles of Dewey, or at least of the Progressive Education Association, and that "knowledge" (the paradigms of Latin) was being neglected in favor of "life adjustment" (the making of blueberry pies).[5] In somewhat more modern terms, the Woods Hole charge was that school subjects (as embodied in textbooks, anyway) had fallen out of touch with "contemporary knowledge," and that teaching techniques were inefficient and failed to challenge. The Woods Hole participants proposed a repair job by means of modernization. The content of the subjects was to be updated and its order of presentation rationalized. The techniques recommended to teachers were also to be modernized, not merely by the encouragement of audiovisual aids,[6] but also by changing the teacher's mode of problem-setting and questioning—in the direction, one gathers, of what came to be known as the discovery method, perhaps itself an adaptation to classroom purposes of laboratory experiments, so called (see Bruner, pp. 20–22). No doubt the changes proposed, and to a considerable extent realized,[7] as a result of Woods Hole satisfied to some degree that "concern for the quality and intellectual aims of education" that Bruner saw as the distinctive aspiration shaping education in that time.[8] But it may also be said, and not unfairly, that the participants brought to Woods Hole an essentially bureaucratic (meritocratic) problem: the narrow problem of improving the schooling of those whom the schools were selecting to "go on," and so to enter that class to which the participants at Woods Hole had themselves gained entrance because of their talents and education, or at least because of their success in school.

II

It is therefore true in the end to say that part of the purpose of writing is to reach others: not to sell them anything or persuade them, but to be quite simply in touch. It follows that we best speak to others when we forget them and concentrate on trying to be straight towards our own experience, in the hope that honestly seen experience becomes exchangeable. At this point the two themes—speaking to yourself and speaking to each other—come together. They are not two directions; they are one and inextricable.

Richard Hoggart

And here we are today, in 1972, gathered together in a Manger Motor Inn, in the State of Florida—and nary a rear admiral among us. What ought to be our concerns today, as we, in our turn, look at the curriculum and consider our responsibility for the preparation of school teachers? What problems ought we to be seeing? What questions ought we to be asking?

We might begin, I think, with some questions about those very questions that Bruner says were asked at the Woods Hole Conference. I have already quoted parts of the passage; I repeat it now in its full form:

> Physicists, biologists, mathematicians, historians, educators, and psychologists came together to consider anew the nature of the learning process, its relevance to education, and points at which current efforts have raised new questions about our conceptions of learning and teaching. What shall be taught, when, and how? What kinds of research and inquiry might further the growing efforts in the design of curricula? What are the implications of emphasizing the structure of a subject, be it mathematics or history—emphasizing it in a way that seeks to give a student as quickly as possible a sense of the fundamental ideas of a discipline? (pp. 2–3)

Think now of the questions carried by those questions, the seeds of their own destruction. "To give a student as quickly as possible. . . ." But why "give"? And why "as quickly as possible"? And what of the neutrality for teaching that seems to be assumed in "give"?

What *are* the implications of building school programs on or around the structures of subjects? Presumably Bruner meant to oppose structures of subjects and mere facts. And he would probably have completed "implication" with some such phrase as "for teaching techniques." Today, however, we have to ask where the disciplines come from or where they exist, the ones that are to be taught by giving students "as quickly as possible a sense of [their] fundamental ideas." Following Dewey (in *The Child and the Curriculum*), some of us would surely want to ask about the consequences of dividing the experience of children, even that of high-school children, according to the specialisms of university departments and their upper-division, postgraduate preparatory courses, which we are perhaps becoming willing to identify with Bruner's "disciplines."

And further, accepting Bruner's probable distinction between structure and fact, we have to ask whether emphasizing the former rather than the latter does in any way change the school teaching-learning experience. Or at least: does the experience change so long as "give" remains the operative and defining action in the teaching act, with its object being the structure of fundamental ideas of a discipline that is representative of the needs and views of its adult practitioners? Is there any change in the values and manners that are conveyed, however informally and silently, by the experience of schooling? Is there any change in the way in which children must see themselves related to schools and schooling?

Why was it "*the* learning process" that the participants at Woods Hole intended to discuss? Such uniformitarianism is surely somewhat surprising in this, as we are so often told, restlessly relativistic age—and among scientists at that. Did no one stop to ask about the conception of even that learning process—or perhaps rather the schooling process—that is contained in Bruner's conjecture that it may be "in the technique of arousing attention in school that first steps can be taken to establish that active autonomy of attention that is the antithesis of the spectator's passivity" (p. 72)? Perhaps those scientists then thought it a nonquestion to ask how "active autonomy of attention" can *be* established by an externally originating technique designed to arouse attention in an individual who is evidently (since his attention must be aroused) uninterested in whatever is being presented, for discovery perhaps. I don't think that we can still think that today.

But where, then, are we today, after Basic Issues, Woods Hole, the Commission on English and the Office of Education with their institutes, Dartmouth . . . and so much more in the way of a New English? "What shall be taught, when, and how?" they asked at Woods Hole. Today we have to ask: What is learned? And we don't mean: What is learned of all that we give in the way of fact and structure, give now so expeditiously and efficiently? We mean rather: What is learned because of what we give? What, for example, is learned by a college freshman who sees himself being given as a possible topic for a paper on *A Midsummer Night's Dream* "Bottom's oxymorons as a mirror of the play as a whole"? We can see this for the "earnest buffoonery" of the academic, in splendid consonance with the dramatic material to which it alludes. But the freshman—what does he infer about English, about literary works, above all about himself when he comes upon a topic like that?[9]

Think now, too, of our cunning passages to the "fundamental ideas" of our discipline, which we began to study at least as long ago as 1962 and the funding of Project English by the Office of Education. Think now of what we give, give even "with such supple confusions / That the giving famishes the craving." Think of a high-school student, the beneficiary of the highest of our thoughts, out in the land of Mencken's nightmare—"out where the grass grows high, and the horned cattle dream away the lazy afternoons, and men still fear the powers and principalities of the air"—a high-school student whose teacher has read this very latest bottling of wine that was soured in the vat, an article published in *English Journal* no longer ago than January and called "Performance Objectives in Reading and Responding to Literature."[10]

Responding, we learn there, is "what most students and pleasure-loving people enjoy doing." There are, it turns out, six sorts of responding: valuing, describing, discovering relationships, discriminating, inferring, evaluating. You may well be confused by the listing of both "valuing" and "evaluating," so I append the explanation given by the author:

Evaluating and valuing resist sharp distinctions but do allow different emphases. Valuing emphasizes subjective, even highly idiosyncratic responses; evaluating emphasizes partly subjective, mostly objective, responses based on objective criteria.

Here, then, a behavior that exemplifies evaluating:

The student, respecting the right of each art form to its own integrity, tells why he does or does not give high marks to a literary work he has read, or to a version of it he has also experienced in the electronic media, or to a review of either he may also have read.

Are we, then, to suppose ourselves to be in the business of turning out Kulygins?

But attend to some other sub-behaviors, as perhaps they are to be called. Here is one from those that exemplify "valuing":

Having read a work like *Hair, Catch-22,* or *Soul on Ice,* the student defends orally or in writing the right of other people to read it regardless of its potential offensiveness.

Is it permissible to ask what genre (using the word as English teachers do) encompasses *Hair, Catch-22,* and *Soul on Ice?* The genre of the potentially offensive, perhaps; or of works provoking the "highly subjective, even idiosyncratic responses" that define the behavior of "valuing," according to the author.

Here is one of the sub-behaviors that illustrate "describing":

Having read a poem, story, or essay, or any other piece containing allusions, the student identifies one and explains how it contributes to the meaning of the work.

"Meaning of the work." There's a question begged for sure. What about globed fruits, to say nothing of real toads in imaginary gardens?

What a fiddle it all is. Note these sub-behaviors—little tests, they are—from the examples of "discovering relationships":

After reading, or listening to a recording of, a contemporary poem or song (e.g., Paul Simon's version of "Richard Cory"); the student explains how the poet relates to the reader—e.g., how the imagery re-creates in the reader the poet's mood or attitude.

Given some narrative verse or prose selections (e.g., from *The Odyssey* or *The Oxbow Incident*) containing verbal phrases at ends rather than at beginnings of sentences, the student identifies the phrases that spell out concretely what is introduced only generally in the main clauses.

After reading, or listening to a recording of, a poem like Dylan Thomas' "Do Not Go Gentle," the student explains how the line-ends and the beginnings of subsequent lines are related (e.g., how they play with each other in such rhetorical games as echoing and punning).

Here finally, as an end to all this, is an example of "discriminating":

Given such comparisons as "the boy looked like a man" and "the boy looked like a bulldozer," the student, *without being rehearsed in trivial distinctions between simile and metaphor* [my italics], distinguishes between more prosaic and more imaginative comparisons.

It must be a very special world indeed, the one inhabited by English teachers. In generality at least, "the student," who figures so largely in these behaviors and sub-behaviors, is obviously pretty much of a piece with the Common Reader. But the behaviors that he is evidently to be trained to perform are eccentric in the extreme, not easily to be imagined as sanctioned by any of Johnson's great terms—not reason, not judgment, not even taste or "fanciful invention." What serious person today would use "recreates" as it is above, in the fifth quotation, or speak so of a poet relating to a reader? As Johnson remarked, and as Aristotle intimated, "The delight of tragedy proceeds from our consciousness of fiction; if we thought murders and treasons real, they would please no more." Who now supposes that a parsing exercise, if that's what it is, as in the same quotation, can lead even to significant abstract understanding, much less to a valued experience? "What mankind have long possessed, they have often examined and compared," Johnson said. To what straits, then, do we seem to have been reduced by time, if now our examination and comparison of poems "like" "Do Not Go Gentle" must be carried on as a search for the "rhetorical games" they contain?

In the course of meditating upon these matters for the purposes of this talk, I found myself wondering how some of my own students would "behave" if I asked them to respond to the article I have been discussing. Perhaps I wanted to test my own responses; more likely I was wondering how successfully I had given the students what I am currently regarding as the fundamental ideas—or anyway attitudes—of the discipline—or art—of teaching. So, following a technique I learned a long time ago, when I was doing class themes, I asked a group of intending teachers to read the article I have been discussing here, suggested that I wanted some kind of report on their "response"—I suspect that the singular is all too accurate—and allowed them fifteen or twenty minutes to write. (What other kind of "response" would provide me the certainty of being able to examine and compare, in the manner of Johnson?) Perhaps I should note that these were Northwestern students; that is, young people who have been successful enough in "good" schools to be admitted to a moderately selective, high-cost undergraduate college, the graduates of which have, I judge, reasonable access either to preferred jobs or to further training in comparable institutions, or did have until lately. I should add that my conclusions about "good schools" derives (as is often the case) from simple ocular inspection. Of course Northwestern has broadened the range of its intake; but the results were not apparent in this class.

The results of my test turned out to be a rather interesting example of duality of consciousness, or fragmental internalization. Most of the students seemed to accept without much question the relation between teacher and child that is assumed in the form of the objectives. It was only in particulars that they found cause for criticism. In other words, while accepting the most general assumption of teachers—the one contained in Bruner's "give" —the students at the same time criticized various particular behaviors or actions in which it was realized in the article. Perhaps they felt compelled to do so only because they had grasped my own feelings about the matter. But of course I prefer to think that something like Trotsky's law of uneven development was working here.

In any event, nearly all the students expressed a conventional, predictable enough, and humanistic uneasiness about the notions of "behavior" and "behavioral." A good many spoke about the conventionality of the objectives: one student wrote, "They all seem too similar to the objectives of some of my high school teachers." Several noticed that new, trendy materials were being used to give the appearance of relevance and contemporaneity to unchanging operations: "just dressing up those tired old writing exercises."

A few students—how easy it is to continue our sorting—saw that, as written, these objectives all assume prior judgments about behaviors that are significant of learning and, correspondingly, about the "learnings" that are valuable. Necessarily such judgments must be based on assumptions or, just possibly, intuitively arrived-at conclusions about aggregate behavior among young people viewed as "students"; that is, as individuals being prepared for roles in the adult world. Thus, having read *Macbeth* and *Antigone*, "the student" is expected, first, to see the plays as having the same "theme"—in itself an odd enough idea, but made the more so when we are given the extraordinary explanation that that theme is "the individual against fate"—and then to write "a brief paper on ways in which the two [plays] are related." The assignment—and it is an assignment—may violate two generations of scholarship and criticism; but it cannot be faulted as a device for sorting out students able—and willing—to perform highly specialized tasks at the request, if not the command, of an external authority. I think several students felt the general stratifying function of these exercises or (technically) alienated work, even though they were able only to insist that individuals should set their own goals or have their own goals recognized:[11] "People should be allowed to live and react, rather than being told how to," one of the students said.

Finally, at least one student noticed that, as given, the objectives contain no slightest interest in feelings. The "Six Kinds of Responses to Reading" reduce "response" to intellectual operations, generally of a rather low order and, hence, easily ranked. The en-valuation of analysis and classification in the objectives is conspicuous, and it seems clear that students would very quickly pick up the corresponding dis-valuation of feelings, especially any of an idiosyncratic sort. One may wonder if "response" is used strictly, to make sure that no mere "reactions" need be included in the material of classroom discourse and activity.

But enough. As I have said before, and no doubt will be saying again—if not ages and ages hence, at least with a sigh—the trouble with behavioral objectives is not, God knows, that they are scientific, or even behavioral, so far as that goes. It is simply that they are all so old-fashioned and silly. In 1925 Mencken learned from *The Social Objectives of School English*, by Charles S. Pendleton, that eighty English teachers, assembled in summer school at the University of Chicago, chose, as the first of 1,581 possible reasons for teaching English, "The ability to spell correctly without hesitation all the ordinary words of one's writing vocabulary"; second in their ranking was "The ability to speak, in conversation, in complete sentences, not in broken phrases."[12] That was in 1925. Can it be said, with any confidence, that we are any farther along today, nearly half a century later? Considering the extremely narrow, not to say mandarin, skills that are used to define school achievement, at least in English, it does seem necessary to begin to suspect that a system which allocates economic, political, and social resources according to educational achievement may differ only in degree, not kind, from one based on, say, inherited property.[13]

III

> "Achievement" in the school system is defined, controlled, and measured in terms of the ability to survive within a culture which reflects the behavior and values of the upper, upper middle, and professional classes.
>
> Michael S. Schudson

Students at Northwestern who have lasted into the upper division, especially those who are preparing to teach English, have plenty of resources for coping with the kind of test of personality that I have been discussing (in which I include my own, by the way). But what effect do such tests have on students who are not members of our community, either the general one of the academically talented (as the phrase used to be) or the more specialized one of English teachers? This is a hard question for us; it is hard for us to know even that it must be asked. For, like the participants at Woods Hole, we have all been successful in the business of schooling. Some—perhaps many—of us entered school feeling that we did so as a right with a very strong sense that school belonged to us. I used the words advisedly: not that we belonged in school, but rather, and strictly, that school belonged to us, that it was ours to use, was there precisely to fulfill a responsibility to us.

And so perhaps we can never know what school and English mean to those who are alien to one or both. But surely we ought to be thinking about such people, especially, for example, when we find teachers who, setting out to "furnish the mind,"[14] take "Out, Out—" and ask about it,

What does Frost say about the saw to make it seem almost alive? What does this do to your feelings about what happens? Does this language make you feel more or less sorrow for the boy? What do you call such phrases, in which a lifeless object is given human characteristics?

What is done when students are left all, all alone with Milton's "On His Blindness," except for pairing it with "To the Virgins to Make Much of Time," thus providing poems with so very marked a contrast in tone "that students will easily discover the difference." That difference, by the way, is said to be that the Herrick poem is "semihumorous"; the one by Milton, on the other hand, is "dignified, sober, and humble," has "a pervasive dignity," a "high seriousness," which are contributed to by the "subjects of the poem . . . : the poet's blindness, his talent, his Maker, Patience—and the nobility of thought in the last line."

What is done when a teacher is told to be inductive, to "direct the students' attention to [Brutus' "I would it were my fault to sleep so soundly"] and ask what it "implies about Brutus"? To that is added: "If the students do not respond with such observations as Brutus is troubled in spirit, is indulgent toward an erring inferior, and is of an introspective nature . . . ask even more specific questions and hint more directly at the expected answers. . . ."[15]

Good students, as they are called, have learned how to deal with such coercive questioning. Presumably they find or expect some reward for doing so and are rewarded for their behaviors and expectations. But then there are the others, aren't there? The ones we have taken to calling "disadvantaged," the reluctant learners, the early school leavers, the "walking C's." I am thinking of the students who rarely achieve success or satisfaction in school, who are accustomed to failure or to just getting by. They read reluctantly, often with difficulty, sometimes without comprehension; at least so far as school reading materials are concerned—which are all we know about, of course. They cannot recognize concepts easily—at least not the concepts the schools deal in—in the language that is used in the schools. Their associative powers are rich and vigorous, as can be seen in their slang and in the lyrics of the songs they listen to, but they ignore or do not respond to the sort of literary subtlety I have been illustrating. Their interests are, therefore, seen to be nonintellectual, material, self-satisfying—in a word, not scholastic. Because school in particular is pretty boring to them, they are thought to be bored by life generally.[16]

These students and what we are beginning to sense, however dimly, about their fate in the schools and the reasons for it, the actual outcome of schooling for them—these matters are bringing us to the very heart of our mystery, to our own peculiar overwhelming question. I mean the question of what it is the schools are designed to do, or can be seen to be doing, when they are considered as instruments of social policy rather than as the sites of a largely aseptic activity, "education," which is thought of as "the development of the special and general abilities of the mind (learning to know)."[17] This is yet another question that some of us today would want to ask about *The Process of Education*.

IV

We know that richer people are better educated, and so we conclude for the moment that if poorer families get more money their children will later be better educated than they otherwise would have been. But this conclusion will always be tantalizingly and endlessly arguable.

John P. Gilbert and Frederick Mosteller

When he was doing *The Process of Education*, it was possible for Bruner to say, "We may take as perhaps the most general objective of education that it cultivate excellence" (p. 9, see also p. 70). Presumably the qualification in the "perhaps" was connected with the fear, to which Bruner gave at least slight expression at the time, that there might be some social danger if the meritocratic pursuit of excellence were to go on without check.[18] At that time, though, he seems to have felt no concern about using "excellence" as a self-explanatory term, needing neither definition nor specification. In the same way, he seems not to have felt any need even to discuss, let alone question, the school-related criteria of excellence. Not for him, a beneficiary of the system, to wonder whether "excellence" is in fact determined by the ratable skills that students demonstrate in the intellectual manipulations out of which school business and testing are constituted. Still less could he question whether educational attainment and test scores give any true measure even of ability, let alone merit.[19]

Today, however, things evidently seem rather different to Bruner. He seems ready to submit Woods Hole and *The Process of Education* itself to somewhat the same sort of question that I have in this talk. For example, last fall (1971), in *Phi Delta Kappan* Bruner took another look at *The Process of Education*. I think it fair to say that he found it wanting in its very assumptions, not only those concerning "education" but also more general ones that concern the political and social structures and powers that are reflected in "education." I think his results deserve recording in a medium with a wider, or at least different, circulation than that of the one in which they first appeared.

To begin with "education"—Bruner now seems to see the indeed very high-priori way that was taken at Woods Hole. "The movement of which *The Process of Education* was a part was," he says, based on a formula of faith: that learning was what students wanted to do, that they wanted to achieve an expertise in some particular subject matter. Their motivation was taken for granted. [The movement] also accepted the tacit assumption that everybody who came to [the new curricula] in the schools had been the beneficiary of the middle-class hidden curricula that taught them the analytic skills and launched them in the traditionally intellectual use of mind.[20]

That comment and the one about education being the cultivation of excellence suggest that Woods Hole was a pretty Platonic affair. I am reminded of that slave boy in the *Meno* from whom Socrates elicits, he says, the principle for doubling the area of a square. You remember the boy's behavior under the relentlessly incremental steps in Socrates' program. I sample the scene briefly, at the point where Socrates is getting the boy to see the error of his first conjecture, that the area can be doubled by doubling the sides.

Socrates How large is the whole space AIKL [the enlarged square]? Is it not four times as large as the space ABCD [the original square]?
Boy To be sure it is.
Socrates Is it only double now to the space ABCD, when it is four times as large?
Boy No, by Jupiter.
Socrates What proportion has it then to the space ABCD?
Boy A quadruple one.
Socrates From a line, therefore, double in length is drawn a square space, not double, but quadruple in largeness.

As is the way in programmed learning, the situation of Socrates and the slave boy implies a model or paradigm of teacher-student behavior in which the direction of learning, the determination of what is valued and, therefore, to be sought for and learned (in the schools, it is, I think, just what is to be learned)—this remains quite firmly in control of the teacher. The student—Greek slave boy, affluent suburbanite,[21] or "disadvantaged" member of what is now rather generally known as "another" culture—is free, or at least random,[22] enough to take his chances in a perhaps rather tedious process of discovering which of his behaviors will stimulate a reward from his teacher. The product of the stimulus-response exchange between student and teacher (that is, the learned datum or, as currently, in some areas of English, the feeling response) is determined by the teacher, for his purposes.

In the case of micro-teaching in the *Meno*, it has to be noted, I suppose, that Socrates' method[23] is assertedly based on the assumption (myth?) that "those very opinions which you [Meno] acknowledge to be [the boy's] own were in him all the time," and that he would "know them without being taught them, having only been asked questions and recovering from within himself his lost knowledge."[24] But in its totality, the situation is hardly very pupil-centered, except in the school sense. The reason for it all is Meno's exasperating—to Socrates, that is—refusal to accept his teacher's assertion "that we do not learn anything; and that all which we call learning is only reminiscence," and his subsequent ironic and crafty question, "Can you teach me to know this doctrine to be true?" Then (making my point quite obvious), Socrates asks for one of Meno's slaves, "that I may prove in him the truth of what I say" (*Meno*, II, 85, 81, 82).

Curriculum designers and classroom teachers may find much of interest in the character and behavior of the boy who comes forward to serve Socrates' purpose, and in the process that they engage in. A boy, and a slave boy, too (and living pretty far from the Nile, for that matter), Socrates' witness is, of course, landless. Thus he has no present interest in, no present use for the geometric principle Socrates is getting him to "recall." Nor can we easily suppose that, dreaming of entering the mainstream of Greek society, he will value the experience he is having with Socrates because of his hopes that some day he *will* possess land, whether floodable or not, that he will need to be able at least to describe, if not also to defend. Or at least we cannot suppose that Plato would have given much consideration to the possibility of such a motivation as accounting for the docility with which the boy submits to Socrates' long interrogation.

Or perhaps I am thinking too much of relevance and merely practical value, to say nothing of stereotypes of class behavior. Plato is silent about the toning of the boy's answers. Perhaps that means that we are free to suppose what we will, according to the interpretations of human nature that we use in our teaching. Perhaps, though we know Socrates' pupil to have been both boy and slave, we are free to think that Plato meant us to see him taking a pure or liberal satisfaction in knowing for the sake of knowing. Or perhaps we are permitted to think that the boy would watch himself as, with the help of Socrates, he recovered "of himself from within himself his [own] lost knowledge" (*Meno*, II, 85) and, watching, would experience the kind of value or pleasure we suppose to inhere in disinterested or artistic activity. Or if, like Plato, we find disinterestedness an unlikely characteristic for even men of the lower and working classes, let alone boys, then perhaps we may still suppose that, in the end, the boy would have found some pleasure, or felt some reward for his appropriate behavior, in the very evident satisfaction that Socrates was taking, at least in the way things had worked out, though perhaps not to any great extent in the boy's own performance.

In sum, the slave boy may be thought of as a very interesting and complex representation or imitation of our own ideal school child. "Come hither, you," Meno says, and it is enough (II, 83). After that the boy becomes a series of responses, all of them given without much reward or reinforcement by Socrates. Not only is the boy, then, docile. He also comes equipped with knowledge, as if from one of our own middle-class and advantaged households, so that Socrates need not consider him as a person. Enough that we should know the right kind of leading question. Between them, Socrates and the slave boy seem to represent pretty well the Idea of learning and learner that was in the minds of the participants in the Woods Hole Conference.

Like all imitations, this one is somewhat removed from the real, not only the reality of the school children which are its object, but also the reality of the society in which they exist as human beings and as objects of the school-children imitation. It was the error of the curriculum planners of the 1960's that they quite failed to see—or if they saw, they did not consider —the social consequences of conceiving curricula to be means of achieving "expertise" in particular subject matters and of devising teaching techniques on the assumption that, for children and young people, learning means acquiring the tools of an intellectual's trade. Even then, as I have noted, Bruner warned that success in a curriculum reform designed "to improve the intellectual level of American schools" carried with it the danger of "the growth of what has been called 'meritocracy.'" And, he said, a meritocracy

implies a system of competition in which students are moved ahead and given further opportunities on the basis of their achievement, with position in later life increasingly and irreversibly determined by earlier school records. Not only later educational opportunities but subsequent job opportunities become increasingly fixed by earlier school performance. The late bloomer, the early rebel, the child from the educationally indifferent home—all of them, in a full-scale meritoc-racy, become victims of an often senseless irreversibility of decision. (Bruner, *Process*, p. 77)

But evidently no one was listening, including Bruner himself, it almost seems. And the reformers just went on and on, resting comfortably on the belief that "those who understood a field well—the practitioners of the field—could work with teachers to produce new curricula," containing "teacher-proof" materials or "courteous translation[s] that could reduce ideas to a form that young students could grasp" (Bruner, "The Process of Education Revisited," p. 19). In short (and as I have said), they operated totally within the refuge of "professionalism."

Today Bruner begins, as it were, outside the school, outside "educa-tion." By the spring of 1970, he says, when asked about the state of Ameri-can education, all he could answer was

that it had passed into a state of utter crisis. It had failed to respond to the changing social needs, lagging behind rather than leading. My work on early education and social class, for example, had convinced me that the educational system was, in effect, our way of maintaining a class system—a group at the bottom. It crippled the capacity of children in the lowest socio-economic quarter of the population, and particularly those who were black, to participate at full power in the society, and it did it early and effectively. ("The Process of Educa-tion Revisited," pp. 19, 20)

We shall kill ourselves, Bruner says in a very moving and important passage, important especially for those who insist that the chief business of early childhood education projects, such as Headstart, is to ready children for school:[25]

We shall kill ourselves, as a society and as human beings, unless we address our efforts to redressing the deep, deep wounds that we inflict on the poor, the outcast, those who somehow do not fit within our caste system—be they black or dispossessed in any way. If there is one thing that has come out of our work with the very young, it is the extent to which "being out," not having a chance as an adult or as a parent, very quickly reflects itself in a loss of hope in the child. As early as the second or third year a child begins to reflect this loss of hope. ("The Process of Education Revisited," p. 21)

Our business today, then, is rather different from that of the partici-pants at Woods Hole. For them it was enough to see that modern scientific materials and something also of a modern view of science-work were put into the hands of teachers. They left untouched, really perhaps unnoticed, the effective purpose of schooling—that is, the sorting and grading of human beings. They did not notice (it was 1959, five years after *Brown* vs. *Board of Education of Topeka, Kans.*) the fact that the school exists to sort out a few winners and to confirm the dispossession of those who have lost.

"What would one do now?" Bruner asks.

What would be the pattern at a Woods Hole conference in 1971? It would not be in Woods Hole, in that once rural, coastal setting. More likely, we would gather in the heart of a great city. The task would center around the dispossession of the children of the poor and the alienation of the middleclass child. In some crucial respect, the medium would surely be the message: the school, not the curriculum, or the society, and not even the school. ("The Process of Education Revisited," p. 21)

Perhaps, then, the questions and problems we formulate will have little to do with all those that have occupied us for the last dozen years or so: for example, determining the constitutive ideas of our subject, arranging them in a properly sequential, incremental, and developmental order, and finding appropriately "courteous" language in which to couch them for children of various ages. As a matter of fact, we might even begin to wonder whether interdisciplinary approaches and multimedia techniques themselves are anything more than secondary matters. For surely our first concern ought to be for the mechanism in the school by which we deprive most children of initiative, of a sense of their own value and potency, of their natural, self-determined desire to learn, and, in sum, turn them from children learning into pupils and students. We need also to look to the social imperatives that help turn us from men teaching into teachers and professors. When we have found out what to do about those problems, then and only then does curriculum become an issue (See "The Process of Education Revisited," pp. 20, 21).

For, as Sir Alec Clegg has said,

—if the only challenge we can offer the young is that of material prosperity, and if we overvalue the quick who can add to it, and we discard the slow who cannot, the former will despise our values and the latter resent our indifference; and we shall blame them both for what is our failing, and there will be much bitterness and much discord in our society.[26]

Notes

1 Jerome Bruner, *The Process of Education* (New York: Vintage, 1960), p. vii.

2 Bruner, pp. 52–53. I have reordered the sentences so as to put first the item that is said to be first in the process of curriculum design, and which indeed would logically seem to be so. The passage is notable for the use of pan-human concepts like "the child" and universals like "the tragic." Is "that have proved themselves" a reference to Johnson's "common reader" and hence to the canon of St. Vincent de Lérins?

3 Bruner, p. xv. The admiral seems to have been the chief administrative officer of the summer headquarters of the National Academy of Sciences.

4 See the list of participants, Bruner, p. v.

5 I have in mind the criticisms of such as A. N. Bestor, Mortimer Smith and the Council on Basic Education, Admiral Rickover, and (earlier) R. M. Hutchins.

[6] I record the presence at the Conference of a person from the University of Kansas City. He was there not to talk about the problems of what we would now call an urban university, but rather to provide information ("input"?) on "cinematography," a function he shared with someone from Eastman Kodak Company.

[7] Cf. Elementary Science Study *Newsletter*, Oct. 1968, p. 1: "Too many teachers and administrators still think we are saying that we are providing a technique—easy lessons about the Discovery Method—when we are really trying to express a way of life, not just of teaching. What we want to say is that anyone who tries to teach children to explore and speculate and try things—if he does not himself explore and speculate and try things— cannot carry it off. And this does not apply just to science or to school hours. Without the rhythm, exuberance, and vitality of natural conviction, the teaching performance will remain just that—a performance. The artificiality, however masked, will be just one more addition to the burden of other artificialities society inflicts on children. It is one more ready smile, too muscular to mean what it suggests; one more bit of intellectual dishonesty children must accommodate in their developing personal philosophies."

[8] Bruner, p. 1. Note that Bruner himself qualifies the concern for quality, etc., by adding after a dash, "but without abandonment of the ideal that education should serve as a means of training well balanced citizens for a democracy." See also his reflections on the dangers of competition and a meritocracy, p. 76.

[9] The topic is not invented. "Earnest buffoonery" is Otis Ferguson's phrase in his great review of the Reinhardt MND, reprinted (from *New Republic*, 16 Oct. 1935) in *The Film Criticism of Otis Ferguson*, ed. Robert Wilson (Philadelphia: Temple Univ. Press, 1971), pp. 87–98. The review, by the way, is probably the definitive comment on High Culture in popular media.

[10] In Vol. 61 (Jan. 1972), 52–58. The quotations I have used are at pp. 52, 53, 54, 55. In the last one, the emphasis is mine, of course.

[11] Robert Zoellner has some rather helpful things to say on this point. See his "Behavioral Objectives for English," *College English*, 33 (Jan. 1972), 418–32, esp. at pp. 424 ff.

[12] *Prejudices, Fifth Series* (New York: Knopf, 1926). The book had just been published by the author, in Nashville.

[13] Michael S. Schudson, "Organizing the 'Meritocracy': A History of the College Entrance Examination Board," *Harvard Educational Review*, 42 (Feb. 1972), 34–69, at p. 69. He is citing Christopher Jencks and David Riesman, *The Academic Revolution* (New York: Doubleday, 1968), p. 151.

[14] The phrase is ascribed to George Winchester Stone in "Will There Always Be an English," a splendid review of our state by George H. Henry, *College English*, 33 (Jan. 1972), 407–17, at p. 410.

[15] This and the two preceding examples are taken from a representative reformed textbook of the 1960's.

[16] Adapted from George Ehrenhaft, "Combatting Apathy: Literature and the 'General' Class," *English Journal*, 58 (Sept. 1969), 840–46, at p. 841. The adaptation consists of the comments and qualifications I have added to his description of "general" students. Cf. his description of "some underachievers,"

> who should have been in the regents (college preparatory) track, and had been at one time or another. But they chose to end their high school days in a general class out of fear of failure, out of laziness or apathy, or out of desire to excel somewhere. They read and write as well as many in the regents classes, but even in the seemingly casual surroundings of the general class they were all extremely quiet, which may suggest why they never found glory as regents students.

[17] From the synonymy under "education" in ACD.

[18] Bruner, pp. 76 ff. See n. 8.

[19] Cf. Schudson, p. 38: "'Achievement' in the school system is defined, controlled, and measured in terms of ability to survive within a culture which reflects the behavior and values of the upper, upper middle, and professional classes." Also his remark: "—even if differentiation of people along the dimension of tested mental abilities should appear

legitimate, it must still be asked whether social stratification along the same dimension is morally justified."

20 "The Process of Education Revisited," *Phi Delta Kappan*, 53 (Sept. 1971), 18–21, at p. 19.

21 Has it been duly marked by historians that, in the parlance of school people, "affluent" in "affluent suburbanite" has come to be taken as a descriptive adjective only? Are they invisible, then, the people who live in the suburban soon-to-be slums, where the American working class (white) was rehoused in the decade or so after World War II—with assistance from the federal government?

22 I am not, by the way, using "random" in the statistical sense. I am thinking rather of what seems to be known technically as "random movement," i.e., "relatively undetermined movement. The term often signifies merely that the observer cannot tell what determines it." See Horace B. and Ava C. English, *A Comprehensive Dictionary of Psychological and Psychoanalytical Terms* (New York: McKay, 1958): "random activity or movement." This, I take it, is what Professor Zoellner refers to (p. 427), when he speaks, in italics, of "a pattern of unspecified and generalized stimuli," in which Stimulus–Response-Reinforcement learning originates or on which it is founded.

23 It is not quite, I should say, the classic Socratic method, for the *elenchos* is used in rather informal fashion, and indeed not all Socrates' questions are formed on the pattern of refutation. His procedure is, however, pretty close to what is known as "Socratic method" in school-talk.

24 It is a nice distinction, indeed, that between "being taught" and being only "asked questions." I am not sure, though, that observing its evident consequences would get us very far along the road that, it seems to me, we probably should be seeking out.

25 On this, see Ned O'Gorman, "Headstart: The Torment of ABC's," *New York Times*, 8 June 1971, p. 37; also Stephen S. Baratz and Joan Baratz, "Early Childhood Intervention: The Social Science Base of Racism," *Harvard Educational Review*, 40 (Winter 1970), 29–50; Grace Lee Boggs, "Education: The Great Obsession," *Monthly Review*, 22 (Sept. 1970), 18–39. I should note that by September 1971, Mr. O'Gorman had swung rather widely to the right; see his "Childhood: The Next Battleground," *Saturday Review*, 23 Sept. 1971, pp. 27–29, 84, where he expresses rather vigorous opposition to "those egalitarian poses so current now among the enlightened."

Another article suggestive of a coming reaction is Michael B. Katz, "The Present Moment in Educational Reform," *Harvard Educational Review*, 41 (Aug. 1971), 342–59. Katz says, "Educational reformers should begin to distinguish between what formal schooling can and cannot do. They must separate the teaching of skills from the teaching of attitudes, and concentrate on the former" (p. 355). But as Katz himself remarks, of course it is "impossible to separate the two; attitudes inhere in any form of practice." And as he makes abundantly, though perhaps unwillingly, clear in his *The Irony of Early School Reform*, in Massachusetts it was precisely the development of the school as the chief or indeed the only institution of education in this country that made possible the detention of children in schools to learn the discipline and attitudes necessary to make them efficient factory workers. And it is precisely the concentration on a very narrow range of skills, especially in the common school, that has rigidified class/racial lines and has allowed the professional and managerial castes, and of course the upper bourgeoisie, to monopolize the advantages of Arnoldian culture, such as they are. On the last point, see Christopher Lasch's review of Oscar and Mary Handlin, *Facing Life: Youth and the Family in American History*, in *New York Review of Books*, 18 (10 Feb. 1972), 25–27, esp. p. 27.

I am not, by the way, arguing "de-schooling." See Herb Gintis, "The Politics of Education" (a review of *Crisis in the Classroom*), *Monthly Review*, 23 (Dec. 1971), 39–51 and "Toward a Political Economy of Education, A Radical Critique of Ivan Illich's *Deschooling Society*," *Harvard Educational Review*, 42 (Feb. 1972), 70–96. On the other hand, we may be "de-schooled" whether we like it or not, as the buildings fall to pieces and the teachers collapse into moral confusion.

26 "The Education of John Robinson," *Listener*, 84 (13 Aug. 1970), 197–200.

Perhaps, though, comfort may be found by some in Lord Snow's interesting ruminations on "the best conditions for scientific creativity" and the differences in scientific contributions among various racial, ethnic, religious groups. "Does scientific creativity," he asks, "depend on educating gifted children wherever they can be identified, with extreme competitive rigor? . . . It seems increasingly that a society has to pay a price, and perhaps a very heavy price, if it is going to cherish excellence." (C. P. Snow, *New York Times Book Review*, 18 June 1972, p. 4.)

To Snow's remark may be added this one by James Reid in his rectorial address at the University of Glasgow last spring: "The challenge we face is that of rooting out anything and everything that distorts and devalues human relations." (*New York Times*, 20 June 1972, p. 37. Reid isn't exactly a walker in the corridors of power; he is a leader—"spokesman," is the *Times*'s word—of the workers in the Upper Clyde shipyards.)

Beyond Literacy*

Alan M. Hollingsworth

Michigan State University

IN THE SCHOOLS and colleges of America the largest departments are nearly always English departments. In the school systems across the land, urban and rural, English is usually the one subject that is still required each year. The Modern Language Association has some thirty thousand members, half of them in English. The National Council of Teachers of English has some fifty thousand members, only a few of whom are also members of MLA. English is indeed well established in the educational structure of America. That fact tells us a great deal about the kind of jeopardy English is now in.

No one today needs to hear yet again that "English is in trouble." Who today does not fully recognize that all of education, English included, is in serious trouble, however difficult that trouble may be to describe and define? English is deeply involved in the status quo in education in the country. It seems unlikely that today's status quo will be around in ten years, or even five. Will English?

It seems probable that all of education in America is now at a kind of turning point. I believe that all major disciplines are going to have to reexamine themselves with thoroughness and in a public way. This reexamination will not be an option. Society is going to force it, is already forcing it. A first step in reassessment, in my opinion, is to try to see where we have been and how we got to where we are, and to thus try to catch whatever shadowy apprehensions we can of natural developments in our future. Perhaps a brief glance at the origins of the field of English will help us recover a sense of the impulses that helped to create it. The account that follows is merely a sketch of some aspects of the origins of English, together with some suggestions about one direction we might well take in the coming decade.

In a sense English began in England.[1] In a sense English began in Scotland.[2] And in a sense English began in the United States.[3]

In 1662, with the return of the Stuart kings, the Act of Uniformity was enforced. Out of this enforcement English was born. Nonconformist ministers were deprived of their living, and dissenting teachers were excluded from the universities and at the same time prevented from teaching in the

---

* Revised from an address to the ADE Seminar in Los Angeles, 29 June 1971. Reprinted from *ADE Bulletin*, No. 36 (March 1973), pp. 3–10.

grammar schools. The consequence was the forming of a number of private schools in the homes of Nonconformist ministers and dissenting teachers. These schools, or academies, were probably illegal, but because they were not connected with the grammar schools or the universities, the application of the law was ambiguous and the government did not choose to force the issue. So these new schools survived—not only survived, but flourished. In 1689, by the Act of Toleration, they were legally established as "Dissenting Academies."

The Dissenting Academies did not see themselves as preparing students for the universities but as offering an alternative that was superior to university education. Many of the same courses were offered as at the universities, but in addition the Dissenting Academies offered modern history, modern languages, and a clear emphasis on mastering the national vernacular. The chief aims of the academies were to prepare Nonconformist clergy for their vocation and some of the middle-class merchants to hold their own in the world of business and gentility. Both aims involved helping students write and speak English well. The curriculum stressed "useful knowledge" and was intended to cultivate manners, strengthen character, and improve the moral sense. Daniel Defoe attended such an academy, Newington Green, in 1676–81. Joseph Priestley taught for six years at the excellent Warrington Academy and produced one of the first English textbooks ever, a composition anthology: *Rudiments of English Grammar adapted to the use of Schools* (1761), widely used.

After the Act of Union and the creation of Great Britain in 1707, English manners and styles, and especially the works of English writers, became all the more popular among the members of the educated classes in Scotland. Apparently the first university lecturing on English was done at Edinburgh in 1748 by a Professor John Stevenson, who taught philosophy and logic.[4] Nothing remains of his lectures other than the reported fact that they were given. One of those who must have heard Stevenson was Adam Smith, a young unemployed man not yet the famous economist, who gave a series of public lectures on English writers in 1748. Smith's Edinburgh lectures were a great hit, and although never published, they were very influential. In his audience was a young student named Hugh Blair. Blair soon began his long career (he lived to the age of ninety-two) as a university lecturer on rhetoric, composition, and belles-lettres, the latter consisting of examples of admirable writing done by English writers. Blair published his *Lectures on Composition and Belles Lettres* in 1759. He and his books were enormously influential, but he was only one among many in Scotland who were interested in English.[5] Lord Kames published *Elements of Criticism* in 1761 and George Campbell published his *Philosophy of Rhetoric* in 1776. In 1762 Glasgow endowed a Chair of Rhetoric and Belles Lettres, and in 1763 Aberdeen offered a course in criticism.

The Scottish university model was, of course, very different from that offered by Oxford and Cambridge. The Scottish student took a four-year Arts course covering a wide range of subjects; the Oxford or Cambridge student took a three-year highly specialized course. The Scottish university was secular, nondenominational; the situation was, of course, otherwise at Oxford and Cambridge. Although both English and Scottish schools once shared the trivium and quadrivium, by the early eighteenth century they had grown far apart. In Scotland, philosophy was the center of the curriculum, especially the philosophy of John Locke.[6] The writing and reading of essays was very important because it was a way of focusing on first principles. Composition had a philosophical aim. The Scottish tradition of rhetoric and belles-lettres focused on the writing and reading of essays for the purpose of philosophical clarification. Literature was used as a source of examples for the would-be writer and thinker.

This Scottish tradition of a stress on rhetoric and composition in the service of philosophy was carried on in the nineteenth century by a number of professors, among them Alexander Bain. Bain, a professor of logic, lectured on composition for twelve years at Aberdeen, drawing on English writers for models and examples. The generation of Scottish university teachers who succeeded Bain included Saintsbury, A. C. Bradley, and Walter Raleigh. As Stephen Potter sees it, gradually, out of the teaching of composition in Scottish universities grew the teaching of English literature.[7]

If English as an academic subject was born in the English academies of the late seventeenth century, and English as a university subject began in the Scottish universities in the middle of the eighteenth century, English as a high-school subject found its start in the United States in 1821 in the decision of the citizens of Boston to found a different kind of school.

Scottish influence on education in English in America can be seen in the appointment of a Professor of Rhetoric at Columbia in 1794 and of a Professor of Intellectual Philosophy and English literature at Dartmouth in 1838. And both Scottish and English influence can be seen in Benjamin Franklin's famous Philadelphia Academy. Franklin published his proposal for an academy in 1749, and the school opened its doors in 1751. There were three courses of study (or departments): the classical, the English, and the scientific. Franklin had strong reservations about the classical curriculum, but he proposed such a course as a gesture of political compromise. Shortly after the academy was begun, Franklin was called to Europe. After several years he returned and was enraged to discover that the trustees and the head of the classical program had rather effectively suppressed the English program. Franklin's beautiful letter in defense of English should be read by discouraged teachers of English at least once a year. "From the beginning, the contempt of your employes [sic] for the new, the English course, has been allowed to damage it. They get you to give the Latin master a title. You gave none to the English principal. To the Latin head you gave 200 pounds; to the English one half as much money and twice as many boys. You voted 100 pounds to buy Greek and Latin books, nothing for English. I flatter myself, gentlemen, that from the board minutes it appears that the original plan has been departed from; that the subscribers have been deceived and disappointed; that good masters have been driven out of the school and that the trustees have not kept faith."[8]

American originality in English was manifested not in Franklin's school or in the appointments at Columbia and Dartmouth but in the decision of the citizens of Boston in 1821 to create a new kind of secondary school. Two hundred years earlier, in 1635, the citizens had founded the Boston Public Latin Grammar School. By 1821 important citizens of Boston were quite aware that many children in the city were not encompassed by such a model. Around 1810 the citizens of Boston had become worried that "the children of the poor and unfortunate elements of the community" were being excluded from the benefits of education and had started programs of study for such children that would help them gain special admission to the academies of the city. But now it was felt that academies were not the proper kind of school for such children.[9]

The proposed new school would give a child "an education that shall fit him for active life, and . . . serve as a foundation for eminence in his profession, whether Mercantile or Mechanical." The school was to give children "the means of completing a good English education to fit them for active life." Instruction was to be in English. There were to be courses in English grammar, "Rhetoric and Belles Lettres." There was to be a course called "Criticisms of English Authors." Blair's *Lectures* were to be used in an abridged form. The new school was to be called the English Classical School, but here there was difficulty. The headmaster of the venerable Boston Latin School did not like the name of the new school. If ancient languages and literatures were not to be taught in the new school, how could it be called a classical school at all? What was classical about English authors? He hoped that the school board would "not suffer so erroneous a use of terms." For whatever reason, the name was soon changed from English Classical School to the English High School.

It is well to note that this new school was specifically designed for the non–college bound. English entered education as a school subject in America for non–college-bound students. The mission of the English curriculum was "to prepare for active life," not for the university.

Boston's new high school became the most widely imitated model in the history of American education. By the time of the Civil War, the high schools were displacing and replacing academies in both North and South. And by 1870 there were high schools modeled on Boston's English High School in most American cities.

After the Civil War, Charles W. Eliot, president of Harvard, began to push his philosophy of the elective system. An important part of his educational scheme was the teaching of English composition and of English literature in place of the classical curriculum. Through the elective system Eliot succeeded in displacing Latin and Greek with English. When Harvard and other schools began in the early 1870's to require composition skills and certain readings on English literature, the struggle between school men and university men for control of the secondary-school curriculum was joined. In 1892 the prestigious national Committee on Secondary School Studies met to define the secondary curriculum of the future. The conference was chaired by Charles W. Eliot; the subcommittee on English had as its secretary George Lyman Kittredge. Many of the problems now afflicting English date from that exercise of authority by the universities over the high-school curriculum.

In 1884 a group of college teachers met in New York to find a way to introduce the study of modern languages, even if it meant displacing Latin and Greek from the center of the curriculum. Most of those present were teachers of French or German, but also present were some professors from the very recently formed Departments of English. When the Modern Language Association was founded, the strongest interest its members expressed was in teaching. But in 1904 E. R. Hohlfield, a charter member, complained that the organization was drifting away from its original purpose. William Riley Parker describes well the development of the organization away from teaching toward research.[10] In the 1950's Parker devoted much time and energy to an effort to get the word "teaching" into MLA's stated aim. A half century earlier, in 1911, a number of MLA members had helped create a new organization, the National Council of Teachers of English, in protest against MLA's increasing disinterest in the teaching of English.

But let us return for a moment to England. While the American high-school movement was blossoming and Charles W. Eliot was campaigning for English and the other modern languages, an extraordinary event was taking place in England—the creation of the first new English university since the Middle Ages.

In 1826 a group of dissenters and freethinkers took the shocking and unprecedented step of creating not a new academy but a new university. They called the new university London University, but the city fathers forced the name to be changed to University College. The new college followed the Scottish model of no church affiliation. It was completely secular, and dissenters and freethinkers were not only to be tolerated but welcomed. The curriculum was that of the eighteenth-century academies: science and the modern languages, including English, instead of the classical curriculum. The College had a definite view of English. English was to be studied as a useful modern language, the most useful for native speakers. English was composition. There would be a factual and scientific study of the English language (which eventually led to the strong linguistic interest of the present-day University College). The new college was an extraordinary synthesis of Utilitarianism and Evangelical idealism. It united the Wesleyan drive for popular education with the Utilitarian view of English derived from Locke.

Not to be outdone by the enemy, a group of Church of England supporters founded a counter-college, King's College, in 1829. The college was Anglican. It was located not in the Bohemian section north of the British Museum, but close to the river near the Inns of Court and the Temple, to encourage the upper middle class to attend. There was to be no crude stress on English as composition; rather, in Wordsworth's vein, English was to be studied because of the moral power of poetry. At University College there was a Professor of English Language and Literature; at King's College there would be a Professor of English Literature and History —history having an ancient and honorable status unlike the study of "Language."

In 1836 the city of London forced the two colleges to join under the title of the University of London. Shortly thereafter, King's College helped to found a women's college, Queen's College for Women, and University College helped to found Bedford College for Women. Each had a definite view of English. At Queen's, English was to be considered in the King's College way. At Bedford, all women were to be trained in practical English and be considered prospective teachers of English.

In 1823 a philanthropic middle-class group founded the London Mechanics' Institute for the purpose of offering technological training and a useful knowledge of the English language to the industrial poor. Very soon there were seventy such institutes in England. Each had a library. One of the surprises to the founders was the curious fact that the technical courses were undersubscribed and courses in English literature were oversubscribed by the students. This gave rise to fears that the institutes might become centers of revolutionary politics. Charles Dickens was a frequent guest lecturer at these institutes. In 1870 the London Mechanics' Institute became Birkbeck College of the University of London. At Birkbeck, classes were at night, since the main purpose was adult education. The University of London provides today a historic panoply of modes of English.

Up to this point English was not taught at Cambridge or Oxford. There is no space here to narrate the fascinating story of how Oxford University was forced by a Royal Commission of Inquiry and by intense public criticism led by John Churton Collins to accept the study of English. Victorian scholars know that in the history of polemics John Churton Collins deserves a very solid place. For twelve years, in journals and the London newspapers, Collins attacked Oxford for not instituting an English curriculum. Such were his activities that in January 1887 the *Pall Mall Gazette* devoted a whole issue as a "Pall Mall Extra" to the support of Collins' effort to get Oxford to accept English. Collins enlisted the public support of Gladstone, Huxley, Froude, Arnold, Pater, Dowden, Jowett, and the Archbishop of Canterbury. The full story of Oxford's fifteen-year delay in accepting English is told in D. J. Palmer's *The Rise of English Studies*, and it is worth any reader's time. When Oxford was finally driven to the wall by the government and public opinion and did take up English studies, it was understood that weaker sorts of students, those likely to be interested in "chatter about Shelley," would be the kind likely to apply. It was thought that English might be an appropriate program "for women and second-class men." English was a "soft option."

Even this brief sketch of the history of English reveals that while the most famous universities of England and America have helped to shape English as we know it, they did not create it. The origins of English are not to be found in the libraries of Harvard, Yale, Oxford, Cambridge. English began in the aim of the Dissenting Academies to prepare young dissenters in the useful knowledge of the native language, in the desire of Scottish universities to help students achieve philosophical clarifications through the study and use of the English language, in the movement for adult education of the lower middle class and of the industrial urban poor, in the desire of the citizens of Boston to provide a worthy terminal education for the poorer classes of the city, in the movement for the education of women in the nineteenth century. In the 1870's, eighties, and nineties in England and America, English was transformed into a university study with graduate status at the same time that it became a high-school program for the college bound as well as for the non–college bound. It was on its way to becoming an elite subject with popular roots. To protect ourselves from the errors of arrogance, we should keep in mind that for the most part the origins of English are relatively humble. We should realize and remember that basic to the growth of English were democratic impulses, that English had—possibly still has—a wide popular base.

One of the recurrent assertions in the many essays of John Churton

Collins in which he proposes the need for the study of English is that English should not be studied alone, should not be studied in isolation.[11] Collins believed that English should be studied in combination with classics, or that English should be studied with the modern literature of a foreign country in a comparative way. I think Collins was right, and I predict a great change in the way English is studied in England within five years of England's entry into Europe. I believe that within that time English will come to be studied in England as Collins proposed a little less than one hundred years ago—comparatively, in combination with a modern foreign literature. For a number of reasons—and this is the main conclusion of my review of the origins of the study of English—I believe that many of us in English must learn more about, much more about, other fields of study, other subjects, other arts, other sets of learning activities. I believe that English must become interdisciplinary, but with caution and no illusions. In the 1970's English must become interdisciplinary, multidisciplinary, cross-disciplinary. We must do this not under the illusion that interdisciplinary work will inevitably produce "new knowledge." Chomsky warns us it will not.[12] And even if new knowledge is produced, we must not exaggerate its importance. As Noel Annan has said, "knowledge has long ago outrun its application."[13] We do not wish to rehearse the kind of interdisciplinary work involved in the general education programs abandoned by Harvard, Chicago, and Columbia. But neither do we wish to forget what of value we have learned from these experiments. To the extent possible we must operate without illusions and visit none on our society.

We must become interdisciplinary, first of all, for self-preservation. The social sciences, especially sociology and behavioral psychology, are writing the humanities out of the future of education. For fifteen or twenty years sociology has been assuming a role something like the role literary culture assumed in Arnold's time. Sociology "has undoubtedly acquired something of the same intellectual-synthetic function for *our* age that the literary imagination could claim in the last century."[14] If literature and criticism are merely reflectors, or mainly reflectors, of times and trends, then it can be argued that sociology subsumes both literature and criticism and assimilates both as mere data. As for behaviorism, it can come as no surprise to English teachers in California to hear that operational psychology, with its crude dependence on quantification, is currently attempting to measure English in the Procrustean bed of behavioral objectives, but much of the rest of the country has this unhappy surprise yet in store. All of this mighty misdirection could have been prevented if we in English had adequately and effectively stated our goals. Since we did not, others are now doing it for us.

When Bloom's *Taxonomy* appeared in 1956 a joint curriculum study committe of MLA and NCTE should have taken the book up as a matter of routine, should have defined it, seen its implications for English, should have acted. That was 1956. Today each department of English should be discussing objectives, including behavioral objectives, through committees within the department and between the department and other disciplines and fields of learning, and through department meetings. We must understand what is happening to us; we must know the enemy. And we must not offer naive objections to the operational psychologists running the behavioral objectives machine. They are well prepared to deal with sentimental humanists. We must be tough, sophisticated, knowledgeable. For an example of a good statement see the "Resolution on Behavioral Objectives" adopted by the membership of NCTE at the Atlanta meeting in November of 1970.

We must become interdisciplinary for a second reason.[15] We must cease to waste time and effort. Anyone who has studied the curriculum of the schools and the universities in America cannot help but be struck by the waste involved. Highly commendable movements and programs are instituted—and wither and die—are forgotten—and are again repeated with no awareness of the past. In *Crisis in the Classroom* Charles Silberman defines "mindlessness" as the main weakness of American education, by which he means "the failure or refusal to think seriously about educational purpose, the reluctance to question established practice."[16] Silberman asks why the very promising reform movements in education in the late 1950's and early 1960's have come to nothing. His answer is that the fact that the reform movement was led by university scholars has proven to be its greatest weakness. The university scholars failed to study the history of education and did not know curriculum even in their own disciplines. "The reformers," Silberman says, "by and large ignored the experiences of the past, and particularly of the reform movement of the 1920's and '30's. They were, therefore, unaware of the fact that almost everything they said had been said before, by Dewey, Whitehead, Bode, Rugg, etc.; and they were unaware that almost everything they tried to do had been tried before, by educators like Frederick Burk, Charleton Washburne, and Helen Parkhurst, not to mention Abraham Flexner and Dewey himself." Because the reforms failed to study educational history, especially that of progressive education in the 1920's, "the contemporary reformers repeated one of the fundamental errors of the progressive education movement; they perpetuated the false dichotomy that the schools must be *either* child-centered *or* subject-centered." The reformers of the 1920's had ignored the warnings of Dewey and others and had chosen the former, Silberman says, while the reformers of the 1950's and 1960's ignored the warnings and opted for the latter, placing all the emphasis on subject matter; "reacting against the banality that child-dictated education had become, they opted for adult dictation. They knew what they wanted children to learn; they did not think to ask what children wanted to learn."

An example of waste that Silberman might have used is that of the neglect of the practice and achievement of Francis W. Parker. In Quincy, Massachussetts, and in Chicago in the 1880's, Francis W. Parker directed his schools in ways of education that have only recently been discovered anew by the proponents of the New English. Parker did not believe in "child-centered classes." Like Wallace Douglas of the Northwestern University English Curriculum Center—the only person whose writings, to my knowledge, show an active awareness of the important point Parker made ninety years ago—Parker believed in placing children at "the center of the educative process"—something quite different from child-centered. The child and the teacher are both involved in the educative process, but the child is at the center of the process. Both are involved; both are needed in the teaching-learning process. In Parker's elementary schools the children wrote the textbooks through the work they did in classes. These works were printed up, bound, and distributed. With an air of revolutionary discovery the Los Angeles school system did this same thing—a valuable thing to do—in 1969, apparently without knowing of Parker's practice in the 1880's. Perhaps the first thing English faculty members should do today is to read Michael Shugrue's history of recent reform efforts in English—*English in a Decade of Change*.[17] Perhaps the next step would be to read Silberman. The third—to read Dewey's *Schools of To-Morrow*.

We must become interdisciplinary, in the third place, to redefine and reassert the unique value of literary criticism. We can no longer assume that literary criticism is valued. One thinks of Benjamin DeMott's statement to the effect that Lit. Hist. and Lit. Crit. are dead. One thinks of William Arrowsmith's denunciations of literary scholarship and criticism at the graduate level. One thinks of Louis Kampf's charge that literary criticism is simply one more way a mindless and inhumane educational system prevents itself from being radically examined and transformed. One thinks of George Steiner's assertion that literary culture in Germany did not prevent Dachau. But one thinks also of the critical work of Frank Kermode, of Northrop Frye, and of Hillis Miller. One thinks of the whole relatively unexplored area of the response to literature. In 1970 at the Association of Departments of English in Los Angeles Caroline Shrodes presented a brilliant paper on the need for a new, an organic theory of literary response, that made quite clear the kind of sophisticated interdisciplinary effort literary criticism ought now to be engaged in.[18] Literary criticism is a unique instrument of analysis and of knowing. We must assert that and prove it over and over again.

We must become interdisciplinary for a fourth reason—to support the great reform in English called "New English." This reform is under way in some early schools in England and in selected schools in the United States, such as the APEX high school in Trenton, Michigan. How much of value from elementary-level language arts can be truly and effectively nurtured and developed in university- and college-level English remains to be seen. The so-called disciplines rest their case, whether they know it or not, on Locke's inadequate philosophy of education and concept of the mind of a learner. How to keep what we offer of value while reinvigorating our discipline with some of the energy and creativity of childhood interest in language is a considerable challenge. Language seen as process makes possible an effort to meet such a challenge.

APEX, surely one of the most important developments in all of education in the last twenty years, is more than a mere application of New English principles.[19] Indeed, APEX was developed simultaneously with New English, and there is no reason to suppose it is directly dependent on Dartmouth. Rather, Dartmouth and APEX are compatible developments out of the pressures of the late 1950's and early 1960's.

Some of the central documents of this extremely important development called "New English" are John Dixon's *Growth through English*, James Moffett's *Universe of Discourse*, Sydney Bolt's *The Right Response*, James Britton's *Language and Learning*, and Wallace Douglas's various essays. We should know these writings and other important documents of New English well. And we should know well not only these but the English curriculum of the past. Thus educated, we should not repeat old errors, and we should also be somewhat wiser in guessing about the future. Helpful in this last regard is to know and be selective about learning theories. Especially important to New English would seem to be a knowledge of Piaget and of Maslovian humanistic psychology. One may guess that Piaget and Maslow have something important to do with our future.

There is another reason why we should become interdisciplinary. I believe each major discipline will soon have to say—we are already being forced to say it—which, if any, major educational problems of the society it is inherently suited to provide solutions for. English will have to offer reading and writing as its work areas. If English cannot help in these areas, whatever else it can provide will soon not be wanted. We must commit ourselves here—but we must commit ourselves not merely to literacy.

In an essay that is stunning in its prescience, R. P. Blackmur defines what he calls "mere literacy" as opposed to what he calls "true literacy." The essay is entitled "Toward a Modus Vivendi," and it appeared in 1955 in *The Lion and the Honeycomb.*[20] In this essay Blackmur makes an astonishing prediction—that in the year 1970 American universities will be in the same fix that European universities are already in as of 1954, that of producing too many Ph.D.'s. Or this is how the problem will appear. The problem, Blackmur says, is literacy. "Literacy is the form ignorance takes in a society subjected to universal education." Blackmur treats literacy as a form of industrial pollution. "Serious literacy," he says, has gone out of style. Mere literacy is totalitarian in its effects. A mass society that is merely literate is just educated enough to be completely controlled. What Blackmur calls for is true literacy—but true literacy means an elite class.

One way to see the major dilemma confronting the field of English is to oppose to Blackmur's views the views of Louis Kampf. Kampf charges higher education, English in particular, with elitism, with self-serving, with cooperation in the suppression of the opportunities of the working classes. "Arnold's ideas can lead only to the practice of cultural elitism—an elitism which is directed toward making the present system more 'civilized.'" Critics, teachers, and intellectuals—often with the best of intentions—have perpetuated and deepened this elitism.[21] Blackmur and Kampf agree that what we are producing is a society in which the form literacy takes is ignorance. Blackmur believes we should abandon the mass and attend to the elite that can become truly literate; Kampf believes that attending to the elite, a mandarin class, is all we have ever done, perhaps all we can do.

I believe that the major task that we in English must undertake in the next decade is to help ourselves and other members of society to become truly literate in Blackmur's sense, but that we must deal not only with the elite but with the great majority. We must center our efforts on something more than literacy—and by *literacy* we must mean forms of communication other than print, but including print. This means a vast interdisciplinary undertaking with linguistics, applied linguistics, anthropological linguistics, psychologies concerned with learning theory, certain areas of professional education, and those parts of sociology and economic history that offer insight into the connections between language and class.

English cannot do all of this alone. But only English can organize the effort in time to matter.

The history of English indicates that this problem—the problem of literacy and true literacy—is the problem which we must historically confront.

In 1904 Albert S. Cook, Professor of English Language and Literature at Yale, gave a talk at Princeton entitled "The Graduate Study of English." At one point he said:

I well remember the impressive conclusion of an address before English students by a professor of Greek a couple of years ago, in which he warned them that English is now on its trial, as Greek had been, and that if English failed to answer the high expectations which had been formed of it, it would fall. (*The Higher Study of English*, 1906)

My sense of things is that that historic moment for English has now come.

We must now attempt to move ourselves and our society "beyond literacy." If we do not, who will? And if we do not, what else will we do?

Notes

1 For this theme I have drawn heavily on D. J. Palmer's excellent *The Rise of English Studies* (New York: Oxford University Press, 1965) and the pioneering British Board of Education Report of 1921, *The Teaching of English in England.*

2 This is Stephen Potter's thesis in his witty and amusing *The Muse in Chains* (London: J. Cape, 1937).

3 So far as I know I alone must take the responsibility for this proposal.

4 *Lectures on Rhetoric and Belles Lettres Delivered in the University of Glasgow by Adam Smith Reported by a Student in 1762–63*, ed., introd., and annot. John M. Lothian (London: Thomas Nelson and Sons, 1963), pp. xxv–xxix.

5 See D. J. Palmer, Appendix I, and Stephen Potter, pp. 104–39.

6 Locke's influence for the better and the worse is dealt with succinctly in *The Teaching of English in England*, pp. 36–38. See also Percival Chubb, *The Teaching of English in the Elementary and the Secondary School* (New York: Macmillan, 1913), p. 36.

7 This is Potter's thesis, but a full-scale study of the Scottish rhetoricians and the rise of English studies would be very useful.

8 William Marshall French, *American Secondary Education* (New York: Odyssey Press, 1957), p. 61.

9 Elmer Ellsworth Brown, *The Making of Our Middle Schools* (New York: Longmans, Green, 1903), p. 299. See also John Elbert Stout, *The Development of High-School Curricula in the North Central States from 1860 to 1918* (Chicago: The University of Chicago, 1921), pp. 1–15. It should be noted that the disadvantaged children being worried about by the good citizens of Boston were male only.

10 See "The MLA, 1883–1953," *PMLA*, 68, No. 4, pt. 2 (Sept. 1953), 3–39.

11 John Churton Collins, *The Study of English Literature* (London and New York, 1891), p. 8ff.

12 Noam Chomsky, *Language and Mind* (New York: Harcourt, 1968), pp. 2–4.

13 Noel Annan, "The Life of the Mind in British Universities Today," *ACLS Newsletter* (Jan.–Feb. 1969), pp. 18–19.

14 Malcolm Bradbury, "Literature and Sociology," *Essays & Studies*, 23 (1970), p. 91.

15 See Harry Finestone, "The Limits of Innovation," *ADE Bulletin*, No. 32 (Feb. 1972), pp. 9–12, for an imaginative and challenging view of interdisciplinary necessities for English, compatible with what I have to say in the rest of my paper, but taking a somewhat different line.

16 Charles Silberman, *Crisis in the Classroom* (New York: Random, 1970), p. 11.

17 Michael Shugrue, *English in a Decade of Change* (New York: Pegasus, 1968).

[18] Caroline Shrodes, "The Scholars and the Anti-Self," *ADE Bulletin*, No. 26 (Sept. 1971). Reprinted in this volume, pp. 37–45.

[19] See *APEX—A Nongraded Phase Elective English Curriculum*, USOE Project 661691 (Trenton, Mich.: Trenton High School, 1966).

[20] R. P. Blackmur, *The Lion and the Honeycomb*, (New York: Harcourt, 1955).

[21] Louis Kampf, "Culture Without Criticism," *The Massachusetts Review*, 11, No. 4, (1970), 663.

Facing Up to the Problems of Going Interdisciplinary[*]

John H. Fisher

University of Tennessee, Knoxville

> Nel mezzo del cammin di nostra vita
> Mi ritrovai una selva oscura,
> Che la diritta via era smarrita.

I HAVE SPOKEN several times in recent years of my belief that the humanities have come to the end of a cultural path and must now seek a new way. In the 5 July 1970 *New York Times Magazine*, Konrad Z. Lorenz, author of *On Aggression*, spoke of the motives that have supported our efforts in the past. "If you have not made use of biology [he says] to understand how species lacking a cumulative tradition act, you cannot grasp the unique nature of human culture. The appearance of language made it possible to maintain a tradition independent of environment. With culture something completely new came into the world: the potential immortality of thought, of truth, of knowledge. An entire people, an entire race, can now perish, and yet their culture can survive in libraries—so that another people, even another planet, can find it and make use of it. This is the real immortality of the spirit."

What could better describe the purpose of English and foreign-language teaching in this country? The only native languages and cultures on this continent are the Indian; all of the other languages and cultures, not excepting English, were imported by immigrants and carry the ethnic and cultural overtones of their places of origin. English is the WASP language, and English literature, which is the staple of our curriculum in the humanities—Chaucer, Shakespeare, Milton, Pope, Wordsworth, Tennyson—embodies attitudes toward government, religion, and social relations that are peculiarly British.

Ninety-five percent of the inhabitants of the thirteen colonies that declared their independence in 1776 were of British extraction. When they declared their political independence, they by no means declared their spiritual independence. For the succeeding two hundred years, we have looked upon England as the wellspring of our culture. Until 1820, Sir James Craigie reports in the *Dictionary of American English*, the passage of new words and new senses for old words was regularly from east to west—from England to the new country. Emerson might deliver his address on "The

---

[*] An address to the ADE Seminar at Northwestern on 12 Nov. 1971. Reprinted from *ADE Bulletin*, No. 32 (Feb. 1972), pp. 5–8.

American Scholar" in 1837, but the Morgans and Newberrys and Huntingtons and Folgers continued to transport English books and manuscripts to this country to the point where Britain began to feel denuded of her treasures and we have today in America richer resources for the study of the Anglo-American tradition than the British themselves. These collections were symbols of an ethos. Throughout the nineteenth century, the teaching of the English language and its principal repository, English literature, was the primary means of acculturating the successive waves of non-English-speaking immigrants. That process was again both practical and symbolic. For, as E. R. Leach wrote in 1954 concerning the dialects of central Burma, "to speak one language rather than another is a ritual act, it is a statement about one's personal status; to speak the same language as one's neighbors expresses solidarity with those neighbors, to speak a different language expresses social distance, even hostility."

By 1900 thirty-five million immigrants had been exposed to English. The shame of their children in the broken English of their parents and their consequent reluctance to preserve and transmit their ancestral tongues is a commonplace of American cultural history. By 1940 sixty percent of the population declared that they were not of Anglo-Saxon extraction. Today in 1973, the English, Scottish, Welsh, and Irish descendants represent some 22% of the population (*New York Times*, 14 May 1973, p. 52). The Census Bureau reports the eight largest ethnic groups as follows: English, Scottish, Welsh, 29.5 million; Irish, 16.4 million; Spanish and Latin American, 9.2 million; Italian, 8.8 million; French, 5.4 million; Polish, 5.1 million; Russian 2.2 million. These account for 102.2 million, or 50% of the total population. One era had drawn to a close.

As Barbara Tuchman chronicled in *The Proud Tower*, the First World War marked the culmination of a half century of increasing international involvement by the United States. The aftermath of the war proved a fiasco, however, and by the time of the Depression of the 1930's, America appeared to be nearly as isolationist in spirit as it had been when George Washington delivered his Farewell Address. Yet the period between the wars appears in retrospect to be the time when the cultural current began to flow from west to east. By the 1930's Hollywood movies had become the pabulum of the world, and since the Second World War, American music, American art, American publishing, American television—not to mention American science, American food and drink, clothing, and appliances— have set the tide running heavily in reverse. American cultural imperialism is now a sore subject throughout the world.

This cultural phenomenon has had its impact upon our study of English and the European languages and literatures. The period of clinging to our English roots and of venerating Europe's superior culture is coming to an end. In the language curriculum, this has the effect of turning us from our nineteenth-century obsession with linguistic solidarity to interest in the varieties and social implications of American dialects. In literature, it has the effect of turning us from inculcating cultural homilies to an interest in the nature of literature in society and to literatures other than the English and the European. The study of language and literature as a cultural rite is being replaced by the study of language and literature as an aspect of human behavior. In a word, the study of language and literature is growing interdisciplinary. But the disciplines it is beginning to mingle with are not only other languages and literatures, and the other humanities such as philosophy or art history, but sociology, psychology, and anthropology.

That is Fisher's Stereopticon. I do not urge it upon you. Many of my most esteemed colleagues will have none of it and say that I am merely stoking a campfire. Be that as it may, I needed to flash the vision on the screen as a background to my real concern for today. For although, along with others, I have been saying glibly that the humanities are becoming—and must become—interdisciplinary, I have never faced up to the implications of such a movement. What does it mean for the student, for the teacher, and for the curriculum?

Merely to ask the question makes one aware of the irony of the current situation. Interdisciplinary study in the humanities is notoriously difficult if it is seriously pursued. For one thing, it almost always involves mastery of more than one language. Not even everything in the social sciences (Levi-Strauss) or architecture (the Greek and Italian urban planners) is available in English. Handling diverse bodies of material is likely to involve quantification, statistics, and, most recently, computer models. Nothing is more superficial than casual or eclectic comparisons of literatures or cultures. This is what has given "social studies" in the secondary schools and undergraduate comparative literature courses in translation a bad reputation. Yet as the requirements of general education are being progressively abolished in college, students are being allowed—almost encouraged—to go their own interdisciplinary ways. In recent questionnaires, MLA found that something over 40 percent of the four-year colleges and universities had reduced or removed their English and foreign-language requirements for graduation. In many cases, this is the result of the wholesale reduction of requirements rather than any special distrust of language and literature—and at least for the foreign languages, the overall effect upon enrollment has not yet been serious. Nevertheless, I believe that going interdisciplinary has now come to carry the implication of doing it all in English and of eliminating requirements so that the student may choose anything he wants to outside of his major. And unless he has his eye on graduate or professional school, the specifications for the major are becoming increasingly flexible.

Furthermore, the liberalizing of requirements reflects practical necessity rather than educational philosophy. As the college cohort grows larger, staffing and administering the required courses in general education grow more difficult. As the variety of subjects offered in college grows larger, it becomes more difficult to decide what to require, and the alternatives grow manifestly less rational (Swahili vs. statistics). Students enter college with widely differing preparations. If they are all put into certain designated courses, the institution bears some responsibility for their success or failure. When they are allowed to choose freely, the institution is less responsible if they choose poorly and fail.

The paradox is that a vast number of the 8.5 million students now in college are the first generation of their families to attend. Their high schools have not—could not have—adequately prepared them for the cafeteria of courses they encounter. They are not clear as to their own objectives or the best way to achieve a coherent education. College advisement is at best an unsteady reed. So hundreds of thousands of students each year end up doing what comes naturally—thumbing through the catalog and signing up for whatever looks interesting.

Need I say that this is not the way to achieve interdisciplinary education? Combined with the traditional departmental major the free elective system may not lead to absolute chaos, because if all else fails, four or five courses in one department are likely to reinforce one another in some way. But if those four or five courses can be chosen for a program in, say, American Studies from fifty courses in literature, art, music, history, economics, sociology, and political science, the student is likely to end up with nothing but a scattering of unrelated courses. (When I say that the future lies in interdisciplinary studies, my colleagues at N.Y.U. like to point out to me that their graduate enrollment in American Studies fell from 80 students to 15 over the last four years.)

A successful interdisciplinary education seems to me the antithesis of the free elective. If that is so, the fact is going to dampen the enthusiasm of some of those who have been enthusiastic about this approach as a way to break out of what they regard as the stultifying narrowness of the departmental major. The key to an effective interdisciplinary education seems to me a "systems" approach, that is, not to think of individual courses or individual fields or departments, but of an interrelated series of courses and independent study activities. We already have the pattern for this sort of work in our interdepartmental "programs" of study. These should be vastly increased in number and variety. There should be programs of literature and sociology, literature and psychology, folklore and anthropology, European literature and the rise of modernism, English literature and the homogeneity of national values, effect of the mass media, and so on, and so on. The rationale for each program should be spelled out in the catalog. The essential point would be that each program would specify a coherent sequence of courses from the freshman year through the senior. Each would imply some progression on the part of the student. This would allow the instructor in the later years of college to act upon presuppositions as to what the students could do—a condition that the free elective system makes progressively more difficult. A student might choose any program, but once he chose it, his sequence of courses would be fixed. He might change from one program to another, but if so he would have to back up and take the curriculum of that program in prescribed order.

Some such plan as this seems to me essential if interdisciplinary education in the humanities is to have any chance of success in the years ahead. Otherwise the departmental major will win out. The individual departments, for better or worse, have over the years hammered out more or less coherent fields of coverage and methodologies. Careers find their identity within the departmental structure, and I do not really see how it could be otherwise. Colleges and divisions are too big and too miscellaneous to form professional homes. Indeed, some departments like English and psychology are themselves growing too large and too diverse. This is one reason that we have witnessed the emergence of new disciplines in the last quarter century: linguistics because linguists did not feel at home in departments of literature; history of science because these scholars did not feel at home in science departments; anthropology because anthropologists did not feel at home with sociologists. But the level on which such new disciplines begin to emerge is not the classroom or the curriculum, it is rather in the scholarly conference and the professional journal.

So a further problem of going interdisciplinary is how to persuade ourselves and our colleagues to do it. Our students are much more ready for interdisciplinary work than most of us. They do not see the difficulties, only the imaginative sweep. Most scholars work more and more intensively with a smaller and smaller body of data as they advance. I am down to learning as much as I can about the language and literature of London between 1370 and 1400, and by the time I'm sixty this may be narrowed to Westminster between 1386 and 1395. And I shall still die before I have fully unraveled the effect of Chancery upon the development of standard English in this crucial period. If I'm told now that I must pick up sociology and anthropology, I'll just dig in my heels, as will most of my colleagues in their fifties. Fortunately the young are more malleable and the generations pass with frightening swiftness. If our generation can become hospitable to serious interdisciplinary work, that is all that can really be asked of it, and the change in the complexion of the profession will come about fast enough. But I think that we can still expect the new era to be represented by professional dedication and scholarship, not merely by willingness to talk off the top of one's head about what he reads in the *New York Times*.

Fortunately there is the device of the staff meeting. Whatever progress is going to be made toward integrating the traditional humanities with popular culture (film, television, the press) and the social sciences is going to be made by small groups of like-minded people planning new programs of scholarship and teaching as teams or task forces. This is the way the great books courses at Chicago and Columbia were—and for all I know still are—planned and staffed. The teachers, drawn from the language departments, philosophy, history, etc., met weekly to sweat out what they would teach and how they would teach it. The weekly meetings did not settle once and for all the neo-Aristotelian or neo-humanistic interpretations of poetry, but I am told that they had a Hawthorne effect that made the general humanities course at Chicago and Columbia in the 1930's an almost mystical experience for many of the teachers and students. And that course, composed of Plato and Virgil and Dante and Shakespeare and Goethe and Flaubert, was a harbinger of what students are asking for today, save that now they would include the Ramayana and the Nō plays. In the late 1940's, also, there was a movement toward courses in "communication" that combined reading and writing with public speaking and study of the media. In the name of quality, we shouted this approach down in the 1950's, but it would appear now that it was on the right track.

History may show that the period from 1955 to 1965 was a regression in the development of the humanities in this country—retreat into a culture-bound attitude which we had earlier begun to grow out of. The cracks in the genteel tradition had begun to show in the 1930's and 40's, and they have begun to show again since 1968. Our problem is to know how to evaluate the strain upon the Anglo-American tradition; not to mistake a popgun for the clap of doom; not to throw the baby out with the bath; but yet not to mistake the cloud small as a man's hand now on the horizon.

Clichés are such a comfortable way to talk and to think. The term *interdisciplinary* itself could so easily decline into a cliché. That would be the final misfortune, for the idea is pregnant with possibility if only we can learn to deliver.

Prolegomenon to a Definition of Interdisciplinary Studies: The Experience at Governors State University

Daniel Bernd

Governors State University

THE NECESSITY to define interdisciplinary studies arises largely out of economic and political pressures apart from the imperatives within the disciplines themselves. When a new university such as Governors State University writes in its guidelines that its program shall be interdisciplinary (without telling anybody what that means operationally), the educational planners are responding to something that they feel to be unsatisfactory with the conventional academic arrangements. "Interdisciplinary" may turn out to be this year's favorite in-word, the successor to "relevance" and "accountability." Even so, it is possible to define and describe what interdisciplinary studies can and ought to be.

First we ought to decide some of the things that an interdisciplinary program is not:

> 1. It is not antidiscipline or nondiscipline. An interdisciplinary program does not attempt to produce a new kind of person who is in any substantial way better educated, better equipped to deal with problems, or *more relevant* than a mere narrow specialist trained in a discipline. We must begin with the premise that there is nothing wrong with the disciplines as disciplines. A good deal of confusion about the state of American higher education could be avoided if we would all stop shouting *mea culpa* about non-sins. Something is wrong, but less with what we are, as discipline specialists, than with what we have (or haven't) done with it; herein lies the source of the exasperation in the public mind about the function of college professors. Like a good psychiatrist, before we

* Reprinted from *ADE Bulletin*, No. 31 (Nov. 1971), pp. 8–14.

can locate the real guilt, we had better stop worrying about matters that we are not guilty of. Irrelevance is not the problem of the disciplines. We ought never to have let ourselves be trapped into arguing that "We can be more relevant than you." To admit that higher education has sometimes ignored important problems and concentrated on trivial matters says nothing about disciplines, a discipline, or a subdiscipline *per se*. As Dean Saul Cohen of Clark University once put it, "Relevance is a problem in education that the disciplines must help to solve, not a quality they either possess or lack." It is well to be clear on this issue before we turn higher education over to the new prophets of relevance. We can't lick anti-intellectuals by joining them.

2. To be interdisciplinary does not mean to be a "generalist." Donald T. Campbell of Northwestern University described the problem well when he noted that to be interdisciplinary we must give up these "Leonardesque aspirations." Omnicompetence is not anything we can or should attempt to train anybody for. An interdisciplinary program does not mean that we will produce latter-day da Vincis, somehow endowed with the benefits of a super-liberal-arts, super-general-education training. I am sure that we have all heard enough from people who rather smugly define themselves as "generalists" in order to assert a moral superiority over somebody called a "specialist" (one who is thereby defined as narrow, obtuse, and otherwise unqualified to run things as compared with a "generalist").

This sort of argument has been going on a long time, often conducted by people who believe that by abstracting somebody's list of great books they will discover a place upon which to stand and move the world—like a well-read Archimedes who doesn't have to know very much about anything in particular, but needs only the capacity to discover the secret levers which the guardians of the disciplines' mysteries so antisocially try to keep to themselves. The baldest expression of this I ever heard was from a dean who averred that if all these subject matters contain such wisdom, why didn't we stop all the nonsense and just teach the wisdom? He was not being ironic, but was simply expressing the notion—more widespread than it ought to be—that relevance, wisdom, insight, truth, and other good things can somehow be squeezed out of a subject matter like the juice of an orange, if we could only design the right centrifuge.

All that I am saying is that we had better face the

truth that the expansion of knowledge means specialization, and that there is not only no need to apologize for it, there is a necessity to affirm its virtues. Whatever interdisciplinary studies are, they cannot provide the rationale for amateurism in education. The point ought to be made clear enough by considering the way English is taught in the American public schools, where almost half the teachers do not have qualifications remotely resembling an English major. Too many teachers literally do not know what they are talking about.

3. An interdisciplinary program is not generated by a social value system imposed from outside the disciplines. Dumping a lot of specialists into the same curriculum and labeling it with some honorific title ("democracy," "humaneness") does not produce an interdisciplinary program. An interdisciplinary program is not a forced association of a congeries of disciplines jumbled together under the aegis of the socially desirable.

4. Just as the problem of interdisciplinary studies is not that of discovering relevance or of creating new super-disciplinarians, neither is it a solution for the problem of research versus teaching. If the activity of research is essentially the activity of creating knowledge (whether anybody else has created it before or not), and if teaching and training have something to do with what happens to that knowledge, then it is difficult to see how the allocation of resources between those two activities (which are not really very separate concerns) is going to be solved by the definition of new programs of interdisciplinary studies. The necessity of making teachers out of researchers and researchers out of teachers will remain with us.

5. An interdisciplinary program is not one in which one or several disciplines are subsidiary or instrumental to another discipline.[1] We should distinguish between interdisciplinary programs and attempts to meld disciplines such as "Core Curriculum," "Communications," or even "American Studies."

There have been many examples of valuable and exciting educational enterprises which involve two or more disciplines, but in such enterprises there has usually been one central or essential discipline which was using another discipline instrumentally to its own purposes. For example, a course in the intellectual and social history of nineteenth-century Europe very well may use painting and novels to illustrate how historical movements were also reflected in the art of the period. But the historian will not talk about the painting or the literature in the same way that an art critic or a literary scholar would. For the social historian, questions of the value, quality, and significance of the art in its own terms would be of relatively little moment. The reverse of the example is illustrated by the desire of English teachers to consider literature *qua* literature rather than as historical data. I believe that it is on this central question of "who is to be instrumental for whose purposes?" that interdisciplinary programs have failed in the past and will continue to fail unless the integrity of each discipline's substance and perspective is maintained. The field of English has always been the particular victim in efforts to design programs that transcend the boundaries of disciplines. English seems to be a universal chemical with which every other discipline wishes to combine, and yet most combinations have not survived. Any high-school teacher who has had to suffer the responsibility for the English portion of a core curriculum will know what I am talking about.

Before we can begin to describe an interdisciplinary program, we should stipulate what we mean by *disciplines*. What we mean by the word is a habit of mind, a way of ordering concepts, methods of looking at phenomena, or a series of methodologies which lead to something called "a field of study." The architectonics of a particular system are what we generally mean by a *discipline*. There is no need to agonize about what disciplines are or ought to be, because few people within one have difficulty identifying themselves. The analogy can be drawn to Kant's metaphor (freely translated)—we look at life through space-time colored spectacles; that is, whatever phenomena we observe are, perforce, observed in time and space. So it is with disciplines—we observe and react to data within the structure of our subject. We read books as "Englishers" because that is what we are. Quite obviously, a historian would not read books in the same manner. In a certain sense, he would not be reading the same books.

What then should an *interdisciplinary* program be like? We were forced to try to answer the question at Governors State University because the guidelines for the University and the College of Cultural Studies told us we had to be interdisciplinary. Unfortunately, guidelines are not deductive, as anybody who has ever written them or tried to follow them has discovered. The appropriate refrain is probably from Prufrock, "That is not what I meant at all . . . at all."

Our College of Cultural Studies is responsible for the disciplines in language and literature, the social sciences, and the fine and performing arts.[2] We have twelve faculty members. The temptation to consider ourselves qualified to teach everybody everything has been great, but we have resisted it.[3] After an extended series of intensive and self-revelatory discussions, we have arrived at a way of preserving our identity and the integrity of our disciplines without taking on the pretensions of a class of Renaissance men and women.

We have been helped in the conceptualization of what we are doing by a volume entitled *Interdisciplinary Relationships in the Social Sciences,* edited by Muzafer Sherif and Carolyn W. Sherif, a book which is a report of a symposium on the subject at Pennsylvania State University in 1967. Of particular use was an essay by Donald T. Campbell of Northwestern University entitled "Ethnocentrism of Disciplines and the Fish-Scale Model of Omniscience," which is easily a prizewinner for titlesmanship in the social sciences. Mr. Campbell's thesis is that which has been outlined above. We must forget our impulses toward omnicompetence (Leonardesque aspirations) and search for another model for interdisciplinary relationships. Basically, Mr. Campbell believes that problems have overlapping areas which various disciplines may illuminate—thus the fish-scale model of omniscience.

We had already begun discovering this model for ourselves before we came across the Sherifs and Professor Campbell. But they have been useful in clarifying the issues for us. We had begun to see that the major problem is, in the Sherifs' words, substantive, not merely administrative, and that we are not going to make interdisciplinary programs take shape by writing guidelines and then carefully not organizing the College along departmental or divisional lines. Suggestions for administering interdisciplinary programs often remind me of Irish folktales where disputes are settled among strong men by locking them in a room together, the winner being the one who can walk out.[4]

After clearing the ground by discovering the negative conditions, it seemed to us that an interdisciplinary program should satisfy the following:

> 1. The problem must be considered a substantive one, not merely administrative in nature.
> 2. The program must be based on disciplines. By interdisciplinary we did not mean nondisciplinary. Nor were we recruiting "generalists" to man the program.
> 3. The interdisciplinary essence, if we may call it that, would not inhere in individuals but in issues or problems that allowed several disciplinary perspectives.
> 4. The issue or problem was just that, not a value or set of values which it would be deemed desirable for the disciplines to support.
> 5. Some device, framework, or methodology must be devised that would generate an interdisciplinary issue, problem, or set of problems, which could be approached in an interdisciplinary fashion.
> 6. Any framework or methodology so generated should include the possibilities for all three disciplinary areas: language and literature, fine and performing arts, and the social sciences.

We invented such a generating device and called it the Interdisciplinary Studies Context (ISC). The Interdisciplinary Studies Context is simply a means of finding issues or problems which yield the beneficial results of multi-, inter-, or cross-disciplinary perspectives, while preserving at the same time the particular integrity of the individual disciplinarians involved in the study of the problem. We are trying to have it both ways: we cannot be other than what we are, but the direction in which we change and develop can be influenced by what we find from other perspectives. The Sherifs have defined one of the major values of interdisciplinary studies as the check on validity which one discipline gives to another by examining the same data through different disciplinary lenses. From our point of view it is not so much "validity" that we are after as discovering new things about our subjects through working with other disciplines.

At Governors State University the first Interdisciplinary Studies Context we invented is called "Popular Culture." Indeed, it was the Interdisciplinary Studies Context that allowed us to work with a subject such as "Popular Culture" at all. It was only after many discussions (some of them less than polite) that we came to see how the concept of the Interdisciplinary Studies Context could work and would be useful in allowing us to work together rather than spending our time in attempts to justify our disciplinary existence. The enterprise of collecting data and defining "Popular Culture" in this country has often had too much of a flavor of polemics about it, giving rise to indignant defenses of the non-popular culture, attacks on popular culture, and attempts to describe it as the domain of newspaper columnists and quack sociologists. Because the basic premise of the Interdisciplinary Studies Context is that every discipline has its own integrity, and because we agreed that a discipline's capacity to contribute or not contribute to the issue at hand says nothing about its value as a field of study, we avoided much of this ill will. In short, the Interdisciplinary Studies Context, particularly in "Popular Culture," gives us a means to study problems without having to consider the territorial imperatives of other disciplines. To give the most conspicuous current example of how not to study a problem, we note that it is not necessary to destroy print in order to understand media.

"Popular Culture" was chosen as our first Interdisciplinary Studies Context because it seemed to afford opportunities for the widest range of faculty contributions. The Black Studies component of the Interdisciplinary Studies Context "Ethnic Studies" was also chosen because of our commitment to a Black Studies program. Even more than in the Interdisciplinary Studies Context "Popular Culture" has it become clear that a carefully defined interdisciplinary program de-escalates problems. Because Black Studies is considered in our College to be under the Interdisciplinary Studies Context rubric, everybody in the College has either a central or a supporting role in Black Studies. Black/white issues in terms of students, faculty, and content are dealt with, literally, in Context. Just as confirmed disciplinarians or subject-matter specialists are not required to assume new identities when they reach out beyond their conventional boundaries (in fact, the Interdisciplinary Studies Context requires that they *not* lose their identities), the notion of context provides a means of working together. Confrontations tend to focus on issues, not personalities.

The nature of Governors State University imposes a necessity for coherent planning. We have no grades; students' transcripts record only their achievements; there are no required courses; and students make individual agreements which define their goals and courses of study. This system requires a good deal more planning than writing a catalog description. The educational program is always *out there*, open for inspection.[5]

Some Interdisciplinary Studies Contexts will be more broadly gauged than others, but the first ones chosen require the insights of all of the three major disciplinary areas within the College: language and literature, fine and performing arts, and the social sciences.

Having invented the Interdisciplinary Studies Context in a university without students (we opened in September 1971), we felt constrained to begin our first session with some kind of program which would demonstrate to students just what we were talking about. This became particularly important to us because Governors State University is a senior institution designed to serve mainly junior-college graduates from lower-middle-income areas. Our students are intensely practical, intensely suspicious of the old ways, and (to put it bluntly) not well prepared to succeed in the conventional liberal-arts educational program. We have told them that we have no majors, and that each student will follow a course of study based upon his educational objectives in the light of the resources of the College and the mandates of the University. Many students would prefer to escape from this freedom into a defined set of units which would guarantee access to a job, to graduate school, or to a raise in the pay scale. We tell them that they must be disciplinarians (have a discipline), and that they must do it within an Interdisciplinary Studies Context.[6]

In order to demonstrate to the students and to ourselves that we have a workable program, all students spend their first eight-week session with us in four mini-modules (we call courses "modules" because the jargon fits our system better) called Exploring Contexts. One major object is to expose all the students in the College to all the faculty. If the students are to work out individualized educational programs based upon institutional resources, they must know what those resources are. Each Exploring Contexts module is designed to demonstrate what an Interdisciplinary Studies Context will yield when an interdisciplinary team works together on the same problem. I will describe the one I have been involved in at some length, one that, as far as we can tell from student evaluation, is working rather well. The module is called "Poverty, Social Dialects, and Social Class." The central problem is to discover how the language one speaks influences one's position and options in the milieu in which he lives. The central text is Bernard Shaw's *Pygmalion*, supplemented by a book of language readings, *The Play of Language*, and the text of *My Fair Lady*. The faculty members include a specialist in dramatic literature (myself), a specialist in social dialects, a filmmaker and philosopher, and a technical theater-musical-comedy specialist. The major teaching methodology chosen was that each of us talked about the problem and the play *in terms of his own discipline* (thereby demonstrating his specific theoretical and technical sets) in the presence of the other faculty members. I was concerned with how to read a play of Bernard Shaw's. The linguist was concerned with the facts of language and the social implications of the relationship between the hero and heroine. The filmmaker and theater specialist dealt with how the problems of producing a play versus producing a musical comedy yield information about the issues. Aside from the very positive reaction of our students, the greatest benefit seemed to accrue to the teachers. The faculty team has agreed that each of us learned several things about our subject that we might not have discovered had we not been working in an Interdisciplinary Studies Context framework. Perhaps the new knowledge is not very significant *in toto*, but it is difficult to weigh the profound satisfaction we felt in the total engagement of our students in the issue before them. For example, I am now prepared to defend an interpretation of *Pygmalion* as Shaw's "black" comedy, in every sense of the word. This interpretation grew out of our students' persuading me that Shaw was really writing a paradigm of cultural imperialism at work. I am not offering this as the inevitable or even very significant result of the interdisciplinary program but only as an example of how being forced to look at things from new perspectives yields sometimes startling results.

Our evaluation of the students' responses was subjective and only yet a feeling, but perhaps the most pleasant result was in the fact that students who were suspicious of the literary enterprise to begin with became caught up with the conflicts in the play and began reading it as literature as well as the embodiment of a social issue. I had thought that to persuade Black Studies students from the inner city of the value of close textual analysis and genre theory in a play about 1913 England was perhaps quixotic, but I found that I was knocking on an open door. They had little trouble with "relevance." It was the students who demonstrated the relevance to me.

Another beneficial side result of this Exploring Contexts module (and the other three modules are having the same experience)[7] is that the Interdisciplinary Studies Context provides a matrix for discovering relevance rather than arguing about it. Thirty percent of our students are black. A goodly share of the remainder are suburban housewives with very different value systems. The whole question of racism within Governors State University and the community in which it exists was neither ignored nor allowed to overshadow the educational program. The Interdisciplinary Contexts and their truncated versions, Exploring Contexts, allow the confrontations to take place through the medium of discussable issues. Without commenting on the desirability or necessity of sensitivity-training sessions or race-relations seminars, we believe that working within the educational program provides a responsible and hopeful means of avoiding the communication problem that has plagued other programs.

It is of course too early to tell whether our particular interdisciplinary program is going to work or not. At least two questions have to be answered:

1. How do you balance the amount of work a student does within a discipline against the interdisciplinary imperatives of the College?

2. How do you have an interdisciplinary program without the methodology of team teaching? Team teaching is much more demanding than individual enterprise.

But the above is the experience of one program in one university. Of much larger importance is how we conceptualize an interdisciplinary-studies program which avoids the failures of the past. I would summarize these necessary but far from sufficient conditions as follows:

Negative Conditions:

1. An interdisciplinary program is not antidisciplinary or nondisciplinary.

2. Its aim is not to produce "generalists" with Leonardesque aspirations.

3. It is not stated in terms of values or themes.

4. It does not solve the teaching-research problem (although it inevitably demands enormous attention to teaching).

5. It is not based on an unequal relationship among disciplines; that is, where one or several disciplines are instrumental to another's purposes.

Positive Conditions:

1. An interdisciplinary program is a substantive matter.

2. It insists upon the identity and integrity of individual disciplines.

3. It brings the disciplines together under the rubric of a problem or issue that allows of and requires a multiple-disciplinary input.

4. It provides some structural framework within which problems are stated and issues discovered.

5. Thus conceived, an interdisciplinary program can be powerfully noetic for each discipline involved.

6. The quality of being interdisciplinary is a quality of programs or structures, not of individuals, although those programs and structures can substantially affect the character of an individual's work within his discipline.

7. Because within an interdisciplinary structure different disciplines act as a validity check and guide to each other, and because of the positive conditions listed above, an interdisciplinary program provides an arena for the solution of problems outside the usual interpersonal and political systems.

Interdisciplinary programs and the pressures to produce them arise in a time of troubles for American colleges and universities, but no one should regard them as anything more than useful ways of dealing with problems that we ought to be considering no matter what the pressures upon us. Interdisciplinary programs have a logic of their own that should serve as sufficient rationale for their support. The rise of the two-year college, the need for reconsidering graduate programs, the plight of the schools are enough incentive for the generation of interdisciplinary programs. What we must not do is to become the prisoners of our critics and search for ever greater immediacy, ever closer fits between the job markets and our educational programming.

In an educational world increasingly dominated by talk of contracts, accountability, performance, production, and efficiency, a world in which centralized planning is more and more used to control the educational aspirations of those we like to think of as a free people, it would be dangerously easy to put forward interdisciplinary programs as the new solution, the means of finally end-running the ivory tower's control over education. The kind of program I have outlined here attempts to avoid that trap by placing problems and issues in contexts where they can be worked with.

Notes

1 For that reason most area-studies programs, dominated by a particular social science, are not genuinely interdisciplinary programs, although they could be.

2 The other three colleges in the University are: Environmental and Applied Sciences, Business and Public Service, and Human Learning and Development.

3 Members of the discipline of English are more subject to this temptation than most. We have usually been too eager to compile volumes of essays on subjects we know very little about and present them in courses labeled "English." A new anthology doth not an interdisciplinarian make.

4 The beginning work was done by an educational anthropologist, a reading specialist, and a graphic artist (Professors Edward Dodson, Jayne DeLawter, and George Brownlee), who were our first faculty members. The original conceptualization inhered in something called "Themes," a terminology I persuaded them to drop because of its unfortunate associations with the thematic-curriculum movement in English, which certainly was not what we had in mind.

5 See Appendix II.

6 See Appendix I for currently approved Interdisciplinary Studies Contexts.

7 See Appendix I for the four Exploring Contexts mini-modules.

Appendix I: The Educational Program of the College of Cultural Studies

The College of Cultural Studies includes the disciplines of language and literature, the social sciences, and the fine and performing arts. Its educational program is expressed in terms of Interdisciplinary Studies Contexts (ISCs). During its first year (1971–72), the ISCs taught were "Popular Culture" and the Black Studies component of the ISC "Ethnic Studies." Projected ISCs include "Language and the Human Condition," "Invention and Creativity," "Ideas in Culture," and "Socio-Cultural Processes."

As an experimental launching device we tested the Interdisciplinary Studies Context concept in our first two eight-week sessions in four abbreviated modules called "Exploring Contexts." The four were entitled "Urban Communities and Systems," "Poverty, Social Dialects, and Social Class," "Pluralism and the Melting Pot: Myth, Reality, and the Future," and "The Arts as a Medium of Social Protest."

Appendix II: Governors State University

Governors State University was established 17 July 1969 as a free-standing senior-division university to serve junior-community college transfer students and others working toward baccalaureate and master's degrees.

The University opened its doors on 13 September 1971, approximately two years ahead of schedule. It currently has an enrollment of five hundred full-time equivalent students in temporary facilities.

The University consists of four colleges: Cultural Studies, Business and Public Service, Environmental and Applied Science, and Human Learning and Development.

Students receive no grades. Rather, students' records reflect accomplishments and abilities; they measure changes effected. Students are encouraged to work at their pace and toward goals they work out with the faculty.

Richard H. Green

University of Florida

MY MAIN CONCERN is with the possibilities of change in the English departments of the long-established, research-oriented state universities. What happens in these departments over the next few years will be of crucial importance to the study of language and literature at every level of secondary and college education and in every kind of institution, because, in the present state of higher education in America, these departments will increasingly influence the patterns of educational practice and standards of achievement in the discipline. If there is to be more, and more rapid, change in the profession as a whole than we have achieved in recent years (and I shall argue presently that there must be), much will depend on what happens in those departments in major public universities which, for reasons which need our careful attention, are instructionally conservative and administratively cumbersome.

The presence at this ADE seminar of representatives of every kind of department, from the newest and most experimental to the long-established and traditional, provides an ideal situation in which to discuss our differences within the larger context of our mutual dependence. In the short run the university departments have the most to gain from our dialogue. As teacher-training institutions, as well as centers of research, we need to know how to adjust our programs and methods to the realities of the careers our students will pursue. It is important for the research-oriented departments to know what students and faculty in the community colleges and new universities do and need; and it is also important for the teachers and administrators in the latter institutions to be aware of our resources, and of our own changing attitudes and educational practices on both the undergraduate and graduate levels.

We must avoid the stereotypes on both sides which cause abrasive rhetoric and refusal to learn from each other. I suggest that we cooperate with each other out of good will and out of mutual self-interest because we are committed to the same educational goals, however differently we pursue them, and because we depend on each other for the vitality and integrity of our profession.

* An address to the Tampa Seminar on Interdisciplinary Studies, 10 Feb. 1972. Reprinted from *ADE Bulletin*, No. 34 (Sept. 1972), pp. 24–29.

The Need for Change

The first realistic step in assessing the situation of English studies in the research-oriented university is to acknowledge the wide differences of opinion among faculty members concerning the need for substantial change. Opinions and convictions on this subject are deeply held, and they reflect both our personal attitudes toward the study of literature and language and our general uncertainty about the future of our discipline. Are we in a period of rapidly accelerating, irreversible cultural change to which institutions of higher learning, especially public institutions, must accommodate by proportionately rapid changes in curricula, teaching methods, and administrative priorities? Or are the degree and rate of change exaggerated, and is the evidence of cultural dislocation being manipulated by educational faddists to serve their own doubtful ends? The relative calm of this academic year and last, in contrast to the upheavals of the late sixties, has relieved many of our colleagues of the sense of doubt and urgency so widely felt a few years ago. Personally, I would take cold comfort from what may be simply apathy or resignation in the face of professional and institutional intransigence.

Even if the evidence of change is massive and alarming, as measured not by student discontent but by such physical, psychological, and moral criteria as we can generally agree on, some will still argue that the obligation of institutions and professors of higher learning—especially in the humanities—is to conserve the traditional discipline and methods and resist the new and fashionable. If it is argued that the coincidence of social and technological change with the nation's effort to greatly expand educational opportunity at the college level demonstrates the need for radical changes in our traditional practice, many of my colleagues would contend that innovation and accommodation should be left to the two-year and four-year colleges, and to the experimental colleges growing precariously within many of the big universities. The research department must be concerned about the allocation of its resources, and it cannot afford to jeopardize the quality of its scholarship. But this is not to say that its scholarly activities in research and teaching should remain static in the face of new kinds of knowledge, new areas of research, and the changing needs of our students. For reasons which I shall develop toward the end of this paper, our best hope for improving English studies in the university, and in the colleges as well, will be our willingness and ability to enlarge our patterns of graduate study and research.

By background and temperament I have a preference for a kind of literary study which builds on past scholarship and favors interpretation validated in the work itself and its place in literary history. Nevertheless, I am convinced that we are indeed in a period of irreversible and accelerating cultural change, and that among the changes are new ways of perceiving literary works in relation to human experience, new media by which our understanding of literary works can be enriched, new audiences with new kinds of perception which demand new means of access to the insight into the human condition which literature can provide. I am also convinced that we must take the study of language and the teaching of writing, both expository and creative, much more seriously than we do, that we must explore the advantages of interdisciplinary study, and that our programs should reflect our responsibility for the training of expert teachers. These convictions are, of course, widely (though not universally) shared in university English departments, and we have made some progress in recent years in accommodating our teaching to the changes in ourselves and in our students. But shifting enrollments, notably toward psychology and sociology, and changing vocational and cultural patterns suggest that we are moving too slowly. We are inhibited less by lack of awareness of the need for change than by outmoded disciplinary practices and inflexible institutional constraints. The remedies, I suggest, are both political and philosophical. We must be much clearer about the purposes of our profession and about the scope of our responsibilities. And we must learn to make more advantageous arrangements for our work both within the department and in its relations with other disciplines in the university.

Obstacles to Change

The obstacles to change in university departments of English are many and formidable, and they will not be surmounted by fervor, exhortation, or grants from The National Endowment, though all of these may help. Those of us who have, over the past few years, taken a larger view of our professional responsibilities have found it easier to argue the need for change than to make it happen. We have observed antiquated undergraduate curricula preserved as if nothing much had changed since the 1930's, designed mainly to prepare a chosen few for admission to prestigious graduate schools, and with luck and stamina and financial support to earn Ph.D.'s. The few best of the lucky few will validate the system and the selection process by valuable and influential scholarship and criticism. But we have also observed the glazed eyes of bored undergraduates who tolerate us with lazy patience and suprisingly civil disregard, and who are bright enough to satisfy our minimal expectations and pass onward through the "major" until they graduate, and we have been depressed by a feeling of waste.

We have lived with equally narrow graduate programs, pleased and excited by the students who do fulfill our hopes for the advancement of literary studies of the kind we profess, and dismayed by the number and talent of those who give up along the way, or stick it out to gain the license which will be some compensation for years invested and the freedom not to do what we all along said they were being trained to do. And if our undisturbed colleagues tell us that these students have gained much of value along the way, we agree but are not comforted. There must be a way, or ways, to provide access to an education more suited to the lives they actually lead and the professional duties they will perform.

At the outset we are encouraged by support from widely different quarters. Deans and vice presidents agree that the humanities are both important and in trouble and that the English department, by virtue of staff and budget size, and by the number and variety of educational and social causes it is supposed to serve, is elected to lead the way through the changing scene of the seventies. But the realities are harsh. In these years of depleted budgets, priorities are often determined by habit and public outcry, and the more conspicuously "useful" disciplines preempt the limited funds. We are encouraged, too, by the good will and support of our colleagues; but new courses and programs, and experimental teaching arrangements, particularly when they involve the cooperation of several disciplines, are commonly resisted. Even many of our students, after general demands for change and relevance, choose the safety of tradition and prescription. We begin to discover the political dimensions of any substantive change in departmental and institutional priorities and practice.

One impediment to change, and a valuable safeguard against costly mistakes, is the principled commitment of some of our best colleagues to the kind of literary study which they practice superbly themselves and to which they regularly attract very good students. One cannot quarrel with excellence, one can only plead for variety of excellence in a pluralistic world of language and letters. The question is not whether our traditional historically-oriented programs are valuable or not, but whether they are all we can and should do, or that they should necessarily be the only aspiration of good minds and devoted scholars and teachers.

By and large our reward system suggests that they are both, and this fact is not lost on the younger members of our departments. Anyone who has spent a dozen years or so on the editorial boards of our high-status learned journals has seen, among the fresh, original, and useful articles, the steady stream of warmed-over seminar papers and chapters culled from dissertations written under the pressures of haste or boredom. Behind these good, but not very good, papers one sees young scholars pursuing uncongenial projects of doubtful value. Our narrowly conceived curricula encourage them to pursue their even more narrowly conceived scholarly interests. Teaching composition is regarded as a chore and is often done badly; explorations of the relations between the literature they know best and that of other periods, other literatures, other arts, other disciplines are high-risk enterprises for which their training has not prepared them and which, in any case, our academic structure makes excessively difficult. Publication of the results of our scholarship and teaching experience will continue to be an essential part of our professional life. I am simply arguing that our writing will be better and more useful if a substantial part of it grows out of a more spacious vision of our profession. To conceive of our discipline in larger, more humane terms is no longer difficult; but to open up new opportunities for our students and ourselves by loosening the constraints imposed by departmental and collegial claims staked out and jealously guarded and worked over for many decades will take imagination, nerve, and political effectiveness of a high order. And until we do, we must expect our colleagues to put a high premium on conformity and safety.

A second major obstacle to change is the department itself as the primary instructional and research unit in the university. Its self-image and its priorities, its status within both the institution and the profession are defined by its doctoral program, a course of historically-oriented study which has changed only superficially over the past thirty years that I have been closely associated with it. There have been some shifts of emphasis, from philology to criticism, from earlier to later literature, from sources and influences to close reading, to larger literary and social structures, but for the most part our attention remains focused on literary history and editorial activity. Really different alternatives in our graduate programs are still too new for us to predict their future. Our undergraduate programs, at least the parts we tend to take most seriously, are designed to permit us to teach what we have learned and to locate and prepare students to emulate the pattern of our own professional careers. We select our faculty from institutions as traditionally oriented as ourselves with a view to covering the traditional historical periods. We judge the progress and distinction of our colleagues largely in terms of their publication in journals which, because we are their editors, enforce the traditional limits of our view of literary study.

If we are at fault, it is not because what we normally do is unimportant or outmoded, but because it is too narrow to serve the needs of students for whom the study of literature can mean as much for their experience of the present as for their awareness of the past. I see no reason why we should not consciously and responsibly bring the experience of literature directly to bear on human individual and social problems. Surely our literature, read in ways that honor its profound and complex fidelity to human experience, affords more insight into real human problems than the simplistic "Dick and Jane" case histories that are often offered in other disciplines as instructive types of behavior and values. But generally we are reluctant to move from the work and its time to the reader and his, to encourage our students to examine their personal problems in the process of their encounter with literature. We often hope that the transaction will somehow take place, but we are reluctant to encourage it openly, partly because we feel that such "applications" will distort the literature, partly because we feel incompetent to act as moral philosophers, much less as therapists. Well, literature can stand to be useful (this was its reason for being until quite recently in a long history) and modest new competencies can be acquired. Or at least we can learn to teach and learn together with our colleagues in other disciplines.

National and linguistic boundaries are another cause of the narrowness which inhibits our effectiveness. Competence in several closely related languages and literatures is the obvious but rare and difficult remedy, but few of us have the luck and talent to make this a general solution and very little in our programs of study encourages this versatility. Again, the least we can do is to cooperate with our colleagues in the other departments, but typically what we do is form a new department of comparative literature with its own instinct for separateness and visions of a minor budgetary barony. For all our historical orientation, we seem unable to cooperate effectively even with our colleagues in history. Those of you old enough to recall the days when a doctor's oral was endured before examiners from various obviously related disciplines will remember the scenes of outrage or resignation when candidates in English knew little history and philosophy, and could not talk about Dante, Cervantes, Racine, and Goethe (I leave it to you to supply more modern equivalents). And the candidates of the other disciplines were usually just as innocent of knowledge of their own English and American literatures. We are shrewder and more merciful now; not having the wit and political skill to make interdepartmental study a viable mode of education, we stick to an ever more narrowly defined speciality and restrict the jury to members of the craft union. I think that, after a long period of more and more narrowly specialized study, we have reached the point where we should encourage a larger, more general view of literature and its relations to social problems of all kinds.

Another conspicuous example of our limitations, this one imposed by the constraints of institutional organization over which we have little control, is our separation from art history, musicology, theater and speech, photography and cinematography, and in general from the creative and performing arts of all kinds. No one would seriously argue that the study of literature would not be enriched by immediate access to skilled performances and expert analysis of the closely related arts. But to achieve this access we will have to bridge gaps not just between departments, each with its own budgetary and staff problems—not to speak of ingrained disciplinary prejudices—but between colleges set apart from each other in space and mission, and governed by separate administrations competing for what each conceives to be its just share of the university's limited funds. It is no exaggeration to say that universities have grown so big in numbers, so complex in structures, so narrow in a multitude of highly specialized academic interests, that contact between faculty members and students whose common interests transcend disciplinary fields is a matter of luck. And when the contact is made, the possibilities of cooperative learning and teaching are administratively almost impossible.

Some Ways to Make It Happen

I am aware of notable exceptions to these generalizations, but if this is a reasonably accurate description of our predicament in the university, what then can we do? First of all, if we are interested in the practical reform of imperfect institutions, we can limit our indulgence in the shock rhetoric which calls for abolishing departments and radically restructuring the university. There is some virtue in outraged condemnation of our faults and utopian proposals for root-and-branch reformation. The outrage is often justified and provides some relief for our frustrations; the visions of what we might become can, at their best, give direction to the slow but necessary process of orderly change. But too much talent, energy, and enthusiasm are dissipated in revolutionary schemes which ignore the essential conservatism of the university and of the legislators and taxpayers upon whom its policies—and our employment—ultimately depend. But this is not to say that we are not, in fact, steadily changing, or that we cannot increase the rate of our accommodation to the needs of the society we serve.

Our first hope lies in the individual scholar and teacher whose versatile talent, energy, and nerve drive him to go beyond the limits of his traditional field to test new ways in which the study of literature can combine with other kinds of intellectual activity for the healthy development of our discipline and our students' needs. Much of our best literary scholarship has been, and is being, produced by those whose learning included other languages and literatures, intellectual and cultural history, and the fine and applied arts of the period in which the literature was made. Currently, much valuable work is being done by those who combine important developments in psychology, anthropology, linguistics, and politics with the witness of literature as cultural event. The most recent, and one of the most important, manifestations of this need to expand the relations of literature with related cultural developments is found in work which combines written literature with the visual languages of contemporary media, most notably that of film in its various forms. The least we can do is free our departmental curricula so that these new approaches have a fair chance in the market of student and faculty interest, and encourage and reward our colleagues who prove that they can do these new things well.

Beyond encouragement of the gifted and innovative individual, I think we can encourage the development of pluralistic standards of excellence in departments. We can, without sacrificing the traditional and valuable study of literature in terms of its historical development, make room for the interdisciplinary skills I have just mentioned, and reward the achievements of those (especially among our younger colleagues for whom the professional risk is greatest) who do new things well, or old things in new ways. And we can make a serious effort to establish within our big departments a sense of community and common purpose so that we will know what our colleagues are doing, or would like to do, and offer our constructive criticism, cooperation, and support.

I suggest that the best practical start we can make in enlarging the scope of our profession and at the same time of serving a clear public need is to develop a program, initially at the M.A. level, to prepare new teachers for the community colleges and to provide in-service opportunities in new areas of study for those already teaching. I need not labor here the already great and steadily growing importance of the two-year college as an integral part of higher education in America. Their faculty members are our colleagues and former students who deserve much better than they have received from us both in the way of professional preparation and that mutually supportive and informative professional relationship which should unite us. Their students will more and more be ours as the community colleges prepare increasing numbers of high-school graduates for entrance to the upper-division and preprofessional curricula of the universities. The diversity of cultural and educational backgrounds, the range of age, maturity, and experience of students in the community colleges challenge our ability and willingness to respond to their needs and our responsibilities.

Beyond serving a clear and pressing need, a program genuinely responsive to the general education mission of the two-year college will be interdisciplinary, broad rather than narrowly specialized, and committed to the improvement of teaching. It will succeed only if we broaden our own idea of the uses of literary and language study and learn to work cooperatively with colleagues in the other areas of the humanities and related disciplines. I cannot think of a situation more demanding in terms of scholarship or more likely to produce valuable research. Nor can I think of a development more likely to force us to reconsider the narrow administrative and curricular structures, in our undergraduate and graduate programs, which now inhibit a more generous view of the possibilities of our profession.

Extended consultation over the past two years with teachers of English in over two-thirds of the community colleges in the state has given us at the University of Florida a fairly clear idea of what an appropriate teacher-training program will entail.[1] It must be developed with the advice and active help of experienced teachers in the two-year colleges. Its foundation should continue to be the study of literature, but the literature studied should not be restricted to that which is representative of English and American, or even of Western, culture. So broad a view of the kinds of literature which ought to be studied implies substantial redefinition of the ways words and listeners and readers interact as well as new efforts to discover in all good literature the problems and aspirations of our common humanity. Beyond literature, even so diversely understood, we must teach the understanding and criticism of the visual languages and arts, especially of cinema.

It should be apparent that I am describing a program which reaches beyond the customary resources of English departments, and that is why I see it not only as valuable in itself but as a powerful agent to change the rigid disciplinary structure of the university. The responsibilities of "English" departments in many of the two-year colleges are properly defined by the term "humanities and the related arts." Any graduate program which tries to train recruits for this kind of teaching, and to extend and enrich the knowledge and skills of already experienced teachers, is properly the charge of what at the University of Florida is called the Humanities Council, representing the traditional humanities departments as well as the humanistic aspects of the social sciences and the fine and performing arts. While English departments have the resources, and I hope the will, to initiate the kind of program I have begun to describe, the wholeness and success of a program fully responsive to the needs of the community colleges must engage the cooperative efforts of many disciplines which rarely act in concert effectively. To bring related departments together in an effort to discover and promote their common interests and thus to develop new areas of research and teaching is a difficult enterprise, but it may be that the needs and pressures of a changing society, transmitted to the universities through the medium of the colleges committed to serve the whole community, will accomplish what no amount of internal planning and exhortation has been able to do. When self-interest coincides with the public interest genuine change may result.

In addition to the general study of arts and letters which I have so far briefly outlined, the program should offer opportunities for the candidate to improve his writing and teaching skills and to learn the techniques of recognizing and correcting writing and reading deficiencies in his future students. The teaching of writing is the major responsibility of the community college English teacher and his training ought to reflect that fact. Indeed, the entire graduate program ought to stress, by precept, example, and internship, the importance of good teaching.

Although I have used the word *program* to outline some of the things we should do, I do not believe that these new, or newly defined, courses should be arranged to constitute a separate program for those who teach or wish to teach in the community college. They should simply be optional kinds of study available to those who find them professionally useful, but meant primarily for those who see them as new opportunities for creative research and teaching. They will complement and enhance, not threaten, our established methods and subjects of research in literature and language. And, if we are successful, we will have gone far toward establishing a community of scholars in the humanities and improving the quality of our conversation and our work.

Notes

[1] The report of the committee which consulted with community college teachers throughout Florida was written by Ward Hellstrom and J. B. Pickard. They are also chiefly responsible for developing the program begun in the summer quarter of 1972. Copies may be obtained by writing to the Department of English, University of Florida, Gainesville 32601.

Interdisciplinary Studies and the English Department*

Barry A. Marks

The American University

I HAVE just recently had the opportunity to address my fellow chairmen in the pages of the *ADE Bulletin* on the subject of the current undergraduate curriculum at American University—not only what it is but something about the process by which it came into being. I can't resist remarking that writing that particular article was a voyage of discovery for me. In the process of recalling what had happened in my department over a period of three or four years I discovered some interesting things about what might be called leadership styles. The article contains, for example, some hints about the uses of confusion as an administrative style. I would deny—in fact I *do* deny—that I have ever deliberately created confusion either for its own sake or for some end which I already had clearly in view. In light of hindsight, however, I detect a principle at work. And, if you will accept me for a moment as pure historian, I would formulate the principle this way: If you create enough confusion and involve enough people in it over a long enough period of time, and if you get the people tired enough of meetings trying to restore order, then even the half-baked ideas of which department chairmen are capable will seem like heavenly blessings. There are a number of qualifications to this principle, but I haven't formulated them. And I don't think I want to. I remember Ishmael's warning in *Moby Dick*: "Look not too long in the face of the fire, O Man! Never dream with thy hand on the helm! Turn not thy back to the compass. . . ." Some things it is best not to think too much about—at least not out loud. I am told, however, that some of you have come here facing problems primarily of strategy and tactics. Perhaps the principle of creative confusion will be adaptable to your own institutions. If it is, no footnotes, please. That kind of credit I don't need. I've got problems of my own.

There's another leadership style which is related to the principle of confusion but which is more fundamental. I want to name this principle and describe it briefly because it will form the basis for the rest of my remarks about "Interdisciplinary Studies and the English Department." I

---

* An address to the Tampa Seminar on Interdisciplinary Studies, 10 Feb. 1972. Reprinted from *ADE Bulletin*, No. 33 (May 1972), pp. 13–19.

call it the gramaphone style, and I have taken the term from Lawrence Ferlinghetti's poem "Dog," which I'm sure many of you know. The poem ends this way:

> The dog trots freely in the street
> and has his own dog's life to live
> and to think about
> and to reflect upon
> touching and tasting and testing everything
> investigating everything
> without benefit of perjury
> a real realist
> with a real tale to tell
> and a real tail to tell it with
> a real live
>   barking
>   democratic dog
> engaged in real
>   free enterprise
> with something to say
>   about ontology
> something to say
>   about reality
>   and how to see it
>   and how to hear it
> with his head cocked sideways
>   at streetcorners
> as if he is just about to have
>   his picture taken
>   for Victor Records
>   listening for
>   His Master's Voice
>   and looking
>   like a living questionmark
>   into the
>   great gramaphone
>   of puzzling existence
>   with its wondrous hollow horn
>   which always seems
>   just about to spout forth
>   some Victorious answer
>   to everything

The gramaphone style necessitates an attitude of listening "like a living questionmark" to real interests and needs.

My point, phrased in the negative, is that I don't believe in interdisciplinarianism as such. Indeed, to name it is to abhor it. I think a program whose first and primary goal is to be interdisciplinary is doomed to failure. I am suspicious of grand designs of any kind, certainly if they are going to force faculty members and students to undertake activities for which neither has any particular bent.

I recently read a description of a new program focused on the city. It proposed to bring together readings from literature, sociology, economics, and city planning. It envisioned motion pictures, architectural walking trips, bus tours, talks by "specialists from the community," and museum visits. It was an imaginative design. I wish I had invented it. The program will be implemented. I estimate it will last three years. If a few big egos get attached to it, it may last five. However long it lasts, it bears all the marks of Madison Avenue packaging. Like the handsome young man in Edward Albee's *American Dream*, it has no heart.

I am myself a product of an interdisciplinary program. Both my M.A. and Ph.D. were awarded by the American Studies program at the University of Minnesota. But what made that program go, back in the late 1940's and early 1950's, was not the program itself, not the combination of courses, and certainly not the so-called coordinating courses; it was rather the intellectual atmosphere created by Henry Nash Smith, who was then writing his prizewinning book *Virgin Land: The American West in Symbol and Myth*, and from which his student John William Ward later wrote *Andrew Jackson, Symbol for an Age* and from which his colleague Leo Marx subsequently produced *The Machine in the Garden*. What distinguished that program seems to me the only really sound basis for interdisciplinary studies: namely, men seriously formulating questions and seeking answers that cannot be dealt with satisfactorily within the confines of a single field, and who therefore need contact with colleagues and students from other fields as well as their own.

I do not mean to say that interdisciplinary study cannot usefully take place without men of Smith's caliber. Neither do I mean that chairmen must sit around waiting helplessly for faculty members with serious questions requiring interdisciplinary study suddenly to come knocking on the door. Indeed, the ones who knock may be the wrong ones.

No, listening to the gramaphone can be an active approach for English chairmen, because literature and the study of literature are inherently interdisciplinary. In the course of a lot of stimulating talking and listening, my own department came to the realization that behind such traditional course labels as "American Literature I and II" and "The Later Plays of Shakespeare" lay various items of hidden agenda. The writers whom we read in our classes concern themselves with literature, but they concern themselves also with the nature of man, society, the physical world, existence itself, and the relationships among them. Herman Melville was interested in the problems and the significance of literature—his own, that of his forebears, and of his contemporaries—and he also was interested, for example, in the complexities of civil government and the dynamics of a viable society. That's not very startling news, is it? Perhaps you will be equally unstartled when I tell you that the faculty of our department has come increasingly to recognize—and what is more important, to acknowledge openly—that it too is interested, deeply interested, in matters which are ordinarily thought to be the special preserve of other academic departments. As professional students of literature we speak on the one hand about love and the social order, alienation and identity, and the presence or absence of God from the natural world, while we hide behind such self-protective labels as "American Literature to the Civil War." Frequently, we are really more interested in what those American writers have to say about alienation and identity than in the causes and patterns of literary development. On the other hand, we have, with massive, false humility, failed to explore and develop the *knowledge* which imaginative writers have to contribute both to our academic brethren in the social sciences, the natural sciences, and the other arts; and to society at large.

Having listened to the great gramaphone of puzzling existence, our department has restructured its curriculum. The new arrangement represents, I think, a contribution to what Dean Halloran (speaking at the MLA meeting last December and referring to the first ADE Interdisciplinary Seminar at Northwestern) described as "the problem of defining the nature and organization of the 'new modes of English and interdisciplinary studies.' "

Beginning next fall our department will organize most of its course offerings under the following five major headings: Studies in Major Literary Works and Writers, Studies in Literary Form, Studies of Literature in Historical Context, Studies in Literary Ideas, and Studies in Making and Performing Literature.

I do not offer this organization of courses as any kind of last word. "Not necessarily," as Robert Frost once said of a poem, "a great clarification, such as sects and cults are founded on, but . . . a momentary stay against confusion." I am proudest of the fact that, for better or worse, I think our answer indicates that somewhere along the line we were asking the right questions. What we are saying to ourselves, our students, and whatever other portion of the world may choose to listen is that these are the dimensions of literary study.

For the immediate purposes of this meeting I think two points need emphasis. One is that our five categories came from a period of insistently asking such questions as "What are we really doing when we study and teach literature?" The second is that our answer is a critically important first step in the process of getting ready for various interdisciplinary ventures.

Let me offer one or two additional, editorial comments. One is that the program provides plenty of room for the traditionalist (student and teacher alike). If a faculty member is genuinely interested in the historical development of literature and wants to use an anthology and teach a survey course in American literature, I think our campus is lucky to have him. For the foreseeable future, there will be a student clientele for such a course. At least two of our major categories are uniquely *for* traditional approaches to literature—"Studies of Literature in Historical Context" and "Studies in Major Literary Works and Writers." In the latter, the fundamental stress will presumably fall on the confrontation by students and teachers with excellence for its own sake. I have not yet met anyone who thinks that such activity is out of place in a university setting. I think I might have some difficulty understanding him if I did.

My second editorial is half apologetic: the category "Studies in Making and Performing Literature" is intended as at least a partial response to the Dartmouth conference with its emphasis on the dramatic-emotional dimensions of literature. (Monroe Beardsley, incidentally, offers a useful term when he speaks of the *transempirical* in literature.) I am apologetic because, in that area, we have not yet done much more than highlight existing courses in creative writing and oral interpretation and to say to our students: We consider these important modes of studying literature. We are currently conducting one experiment: a course called "Experiential Reading," in which we are combining literary criticism with exercises in "creative writing" and oral analysis. In general, however, the role of literary composition and performance deserves more attention than we have given it to date—not only because it might become more fully integrated into our department's program but also because it is potentially of enormous importance in an educational system and a society which are on the one hand becoming increasingly dominated by the yes-no logic of the computer and on the other hand are groping rather wildly for such forms of counter-logic as "simulation games" and the many varieties of "encounter groups." Literary professionals have centuries of experience in the relationships between the verbal and nonverbal, the logical and nonlogical, which can, I think, be made more available than it now is.

My third and last editorial on our five categories of literary study really follows from the last. My own private hope is that, in the long run, the work that we will do under the heading of "Studies in Literary Form" will produce a much sharper sense of literature as a *mode* of vision than I think the profession now has. Unless I miss my guess, many English teachers, particularly when confronted by nonspecialists, tend to be apologetic when they are moved to talk about matters of form and technique, feeling that these are somehow precious subjects, less important and vital than something called content, i.e., what the author is saying about life. The fault, if fault there be, is with the profession, not with literature.

Let me illustrate my meaning by citing a recent book by Thomas Edwards of Rutgers called *Imagination and Power: A Study of Poetry on Public Themes*. Professor Edwards says his study is about a dramatic situation which he finds frequently in the poetry of the last four-hundred years. The situation is "A man who is a poet finds himself writing (for whatever reason) a poem about men who are not poets but 'public men'—kings, soldiers, politicians—or about the 'public conditions' that seem the consequence of what such men do" (p. 1). A few pages later he observes that the ordinary citizen's relation to politics involves "an imaginative act," not unlike poetry itself. His point is that our sense of who President Nixon is or who Governor Wallace is, is necessarily an invention based on severely limited information. So far, so good. That the imagination plays an enormously important role in everyday affairs is insufficiently thought about by most of us; neither is it a great surprise. What really struck me was this next passage from Professor Edwards' introduction. He has been talking about exposés of public figures for which he notes the public has a "vulgar hunger." And then he makes this comment:

But if simple mediations between power and humanity will not do, even complex ones can at best be only tentative. If no new perception of the public case is achieved, the poem is dead; yet complete transformation makes the poem only a glibber version of the politician's own magical rhetoric, which smoothes all conflict into the glassy calm of easy solutions. *But if the poet ends by being unsure about the value of opposing positions, this is only to say that he has reached the centre of politics and accepted its painfulness and its necessity.* (p. 6) (italics added)

I don't know how aware Professor Edwards was of the implications of this last remark. It seems so unexceptionable to one whose training has been in literature that I doubt he thought very much about it. What I hear Professor Edwards saying is that political truth is paradoxical (or at least contradictory). When one finally sees a political situation whole, what he sees is the approximately equal value of opposing positions and courses of action. And I think artists and critics habitually assume the same to be true of all realms of experience. Why? Because literature is inherently—if not exclusively—counter-logical. From the first day we explain to our students that drama consists of conflict, complication, climax, and resolution, we may think we are merely telling them about the basic mechanics of an art form. In fact, we are implicitly telling them about a basic assumption of our discipline and one which strongly colors the way writers and sensitive readers see the world.

In at least superficial ways this basic disposition to see the world according to the "both-and" method of literature as contrasted with the "either-or" of more empirical-rational logic is a very ordinary human phenomenon. I think we heard about this aspect of "literary methodology" from a very interesting source recently. President Johnson told a story during one of his T.V. interviews with Walter Cronkite. The story was slightly garbled, but what it came to was this. On one occasion Johnson's advisers were unanimous in urging him to send aid to India on an emergency basis with, essentially, no strings attached. Johnson was apparently disturbed by the very fact of this unanimity. So he commissioned former ambassador George Ball to prepare a brief arguing the case for giving the aid only on the condition that India use the famine-inspired emergency as an occasion for adopting long-range as well as short-range answers to her problems. As President Johnson told the story, it was only after he had had a chance to weigh Ball's argument that he felt ready to accept the hitherto suspect unanimity of his official family. It was only after he had come to see opposing options as approximately equal in value that President Johnson, like Professor Edwards' poets, felt he had "reached the centre of politics." It was only after he saw political reality as a contradiction that he thought he was seeing truly, and was ready to make his choice.

A basic principle of traditional, Aristotelian logic is the law of noncontradiction. It holds that "a" cannot be both "a" and "not-a." The Coleridgean proposition that the function of the imagination is to reconcile contradictory opposites establishes a counter-logical position. Oedipus, at once hero and villain, scratches his eyes out and proclaims finally that he sees. How does Fitzgerald's *The Great Gatsby* end? With that wonderful cluster of paradoxes—"So we beat on, boats against the current, borne back ceaselessly into the past." Literary techniques imply ways of seeing the world. And I think that closer inspection of some of literature's most basic techniques will eventually promote interaction between literature and other, empirically and rationally based, academic disciplines. I think my reference to President Johnson's use of an essentially literary method—no matter what your imagination tells you about his chances of ending up with horns and a long tail or with harp and angel wings—suggests that, if we had a better understanding of the forms and techniques of literature, our contribution to the grand public could be increased also.

So much, then, for the broad outlines of the answer that my department has come up with for organizing a curriculum. I would like to think that our categories for the study of literature might be useful elsewhere. I recommend strongly the gramaphone *process*. If each of you went back to your home institutions and encouraged your faculties to review the nature of literary study and came up with very different answers from ours, I think both your departments and the profession broadly would be richer for the experience. I also think you would find yourselves better prepared for vital interchange with colleagues in other departments as well as with society at large.

I come to a second corollary of the gramaphone approach to interdisciplinary pedagogy. If careful listening is likely to produce new and outward-looking ways of studying literature within our departments, similar listening is likely to turn up a remarkable readiness for cooperation on the part of colleagues in other departments. I have already mentioned simulation games and encounter groups: their use by departments of political or administrative science suggests a certain dissatisfaction with the theoretical, verbal, narrowly intellective ground rules of those disciplines. The authors of games about how cities work want to give students something more than mere descriptions of the interrelationships among the social, political, and legal dimensions of power or of the many-sided, sometimes conflicting, sometimes congruent relationships among the mayor, the city council, the governor, the state legislature, the president, the congress, private pressure groups, and so on. They want to communicate also a *sense* of these relationships. And I think they want, further, to communicate something of the incalculability of politics about which their academic disciplines tell them a great deal in general and very little in particular.

If your campuses are like my own, I think you might be surprised at the number of faculty members outside our English departments who assign works of literature in their courses. And not just in philosophy and history but in sociology, political science, nursing, and business as well. Actually, I have two observations to make about this phenomenon. One is that it indicates some readiness for interdisciplinary cooperation. The other is: Tread lightly. My father-in-law, who was an executive in a movie company for many years, used to complain that everyone seemed to have two businesses in which he considered himself expert—his own and the motion picture business. I have found professors of social psychology and history and business administration who were thoroughly satisfied with their literary expertise and didn't need my help at all, thank you. At the same time, I remember talking recently with a political scientist who was very open to suggestion. He was preparing a paper on the rationale for using literature in political-science teaching and even research. In the course of our conversation I said to him that I thought one of the advantages of literature is that it can provide insight into an aspect of politics that is ordinarily hidden from the political researcher by the very nature of his discipline. I had in mind the relation between a man's role as politician and his role as a family man. I mentioned to my friend as an example the way Robert Penn Warren treated these two aspects of Willy Stark in *All The King's Men*. Stark's wife is extremely upset by the ruthlessness with which Stark treated one of his close political associates because she sees it as a metaphor of his increasingly loveless treatment of her. In turn, the absoluteness of Stark's commitment to a pure, wholly unpolitical hospital is, in part, at least, his way of exorcising his guilt about his wife's unhappiness. But I mention here my conversation with the political scientist not so much to prove the relevance of literature to the study of politics (my friend, after all, was already convinced of that) as to suggest the potentiality for full, scholarly cooperation: the fact is that my political scientist friend was astounded by my observation. He has actually used *All The King's Men* in the classroom, and yet he had not been aware of the major difference between the novelist's concern with the whole man and the political scientist's concern with political roles. And he had of course missed a major opportunity to broaden the perspective of political science which had been right there beneath his nose. Conclusion: approach your colleagues in other departments warily but confidently. We have not only literature itself but critical skills and insights which are needed, if not always or immediately wanted.

In addition to the fact that other academic departments actually use literature in their classrooms, I want to mention at least briefly one other characteristic of disciplines other than our own which seems to me to present a potentiality for interdisciplinary exploration. It is not unusual for social scientists to adapt literary concepts to their most fundamental theoretical frameworks. One of the most important concepts in the field of sociology is that of social *role*. Sociologists have used the notion long enough by now that they have undoubtedly forgotten its metaphoric base. Erving Goffman recovered some of that original metaphor in his *Presentation of Self in Everyday Life*. Goffman's methodology is sometimes referred to as a dramaturgical model. Recently, I am told, psychotherapists have begun to use the term *theme* to distinguish between the underlying clusters of thoughts and feelings which remain relatively constant in a client and the explicitly verbalized subjects which sometimes shift rapidly. And I might add also the term *scenario*, which is not in widespread use by scholars, but which has within the last four or five years become popular in circles where highly trained professionals and highly placed men of affairs meet to do the public's business. This use of literary terminology outside English departments deserves to be listened for. It represents another kind of potential for our doing serious business beyond our own walls.

A third corollary to the gramaphone style is piecemealism. I believe in piecemealism for many reasons. The process of rethinking literature and the study of literature will certainly have a different impact on different faculty members. Faculty members in other departments will be at many different stages in their willingness and ability to think about literature or about literary scholarship. I think it highly desirable that individual faculty members be able to play out their interdisciplinary hands in different ways. And I would add that I am very skeptical indeed about what many presume to be a student demand for interdisciplinary study. Long before I saw the article "No Use for Illusions," (*Life*, 4 Feb. 1972), my crystal ball had begun to tell me that those of us who have a commitment to educational change were going to have to operate in the future without the benefit of the external pressure of so-called student unrest. It means we will have to move with a keen eye for the genuine. It means, I think, we should be wary of massive changes which might require forcing new programs on large numbers of students as well as on large numbers of faculty. I think for now our aim should be variety and small-scale experimentation. And the motive power should be the concern of individual faculty members for what their own sense of their profession tells them needs doing.

I don't want to stop to talk about the institutional environment which may be necessary for the flourishing of interdisciplinary study. I am aware that my remarks are partially conditioned by the institutional framework in which I operate. I know that many of you are much concerned about precisely this subject. I am aware that various kinds of institutional flexibility are essential. I hope, however, that Professor Green is going to address himself to these matters and you will forgive me for not doing so.

Let me give you a small sampling of piecemealism at work. The first instance is a senior faculty member whose departmental specialties have been Shakespeare and the history of the language. She has been a teacher and scholar long enough to have a healthy skepticism about so-called educational reform. She also has a very broad range of interests. This past fall she offered a course in our department called "Shakespeare and Politics." The catalog description read as follows: "Study of Shakespeare's dramatic portrayal of the struggle for political power. The position and duty of a king. Plays to be covered: *King John, Henry VI,* 3 parts, *Richard III, Richard II, Henry IV,* Parts I and II, *Henry V, Coriolanus,* and *Julius Caesar.* Includes considerable reading in historical and philosophical background material."

A large number of her students were majors in political science. She has been asked by our School of Government and Public Administration to give the course again. During the current semester she will be working with a number of SGPA students who have asked to work with her on an independent study basis. These students will be focusing their attention on such subjects as Shakespeare's view of the orderly succession of power, the nature of stable government, and the characteristics of the wise ruler. She experienced some difficulty getting her students to read Shakespeare's plays as plays before leaping to conclusions about Shakespeare's views on politics. She found she had to refine *her* understanding of the various aspects of the political process to which Shakespeare's plays addressed themselves. Both kinds of trouble seemed sufficiently important to warrant attempting the course again next year as part of our department's normal offerings. She will do so. And I assume she will not continue to do so when and if the subject runs dry. My own private hope is that one day soon she will publish an article or two in the *American Political Science Review,* based on what she is now just beginning to discover.

A second instance is another of our faculty members who last year team-taught a course with a member of our department of philosophy and religion. The course was entitled "Man the Mythmaker." It represented a convergence of interests between the member of our department whose major field (conventionally defined) is Modern British Literature, and the philosophy-religion man, whose field is Old Testament. They gave the course together a year ago and again this fall. It was listed in our catalog in a special section designated "Interdisciplinary Courses." Next year the member of our department will teach the course with a different member of the philosophy-religion department, and the course will be listed in the catalog as both a literature course and a philosophy-religion course. Depending upon whether the students want credit for it for literature or philosophy-religion, they will register under different course numbers. They will, needless to say, meet in the same classroom. I do not for one moment believe that interdisciplinary studies necessarily means team teaching. In this instance, on at least a shortrun basis, it makes sense.

A third instance is a new member of our department who did his Ph.D. under Norman Holland at SUNY at Buffalo. Last fall I was able to arrange for him to *take* a course—as a student—as part of his teaching responsibilities. (Some day, incidentally, I hope to be able to do more of this kind of thing as a part of our normal procedures.) He elected, because of his background in psychology, to take a course in counseling. Let me now simply read to you some passages from a memo he gave me this past December.

Before the semester began, my theoretical knowledge of psychology—of psychoanalysis, in particular—was fairly comprehensive. However, I had rarely attempted to bring this knowledge to bear in my day-to-day life, neither in my classrooms nor in other contacts with people. Of course, I had subjected texts to detailed psychological scrutiny with some success, but they are not quite the same thing as a person sitting in a chair a few feet away. Texts can never actively resist, nor evidence their uneasiness before my interpretations. An important function of my experiences in the Counseling Center, then, was the testing in practice what I had previously known only in the abstract. . . .

When I was able to attend fully to the client, I discovered that not only was my theoretical knowledge of psychology more or less sound, but also, and to my surprise, that my literary training was extremely helpful. As a student of literature I have had to sensitize myself to language, to words and their contexts; learning to permit a text's meanings to emerge and form thematic clusters of themselves rather than impatiently imposing my preconceptions. This ability to "hear" and locate a text's thematics proved excellent preparation for listening to clients talk about themselves, and for coming to an understanding of their situation, or their thematics.

Obviously, there are differences. The words the literary scholar concerns himself with are frozen; he may circle about them slowly, teasing out their nuances over a period of time. The clinical psychologist, on the other hand, must contend with words in motion, with speech, and he cannot retrieve the exact context of a client's statement once it has been spoken. But, if the clinician's goal is more immediate and his data more elusive, his task is the same as that of the literary critic: understanding and coming to terms with the words of another, words which evidence the speaker's unique mode of being-in-the-world.

Because of literary training, in the clinical setting I was alert to a client's metaphors, his unique phrasing and sentence construction. These verbal cues provided new data which could then be integrated with more explicit content of the client's statements, in a manner analogous to the way a critic aligns metaphor in a poem. The resultant description was thus more full, and because it utilized data not always considered, I was often able to arrive at diagnostic statements quicker than those who lacked my literary background. In a sense, having been trained to read books, I was better able to "read" clients. . . .

In an effort to follow up on these observations, I have proposed to the Psychology Department that I offer a course to their clinical students, in literary analysis and interpretation. As I presently conceive it, the course will proceed in three steps: (1) the interpretation of poetry and fiction, to learn the fundamentals of thematic analysis; (2) by utilizing transcripts and case histories, applying these same methods to clinical work; and (3) concluding with a study of various theories of language (e.g., Heidegger, Quine, Skinner, Jakobson, and Chomsky).

My course proposal was greeted enthusiastically by the graduate students with whom I worked all semester. The Chairman of the Psychology Department and the Director of the Counseling Center have both given their approval. . . .

Next year, one member of our department will use literary materials and the techniques of literary criticism in a course in the department of psychology.

Next year also two of our Ph.D. candidates, for whom interdisciplinary study and teaching are requirements, will be giving courses based on their special interests. One will be combining an interest in literature and history; the other will bring literary and philosophical analysis to bear on certain problems in ethics. The courses will be available to incoming freshmen as an alternative to our required course in Composition and Reading.

I will not attempt to defend the piecemeal approach any further. I have been defending it since I read from the Ferlinghetti poem. It makes bureaucrats uncomfortable, whether they be deans or foundation executives. When it's time to place one's bets, however, I think the wise educational administrator will put his money on men and women with ideas rather than on the grand format, whether traditional or radical.

In closing, I would like to italicize one last point. I have said that one of the principal criteria for measuring the value of any interdisciplinary effort is whether or not the faculty members involved have a *serious* interest. I will go way out on a limb. In listening to a faculty member describe his concern with the relations between literature and other disciplines, I would urge chairmen to ask themselves whether or not, somewhere along the line, the faculty member is likely to publish his discoveries in the journals of a discipline other than English. I don't offer this criterion as an absolute. I think it's a useful rule of thumb. If we are going to be interdisciplinary, I don't think we should merely play at it. We should subject ourselves to the highest standards of both or all of the disciplines in which we propose to work.

I strongly recommend to you Leo Marx's article "American Institutions and Ecological Ideals," which appeared in the 27 November 1970 issue of *Science*. At the core of that article is the striking claim, based on his book *The Machine in the Garden*, to which I referred earlier, that literature provides the only source of an American ecological tradition or of what he calls the "literary-ecological perspective." In part, what Professor Marx is saying is that imaginative writers have always been accustomed to speaking from an integrated vision of man, society, and the physical environment. As he puts it, the classical American writer, beginning with Cooper, Hawthorne, Thoreau, and Melville, has dealt with "a particularized setting (or landscape) inseparable from the writer's conception of man." The article is distinguished, basically, by two things. One is Marx's scholarship. He had done some homework about both literature and ecology. The second is his assumption that as a literary critic and historian he has something of value to say to a scientific audience. Finally, I think, this is the combination for which we need to keep our ears peeled: men and women who have done or will do some homework and who, untrammeled by false modesty, believe that they have something substantive to contribute to other fields as well as something to learn. I can think of no better definition of an interdisciplinary student and no better basis for interdisciplinary studies.

Science, Literature, and the New Consciousness*

Irving Deer

University of South Florida

ORTHODOXY, whether in literary criticism, pedagogy, or religion, is fast becoming a thing of the past. The climate of opinion is simply set against it. Too many political, religious, and educational orthodoxies have been too divisive, too restrictive, and too destructive. They no longer attract a generation dedicated to participating in determining its own destiny and to seeking wholeness and fulfillment. This is true whether we think of the personal struggle to fulfill one's own potential, or of one's struggle to achieve harmony with others. Man is both a subject and an object; he has both an inner and an outer life. Never before in this century have so many felt the necessity of achieving wholeness by reconciling the two, and the possibility of achieving it by rejecting, or at least recognizing, the fragmentariness of orthodox visions which have for so long replaced wholeness. Even the orthodoxies of science are suspect. That may be the most significant indication of the post-modern age into which we are moving.

This is not to say that religion, literature, and art are dead. They are visions of wholeness. Only the orthodoxies, the long-accepted ways of attempting to get at the visions they contain, are dead. For those who sense that they are visions of wholeness, only the Establishment ways of pointing out those visions are suspect.

Along with most other professors, including the science professor, to students today the English professor is a member of the Establishment. Despite his dedication to helping his students discover the vision of wholeness which literature presents, he is as suspect as any other member of the Establishment.

To be sure, this has always been true, and there has always been for most serious English professors a gnawing sense of the somewhat paradoxical activity their profession demands of them.

The problem is not merely that we are aware as never before that the "situation" of the literary work has many elements, and that whichever one we emphasize, whether it is—to use Abrams' taxonomy—the writer, the work, the world imitated, or the effect on the audience, the "whole" reality of the work is reduced to a partial view. The problem is also that we are aware —again as never before—of the essential relationships among the elements,

---

* Reprinted from *ADE Bulletin*, No. 34 (Sept. 1972), pp. 37–45.

relationships that must be grasped if we are to have any sense of the wholeness that makes up the situation of a literary work. The conception of the elements within a work of art as organic, so heavily stressed by the New Critics, has now been extended outside the work, to identify the work itself as one organic element among many, including those elements that make up the historical, social, and philosophical context of the work. Without that larger organic sense of the significance of a literary work, without a sense, that is, of its interdependent relationships with other elements that make up the whole of reality, the study of any literary work, from any angle, seems irrelevant today. Without it, no matter how professional our approach to literature, we are coming more and more to feel uneasily specialistic, divisive, and reductionist. And, unfortunately for our enrollments, our students are reaching the same conclusions.

All this by way of preliminaries. If the analysis I have just made of our present situation has any validity, it seems to me that we must take a more genuine interest in disciplines outside our own, especially in those for whom we have had no inclination—those outside the humanities—like the sciences and social sciences. Most of us have long recognized, at least in a general way, the value of history. It is essential now that we begin to recognize the value of the history of science, and that we develop an interest in its particulars as well as in their ideational significance.

The problem, of course, with trying to encourage most members of our profession to take a serious interest in the sciences, or even in one science or social science, is that we have been brought up to think of science as the enemy. Brought up on Eliot's formulation of the "dissociation of sensibility," literary critics, scholars, and professors have become firmly convinced that science, more than any other cause, has brought about the death of metaphor, the very stuff of literature. Given this conviction, not to mention the time-consuming strain of learning something specific about another strange, difficult, and even apparently hostile discipline, how can a serious interest in science be justified and promoted?

If we are to judge from the lowering enrollments in English classes, the many dire predictions of even greater cuts, and the growing interest in interdisciplinary courses as one possible means of stemming the tide of the exodus, a serious interest in science may no longer remain something considered useful only by a few hardy and imaginative souls. It may be rapidly becoming a necessity for the professional survival of English studies. The fact is that language, logic, and literature are suspect. We may not wish to take that fact seriously, but our rapidly lowering enrollments, among many other indications, tell us that it is nevertheless a fact. Our growing dedication to formulating and implementing new pluralistic conceptions of English departments is an admission of how hard that fact hits us, whether or not we want to admit it publicly. The question I am concerned with at the moment is how a serious interest in science—say, in the new physics—can help us to cope with the problem that we are fast losing the interest (and the respect) of students, and along with them, of those who control the purse strings and administrative structures on which our very survival as a discipline depends.

However detrimental we may feel that science has been to the health of metaphor, we must recognize that it has exerted a great influence on the shaping of our world view. We may feel that this is precisely why the newly emerging world view is now working against the continuation of respect for our traditional approaches to literature. But, however we feel, we must understand our world view if we are ever to deal with what it is doing to our profession. We are in grave danger of misunderstanding it unless we understand some of the important ways in which modern science helps to shape it. Let me put it another way: I am arguing that a serious interest in science, in the new physics, for example, can greatly help us to understand the values, attitudes, and metaphors coming into acceptance today that mitigate against a continued respect for our professional enterprise along traditional lines. Let me briefly examine an example of the effect one idea in the new physics is having, the idea of complementarity. I am not arguing about the value of its effect—pushed too far, any analogy, like all arguments from analogy, can be abused—only that this effect indicates something of the ways in which the new science is influencing the current view of the world and the search for wholeness.

Gerald Holton, the physicist and science historian, tells us that "each age is formed by certain characteristic conceptions, those that give it its own unmistakable modernity."[1] He argues that "the renovation of quantum physics in the mid-1920's brought into public view just such a conception, one that marked a turning point in the road from which our view of the intellectual landscape, in science, and in other fields, will forever be qualitatively different from that of earlier periods" (p. 1015). Holton is referring specifically to the idea of complementarity which Neils Bohr introduced to an audience of most of the world's leading physicists at the International Congress of Physics in Como, Italy, in 1927. Bohr's talk had been prompted by his recognition of what Holton calls "the profound and persistent difference between the classical description and the quantum description of physical phenomena" (p. 1015). His proposal "was essentially that we should attempt not to reconcile the dichotomies, but rather to realize the complementarity of representations of events in these two quite different languages" (pp. 1017–18). In the older, "classical" physics, objectivity was an attainable ideal, at least in theory, and a clear subject-object separation was assumed to be a possible and desirable ideal. In the new physics, devoted to the subatomic realm, "the only way the observer (including his equipment) can be uninvolved is if he observes nothing at all" (p. 1018). Physics had, in Gamow's terms, "become declassicalized."

Bohr, in a 1949 summary of his 1927 talk, pointed out that it was "decisive to recognize that, however far the phenomena transcend the scope of classical physical explanation, the account of all evidence must be expressed in classical terms" (quoted in Holton, p. 1018). For the new physicists, "light behaves as a wave motion on some occasions and as a corpuscular radiation on others."[2] How can light be waves and particles, even under different experimental conditions? How can a thing, a phenomenon, be two different things? Is one experiment more accurate than the other? Bohr said no; he argued that "the wave and particle descriptions were complementary." As he said: "Evidence obtained under different experimental conditions cannot be comprehended within a single picture, but must be regarded as *complementary* in the sense that only the totality of the phenomena exhausts the possible information about the subjects" (quoted in

March and Freeman, p. 134). The point is that nature's wholeness cannot be visualized or diagrammed as assumed in previous classical concepts. As Holton says, "the separateness of the accounts is merely a token of the fact that, in the normal language available to us for communicating the results of our experiments, it is possible to express the wholeness of nature only through a complementary mode of description" (p. 1018). But, as he goes on, "the apparently paradoxical, contradictory accounts should not divert our attention from the essential wholeness. . . . Unlike the situation in earlier periods, clarity does not reside in simplification and reduction to a single, directly comprehensible model, but in an exhaustive overlay of different descriptions that incorporate apparently contradictory notions" (p. 1018).

In an age painfully aware of the long disjunction between subjectivity and objectivity nurtured by "classical" Newtonian mechanistic science, of the extreme fragmentation men feel within and without, and of the desperate search for wholeness, expressed everywhere in our arts and incessantly examined in our philosophy, Bohr's ideas and the changes they represent in science come as a godsend. They imply a new—this time a scientifically recommended—necessity for thinking in terms of wholeness, not, as the old science had implied, an ideal of pure objectivity, an exclusive concern with the fragments of experience accessible only to strict causal analysis. Along with a number of other ideas "that have profoundly shaped and changed twentieth century thought in science and with it the whole conception of nature and man,"[3] the idea of complementarity has become one model of the thinking dedicated to overcoming fragmentation.

There are a great many other ideas derived from the sciences, including others from the new physics, which also discourage reductionism in the sciences, and encourage concern with wholeness. The recognition that subjectivity plays a part even in science, the most objective of endeavors, is perhaps the most obvious sign of both the scientific and the philosophical acceptance today of the idea that wholeness, whether in the physical or the metaphysical realm, is both a subjective and an objective affair. Science itself is suspect for its past ideal of eliminating the subjective component and for thus encouraging a reductionist world view.

However, despite its apparent acceptance of subjectivity today (some physicists do not accept Bohr's hypothesis), science still remains suspect for a number of reasons other than its past exclusion of subjectivity. Most of these have to do with its purely rational, one-sided approach to wholeness. While it recognizes the old simplistic mechanical models for what they are, it is suspected of merely substituting more complex, more sophisticated machines. If man and the world are no longer treated as simple machines, are they merely seen as more complicated machines? Such questions remain.

To overcome the suspicions against science, and perhaps their own self-doubts, scientists are trying a number of tactics, all of which reveal a self-conscious concern for a holistic approach to both physical reality and human fulfillment. Among these tactics are:

1. The continuing recognition and examination of science's new, more complex role, as Werner Heisen-

berg puts it, "as part of the interplay between man and nature," or as he says, the recognition that the Cartesian dualism "is no longer suitable as the starting point for modern science."[4]

2. The continuing recognition that because the procedures of science—its method of separating, explaining, and arranging—change and transform their objects, they must always be conscious of their limits.

3. The recognition and increasing awareness of the limitations of any one-dimensional approach.

4. The improvement of methods of analysis to get more sensitive procedures, a tactic which requires a greater awareness of what the complexities are, what questions need answering, and what help can be gained from working across scientific disciplines or borrowing and modifying procedures from one discipline for use in another.

5. The recognition of the relationships between scientific knowledge and social and cultural problems.

6. The exploration of relationships between scientific conceptions and epistemological and metaphysical problems.

Designed to overcome fears by both scientists and nonscientists that science is reductionist, both in its search for the whole of physical reality and in its attempts to help men achieve wholeness, these tactics are all interrelated approaches to the same problem: the problem of utilizing science as a means to an end, the end of wholeness itself. Any one of these tactics, if pushed far enough, leads to the others in both theory and practice. Each implies what is important in an age painfully aware of the fundamental distinction between any partial perspective or systematization of the existent world and that world itself: the necessity for interdisciplinary approaches to both scientific and more general concerns. The problem is implicit in some remarks by C. H. Waddington, the chairman of the department of genetics at Edinburgh. He says, "The existent world is obviously of infinite dimensions. You can never exhaust its content by concepts, otherwise you would only have to think of those concepts to re-create it. There is therefore a very extensive loss of dimensionality at that point when you pass from existence to concept, but"—and here he goes on to make a point of some significance to teachers of literature—"whenever you go from one level of discourse to a more abstract one you lose dimensionality."[5]

These remarks were made at a symposium of specialists in the life sciences arranged by Arthur Koestler and held at Alpach in the Austrian Tyrol in 1968. The concluding paper, Victor Frankl's speech "Reductionism and Nihilism," summarizes the symposium's aims and runs the gamut in suggesting examples of tactics for remedying the drastic situation caused by an increasing trend toward specialization in the sciences. Not that he believes that we can do without specialists today. Just the opposite. History cannot be reversed, and the world needs specialists. But they must know what they are doing. As Frankl says,

I for one think that the present danger does not really lie in the loss of universality on the part of the scientist, but rather in his pretence and claim of totality. That is to say, when a scientist who is an expert in the field of biology attempts to understand the phenomena of human existence in exclusively biological terms, he has fallen prey to biologism. And at the moment biology becomes biologism, science is turned into an ideology. (p. 397)

It is the scientist's responsibility "to embark on reductions . . . but he must be aware, remain aware of what he is doing" (p. 409). To Frankl, a man is a reductionist "only if he makes reductions in a scientific way, but is not aware of what he is doing" (p. 413). Such a man seems to Frankl to be the modern purveyor of nihilism, the man who, like Frankl's junior high school science teacher, is fond of telling his students "that life in its final analysis is nothing but combustion, an oxidation process" (p. 398). Imagine, says Frankl, "what it means that thousands and thousands of young students are exposed to indoctrination along such lines, taught a reductionist concept of a man and a reductionist view of life" (p. 399).

The remedy Frankl suggests against the dangers of reductionism is an interdisciplinary approach to scientific problems, the same remedy stressed by the other participants in the Alpach symposium. As he says, "we should take the lesson of stereoscopic vision, i.e., we should not mind apparent contradictions, but should embark on a stereoscopic style of research, as it were. I mean multidisciplinary approaches as they are carried out in interdisciplinary research" (p. 414). He illustrates his own interdisciplinary approach by explaining that in his lectures on the treatment of a patient with a brain tumor, he first discussed the patient's reflexes, "as if he were a closed system of reactions and responses," then his psychogenic neuroses, and finally his "human dimension."

While the scientist's first professional responsibility is to the improvement of his discipline, so that he and others can use it to acquire new scientific knowledge, his first responsibility as a man is to the improvement of the quality of life for all men. As the life sciences and physics are beginning to show, the tactics for overcoming the limitations of the sciences and the suspicions against them have led many of the most outstanding scientists inevitably to attempts to fulfill their responsibilities as men. Recognizing that man is engaged in a subject-object relationship with nature, and that even as a scientist he is therefore both creating, as it were, and discovering the part of total existent reality his experimental conditions allow him to see, he seeks help from his fellow scientists and tries to remember what he is doing so as to refrain from generalizing about either the whole of physical reality or human wholeness. And, because he has discovered only recently that what he sees in nature is in a sense a picture in his head, he is struck with renewed wonder at the complexity and mystery of things. Epistemological and metaphysical questions press on him. If he is involved in what he sees, how can he tell what constitutes genuine knowledge and what ultimate reality? He feels in his own way what Michael Polanyi, the famous scientist–social-scientist–philosopher, urges him to understand: that even the most objective endeavors of men require subjective involvement, that without such involvement discovery would be impossible, and that, because of such involvement, no separation between the sciences and humanities is possible.[6]

The fact that so many atomic physicists, for example, engage in philosophical speculation today illustrates the growing tendency for even most advanced specialists in disciplines outside of philosophy to engage in metaphysical and epistemological concerns. Like a great many other important ideas deriving from recent science, the idea of complementarity represents a revolution in science grounded in a new consciousness of the distinction between the fragmentary approaches of individual sciences and the wholeness each strives to reveal in physical reality and to help men achieve as human beings. This new consciousness leans heavily toward encouraging a new interdisciplinary conception among the sciences as well as between them and other disciplines.

Bohr's ideas represent a revolution in physics which amounts not only to a reversal in the thinking about the relationship of the observer to what he observes in nature, but—and this is very important—also to a fundamental change in the methodology of science. If we keep in mind the idea that classical Newtonian physics has served "as the model for the interpretation of the biological, social and behavioral sciences," and that the new physics provides a new model, we can imagine the magnitude and significance of the changes this model may bring. Floyd W. Matson, for example, in *The Broken Image*, sees it not only as a means of suggesting "new connections" among the various fields of the sciences and social sciences, but as a possible way to overcome the "broken image" of man's understanding of himself brought about by the adoption of Newtonian physics; a way, that is, of integrating the sciences and social sciences "into a new, human view of indivisible man."[7]

It is not only among social scientists like Matson, scientists like Bohr, Heisenberg, Conant, Schrodinger, Jeans, and Holton,[8] and philosophers like Petersen, that a wider view of the significance of the new science is held. English professors, in various roles, have also begun to investigate the significance of the new science for their own central concerns. As long ago as 1962, two English professors, Paul C. Obler and Herman A. Estrin, edited a book entitled *The New Scientist: Essays on the Methods and Values of Modern Science*.[9] It contains essays ranging from the relationships between science and the life of the mind to those between science and society and between science and education. Everywhere in these essays is the assumption, often explicitly stated, that an understanding of science today is essential for an understanding of the world picture, something presumably of interest to English professors.

A more direct application of insights from the new physics to the actual practice of teaching English is provided by the Shakespeare critic Norman Rabkin in his book *Shakespeare and the Common Understanding*,[10] the title of which is an obvious echo of the title of Conant's book *Science and the Common Understanding*. Rabkin's purpose is to provide a new conceptual framework for understanding Shakespeare based on the idea of complementarity. As the cover description of the book indicates, "it defines Shakespeare's way of seeing . . . as *complementarity*—an approach to experience in which 'radically opposed and equally total commitments to the meaning of life coexist in a single harmonious vision.' It demonstrates that this mode of vision is at once wholly Shakespearean, basic to much significant aesthetic experience, and central to the way in which the world is seen today." With this approach, Rabkin offers an explanation for what makes so many of Shakespeare's plays problems, and significant clues to a new method for unraveling some of the most perplexing problems. What makes the plays problems, he argues, is what makes them Shakespearean, the way in which Shakespeare sees the world. This, Rabkin feels, is a way of seeing which the new physics is helping us to understand. With science promoting a vision that accepts contradictory readings of experience, a new interdependency between subject and object, a new sense of the significance of ambiguity, ambivalence, and paradox, and a new sense of the distinction between fragmentation and wholeness, we are in a better position than ever before since the rise of Newtonian science to understand and appreciate what literature, both past and present literature, communicates.

Just as scientists today are working along large-scale and often interdisciplinary lines—often as teams of specialists from different disciplines—English professors are beginning to recognize the need for interdisciplinary approaches to the teaching of English and related disciplines. Henry Wasser, for example, an English professor at the City College of New York, sees a way out of the impasse over American Studies by modeling it on Bohr's principle of complementarity. As he says,

I hold that the hypothesis of complementary relationship promises much for future scholarly study. In this relationship the scholar realizes that there are different but equally or nearly equally valuable approaches. Often in the manner of physics one view does not dominate another but rather explains the same set of phenomena or facts in different ways reaching different conclusions. One approach may supersede another by explaining more. Here the differing disciplines involved in American Studies are each utilized—*here at the juncture* of the tracks of the sociological, the literary-critical, the psychological, the philosophical, the economic, the historical a series of insights are provided. With this hypothesis the whole of American culture is grasped.[11] (my italics)

If it is here, at the juncture of the various significant tracks, or, to use a term from Marshall McLuhan, at the "interfaces," that we can grasp the wholeness of culture, why should it be so difficult for us to understand that the wonderful metaphor of culture we call a literary work can also be grasped in its wholeness through a similar interdisciplinary approach? Literary critics have for many decades snubbed literary scholars—the textualists and literary historians, for example—and now do the same to the linguists, the literary scientists, on grounds that they are reductionist, which is sometimes but not always true. The linguists' approach is no more or less reductionist than mere formal analysis, the mainstay of the New Critics. Any approach to literary criticism, or the teaching of literature, whether purely formalistic or not, based on the conviction that only what is in the work counts, if this approach pretends to get at the work's wholeness, is as reductionist as generalizing its wholeness from its typographical or its linguistic character. This is precisely the kind of reductionism Frankl criticized scientists for indulging in too often: the taking of the part for the whole. It is the particular form of nihilism, to use Frankl's concept again, foisted by teachers and critics of literature on the educational enterprise and on themselves, despite their conscious pursuit of wholeness.

To begin to recognize this is like suddenly recognizing that, despite your firm conviction that you are not prejudiced against women or blacks, you really are. It is to begin to realize that the structure, call it a "fiction," you have imposed on reality—both the reality literature expresses and the reality of the world for which it is a metaphor—is not reality itself but merely a model, a reduction from it, by which you hope to get at the reality. It is to recognize, to use the idea so well expressed by Colin Turbayne in *The Myth of Metaphor*,[12] that you have mistaken your model for the reality you merely meant it to probe. I am firmly convinced that our best students sense that we are doing this, and that this is their main reason for leaving our classrooms as well as those of our academic colleagues in other disciplines, including the sciences. Whether or not they can articulate their discontent, they are fed up with the nihilism foisted on them for so long in the name of specialization. Even if we cannot see the elitism in our disciplinary purism, they can. This is why even our majors ask so often these days, "Why teach literature?" Not that they resist reading; they are reading more than ever—the Vonneguts, the Barthelmes, the Cortazars—but they are reading on their own, and what is more to the point, they are reading—and going to Bergman and Kubrick movies, and listening to pop music—for purposes which we seem to deny. They sense that contemporary literature, and pop culture in general, is attempting to express the totality of experience for which they are groping. Where we define and describe, they participate and explore. When they want to expand their consciousness of the world, we impose on them the reductionist tactics for contracting it.

Perhaps a personal experience will illustrate what I am talking about. I have had the experience of teaching Kurt Vonnegut's *Slaughterhouse-Five* to students who had already encountered it in another course. They have responded to Vonnegut with great intuitive enthusiasm. But what they have learned about Vonnegut from a number of instructors is that (a) he uses science-fiction techniques, (b) he uses some filmic transitions (Isn't that original of him!), (c) his names are symbolic of certain ideals about contemporary society, and (d) one can play anagrams with a lot of his place names. The students, in other words, have learned to play literary tricks with the novel. It is a tribute to Vonnegut that they enjoy the novel despite the efforts of their professors. No one has asked the questions which would help them to understand why the novel means so much to them. As soon as I ask, "Why would Kurt Vonnegut use science-fiction forms? Why would he try to use film form?" they begin to examine the relationships between fiction and the total culture in which they live. They discover that Vonnegut is using science-fiction and film techniques as a way of sharing with them the experience and understanding of reductionism and chaos foisted on men today in the name of technology, progress, and a thousand other labels. They experience with Billy Pilgrim the sadness of his plight, and that of all men today, when they succumb to the pressures for conformity or anarchy, the social equivalents of reductionism and chaos. But because they understand his plight, as he does not, they are not reduced to his state of inertia, fantasy, and retreat so dramatically rendered in Billy's repeated refrain: "So it goes."

The more one knows about science fiction, film techniques, and contemporary culture, including modern science, the better one is able to help students see their juncture and the insights it offers them. If they can get enough help, they can even discover the ways in which science fiction may be used as a criticism of scientism itself, and the ways in which film can both express to them and cushion them from their own restrictive concepts of reality. All of these insights are gained, not by sticking with strictly literary approaches, but by connecting the forms and techniques of literature with what goes on in the larger contemporary world. In the process, the student brings to bear what he knows about the psychological effects of transitoriness, what he himself understands about the ways technology dehumanizes him, and what he himself recognizes about how social and domestic institutions can reduce men to mere artifacts. From that starting point, he comes to know a great deal about the nature of the culture in which he lives—and finally, about how Kurt Vonnegut's novel not only expresses much of what he already knows and feels, but also how it helps him to probe and explore the directions by which he might travel if he is to know himself.

A literary work can thus serve as a juncture for the student between himself and the world. When we ask why a novelist uses a certain form, his novels can become windows to the world, not mere reflections of themselves and collections of literary devices. They can involve the student in the world, in the various ways of seeing it which many disciplines offer—the sciences, the humanities, and the social sciences. The alternative is that the student mistake not only our models of the novel for the novel itself, but, more importantly, our models of the world for the world itself. If he makes this mistake, he is set adrift with neither a self nor a world view; he becomes a purveyor of the very nihilism against which we had hoped to protect him.

That growing numbers of English teachers are approaching literature in interdisciplinary ways analogous to those I suggest with regard to Vonnegut's novel, and that they are coming to feel the need for interdisciplinary approaches to English study, are signs that the profession has been absorbing, without necessarily knowing it, a world view greatly influenced by the new sciences, including the new physics, and by such ideas as Bohr's complementarity principle. A recent book in literary criticism, for example, which hints at this is Stephen Booth's *Shakespeare's Sonnets*.[13] Booth's approach to the sonnets is like that which Holton suggests Bohr implies as essential to an understanding of physical reality: "clarity does not reside in simplification and reduction to a single, directly comprehensible model, but in an exhaustive overlay of different descriptions that incorporate apparently contradictory notions" (p. 1018). Booth examines the many structures and patterns operating in the sonnets, in the formal, logical, and syntactic patterns; the rhetorical and phonetic structures; the patterns of diction and their interrelationships. In a review of the book for the *New York Review of Books*, Frank Kermode praised it as the best of the new books of Shakespearean criticism. As he said,

There may be, there is, a moment when one intuits in the complex mesh of conflicting patterns an order; and Booth says that such moments are the happiest the human mind can know, moments when it is beautifully poised on the threshold of comprehension, like, perhaps, the mind of the poet. These large claims suggest that criticism is regaining its confidence as it acquires new techniques, which it movingly represents as able to increase our happiness or mitigate our pain. Criticism may thus be both difficult and humane.

Booth's analysis of the sonnets on these new principles seems to me of a high order of criticism and humanity. . . . Any way I can look at it his achievement seems to me extraordinarily impressive.[14]

I am not saying that Booth is influenced directly by Bohr's ideas.[15] But his approach to the sonnets is harmonious with the peculiarly contemporary way of seeing suggested by Bohr (and Rabkin), and cannot have been conceived except as it arose from a climate of opinion favorable to multidisciplinary analysis, nurtured by modern science.

Perhaps, for our purposes, the most important sign that the profession of English is beginning to absorb the lessons of the new science, including the new physics, is our growing interest in interdisciplinary approaches to English study. Among those eminent in the profession who have for some time advocated a new interdisciplinary approach to English studies is John Hurt Fisher, until recently secretary of the most scholarly, prestigious organization in the profession, the Modern Language Association, the bastion of specialization. If we look at some of Professor Fisher's recent comments on the kind of interdisciplinary study he feels is essential today, we can see that he is advocating a model for English study very similar to the model based on Bohr's ideas about complementarity and advocated by Henry Wasser as a solution to the search for a conceptual approach to American Studies.[16]

After quoting Konrad Lorenz to the effect that " 'The unique nature of human culture' " cannot be grasped without an understanding of the lessons of recent biology, Fisher concludes that these lessons very effectively describe "the purpose of English and foreign-language teaching in this country" (p. 6). He is speaking most specifically of what Lorenz says biology can teach us about " 'how species lacking a cumulative tradition act.' " The tradition of English study in America, based as it has been on a culture other than our own, has been in the position of such a species. However, since the thirties, the "cultural current" seems to Fisher to have been running from "west to east." With "the tide running heavily in reverse" for some years now, "the study of languages and literature as a cultural rite is being replaced by the study of language and literature as an aspect of human behavior. In a word, the study of language and literature is going interdisciplinary. But the disciplines it is beginning to mingle with are not only other languages and literatures, and the other humanities such as philosophy or art history, but sociology, psychology, and anthropology" (p. 6). I would, of course, add the other sciences, including physics.

Having quickly established the case for an interdisciplinary approach to English studies, an approach which includes fields of study not included in previous conceptions of interdisciplinary programs with such labels as "humanities" or "communications," Fisher argues for an interdisciplinary conception very similar to that Wasser based on the idea of complementarity.

The key [Fisher tells us] to an effective interdisciplinary education seems to me a "systems" approach. That is, not to think of individual courses or individual fields or departments, but of an interrelated series of courses and independent study activities. We already have the pattern for this sort of work in our interdepartmental "programs" of study. These should be vastly increased in number and variety. There should be programs of literature and sociology, literature and psychology, folklore and anthropology, European literature and the rise of modernism, English literature and the homogeneity of national values, effect of the mass media, etc., etc. The rationale for each program should be spelled out in the catalog. The essential point would be that each program would specify a coherent sequence of courses from the freshman year through the senior. (p. 7)

The problems approach suggested in the titles of programs Fisher uses as examples—"European literature and the rise of modernism, English literature and the homogeneity of national values, effect of the mass media"— suggest an affinity between his ideas and those of a number of other prominent advocates of an interdisciplinary approach to "language and literature as an aspect of human behavior." Like the prominent English and anthropology scholars who planned the conference on anthropology and literature which culminated in the Winter 1972, issue of *Daedalus* (*Myth, Symbol, and Culture*), Fisher is saying that a real interchange can take place only when the contrasting methods of different disciplines are brought to bear on "similar problems." The *Daedalus* team is talking about a "real interchange" among scholars from different disciplines who come to see that they are working on similar problems from different angles. Fisher is talking about an interchange between English teachers and their students. But the principle is the same. Fisher is trying to get us to see that specific problems treated from a number of vantage points are much more meaningful than if they are treated only from one. If we recognize that the one vantage point until now predominant has been, as Fisher has explained, that of a culture not our own, we can get some idea about why traditional approaches to English studies are suspect today.

But there is more to the resistance to English departments today than the mere suspicion that they are teaching literature that implies values from another culture. If that were all there was to the problem, we could simply switch to teaching courses in American literature and American culture, whether along the lines Wasser suggests for American Studies or along other lines. Why, then, would Fisher suggest the necessity of relating the sciences and social sciences to English? Obviously, the sciences and social sciences are not bounded by American or any other national cultural concerns. The problem is one of vision, not revision along patriotic lines. Students are dropping out of science courses as fast as they are dropping out of English courses. They are simply dropping out of college, whatever their majors. When one asks them why, their answers reveal that what they want is the freedom to see significant human problems in the round, to get some sense of wholeness again, some sense of what it means to have a wider consciousness, a great many options, and a sense of significance as subjects as well as objects. They want to be participants in the act of discovering whatever they can discover of wholeness.

If we go at the problem of trying to recapture enrollments by merely providing unlimited numbers and types of courses, like, say, science fiction, writing for profit, and sex in literature, we are not only in great danger of losing the integrity and value of our discipline to a kind of supermarket concept of English; we are also in danger of losing even more students, especially our best.

I am not arguing that good courses on, say, science fiction or pornography and literature are not possible. Far from it. I myself have long been a staunch advocate of courses which relate popular culture to literature. What I am saying is that unless we know what our professional aims are, our academic ideals, and create new courses in keeping with them, we are in great danger of merely serving the winds of fashion for the sake of numbers. A program based on constantly shifting fads and fashions will turn us into admen or T.V. producers intent on hawking our wares, an occupation few English teachers are competent to perform. We may hit it lucky here and there for a time, but in the end, like all television producers, we will be replaced by new producers with new program ideas.

Our emphasis on numbers may momentarily confuse us. I believe, however, that our real concern is over losing students who might major in English if we were doing our jobs in ways that were meaningful today. We preach wholeness, and practice divisiveness. How else explain the general disdain of most members of our profession for other disciplines, most notably the sciences? Students are not down on literature; they are down on us for the ways in which we teach it. Most bright students today probably read more contemporary novels than most English teachers. Of course that is because we are not all specialists in contemporary fiction. We are democratic in our divisiveness. We practice it not only against other disciplines, but even against those parts of our own which fall outside of our immediate specialized interests.

I am not arguing that we should read everything and know everything either inside or outside of English. There is only so much time available. What I am arguing for is the idea that there is a new vision emerging today, a new consciousness much influenced by the new sciences, and expressed as interest in interdisciplinary studies of the types to which I have referred. We ourselves must at least understand, if not have, this new consciousness, so that we can plan our programs and do our teaching in harmony with it. Because students demand recognition of this consciousness, it must be the basis of any worthwhile institutional conception of which we hope to remain a significant part.

Our greatest danger is from ourselves. Knowing ourselves to be men and women of good will, dedicated to helping our students understand great literature, we have lapsed into a kind of unconscious elitism entirely out of keeping with what is happening today. What complicates the issue is that our main concerns with literature center around the very things the best students today seem to want: freedom of choice, wider consciousness, a fusion of subjectivity and objectivity—in a word, a vision of wholeness, the only means by which the intense sense of fragmentation today can ever be overcome. Knowing that literature communicates wholeness, and that we are dedicated to teaching literature, we assume that everyone, including our students, should prize our efforts on their behalf. What we fail to understand is that the way we are going about it too often belies our goals. If we approach the "wholeness" that literature contains from only one special vantage point, or a few related literary vantage points, how can we hope to persuade generations nurtured on the relativistic, antiabsolutistic ideas of modern science that we are anything but narrow-minded elitists who think our way of getting at the whole truth is the only legitimate way? Moreover, unless we understand the vision implicit in the literature, art, and science of our time, how can we understand what is of value in it, or for that matter, what its dangers are? How can we understand the present generation if we insist on doing so only by retaining older forms of consciousness? By practicing a narrow, literary, specialistic approach to English studies, we are practicing fragmentation and divisiveness while preaching wholeness and union. It is about time we began to see this. With the rapidly growing distrust against us today, it is essential that we see it. How better to begin seeing it than by striving to understand how the sciences are helping to shape today's consciousness of wholeness? If we can work on problems similar to those which interest our traditional opponents in the "two cultures" debate, if we can understand what each of us can offer the other, how better to signal our determination to practice from now on what we preach?

Notes

1 "The Roots of Complementarity," *Daedalus*, 99, No. 4 (1970), 1015.

2 Arthur March and Ira M. Freeman, *The New World of Physics* (New York: Knopf, 1963), p. 120.

3 Gerald Holton, Introduction, *Daedalus*, 99, No. 4 (1970), 723.

4 "Nature and Contemporary Physics," *Daedalus*, 87, No. 3 (1958), 107.

5 "Discussion," in *Beyond Reductionism: New Perspectives in the Life Sciences*, ed. Arthur Koestler and J. R. Smythies (Boston: Beacon Press, 1971), p. 412.

6 *The Study of Man* (Chicago: Univ. of Chicago Press, 1958), passim.

7 *The Broken Image* (Garden City, N.Y.: Doubleday Anchor, 1966), cover description.

8 Not to mention other historians of science like Alexandre Koyre, Thomas Kuhns, Henry Margenau, and Giorgio de Santillana.

9 *The New Scientist* (New York: Doubleday Anchor, 1962).

10 *Shakespeare and the Common Understanding* (New York: The Free Press, 1967).

11 "Principled Opportunism in American Studies," *American Studies in Transition*, ed. Marshall W. Fishwick (Philadelphia: Univ. of Pennsylvania Press, 1964) p. 176.

12 *The Myth of Metaphor* (Columbia, S.C.: Univ. of South Carolina Press, 1970).

13 *Shakespeare's Sonnets* (New Haven, Conn.: Yale Univ. Press, 1969).

14 "A New Era in Shakespeare Criticism?" *New York Review of Books*, 5 Nov. 1970, pp. 36–37.

15 Kermode is. See his *The Sense of an Ending* (London: Oxford Univ. Press, 1966), pp. 59–62. He is not altogether impressed with many of the arguments by analogy to the principle of complementarity. But his insights into it as a "concord fiction" in our age are very illuminating.

16 John H. Fisher, "Facing up to the Problems of Going Interdisciplinary," *ADE Bulletin*, No. 32 (Feb. 1972), pp. 5–8. Reprinted in this volume on pp. 90–94.

Planning Qualitative Disruption*

William M. Birenbaum

Staten Island Community College

SO FAR I have had a fascinating career in what is loosely called "experimental higher education" in this country. Indeed, as I see it, mine has been among the most disinguished records of failure in this field. It began with the third or fourth revision of the so-called Hutchins College at the University of Chicago, where I first taught. (That college was revised so often, one lost count of which version was being shaped.) I escaped to Wayne State just in time to participate in the architectural effort for Monteith. Shortly after I became dean at the New School for Social Research in New York, plans developed for an "experimental" upper-division college. Experimentally, things were just shaping up well during my adventure at Long Island University, when I was "invited" to leave. That disaster provoked an invitation from the people of Bedford-Stuyvesant in Brooklyn to help them design a new college for the half-million black people living there. The Bedford-Stuyvesant project went forward during the bitter battle of Ocean Hill–Brownsville for the decentralization of the public schools. Bedford-Stuyvesant produced an unusual and exciting design—an antisuperblock, decentralized, street-oriented "campus," a curriculum aimed at breaking through the traditional barrier between formal learning and informed action, and a community structure based upon cooperative principles—a sharing of economic and political power among employees, consumers, management, and the community-at-large. (Details of the plan are stated in my new book, *Something for Everybody Is Not Enough.*)

The projected launch of the Bedford-Stuyvesant college priced out at about $32 million, a cost which did not attract an overwhelming number of buyers. Finally, only City University proved able, ready, and willing to pay the price—a curious result, because in the view of most people in the community at the time, City University was the enemy, and the whole experimental effort was meant to be an end-run around CUNY's indifference to or traditional view of Bedford-Stuyvesant's educational problems. The community's leaders felt that if CUNY had done what it should have

* An address to the ADE Seminar at City College, New York, 15 April 1972. Reprinted from *ADE Bulletin*, No. 34 (Sept. 1972), pp. 18–23.

done, there would have been no need for the new college. In any event, the opposing team bought the project, and the college opened last fall. What opened bears little resemblance to what was designed, as is typical in this business. While the design, or the essentials of it, is now being tried in Seattle, Minneapolis, and Chicago, it will probably never see the light of day in Brooklyn, which gave it birth.

After designing the college in Bedford-Stuyvesant, I went to Staten Island Community College. I've been there three years, and if I finish this year it will be the fourth, which is as long as I've been in any job so far. I face this with some trepidation too. I think we're doing pretty well at Staten Island. The College, after only three years, is in considerable chaos. Allowed a little more time, we can really mess it up. We're making modest progress in this regard.

Every place I've gone I've always been told that the blackboard is clean. Be bold, innovative, experimental! Write your own lesson! That has always been misleading, because everywhere I've gone I've found out the blackboard is clean if you start from one given, a necessary precondition for boldness. The given in each of these situations has been that you can't think about a college unless you proceed from the premise that you have a campus. Everywhere I've been, from Brooklyn to the greenery of Staten Island, I am told to be experimental, innovative, to encourage people to do their thing—but to remember that a college has a campus or it is not a college.

The idea of *campus* derives from the Latin meaning of the word—"an open plain or field." That's something we didn't have in Bedford-Stuyvesant, in the middle of Detroit, on Chicago's South Side.

As an educational institution, the campus derives from the tradition of the medieval monastery. The monastery, as you know, was always put purposely where the people weren't—on open plains remote from centers of population or on mountain crags difficult to get to. And even though it was put where the people weren't, it always was surrounded by a wall. The monastery was based on the conception of enclosed turf and definitive acreage inside the wall. The wall always had one main gate, and it always had a principal officer who presided at this gate—the keeper of the key. He represented the authority that this system, through its wall, imposed. The wall had the traditional purpose of walls. It was meant to regulate with great care what got in and what got out—the terms of entry and exit. Now, every monastery had its secret passageways—its tunnels and its hidden gates, where those who really were in charge could go out and do their thing in the wee hours of the morning or late at night. But for the official clientele there was one main gate and one keeper of the key to the gate. For them the system was an isolated enclave.

While I was at Long Island University, the C. W. Post Campus was developed. The Post family gave this lovely estate, a manor in Nassau County on Long Island, to the University to make into a college. When it was given it consisted of a manor house, a gatehouse where the keeper of the gate lived with wife, stables, and acres and acres of what exists in Nassau County, namely, potato fields. The first thing the Board at L.I.U. decided, before it touched another thing, was to put a wall around the acres to distinguish those potato fields from other potato fields on Long Island.

Then they developed the enclave on the inside. It was a typical case of what I mean by the educational wall. It was not exceptional at all—pick up any college bulletin, and you will see that the introductory pages describe the size and shape of the campus, its apartheid virtues. The University of Utah consists of two thousand acres; its campus overlooks downtown Salt Lake City; and so forth, and so on. The enclave is spatial, and the wall is meant to say to everything beyond it that it is a *special* place, specially apart.

Invariably this enclave is not only territorial; it is also temporal. From coast to coast in this country, from Pomona to Parsons to Princeton, the undergraduate educational system designed to produce red-blooded, liberally educated, employable, flag-waving Americans is more or less 120 credit hours big. I've tried to discover the origins of this credit-hour system, and I've yet to pin down authoritatively exactly when it started. But I do know for a fact that it was close to 120 credit hours big before we had electric lights and Model T Fords, not to mention split atoms and moon walks.

This 120-credit-hour-system presents a slight problem because we have been writing down what we know one way or another for about six thousand years. We came into World War II with a horrendous pile of it, and since World War II, to look at it just quantitatively, the pile has been escalating by a hundred percent each decade. The pile of what there is to know is horrendous. And the temporal space in which to put it is fixed. This enclave, therefore, is not only so many acres big, it is 120 credit hours big. Now, the typical so-called course is three of these coins of the realm, and three into 120 equals forty courses. There are twenty campuses in the CUNY system, all of them have bulletins which list these courses, and so far I've counted over fifteen thousand courses offered by the City University this year. The curriculum for an individual human being should consist of about forty units out of a possible fifteen thousand, and this is supposed to produce the ideal result, a liberally educated, red-blooded, employable, well-informed American citizen.

We've invented in this country a neat, mature system for accommodating this oversupply of knowledge. It's a system which I call the shafting of knowledge. What we've done is to take the six-thousand-year pile of knowledge and categorically organize it in a series of disciplinary shafts across the territorial, temporal enclave which we call a "campus."

We've always talked about this campus as if it were a community. We've acknowledged that it is also a bringing together of humans whose relations somehow have to be accommodated. Hutchins used to call it a "community of scholars." I've yet to find one of these, but I allow for the possibility that one exists somewhere.

In any case, we all talk about the campus as if it were a community, and because of that we have somehow had to devise a political system to accommodate the shafting arrangement of the knowledge pile. The way we've done that is to departmentalize the shafts for the purposes of negotiating the nitty-gritty power elements among the people brought together in the "community." The departmental system is a way of handling the disposition and negotiation of academic wealth and the interests of the people who are brought together in the campus community. We can think of the department arrangement as a series of shafts, each headed by a precinct captain (the chairman). He reports for certain purposes to a ward leader (dean), who in turn reports to the leader of the party, the president or chancellor. The transaction of the nitty-gritty business of the campus community proceeds in terms of this kind of political structure.

I have recently had the extraordinary experience of looking closely at some fifty college bulletins. Their introductory pages all contain certain common denominators. They all tell you that their campus is the best thing that ever happened. I have yet to open one that does not say, "We are the best conservators of the past; we commit teaching better than anyone else; we're relevant; we're innovative and experimental; we've got everything." All of them say that, including Parsons. They all say that there is a prescribed way to get in and prescribed way to get out. If you follow the directions carefully (sometimes they are very complex, and you have to read them more than twice to understand), you can bake yourself into an educated cake. But they all provide essentially the same recipe for the same cake.

These college bulletins all say to the consumer: "If you want to get in, you approach this college modestly up at the top to one of its knowledge-shafts, proclaiming publicly there that you are ignorant." Then, by some mysterious means, this system determines who shall be kept out. This is called Admissions. After you are allowed in (if you are), the recipe prescribes quiet sinking in the appropriate shaft. The deeper you sink into the shaft, the greater the pressure becomes down near the dregs. Finally you hit bottom, and then there is a public ceremony and you are ejected. At the point of ejection, the system proclaims *not* that *you* are educated (that is not the point of commencement), but that *it* has educated you; not that you are educated, but that the system has done its job. You are issued a union card to put in your wallet or hang on your wall, so you can show the world that the system has done its job.

The shafts arranged in the campus enclave work the same on the faculty side. A young Ph.D. from N.Y.U. or Columbia arrives and beseeches the system to let him in. If the system lets him in, it admits him at the lowest rank (at the top of the shaft), and then it gives him the schlock assignments, the freshman courses scheduled at an inconvenient hour with a dull subject matter. So he begins to sink. As he sinks he is supposed to demonstrate to the world that he really is becoming a monopoly purveyor of what is in the shaft. He does this through interesting talks, publication, and research, keeping in mind that it is political to shake the chairman's hand, to smile at the right moment, and not to say anything too offensive to his colleagues. If he does all that and keeps his nose clean, pretty soon he sinks to the bottom of the shaft and is awarded the highest rank with tenure. That's a moment of crisis, a period of professional menopause, because it raises the question of what you do next. If you're still young, with your whole life ahead of you, it's an especially trying "success."

A curriculum is primarily the result of a series of decisions by various people in the shafts to exclude substantial parts of the knowledge in a six-thousand-year-big pile. The bulletins always proclaim that the curriculum is the distillation of ultimate truth, but as I have observed curriculum committees in the places I have been, I find it hard to believe that the curriculum has much to do with distilled truth. Instead, it is a treaty, where people with conflicting interests confront this six-thousand-year-big pile and decide not so much what should be in as what should be out. That decision, of course, is primarily reflective of a certain group of people's values at a particular instant in time, as they negotiate their conflicting interests.

The typical faculty of the typical undergraduate college in America has not reexamined the whole curricular treaty for seventeen years. Going back seventeen years from 1972 to 1955, reflect for a moment on the ages of the people who met in the typical American undergraduate enclave to decide what to keep out, and the character of events in 1955. When black, or Italian, or Jewish, or poor, or rich students come into a history department or an English department now and say, "Your curriculum doesn't appeal to us," what I understand them to be saying is: "The treaty you made back in 1955 or whenever you made it may properly need reexamination." The typical faculty rejoinder, of course, is: "You don't know what you're talking about. Scholarship transcends time, the truth is eternal, don't talk to us that way." There is a little difference of opinion here which can sometimes become rather serious.

If I'm right about what the curriculum is, this best explains why faculty meetings never encompass any significant discussion about it. It is dangerous to raise any fundamental question about the treaty in the typical faculty meeting. For example, let's assume the precinct captain in charge of the life science-biological science shaft were to stand up in a faculty meeting and look diagonally across the shafts and say: "Gentlemen, the last time we examined our treaty was seventeen years ago, and at that time we all knew physics was red-hot. When we divided up the coin of the realm and decided who gets what share of the credit-hour treasury we gave physics a big piece. But we all know what's happened to physics in the last two decades, and we all know that life science-biological science is now red-hot. We've got genetic codes and transplants and all sorts of marvelous things going on. We want six more pieces of the treasury." Everybody listening knows that if this precinct captain gets six more it comes out of somebody else's hide, because the overall size of the undergraduate pot is limited. The question is whose. The whole network of the agreement is shaken. I'm sure that the rage for kicking ROTC off campus a few years ago had less to do with the principle of whether the military should be on campus than with everybody's knowledge that ROTC preempted six to twelve low-grade pieces of the treasury.

Superimposed on all of the vertical shafts of knowledge are a series of horizontal control systems meant to apply to all of them, with malice toward none and justice toward all. One horizontal control system is Admissions, the standard by which it is determined who shall be kept out. Another is the credit value placed upon time. Still another is the highly scientific, though little understood, machinery through which we judge the quality of people by the devices through which faculty members recommend the promotion, reappointment, and tenuring of each other.

These and other horizontal control systems transform the campus enclave into a rather rigid grid that looks like a checkerboard. The best way to get through this is to get yourself in the psychological frame of being comfortable when you are boxed in, stuck in a square. Any fool who can do that can beat the system. That's why Open Admissions is no big deal. If you've got enough human energy to survive any high school in this city to the point of graduation, if you're still warm, and if you have a verbal skill good enough to read the bulletin or talk to a counselor, you can beat the grid. The same is true for the faculty. Anybody who can survive the machinery through a master's or a Ph.D., especially at weird, i.e., "excellent," places like Columbia, can approach the top of one of these shafts, beg to get in, and be comfortably shafted through the course of professional life.

The grid works pretty much the way it looks. It looks like a map of Manhattan, and just as in Manhattan, if you follow along the block carefully observing STOP signs and DO NOT WALK signs at the corners, you have a fair chance of getting from one place to another without getting killed. In Manhattan you're in real trouble if you come to a corner and you start to cross the street diagonally. Similarly, if you attempt any diagonal motion across the campus grid, you're in great peril. Any activity in the grid other than straight up and down is dangerous. Circular activity is disastrous. But vertical activity—sinking—is relatively safe, and any fool can negotiate it.

This campus grid is separated from another one above it, or before it, by the phenomenon of being eighteen. As I talk with my own students and with students around the country, they tell me that where they've been before they reach the college grid is very similar. Consequently, when they get into the college grid they know the basic rules of the game, even if they don't read the bulletin. As I understand the best evidence of the science of human and biological development, there is no period in human life from minus nine months to plus twenty-five years that is less meaningful than age eighteen. In terms of the unfolding of motor skills, emotional development, and learning capacity, eighteen is about the least significant age. But that's just the age when the switch from grid to grid is prescribed, compelled.

At the bottom of the campus grid, or after it, there is still another grid, separated by the phenomenon of ejection and by an age level close to twenty-two. The graduate and professional schools are identical grids, except that the boxes are a lot smaller and more rigid. Alumni of my present college who have gotten jobs in such places as the sixty-second floor of the Chase Manhattan Bank in the Wall Street area tell me that not only the job and the bank's organization, but even the building in which they work conforms beautifully to this pictorial revelation of how life should be. Let us not mention experience in the U.S. Armed Forces. Let us not mention what the bedroom communities in Connecticut, New Jersey, and Long Island look like from the air, or how they work on the ground when you live in them.

The best argument in favor of the multiple grid system, of this neat way of processing people, is that it is not disruptive. It is a perfect way to perpetuate a standardized version of how life should be in this great free society. It stands for what I, of course, would consider to be an anti-intellectual proposition: that education should not be disruptive. Or, to put what I stand for positively, education, particularly at the collegiate level, must be disruptive. The only issue about disruption involved here is a qualitative one. My view of the disruptions that have happened is that they have been of a low-grade quality, and I am concerned about the quality of the disruption.

Obviously the campus grid is a monopoly system, and I feel that it is therefore very un-American. Rewards in the system are determined by the extent to which one can prove he is a consummate monopolist within the terms of the shafts. To break a monopoly, obviously there are several key points of attack. One is to challenge the single entry and exit, the power of the gatekeeper, by knocking holes in the wall and creating alternative ways of getting in and out. If you do that and you still want to control what goes out, you take the risk of not being able to regulate what goes in. That causes special problems inside. Another way is to challenge the monopoly situation in one of the shafts, and if you do that you've got new problems.

To give you an idea of how the shafting of knowledge works in the real world, let me tell you about what happened a couple of years ago at my college. When Open Admissions threatened at City University, the Board issued policy proclamations on the front page of the *New York Times* in May of that year, saying: "We're going to have Open Admissions in this place." As is typical in City University, there was no budget in May. Budgets don't happen in this system until June or July for implementation the following September. But there are directives in May, and mine came from headquarters and said: "Did you read the *New York Times* lately? You're going to have Open Admissions, and in the case of your campus next September you're going to have two thousand more freshmen than last September." You don't build new campuses between May and September, especially when your budget isn't available to you even in July. But I dutifully called in my precinct captains and said, "Ladies and Gentlemen, you all read the *New York Times*, and you know we're going to have Open Admissions. That means two thousand new human beings in this place, and the presumptions are that none of them can add and subtract or read and write."

The news about people not being able to add and subtract or read and write wasn't really surprising, because I'm under the impression that the students we've received at the College since it opened fifteen years ago have not been able to read and write or add and subtract. As a matter of fact, as a president receiving memoranda from my faculty, I'm under the impression that some of *them* can't read and write. There's a little problem here. Being able to read and write is a matter of degree, so all that Open Admissions meant was there would be fewer people who could read and write well.

Of course, none of my precinct captains really believed all this in May. They thought that the legislature or the City Council or somebody would have the good sense not to provide the money, and that once the Board had its kick out of the publicity on the policy, the whole thing would quietly go away. So they all sat around and laughed about the prospect of two thousand more freshmen who can't read or write.

But I did dutifully what anyone who plays this game should do. I went to the English shaft and I said, "Gentlemen, two thousand more freshmen, assuming the budget comes in, prices out to seventeen more full-time lines (pieces of the treasury) for you. You're my monopoly in this production field, and I'd like to know, are we ready?" They said, "What do you mean?"

And I said, "Well, you know, how is the monopoly doing?" (Incidentally, I've asked that question many times in my career in many monopoly areas, and I've yet to have a monopoly tell me it's not doing great. They always tell me they could do better if I wasn't such an SOB, but given the fact that I have been fouling up, I am told the monopoly is doing great.) So I was told they were doing great, and I said, "Well, I don't know anything about English, but I hear there is something called reading, and I hear that there are new ways of teaching people to read and write and talk, and are we ready?" I was told what you'd expect: "We are a good English department, and good not only means Milton and Shakespeare, it means we're hip. We're a two-year college, and we've got Russian literature, black literature, Latin American literature, and Spanish literature. We're really hip. But we are a college English department and don't talk to us about high-school remediation." In late June, with a budget finally in hand, as party leader I assembled the precinct captains and the ward leaders again, and we had another talk. I said, "I've got seventeen lines in this budget to use for what is called English in this college." And that monopoly stood up through its leader and said, "Those are ours." Then he opened his briefcase and asked me to put them in there. I, of course, took out the memorandum about how hip they were, and I said, "Look what you wrote me just three weeks ago. I hereby proclaim that those seventeen are not yours."

The monopoly was shocked. They said, "Who else's could they be?" They said, "The job is English." I took the position that maybe we should have another English department. I couldn't think of anything else to do. It was late June, and two thousand new students were due in September.

Then we had the final faculty meeting of the year, and a distinguished monopolist from physics stood up in the meeting and said: "Mr. President, is it true that we're going to have two English departments in this place?" I said, "Yes, sir." And he said, "Do you mean to say that you think that's good?" Well, I'm in Staten Island, and it's the only borough of this city that voted for Nixon. I have to do business out there, so I choose my public language carefully. With some innocence I thought it might be a good idea at a faculty meeting out there to say, "Yes. Competition is a good thing."

Well, I was immediately threatened with a union grievance under the preamble to the contract with my faculty, which reads, "Both parties to this contract pledge themselves to uphold the academic character of the institution." The allegation was to read, "Any president who stands for competition with the shafted enclave is subverting the academic character of the institution." The message from the monopolies was clear: leave our shafts alone.

The trouble is that neither the present state of our knowledge nor the thrust of the events of our time allow for things to be left alone. It is a time when being shafted is less popular. It is a time when knowing compels fresh assaults upon the line between thinking and acting.

The most that can be said about the adults in any of our learning situations is that those in charge do not know certain things which those of whom they are in charge do know. And vice versa. Our classrooms are a common meeting ground for a sharing of ignorance in which different parties to the transaction know different things and have some real things to share. It is all of these things that make this uptight, neat version of how to do it very much on the line at this point. And my own feeling is that the way the country is, and the way people are living in it, the state of the knowledge, the impact of the technology, and the aspirations of the people will compel alterations of this. We no longer have a choice about it. The question is whether or not we will maintain some measure of rational control over the nature of the change.

The Relevance of Language*

Roger Starr

Center for Urban Problems

I AM DELIGHTED to be here because I enjoy to the last drop the pleasure of interdisciplinary life. Much of my time is spent trying to deal with the housing and planning problems of New York City. The people with whom I come into contact may be architects or builders or economists or public administrators or community leaders. I am not any of these. I therefore am able to make very dogmatic statements about each of their specialties and then to wiggle out between the slats when challenged.

I intend to do the same here this afternoon by explaining at the very beginning that my field is not language. Although I must admit to being a fellow traveler of language, I will claim immunity from professional rebuffs when you individually and united announce important disagreements with my points.

The problems of the urban centers which increasingly absorb the interest—though perhaps not the physical activity—of your students are nothing if not interdisciplinary. We talk of improving the housing condition of low-income families and find that, while there are some who are only housing poor, there are others whose poverty is so serious a part of their personalities and their lives that one cannot do anything significant about their housing problems until their poverty problems are also attacked. Then one finds that one can do very little about their poverty until one has dealt with their education. And education is impossible without dealing with motivation. Motivation cannot be approached until one has seen the family and household in its setting, and then, lo and behold, we are back to the housing problem.

We cannot come to grips with the question of environmental deterioration unless we are willing to deal seriously with the problems of employment and economic activity. Although we are surrounded by romantics who tell us otherwise, the same economic activity that produces employment also produces environmental deterioration. If one is unwilling to face the consequences of the added cost of dealing with environmental deterioration for people of limited income, one has not begun to glimpse the complexity of interrelationships on what Kenneth Boulding has called spaceship earth. Yet in all these interdisciplinary connections there can be found one common element. That common element is politics, *politics* used in its very

* An address to the ADE Seminar at City College, New York, 14 April 1972. Reprinted from *ADE Bulletin*, No. 34 (Sept. 1972), pp. 48–53.

broadest sense as the art of reconciling the interests of diverse and opposing groups. Whatever may be the fundamental nature of the relationship between men and objects, and no matter how that relationship may change under new, even revolutionary demands, the need for politics survives. This continues to confound those who believe that some magical change which they title revolution will somehow cause all human differences to vanish like smoke. We groundlings who find it impossible to believe in the evanescence of group interest must continue to struggle for continuing reconciliations lest some group or other impose its own form of reconciliation on all the rest of us.

The political problem of the city has become more and more complex as the traditional forms of organization have lost their strength. To me, in retrospect, the old party clubhouse that dealt in favors and services rather than ideology looks better and better, but my recollections are merely wistful. There seems to be no chance of recapturing a world in which men and women identify themselves as simply as they once did by reference to their political party, their religion, and their basic philosophy of life. We have now succeeded in finding a dozen different ways to describe ourselves. We have become consumers, environmentalists, women's liberationists, community-control advocates, racists, antiracists—the list is endless. I suggest that as political loyalties melt, the frail web of language is left to bind together by itself the multiple identities.

I suggest that, in the past, free institutions depended on a human practice which these multiple identities make more difficult—the habit of living peacefully with one's disappointments. If, in fact, this habit has been broken, language must take the place of the habit. Language must somehow take on the responsibility of helping to make no disappointment so severe that it cannot be borne peacefully. Language can do so by helping to explain the uses of patience and reason, by helping to discover a way to break into that endless circle of interdisciplinary problems that frustrate urban men and stimulate their animosities.

Of course, many would dispute these few words in praise of language and reason. For these individuals, the problems of the time have become so acute that language no longer expresses them. One must, therefore, experience the world with the solar plexus instead of the eyes and brain. A member of the board of trustees of a New York school with which I am familiar recently told the parent body that classroom activity was worthless. To teach about the city, he counseled closing the school so that the pupils could spend their time on the streets, becoming familiar with street language.

I have no objection to bringing young people into contact with real life; in fact I consider that the very center of educational purpose. Nor would I waste my time trying to keep young people from learning street language; but anyone who spent time as an enlisted man in the army has learned that while there are some emotions which can be conveyed only in the language of the street, there are far more which cannot be so conveyed, and the vocabulary of the street does not gain in force or ingenuity by repetition. There are very few poets in the street, and those who try too hard to convey more meaning than the limited vocabulary will carry end up short of truth, short of poetry. Their humor is as limited as the tedious polysyllabic pendantry that Mr. Bing Crosby produces for the television coverage of his golf tournament. The problem with attending exclusively to the language of the street and the visceral sensations that are engendered by some of the horrors that fill them is that, first, our own perspective may be more blunted than sharpened by the overwhelming nature of the exposure, and, second, that without rationalization and the application of principles, exposure to the raw data leaves us and the data themselves exactly as they were before.

I am arguing that language and the accompanying conceptualization are vitally relevant to a concern for urban problems. This, however, does not mean that all language aids in communication or that all conceptions are equally valid. Those of us who have primary responsibility for the feeding in of vocabulary and concepts to the human brain have an awesome responsibility. It is one of the ironies of our time that we see the difficulties of this process much more clearly in dealing with machines than in dealing with human beings. The art of implanting information into a computer has developed to its present high point in large part because of the early recognition that it is impossible to get more out of a computer than one puts in. We would not be willing to make so absolute a statement concerning the human mind. But nevertheless it is, I suspect, very generally the case that a slovenly vocabulary, a misplaced sense of metaphor, an unwillingness to attempt to distinguish between vital shades of meaning, and a sentimental acceptance of careless conceptualization defeat the usefulness of language for all of us in an urban society.

If we are indeed to maintain our relevance to the urban problems around us, three major activities should encourage a large effort on the part of language teachers and language specialists.

The first of these is the clarification of metaphor. Much of the language system in which we deal has been set down in literary form and it is with this literature, some classic, some immediately contemporary, that we try to work our wisdom on our students. One difficulty with literature is that its technique consists largely of the explanation of meaning by the exploitation of similarity—a process which we may call metaphor. Even street language uses metaphors, as in the invitations to commit the most curious obscenities in which the inviter neither means precisely what he says nor expects a literal acceptance. He is metaphorically offering the definition of a sense of humiliation he wishes he could inflict, while a literal acceptance of the invitation would be regarded with intense embarrassment. In using the metaphor, the curser is suggesting a similarity which he knows should be pursued only to a certain point, and his auditor is well aware of the limitations imposed by usage on what has been said. Metaphor in classic literature imposes no real danger to one's view of reality, because one recognizes that the metaphor consists of an incomplete or partial identification, and one does not really believe that Hamlet is exhorting his flesh to melt, dissolve, and cover the stage with a sudden dew. However, when we deal with contemporary literature about the city—or indeed about any other contemporary subject—we stand in great danger of confusing the vehicle of the content with its tenor, and believing that the works of literature are truly literal at the moment when they are striving to be simply symbolic.

Sometimes the confusion is easy to make. James Baldwin, writing about Riverton Houses, described their middle-class black residents as so humiliated and disgusted at living in this complex owned by the Metropolitan Life Insurance Company that they regularly emptied their bowels in the halls and elevators. When the residents of Riverton Houses complained, quite properly, that this was a slander on their personal deportment and that there was no word of truth in what Mr. Baldwin had written, Mr. Baldwin replied that he had not been trying to write a literal truth but had only been describing symbolically what he imagined their feelings to be. Those readers who came across Mr. Baldwin's words before the correction was made may be excused for making the mistake that his words naturally led to. They would have absorbed a fatal misunderstanding of class pride and dignity among a large fraction of the urban population.

A more difficult and intricate confusion occurs in a celebrated passage in *The Great Gatsby*, the passage describing for the first time the Valley of Ashes. We first encounter this phenomenon at the start of Chapter Two, where Fitzgerald tells us that the motor road that joins West Egg to New York City bends out of its normal path to avoid what he calls a "certain desolate area of land." This, he tells us, is a valley of ashes, where the heaped-up material assumes the ghostly, insubstantial appearance of houses, countryside, gardens, even people, but all seen through a miasma of what the author calls "powdery air." Occasionally, "a line of grey cars," Fitzgerald says, "crawls along an invisible tract, ash-grey men swarm with leaden spades and stir up an impenetrable cloud, which screens their obscure operations from your sight."

The passage is so crucial that Lionel Trilling talks of its "ideographic" use, characteristic of Fitzgerald's own literary economy. It is obvious that the Valley of Ashes has a certain symbolic or metaphorical significance for the author; indeed some of the book's crucial action takes place at Wilson's garage, in full view of the same Valley of Ashes. It seems to me that for Fitzgerald the Valley of Ashes represents the narrow and difficult passage that separates the new, urban, socially disordered world of New York City from the still socially rigid and regularized—though already somewhat tainted by contamination—world of West Egg and most particularly East Egg. The passage between the two, like the mythical passage between this world and the netherworld, is a dangerous and narrow one; the danger springs from the social disorganization of the city, so aptly symbolized by the ashes from which the combustibles have been extracted, leaving behind only the clay shell, which, like the city itself, is an inadequately glimpsed imitation of life, rather than life itself.

Surely the metaphor that those who pass through this valley on the way to the city must abandon hope because they are entering a world of insensate and thoughtless extraction of human values—this metaphor that the city world is as pointless as a pile of ashes—works splendidly. The valley provides a setting that emphasizes the lack of clarity and lack of class in the lives of the Wilsons and their relationship to Tom Buchanan.

My problem arises only when someone takes this description of the ashes as literal truth, and reacts to the ash pile and the effort to deal on a realistic worldly level with ash disposal and recycling under the miasma of the emotional overtones that Fitzgerald discovers in the Valley. Effective though the metaphor may be for Fitzgerald's purpose, filling us with a sense of loathing for the ashes that carries over to explain emotionally the action that takes place near them, the practical reality of the ash pile is anything but wasteful. For the student of urban affairs, that ash pile represents not disorder, but its converse, a recycling order of high technological importance which, regrettably, has been lost. The ashes were a reusable by-product of coal combustion. They were carefully collected in Corona, Long Island, for future use. The uses included the manufacture of cinder block, the development of cinder concrete, which happens to be the material out of which most of the floors of New York's skyscrapers are made. The cinders, incidentally, helped to fill Horse Creek, and now constitute at least some of the material which underlies the public-housing site of Forest Hills about which you have all heard so much.

I raise the issue not to quarrel with Fitzgerald's use of metaphor. Rather I call attention to the responsibility that falls on the shoulders of language teachers when metaphor is used. We cannot read Fitzgerald intelligibly unless we respond with the emotions of revulsion that he wishes to bring out in us by his use of the Valley of Ashes. On the other hand, we cannot respond intelligently to the waste-disposal problems of the city if we are unable simultaneously to understand coolly and unemotionally the nature of the urban wastes and the kinds of technology that must be developed to reprocess them fruitfully. Somewhere, in this metaphorical confusion, lie buried a number of metaphorical phrases—*dead-end job* comes to mind immediately—which, in part, may owe their current usage to metaphorical confusion between description applied to the job for one purpose, and the full significance of the job when perceived within another frame of reference.

A more ambiguous metaphorical use of the urban reality turns up in *The Tenants*, Bernard Malamud's new novel, the theme of which seems to me this very same conflict between the visceral and the rational perceptions of reality which I have been discussing. In the novel they are embodied in the sexual, artistic, and bloody rivalry between an established Jewish writer and a striving black. I am concerned at this moment only with the literal reality in the background, a tenement house in which the Jewish writer, Lesser by name (and I am sure not coincidentally), is the only remaining legal tenant. For the purposes of the story we are shown a confrontation between the landlord, Levenspiel, and the tenant, Lesser, in which the landlord pleads with the tenant to accept relocation into another building so that the tenement may be demolished. The tenant says he cannot leave his apartment until his book is finished. The scene between the two Jews bristles with ironies; neither has quite the strength appropriate to his role. Lesser simply cannot finish his book—he is no longer quite the writer; Levenspiel cannot muster the will to get his solitary tenant out of the building—some ambivalent respect for the artist seems to have robbed him of the insensitivity which a landlord really needs. Artistically, the relationship between these two imagined men is brilliant. But it is my duty to tell you that as housing, the whole business is nonsense.

I will not bother with the economic details, all dubious, by which Levenspiel explains why he is building only a six-story building on the site. Or with the absurdly low cash offer made to get Lesser out. But I must point out that anyone who took literally the basic situation—one lone tenant living in a tenement house with no one breaking into the other apartments, setting fires on the floor, and eventually bringing the building down in ruins—would be putting his own life in jeopardy. Anyone reading this work for its revelation of black-white relationships in art (together with overtones hardly in place here) has come to the right place. But if one reads the metaphor incorrectly and believes that this is a book about a housing problem (bemused, possibly by the "Tenants" in the title), he is taking his life in his hands. Some of this clarification is the business, it seems to me, of the teachers of language.

It seems to me that the custodians of language must recognize that certain distortions of literature are almost inevitable, that the creator of literature almost invariably overvalues the past simply because it is rich in meaning and allusion and tends to undervalue the present and to be suspicious of change simply because it comes to him, as it were, naked, unfledged, bare of illusion. If we are to preserve the usefulness of language we must be constantly alert to the need for clarification of metaphor which will not in any way diminish the suggestiveness of metaphor, but which will at the same time not damage its literal meaning.

A second task of the guardian of literature is the pruning away of the meaningless word. Certainly the proliferation of communication has meant a flowering of words. Many people are trying to say too much in too short a time, and they have developed a new jargon loaded with flabby concepts, improvised meanings, words that constitute little more than a stutter. I am tired, and I presume you are, of people banks and people tires. I am tired of juxtapositions like "we are for people not automobiles" when what is meant rather is that we, whoever we may be, believe the rights of pedestrians are superior to the rights of automobile drivers. Both classes are nevertheless people.

Among all of these words, the one which it seems to me most effectively blocks communication is the word *community*. On every side the community expresses itself; or, rather, individual speakers announce that they are merely the open mouths through which the still, small voice of the community is heard. I have learned by now that it is really not the doll on the ventriloquist's lap who is speaking. The voice is coming from the ventriloquist himself, whatever he may wish you to believe.

Unfortunately the word *community* carries with it a number of overtones in language which cannot be stripped away without a mighty effort. The community is a monad, a single unit in speech. In reality the urban community does not exist as a unit, nor does the so-called black community, nor does the Jewish community except on very rare issues. The word *community* suggests a common interest and a common purpose. It extends deep into the past and can be projected far into the future. It is the nature of the American city today that its past is recent. The city is the product of vigorous change, and its future is uncertain, lying in the shadow of future change that may rival the past change in its depth and complexity.

What speakers mean when they refer to the community wanting this or demanding that is that some people living roughly within certain specific geographic limits have expressed a desire for this or for that, and that the listener is to attach to their demands a significance which the demanders have not truly earned.

The clarification of the word *community*, the stripping away from it of all the frequently illegitimate overtones, becomes a primary responsibility of the guardians of language, if language is to be used to deal effectively with the reconciliation of diverse interests within the city. I could list a dozen other terms which require the same careful attention from the guardians of the language if they are not to contribute to repeated and broadening misunderstandings. The very word *change* itself, which seems to have come into vogue because of a natural impatience with the frequently elusive promise implicit in the word *progress*, nevertheless causes us a measure of trouble. Change is a temporarily neutral word, but the speaker means to attach to it a set of unspoken and perhaps unconceived implications. Those of us who wish to guard the language so that it will remain useful should urge those who speak of change to clarify explicitly the kind of change they have in mind. The exercise will be useful for both parties.

Finally, I see a third activity for the guardians of language which makes their work relevant to the urban crisis. The activity is the development of a forceful and effective rhetoric. The power of invective has been augmented, not diminished, by the disappearance of the political machine. While it was possible until recently to obtain political power in the city by faithful service—mere loyalty to the interests of the party—the diminishing of the party's importance has meant that each striving politician must create his own system. In a world in which the media have become so important, the opportunities for language should have been increased. And yet, how few of the young politicians seem capable of taking advantage of those opportunities. I think that we hear so many words that we have come to disbelieve their power; yet, every once in a while, a new voice breaks through with the use of words that startle, threaten, and eventually command attention. Sometimes the words are and must be abusive. I think of Robert Moses as a man who without direct access to any of the sources of political power managed to work his will in New York because his tongue inspired something akin to terror. I think of Adlai Stevenson, whose wit (and incidentally, for the most part it doesn't read very well; it was *spoken* wit) commanded the allegiance of a certain generation of Americans who could not begin to tell you what, if any, were his accomplishments in political office. I think of Martin Luther King, with a very different style, who yet managed by linguistic methods to effect major attitudinal changes in both the black and the white people in this country. I will not deal in detail with the present Vice President of the United States, but surely the language in which his pronouncements were cast gave them an audience they would otherwise never have achieved. I can think of a few other random sentences spoken by political figures in the past years that have become a part of the language and helped to shape the intellectual environment of American political life.

I am not suggesting that teachers of language should become teachers of rhetoric, nor do I believe that we can or should return to the oratorical processes of an earlier day. I do believe that precision and clarity of speech continue to wield a power that affects the fate of men just as the clarity with which it grasps a metaphor or eliminates the meaninglessness from discourse helps to clarify the understanding. It seems to me that this high calling is one of which you should be justly proud.

Selected Bibliography

Hall, Peter. *The World Cities*. New York: McGraw-Hill, 1966.

McQuade, Walter. *Cities Fit to Live In*. New York: Macmillan, 1971.

National Research Council. Ad Hoc Committee on Solid Waste Management. *Policies for Solid Waste Management*. Prepared for the United States Bureau of Solid Waste Management. Washington, D.C.: Government Printing Office, 1970.

Owen, Wilfred. *The Metropolitan Transportation Problem*. Revised edition. Washington, D.C.: Brookings Institution, 1966. Paperback available from Doubleday.

Starr, Roger. *Urban Choices*. Baltimore: Penguin Books, 1967.

Teaching and Revolution*

Harold Taylor

Past President, Sarah Lawrence College

I BEGIN with some general remarks about teaching and revolution and the relation between art and mass culture before becoming more specific about the education of teachers of English for the high schools. My notion of what teaching is extends to the idea that one enters the life of other persons with a view to influencing their lives in directions desirable for those persons. The formalities of teaching are simply those conventions adopted by professional academics within the conventions of the educational institutions that have developed in this country and elsewhere. Very seldom is the matter of how one's life influences another life, or the conception of changing one's own life and in so doing changing the lives of others, considered to be a function of undergraduate education or of education in general.

In most of my work, I've tried to look at education as the context in which one designs environments rather than as formal course work or formal anything. The thrust of my arguments over the past thirty years is the result of my experience as a teacher. Whenever there is a convention which has arisen because of the professional interests of academics, I have wanted to question it and to see what else might be done that is more informal, more direct, and more personal.

In this particular period in American history, we have entered into a situation in which the personal relationships between teachers and students, between blacks and whites, between the old and the young, between the politicians and the electorate have become fragmented and conventionalized, and in some cases destroyed. Quite often personal relationships are not possible, and the exacerbation of tension has gone so far that students, for example, in their relations with teachers and administrators, have sometimes become incapable of understanding or unwilling to understand why any relationships are desirable. To a degree this is the result of a revolution in society whose roots go back a hundred years at least, but whose character during these last ten years has been determined by changes within the culture, within the society, some of them due to the existence of a new mass culture born when we entered the era of the mass media.

I use the word *revolution*, along with the conception of teaching I hold, not in the conventional sense of a revolution such as the French had

* An address presented at the 1971 ADE Seminar in Los Angeles. Reprinted from *ADE Bulletin*, No. 27 (Nov. 1970), pp. 33–43.

156

when they changed governments; or the Marxist revolution, which uses the intensification of class conflict in order to put one group of people in power and throw the others out. The classical modes of revolution are there to be worked with, and in some countries and in some parts of our society there are people who wish to make a revolution of the classical sort. I am thinking of the revolution in taste, in cultural values, in sensibility, in technology, in the applications of technology to contemporary social systems here and abroad. I am using the term to indicate that change has now become so rapid that what used to be done through evolutionary process is now done so fast that one can call it a revolution. The revolution I am thinking about is the revolution in education, in which the social disorders both on and off the campuses are partly due to social changes which have occurred with such rapidity that institutions have been unable to accommodate themselves. The range of problems runs all the way from the failure of the society to accommodate itself to the legitimate needs of the blacks to the failure to meet the needs of students.

The institutional forms are being broken in a revolutionary way. Some Puerto Ricans in my city of New York took over the buildings at City University a few years ago, and what would have taken fifteen to twenty years to achieve—an open-enrollment policy—was achieved in about five weeks, against the will of a large proportion of the faculty, the Board of Education, and any number of other persons. Now, it is for that kind of rapid change, from one set of conventions into radically new situations in which no one is sure of what is happening, that I am using the term *revolution.*

I would like to make one or two remarks about the relationship of this process to the mass culture. The student in contemporary America and in world society is the link between the mass culture and the various elites in the intellectual community, some of them composed institutionally within the university community itself. We have here in America for the first time in history a mass culture in which the intellectuals and the students, the older generation and the younger generation, the academic professionals and those who have nothing to do with education or the academies are all in the same culture and are all aware of the same cultural environment of world society. They all receive the same reports, and a fourteen-year-old discusses the war in Vietnam with the same apparatus of information, on the whole, as his father and mother. The student coming into college as a freshman, having absorbed values and attitudes from the mass culture, provides a way for the problems of the mass culture to be presented on the campuses—problems including the social, political, and economic issues which in former years did not exist on the campuses and were largely ignored outside them. The mass media and the mass culture make a total environment which can now be seen to have a strong effect on the high school and the college in two ways. First, that environment has brought white middle-class values to the campuses. In the past one found the sorority-fraternity system, a transferred model from the outside community with its elite country-club style of white racism, brought to the campuses and institutionalized by student organizations as well as by the universities themselves. That is still going on. Secondly, on the other side, the minority of rebellious, dissident, and sophisticated students, having been educated within the mass culture, having developed their own styles and their own conclusions and their own forms of philosophy, then try not only to change the society outside the university through operating on the campus to overthrow the conventions, but also to introduce new values from the mass culture into the university.

The mass culture has had other effects on the elites. It has destroyed the idea of a separation between high culture and popular culture—or rather, it has destroyed not the idea of the separation but the reality. That has happened because of the full acceptance of commercialism and mass art for profit by painters like Warhol, and by the injection of art forms from the popular culture into contemporary theater, dance, music, and the visual arts. Anything is art which acts as art and is accepted and believed in by audiences, practitioners, critics, and observers.

Recently, for example, the American Ballet Theatre at Lincoln Center gave the opening performance of a new ballet, *The River*, with music by Duke Ellington and choreography by Alvin Ailey. The tradition of the elites in ballet, opera, and symphony music has made a distinction between popular music, jazz, and "serious" or concert-hall music, in spite of the fact that the art forms of jazz, folk music, dance, and popular theater have always had their own authenticity within the history of culture.

The opening of *The River* marked the first time that a black choreographer whose main experience in dance came from the indigenous forms of the popular culture choreographed a work danced by whites in classical style with music by Ellington, writing this time for a full classical orchestra which usually plays music by classical composers, some of whose work has been influenced by the jazz sounds and styles of Ellington's previous writing. This time Ellington and Ailey came into the preserve of the white elites to join Stravinsky, Brahms, Jerome Robbins, Balanchine, and Tudor, with art forms new to themselves and new to the world of the classical ballet. Ellington wrote the ballet scenario; here, in part, is what he says about it:

The river starts out like a spring and he's like a newborn baby, tumbling and spitting, and one day, attracted by a puddle, he starts to run. . . . Then he goes over the falls and down into the whirlpool, the vortex of violence, and out of the whirlpool into the main track of the river. He widens, becomes broader, loses his adolescence, and, down at the delta, passes between two cities. Like all cities on the opposite sides of deltas, you can find certain things in one and not in the other, and vice versa, so we call the cities the Neo-Hip-Hot-Cool Kiddies' Community and the Village of the Virgins. The river passes between them and romps into the mother—Her Majesty the Sea—and, of course, is no longer a river. But this is the climax, the heavenly anticipation of rebirth, for the sea will be drawn up into the sky for rain and down into wells and into springs and become the river again. So we call the river an optimist. We'll be able to play the ballet in any church or temple, because the optimist is a believer. ("Our Local Correspondents," interview with Whitney Balliett, *New Yorker*, 27 June 1970, pp. 54–55.)

The scenario has elements of the Joycean image of the "riverrun" and *Finnegans Wake* in its cyclical concept of nature, although it is doubtful that the concept came to Ellington directly from Joyce. It was Ellington's extraction from his experience in the popular culture and makes one more link between that culture and the new forms of art.

I cite the example of Ellington and Ailey from among many other instances. The existence of the mass culture has now made possible a whole new array of art forms produced by young people, in the underground press, in new kinds of dance theater, in the new kinds of acting and street theater, in the new forms of the rock musical, and in new poetry. The young have invented their own art forms within a popular culture. Whether we look to Theodore Roszak's description of the counterculture, simply observe our own students, or become serious students of the popular culture which the students and nonstudents have created, we find distinct differences in this generation of the young, a generation which presents itself with a much greater awareness of the meaning of art than the generations of the past.

This generation has derived the meaning of art from the popular culture, and we are now in the middle of a culture which uses films and tapes and multimedia and which thinks of mountains and the contemplation of nature as an aspect of philosophy. In some instances this view of art and philosophy brings its adherents to the Eastern philosophers, or to African dress, or to flowers and beads and particular styles of clothing intended to assert something about a culture different from the conventional ones advertised and propagated and developed within the school and college curriculum. For the first time there is a strong thrust from the mass culture itself in a direction in many ways contrary to the direction in which school and university curricula are moving.

This is also true in the social sciences and the humanities, where students have created their own forms of curriculum and are refusing to have much to do with the conventional curricula of English or social-science departments. In some cases the more severe critics among the students and the more militant educational reformers are refusing to accept the curriculum as it stands and are making their non-negotiable demands in curricular terms rather than in terms of the political or social rules mandated on the campus.

After this preliminary review, I would now like to turn more directly to the question of developing teachers for the high schools in what one can call the humanities, but with special reference to English departments. There are programs of change going on across the country under the leadership of persons who have taken responsibility for change in the content of the English curriculum.

I assume you would agree with me that it is the education of the sensibility which is finally at stake, and that in teaching English literature through the departmental system or in any other way, the total purpose is to develop a sensibility through which students and the culture at large may raise the level of esthetic, social, and personal taste. I also assume agreement with the proposition that this is the prime reason for the work we are doing in the universities and colleges. That is not entirely true, of course, since the entire world is a cradle for sensitivity and for sensibility.

But the distinctive characteristic of the work of the humanist and of English departments within the humanities is to induce the quality of sensibility by which one judges all personal values and, in the long run, all political and social values. I think that in the work we do together—those who are teaching philosophy, anthropology, English, and any of the other subjects which naturally flow together into something called the social sciences and the humanities—we care very much that what we do makes people more sensitive to themselves and to the conditions of their lives, that we are able to expand the possibility of esthetic experience of all kinds and to raise to a higher level the student's judgment of reality, of the world around, and of the quality of the human act, whether it be political, social, or personal.

It is in this area that in the past we have not paid much attention to the development of teachers whose own sensibility has been affected by what they have done in the programs of teacher education in which they have been involved. I had the privilege of doing a two-year study of the general education of teachers and, specifically, their education in world affairs. I found that most of the teacher-education programs were so barren of esthetic or of intellectual content that those teachers who have been through the conventional programs in the humanities and social sciences have had their sensitivity deadened by what they have been forced to do. The education courses which they had been forced to take were either trivial or boring or deadly or all three. In any event, they were irrelevant. Teaching as a way of entering other people's lives and a way of creating new cultural forms and liberating the ideas within other people had not been their enterprise.

As a result, some of the most interesting young poets and writers and dancers and actors refuse to have anything to do with teaching either in the secondary or the elementary schools because of the necessity of taking a degree through the requirements of a B.A. and of a teaching certificate for the high school or for the elementary school. They have preferred in most instances to go into the free-school movement and start their own schools or to work in the experimental college movement or drop out of college altogether. Among high-school students who have not thought of becoming teachers, many have dropped out and formed rock groups, dance groups, dance-theater groups, or theater groups in general—street theater, guerrilla theater—and are writing their own poetry for each other.

My main argument in *The World as Teacher*, a book about teacher education, is that we need to pay direct attention to the quality of teaching available to us in the lives and actions of students themselves. When we think, for example, of the way in which high-school students are capable of tutoring those slightly younger than themselves, the way in which students in junior high school can work with students in elementary school as tutors and discussion leaders and assistant teachers, it is easy to see how to go on from there. A new kind of person, with literary interests fairly well developed and with an interest in teaching, is coming to the universities from high school. What we must do is to create a new situation for him in which he becomes a teacher as a freshman and is encouraged to continue his work in poetry or a field directly allied to poetry, dance, and the arts of theater. We must create a situation in which we remove the formal requirements of the departments of English or departments of any kind and give him a third of his time to carry out one or another form of teaching.

If he is particularly gifted as a teacher, we could perhaps give him a group of eight or ten other freshmen or have him located in a local elementary school, teaching poetry and literature in whatever way he wishes to work out with members of the English department or anyone else in the university community who can help him. With the other two-thirds of his time, he could work in an individually constructed curriculum in which studies in literature, social science, and the natural sciences are planned, not necessarily in the conventional courses, but in ways which can engage his attention in making a curriculum for himself. Over the first year, we could have him work possibly in three areas rather than in the conventional five courses.

In other words, we must take seriously the fact that we have here young men and women with literary gifts that should be cherished and nourished and who, at the end of four years, we would like to develop as teachers of literature in the secondary and elementary schools. I would like to see us do the same thing with young dancers, young composers, and young musicians, and I would like to see us reach out into the high school and into the mass culture, to those young people who are making their own art forms and who are representatives of the youth culture, and to the new young poets, and deliberately construct favorable situations for them on the campuses by whatever we do in the English departments.

I would like to think of chairmen of English departments as, in a sense, presidents and deans of their own colleges, as if there were a college to be built with the talents of the faculty members within one's own department. The students not only would be students working with the faculty in English, but would be educational planners, reformers collaborating with the faculty. The chairman of the department would be—if the word is not too strong—a spiritual and educational leader, a person who works with the entire group of colleagues and students within the area of the English department in creating new educational reforms which could improve the quality of teaching within the English department while the department was engaged in trying to work out new ways of producing new teachers for the secondary schools and for the future of the college community.

I would like us to look at the content of the English curriculum in its relationship to the other arts, and to think of the work of teaching English as that of deliberately working within an art form in which the use of poetry, the novel, and the play is directly related to experience of dance, theater, sculpture, painting, design. I am not suggesting we turn our English classrooms into studios. I am suggesting that if one thinks of language as the tissue which holds together the variety of art forms which go to make up the entire field of the creative arts, then the teaching of language, which in this case happens to be English, is the way in which one can come to a deeper understanding of all forms of art and therefore all sensitivities to life.

That is to say, if one works directly with dancers or actors or composers, the first thing one finds in writing scenarios or in working with musicians is that these persons write differently from the young person who is going to become a teacher or is moving through the English curriculum toward the goal of an increase in sensibility. Those who are writing within the context of dance and theater have a simpler, more direct route toward their own expression of what they want to say, because they are not being asked to comment on someone else's writing or to write in essay form. They are being asked to perform the ultimate creative act of writing their own poetry and prose. There are stimuli to expression through language which come from dance, from sculpture, from design, from society, from all the other arts, and one finds an elevation of the quality of talk when, for example, the talk stems from the discussion of dance with dancers who are choreographers and work with those who write scenarios and do the dancing.

Let me be quite specific about this. At Sarah Lawrence, I had an enormous passion for getting more of our students into the teaching profession. We had a program of experimental education which had many advantages not usually found on other campuses because of the peculiar good luck we had to be able to do whatever we wanted without anybody saying we couldn't, and I wanted to have the word go out through the minds and bodies and hearts of our students. Therefore, anything I could do to develop what would be called formally a teacher-education program, I did, and the faculty and the students developed two or three things which are directly relevant to what I am arguing for now.

One of the projects had to do with the students of theater, music, and dance, along with the young poets and writers and others who were primarily concerned with literature. Those students began teaching children on Saturday mornings in the fields of their own concern, and we organized a program for children in Westchester County, mainly in Yonkers and Mount Vernon, where there is a mixed population of black and white, poor and middle class, starved for intellectual and esthetic experience. The starvation is common in most cities, whether they are suburban towns or central cities. There is a deep, deep hunger for direct experience in all the arts.

We found that when mothers and fathers brought three- and four- and five-year-olds over to the campus to the performances for children produced by Sarah Lawrence students who wrote new works (for example, short operas, or plays, or music for the college orchestra accompanied by the chorus with the children brought into the singing both on and off the stage), the mothers and fathers themselves were moved to a deeper understanding of what the arts meant. The first thing we knew, we had an entire community moving toward a deeper understanding of what art meant and a perceptible shift in the attitude of public-school teachers and others about what you could do with the arts in the schools. The children went back from these classes and performances and began to do some of the same things in their own schools.

On the other side, in terms of the Sarah Lawrence students, they found that by teaching children through the arts—teaching them poetry, having them write poetry, having them write music, having them form percussion orchestras which then could play for young dancers who would make their own choreography at the age of five and six, or having them write their own scenarios—they became so much more deeply involved, both in the art forms they cared about and in the teaching of these art forms, that the quality of their own concern as students and as potential teachers was greatly enhanced. The whole college became different because they were teaching children in the arts.

In the structure of Sarah Lawrence we did not have formal departments. We had groups of people with common interests. In literature we had poets, novelists, writers, and scholars. One year I appointed Randall

Jarrell and Mary McCarthy and found myself turning up as the fairly unattractive figure of a college president in *The Groves of Academe* and in Jarrell's *Pictures from an Institution*. From that point on, I was very careful about what novelists I appointed. In any event, teachers on the campus included Joseph Campbell, Horace Gregory, Genevieve Taggart, and Robert Fitzgerald. We always had a group of poets and writers. Those who were more formally educated as teachers of literature rather than as writers had the attitude of writers. We shared a common way of thinking about literature, and we thought about the pleasures of the intellect available to our students as a natural outcome of the presence of interesting teachers of literature. We had an atmosphere like that of the Black Mountain environment in the arts which affected the whole campus. It was impossible to come to the campus as a student or as a faculty member and not be affected by what one could call a certain kind of sensibility. The student might find herself with a roommate who was a dancer, or dancers were quite often infected with an interest in physics through having roommates who were mad for that particular form of study experience.

Out of this approach to the arts and to teaching the arts to children, we developed an elementary-school program with teaching certification which met the state certification requirements. We met the requirements simply. Since we don't have a credit system or examinations or grades or lectures, we met the requirements by whatever devices seemed appropriate to us. When the certification people wanted ten credits in the philosophy of education, we did some counting. One hundred and twenty credits are usually given for a B.A. degree. We divided 120 by four for each of the years, which is 30 a year, we divided that by three, since we only work in three areas or courses at one time. We then had 10 credits in philosophy for whatever the student did for a third of her time in the philosophy of education. That met the requirement, and we called whatever we did in the philosophy of education by the correct title. The work in philosophy and history of education was brilliant in the case of some of the students.

One study project might deal with the place of women in the history of the arts and educational institutions, or with the beginning of the women's college movement. There were many original, fascinating projects which our students did in courses they designed with the help of the faculty. These were much more illuminating to them than the alternative of taking the usual education courses given in colleges of education in order to meet the credit requirements. We took the world as our campus, the full panorama of all art forms as possible content, and went at it. The teachers who came out of that program, whatever virtues or defects they had, had an enthusiasm and a quality of sensitivity to the arts and to children the like of which I have seldom seen in schools, colleges, and teacher-education programs.

We did another thing which might interest you. We decided that somebody should do something about the M.A. This was before the Master of Arts in Teaching became as popular a solution for secondary-school teaching as it later became. We called a conference of colleges in our neighborhood along the eastern seaboard to talk about the M.A. as a teaching degree. The people who came made the usual negative remarks about the Ph.D. and what a useless teaching degree it was and agreed that the universities should take the leadership in moving the degree into a better situation than the one that now exists. But we concentrated on the M.A., and we accepted the proposition that the M.A. was a perfectly good degree and, if properly treated, could become the mark of a college graduate who is skilled in teaching and deeply aware in scholarly terms of the function of the scholar in society, particularly as a scholar-teacher in the secondary schools or in whatever other part of the educational system the student wished to enter after earning the M.A. degree.

The degree we worked out, which seems to me to be applicable to the problems of chairmen of departments of English, is based on the conception central to the Sarah Lawrence style of education: that there should be no formal requirements, no grades, no exams, no prerequisites, and no required subjects in order to graduate. We assigned the entering graduate student to a given faculty member, and in a fairly elaborate prequestionnaire—a general, open-ended set of questions which we gave to the entrant —we found out as much as we could about what that person had done.

In the arts, quite often we had applicants who had decided to become teachers after practicing one of the arts for several years and wanted to come to us in order to take the degree in congenial circumstances. We found that it was perfectly possible to make an arrangement whereby the student, having applied to us, was asked to describe the goals and interests he or she had in mind, what the student had done in literature, what was in the record aside from courses taken and credits won, and to ask the applicant to suggest what kind of curriculum would be appropriate. We then assigned that person to a faculty member who agreed to accept the student, and the two of them would work out a year's program (or a year and a half, or two years, or whatever seemed the appropriate length of time) of studies, activities, and experiences, off and on the campus, which seemed appropriate for that person. This would, of course, involve work in the schools. If the person were going into secondary school, this would take an extended period of three or four months at some point in the year and a half as a normal part of the graduate student's experience.

We found that the relationship between the person concerned with literature and the person involved in the other art forms was such that quite often a student who had never written for dance would find himself or herself writing short poems to be danced or to be set to music by local composers, writing scenarios for plays, and collaborating with others in doing small theater pieces—in general moving past the technical notion of preparation for teaching as a matter of going through surveys of English literature and covering the periods of the field. Our literature program was based in the experience of writing, reading, and learning. The course content in covering materials important to one's preparation for teaching in the high schools was done on an individual basis, and students worked in courses which seemed appropriate to that purpose. But mainly the reading would be done by individual choice and in small groups by people who were preparing themselves together to become teachers.

I suggest that something of this sort could become the basis of a serious experimental program in many departments of English. It is not necessary to change the entire departmental structure to do it. It is possible to do this kind of thing with those students who would like to try it that way, and with those faculty members who would like to join them. This style of education is a little rangier and harder to administer in practice than the conventional ones. The departmental chairman who does not feel temperamentally tuned to it should not try, nor should chairmen of departments or other educational administrators push people into things they are not interested in doing. The system won't work that way.

I conclude my survey of practical suggestions with some brief remarks about another set of personal experiences which may have some relevance to your present discussions. In a six-week period as visiting professor at the University of New Mexico, I came to know the members of the English department quite well, along with the members of the university's American Studies Program, whose director is a brilliant young scholar, Joel Jones. As you know, such programs vary widely in content and style from one university to another. American Studies at Yale is different from something called by the same name at Berkeley.

I learned that at the University of New Mexico, the title American Studies gave an opportunity to educational planners, who in this case were imaginative and enterprising, to do any number of things which liberated the graduate student and prospective teacher into a field in which he could be called a specialist. At the same time, this did not confine him to a set of studies which made the specialism specialist in the bad sense. One can think of the total American culture historically, politically, esthetically, or any other way, and a whole series of appropriate intellectual activities can be invented for M.A. and Ph.D. students entering American Studies which they would not be able to engage in if this were a program for a Ph.D. in English. I argue that it is high time we shifted radically from the obsolete English Department conception of the Ph.D. in English to something closer to the University of New Mexico idea of American Studies.

I was interested in reading Richard Poirier's piece in the *ADE Bulletin* in which he raises the question, "What Is English Studies, And If You Know What That Is, What Is English Literature?"[1] I found the piece badly argued and confusing but it made a final point which, although it does not follow from the arguments made in the body of the article, seems to me to be the most important point to consider in the whole matter of reorganizing English Studies. "English Studies," says Poirier, "must come to grips with different languages of popular culture, with newspapers, political speeches, advertising, conversation, the conduct of the classroom itself. Until proven otherwise, none of these need to be treated as if it were necessarily simpler than any other or than literature. The same hard questions for all, as Richard Hoggart would have it. Far from meaning that English Studies would thereby slight what it calls literature in order to expand operations, what I propose would give literature a real fighting chance to prove, if intensely enough encountered, not its cultural superiority, whatever that might mean, but its superiority as a training ground for all other efforts in the struggle for expression." (p. 3)

I would like to agree with Mr. Poirier and take the idea one stage farther. It is a time when students in every part of the university are looking for ways in which their intellectual interests can be seriously aroused and sustained. I mean not only the activist students who are already intellectually mobilized and at work on studies in the social sciences and humanities which are useful to them in their action programs. I mean the students who feel vaguely uneasy about having no intellectual interests and can find no way of getting them in the endless expanse of required courses they see ahead of them as they credit their way to a degree. Many of them found themselves discussing serious political, social, and educational issues for the first time at the Moratorium Day on 15 October 1969, others found themselves involved in Earth Day on 22 April 1971, and thousands of others became involved in the campus strikes following Cambodia and Kent State. The rest of the time through the rest of the universities there are very few places where the most serious issues of contemporary life, as they are to be found in contemporary literature, theater, poetry, newspapers, magazines, television, radio, can ever be encountered in compelling form.

What better place could there be for dealing with these issues than the English department, conceived not as a department for covering the materials of the traditional curriculum in English, but as an intellectual and cultural center for the whole campus where experimental courses, study projects, expressions of the rock culture, film reviews, student mimeographed magazines for poetry, short stories, criticism, scenarios for ballet, theater pieces, novels, filmmaking, mass meetings on the role of the arts in stopping the war—anything which seemed like a good idea—could be generated for all who cared to come, for credit or not for credit. If English Studies is translated to mean studies and activities in the use of language as expression and in the development of sensibility, or studies in the way language becomes the living tissue which holds the arts and the human community together, then all this is indicated and more besides. There are precedents for this, including the famous one at San Francisco State, where Caroline Shrodes has played so magnificent a part in creating new forms of teaching and learning through the expansion of the idea of the English department into the idea of a cultural center.

Which brings me to my final point. There are a great many academic professionals on the campuses who consider any effort to move past the conventions and formalities of the past into an inventive educational future as pandering to ephemeral student interests or betraying the tradition of scholarship. My view is that that is what we are now doing all the time— betraying the tradition of scholarship.

I turn to another professional, this time a professional critic who has taught for a time in American universities, A. Alvarez. In a review of the new book by Nabokov and Appel, *The Annotated Lolita*, Alvarez writes about the present difficulty of the English professor. "Teachers of literature," says Alvarez, "are fighting a losing battle against the indifference of their students, who believe, like all students, that wisdom begins with them. But, unlike most earlier generations, they also think themselves revolutionary, which means they no longer have time for the past." Eliot, Coleridge, Shakespeare, Alvarez says, have become irrelevant in their eyes. "In comparison, real literature is what comes at them through a P.A. system and a haze of potsmoke, to the sound of finger bells and guitars. In the circumstances, the only hope of their professors is to try to keep up to date, and tempt the kids at least into the near past with works that were outrageous when the professors themselves were students."[2]

Alvarez is dead wrong; partly right, but finally dead wrong. He should go to Central Park in New York to the Shakespeare Festival's free performances of Shakespeare and see the young people there enjoying the plays. You do not have to lure the students into the near past to the favorites of the professors. Why should the students be lured there in any case, merely to meet authors who were at one time outrageous? The students have their own outrageous authors, and they are going to get more. Some of the students themselves are already outrageous authors.

When the students demand relevance in their studies, they are not demanding merely that their professor deal with current issues, with contemporary situations, authors, and crises. They are looking for intellectual excitement and a feeling that what they are studying genuinely matters.

They will respond to Hobbes, to Plato, to William James, to Freud, to Dickens, to Balzac when they are taught in such a way that the true meanings of the works are not destroyed by analyses, interpretations, and literary fingering of all kinds, and they can get close to the authors and the ideas for themselves. They cannot respond when the mode of response is already conditioned by the enforcement of the conventions which make all reading a preparation for a test and all attendance at class the occasion for listening to explanations and descriptions of what the academic profession in literature thinks all young people should know about all authors.

I propose, then, that we recognize the fact that we are teaching in a revolution and that the revolution is a real one demanding radical changes in order to meet a real situation. If we do not do the teaching which the students are either demanding or ignoring, they will learn in their own ways, and those ways will take them farther and farther from the academy and its collection of museum items mounted in display cases called the syllabi of English departments. Where they will go is to some degree predictable, and I cannot help feeling that at this point it will be a better place than the one they have been in for so many years.

Notes

[1] *ADE Bulletin*, No. 25 (May 1970), pp. 3–12.
[2] A. Alvarez, "Tale of a Tub for Our Time," *Saturday Review*, 13 June 1970, p. 27.

Interdisciplinary Studies: Variations in Meaning, Objectives, and Accomplishments*

Henry Winthrop

Department of Interdisciplinary Social Sciences
University of South Florida

I. Introduction

IN THE present paper I propose to deal with one type of interdisciplinary curriculum, which can be built upon *material borrowed from related departments*, whether or not the specialists in these related departments choose to teach the interdisciplinary course offerings so constructed. By this remark I am recognizing the fact that occasionally a generalist who does not hold a Ph.D. in any of the specialized fields that have made a contribution to the construction of such interdisciplinary course offerings may be the one to take on the responsibility for teaching the courses so constructed, rather than a specialist from one of the contributing areas. The important thing about the interdisciplinary curriculum I propose to discuss shortly is that its goal is to be "responsive to the needs of American society and to our schools." The chief mode of responsiveness by our schools should be, I venture to guess, the devising of curricula that are "relevant" (a much abused word) to the issues of our time. If we wish to be realistic we should recognize that most of our contemporary issues are, in fact, interdisciplinary. They are interdisciplinary in the sense that the findings, methods, and occasionally the values (as in economics) of several of our traditional academic disciplines have a significant, even though partial, contribution to make toward the understanding and resolution of these same issues.

The particular type of interdisciplinary curriculum that, I believe, will satisfy the intent of the second conference is at the present time the major portion of the course content of the Department of Interdisciplinary Social Sciences of the University of South Florida. The courses in that department have several objectives. One of the objectives is to marry questions of social fact and theory, on the one hand, to questions of social value and the formulation of a public philosophy, on the other. Since the intent was to *relate* questions of fact to questions of value, via some of the social problems of the American community, we took pains not to *confuse* facts with

---

* An address to the South Florida ADE Seminar on 12 Feb. 1972. Reprinted from *ADE Bulletin*, No. 33 (May 1972), pp. 29–41.

values. What we wanted was a partnership rather than a case of mistaken identity. As a result of the effort to unite questions of fact and questions of value in dealing with the needs of American society, the interdisciplinary curriculum of the Department of Interdisciplinary Social Sciences captured the interest of English and humanities majors, as well as social science majors, for whom that curriculum was, of course, primarily intended. It therefore served potentially to provide bridges linking not only these three areas but others besides. This curriculum is an ongoing one at the present time, and therefore a discussion of its philosophy and its content will be revelant to persons interested in interdisciplinary innovation. In the first part of this paper, I propose to deal with that curriculum, first, by citing the issues and needs of American society with which our courses deal; second, by describing the sense in which the term *interdisciplinary* has been used in the curriculum of the Department of Interdisciplinary Social Sciences; and, third, by describing some of the thematic content of some of the different courses within that program.[2]

II. Issues and Needs

There are many socially significant problems, many important controversial issues, and many unrequited needs of the American community to which the interdisciplinary curriculum of the Department of Interdisciplinary Social Sciences is addressed. Only a few of these problems, issues, and needs can be dealt with in a relatively small curriculum serviced by only a few faculty members. However, it will increase the reader's understanding of the sense in which the innovative, interdisciplinary curriculum of the Department of Interdisciplinary Social Sciences tries to serve the needs of American society and the schools, if I present without comment a sample of some of the problems, issues, and needs taken up in our courses.[3]

Among these problems, issues, and needs are the following:

1. Automation and cybernation: their current and anticipated social, economic, and industrial effects;

2. Environmental pathologies of the technetronic civilization;

3. The quest for community, that is, the illnesses of the large-scale, industrialized urban center and some of the proposals for achieving authentic community in the sense of a philosophy of the good life and in the sense of physical design of community;

4. Forms of alienation in our techonological society;

5. The nature of the quest for personal identity and the cultural and social forces which tend to abort that quest;

6. The contemporary social problems created by the impact of science, technology, and invention in Western society;

7. Studies of the future and some of the problems with which this new field is beset;

8. The dimensions of value in a complex social

and technological milieu, and some of the relationships of the planning and policy sciences to these dimensions of value;

9. Modes of communication, their relationships to some of the issues in the social and behavioral sciences, and the factors obstructing or breaking down these modes of communication;

10. Some of the problems of contemporary American culture and some of the social and psychological factors that give rise to them;

11. The value patterns of modern technological societies and some of the existing proposals for world order that these patterns necessitate;

12. Some critiques of the social fabric of Western society and the variety of social and psychological causation used to account for existing forms of social pathology.

The preceding themes, then, constitute a sample of the concerns taken up in one or another of the interdisciplinary social-science courses in our Department of Interdisciplinary Social Sciences. They are set forth here in order to illustrate the innovative aspects of one type of interdisciplinary curriculum, one that falls easily within the purview of the interests of students specializing in literature and the humanities, in spite of the fact that the courses involved have been designed for social-science majors.

III. Meanings of the Word Interdisciplinary

In this section I propose to discuss briefly several of the meanings with which the term *interdisciplinary* is customarily invested. Thereafter I shall concentrate at some length upon the meaning we have attached to the particular bloc of course offerings within the Department of Interdisciplinary Social Sciences.

There are five fairly common uses of the term *interdisciplinary*:

1. the survey-type approach
2. the problem-orientation approach
3. the subject-matter approach
4. the field-theory approach
5. the General Systems Theory approach

The survey-type approach, which has been in use for more than fifty years, seeks to provide the student with a fuller grasp of the information and the theories that may be relevant to the understanding of a given problem, issue, need, or area of interest. It does this by making use of lectures from different, but traditional, academic specialties. The text that is usually employed for a survey-type course contains reading matter from the several different academic areas that are germane to the problems, phenomena, issues, needs, or interests which are the foci of attention. The survey course may be taught solo by a faculty member who is sufficiently familiar with the elementary materials employed to handle them adequately, even though he may be a specialist in only one of them. Or the course may be taught as a team venture, with different specialists being brought in at different times to lecture on the material which properly falls within their bailiwicks.

In the problem-orientation approach, information is drawn from several specialties, and a deliberate and original attempt is made by the instructor to show the bearing of these different selections on the genesis of the problem, the various social expressions of the problem, and the selection of an optimal solution for that problem from a set of solutions that have been proposed by experts. In addition, attention will also be focused upon other problems generated by the problem of direct concern, that is, the problem which constitutes the lecture theme itself. Finally, the relationship between questions of social value and the solutions proposed for dealing with the problem in question are highlighted by the instructor.

In the subject-matter approach to interdisciplinary study the concern tends to be a fairly abstract one, interesting in its own right. Thus a group of researchers or specialists may be interested in obtaining a unified picture of an area of concern to which, let us say, some of the different social sciences are relevant. They will therefore have different specialists in these same social sciences report on what their specialties have to say about the area of concern and, in addition, what the relationships of these specialties are to each other with reference to the area of concern.

Let me provide a concrete example. When the Viking Fund was interested in the very general theme of "interdisciplinary integration in the human or man sciences," they funded the editing of a book by John Gillin.[4] This book brought together the thinking of a number of specialists in anthropology, psychology, and sociology, in relation to the general theme. Most of the chapters in this volume also concentrated on the relation of pairs of these disciplines to one another, where the pair itself had a bearing on the general theme. For these three social sciences there were, of course, three such pairs. A second example of the subject-matter approach is the work of George Katona, who has been trained in both economics and psychology.[5] Katona has attempted to analyze various types of economic behavior by viewing such behavior alternately from the theoretical standpoints of economics and psychology. The types of behavior to which Katona addressed himself were consumer behavior, particularly spending and saving; business behavior, particularly production and pricing; and behavior during periods of economic fluctuation, such as inflations and business cycles.

In the field-theory approach the term *interdisciplinary* entails the effort to find a common set of abstractions that will apply to several systems— e.g., the psychological system, the social system, the personality system, and so forth. Grinker's well-known volume is an example of approaches of this sort.[6] In this context the concept of a "system" refers to an effort to find a common language for scientifically organized sets of observations concerning aspects of human behavior that can be segregated intellectually from the total manifold of human behavior, where the segregation will yield results that are scientifically fruitful. Furthermore, the "systems" under study can be applied to individual behavior, in contrast to aggregate or mass behavior.

The most scientifically respected, most technical, and most fruitful use thus far of the term *interdisciplinary* has been in the approach of General

Systems Theory. Here the basic effort is to develop mathematical models that will apply to two or more traditional fields, in the social sciences alone or among any set of traditional disciplines no matter where located. The yearbooks of the Society for General Systems Research publish work in this vein.

The preceding, then, are five of the more common meanings attached to the term *interdisciplinary*. In the next section we shall expand more fully on the problem approach and, in passing, contrast it with the survey-type approach.

IV. Characteristics of the Problem Approach

The sense in which the term *interdisciplinary* has been applied to the bloc of courses in the Department of Interdisciplinary Social Sciences has invoked the *convergence* concept of the term *interdisciplinary*. By the convergence concept I refer to the following basic considerations:

> 1. A problem or phenomenon under study possesses aspects that are *customarily* dealt with separately by different academic specialties.
>
> 2. Information is drawn from these separate specialties that sheds some light on the problem under review.
>
> 3. An attempt is then made to show not only the relationship of the segments of information used to one another but—what is more important—an attempt is made to show also the sense in which all the information selected "converges" on an effort to understand the problem or phenomenon as fully as possible.
>
> 4. An effort is made to bring out the sense in which the problem under focus is related to other important problems and phenomena generally thought of as quite independent of one another. One major task in this fourth step is to show that we are really dealing with an envelope of problems.

This last step is the most significant aspect of the convergence approach and I have used it in several principal ways in my book, *Ventures In Social Interpretation*.[7] For instance, one of the themes of this volume is that many of our social pathologies are part of the social costs of rampant and unregulated urbanization and industrialization. These two forces, together with others like technological development, help to create these social pathologies, which can be regarded as a nest of contemporary problems to be liquidated. But there are relationships among these pathologies and among the effects they produce. As a result, the pattern of these relationships becomes exceedingly complex and very difficult to understand. One can proceed in the direction of mastering the complexity by analysis and planning or by trying to reduce the complexity of modern life, hoping thereby to retain its leading benefits while sloughing off many of its attendant social pathologies.

In the fourth step of the convergence approach we can therefore proceed in one of two alternative directions. On the one hand, we can try to show (a) the relationships of these pathologies to industrialization, urbanization, and advancing technology, (b) the relationships of these pathologies to each other, and (c) the relationship of planning and policy considerations to the grasping of the social complexity we have produced and to the liquidation of these pathologies themselves. On the other hand, we can try to show how these pathologies might be eliminated, not by trying to grapple with the social complexity we ourselves have produced, but rather by trying to reduce that social complexity itself. One method for achieving the latter objective is to suggest modes of community life that will prevent the appearance of the types of social complexity that are now headaches for Western man, while retaining all the benefits and advantages of large-scale, urban living. The preceding considerations constitute the framework for the fourth step of the convergence approach when this approach is used in relation to the task of grappling with those social ills that are the result of the unnecessary, institutional complexities of our lives. Quite obviously, the convergence approach will take on different forms of expression and procedure when we are dealing with a different focal problem.

A simpler but somewhat amusing example of the convergence approach was provided by John Fischer, while discussing in his column in *Harper's* the attributes of a modern university that would justify the statement that the education it offered was truly relevant to the modern world.[8] Fischer calls such a university *Survival U*. His example is so apposite and so profoundly perceptive that I will quote it in full at this point.

Another case study will analyze the proposal of the Inhuman Real Estate Corporation to build a fifty-story skyscraper in the most congested area of midtown Manhattan. If 90 per cent of the office space can be rented at $12 per square foot, it looks like a sound investment, according to antique accounting methods. To uncover the true facts, however, our students will investigate the cost of moving 12,000 additional workers in and out of midtown during rush hours. The first (and least) item is $8 million worth of new city buses. When they are crammed into the already clogged avenues, the daily loss of man-hours in traffic jams may run to a couple of million more. The fumes from their diesel engines will cause an estimated 9 per cent increase in New York's incidence of emphysema and lung cancer; this requires the construction of three new hospitals. To supply them, plus the new building, with water—already perilously short in the city—a new reservoir has to be built on the headwaters of the Delaware River, 140 miles away. Some of the dairy farmers pushed out of the drowned valley will move promptly into the Bronx and go on relief. The subtraction of their milk output from the city's supply leads to a price increase of two cents a quart. For a Harlem mother with seven hungry children, that is the last straw. She summons her neighbors to join her in riot, seven blocks go up in flames, and the Mayor demands higher taxes to hire more police. . . .

Instead of a sound investment, Inhuman Towers now looks like criminal folly, which would be forbidden by any sensible government. Our students will keep that in mind when they walk across campus to their government class. (pp. 20–22)

In this example we see with conspicuous clarity one of the major functions indicated for the fourth step of the convergence approach, namely, pointing out the extent to which different social pathologies or problems, usually thought of as independent, are really deeply related to one another. One must note that the *relating* operations in the passage quoted are above and beyond the mere gathering of information from several specialties. These relating operations are among the functions of the instructor, and the flexibility with which they can be handled opens the door to creative and innovative teaching on his or her part. It is here that we can see why the survey type of course—which is what most people mean when they use the term *interdisciplinary*—is not truly interdisciplinary at all. Information gathered eclectically for a survey course or for a book of readings is not information that has been related in the convergence sense of the term "interdisciplinary." It is taking an inordinately long time for academics to realize that there is nothing at all interdisciplinary in the survey-type approach. There is no gainsaying the value of being intellectually eclectic. But to be eclectic is not the same thing as being "interdisciplinary" in any sense of the term.

One should also note, in addition, that since the convergence approach is problem-oriented, the person who uses it may not be a specialist in any field at all. To be a specialist is to be subject-oriented, not problem-oriented. That is precisely why specialists approve of survey-type courses and call them interdisciplinary. But they are confusing eclecticism with intellectual integration.

V. Practitioners and Advocates of the Convergence Approach

A number of distinguished and activist social critics and reformers in this country have recognized the practicality and necessity of a convergence stance in educational matters, as well as the potential of the convergence-type approach for conveying a fuller understanding of our complex social problems and issues. Among these individuals are Ralph Nader and John Gardner, as well as the active leadership of such organizations as Common Cause, The National Urban Coalition, The Center for The Study of Responsive Law, The Citizens for Local Democracy, and many others. Ralph Nader in particular has made practical use of the convergence approach in two fundamental ways: (1) in attacking social and administrative abuse and neglect he has made his work on behalf of the public interest most significant by being cross-disciplinary in his approach; and (2) he has reiterated his conviction that there can be no meaningful understanding of our difficult social problems and no effective solution of them without making explicit the value goals we hope to achieve and allowing these goals to constrain somewhat the direction of our efforts. In a recent article discussing the rise of student Public Interest Research Groups (PIRGs)—groups of students working on environmental, consumer, property-tax, housing, and municipal-government problems—Nader noted that such groups provide students with an opportunity to combine their studies and extracurricular interests with training in recognized community problems.[9] He went on to remark:

> For too many years, millions of college students have dissipated their energies on courses and subjects that bored them because of their remoteness from the realities of the times or their lack of pertinence to the great public needs that knowledge should recognize. Boredom or lack of motivation continues to plague

campuses across the country in a massive epidemic of wasted talents. What students are beginning to experience is that they get a more thorough education in their field of study if they can work on investigating and solving problems that challenge both their minds and their sense of values.

This is the appeal of the PIRG idea. It provides a continuing opportunity for students to connect their growing knowledge to public problems and solutions in the society. Science and engineering students can work on pollution prevention projects that challenge their technical knowledge and their sense of what science and engineering should be doing for human betterment. Political science and economics students will be able to test textbook principles in the context of everyday consumer or governmental problems and develop a deeper understanding of factual and theoretical research that relates to people. (p. 11)

In these remarks we can see clearly not only the interest of Nader and the PIRGs in convergence-type analysis and in the honest expression of the values that will guide research but also the awareness of the fact that to cope successfully with the public interest demands always that we recognize ourselves to be dealing with an envelope of problems in exactly the sense emphasized in John Fischer's example of The Inhuman Real Estate Corporation, which wished to build a fifty-story skyscraper in the most congested area of midtown Manhattan.

It should not be assumed that the convergence approach to interdisciplinary studies is limited to intelligent activists like Ralph Nader or John Gardner. We find the recognition of the usefulness of the convergence approach in academic scholarship as well. Thus when Ben Seligman wrote his distinguished volume on the theme of automation and cybernation and their social and economic effects, he remarked in the Preface:

The writing of this book, which has absorbed the largest part of my free time during the last three years, represents fundamentally an exercise in what is now called "interdisciplinary research." It is a study not only of the technology of automation but also of its economic, social, psychological, and philosophical implications as well. There was no intent to trespass as a stranger upon the domain of disciplines outside the realms of technology and economics, yet I feel strongly that any social scientist must use the materials of other disciplines if his own analysis is not to flounder. I have therefore searched diligently all the social science literature for guides and insights that might prove useful in grasping what automation is doing to our civilization. I am convinced that, in the study of our new technology, interdisciplinary considerations are essential.

The social scientist must deal with such problems as with a palimpsest. He pulls back the upper layers of his subject to expose the fragmentation of work, the rise of the specialist, the final victory of technicism. These developments are reflected in the positive stress that modern science and technology place on process—how a thing is done—rather than on normative criteria. Seldom is the question asked, "Why?" It seems to the practitioner of modern technology an unmeasurable query devoid of meaning, because, in our advanced technological culture, what is relevant can be only something that is measurable, quantifiable. Under such a regime there is no need to inquire after human ends and human purpose.[10]

Readers of Seligman's volume will have little difficulty in recognizing that it has been executed in the spirit of what we have described as the convergence approach. They will also note throughout its insistence on the meaninglessness of discussing the social and economic effects of technology

—whether automation or other inventions—without invoking questions of social value and personal morality, or, in Seligman's own phrase, "normative criteria."

VI. The Thematic Content of a Sample of Currently Offered Convergence-Type Courses

A somewhat sharper focus can be brought to bear upon the actual expression of the convergence-type approach to interdisciplinary endeavor if we list some of the Social Science Interdisciplinary (SSI) courses now offered in the Department of Interdisciplinary Social Sciences of the University of South Florida and, at the same time, note briefly some of the content of the courses so listed. For this purpose the brief descriptions of the potential content of the four courses shown below will serve to clarify somewhat the nature of the themes involved in the convergence approach. I have used the phrase "potential content" to refer to a pool of themes only *some* of which are selected for classroom treatment in any quarter. Since the selection will vary from quarter to quarter, almost all of the themes in the pool will receive classroom recognition and treatment sooner or later.

The courses in question are the following:

A. "Community Planning" (now called "The City of Man")

A sample of problems dealt with: (1) the meaning of community, (2) physical pathologies of the modern large-scale urban center, (3) social pathologies associated with urban living, (4) urban housing problems, (5) proposed new concepts of community, (6) proposed new forms of town planning and community formation, (7) new technologies for small-scale community living, (8) new tools for retaining the amenities of the big city in the small-scale decentralized community, (9) planning techniques for community, e.g., input-output analysis, aggregative and intersectoral planning. (See the outline of this course below.)

B. "Social Issues of Our Time"

1. *Automation and Cybernation*

(1) Automation and cybernation and their social and economic effects, (2) the implications of the information-processing revolution for changes in social and cultural life styles, (3) the implications of teaching machines for education, (4) the new consequences for man-machine relationships of computer technology, (5) the problems of artificial intelligence, (6) "Shaky," the robot who is expected to excel man in his cognitive functions in ten to fifteen years, (7) mankind's adaptations to a workless world.

2. *Total Environmental Management*

(1) Soil degradation and destruction, (2) radiation pollution and genetic damage, (3) air and water pollution, (4) the poisoning of edible species in the life cycles supplying men with food, (5) nutritional pathologies stemming from industrialism, and protest against them arising from the consumer movement, (6) dangerous hard goods, dangerous toys, etc., (7) conventional and nonconventional forms of waste, (8) technological waste and its measurement, (9) pharmacology, materia medica, and iatrogenic

diseases in the metropolis, (10) agricultural waste, (11) the effects of industrial waste on flora and fauna in the environment.

C. "Human Relations and Productivity" (This course should properly be named the *Social Impacts of Science and Technology*)

1. *Social Effects of Science and Technology*

Demographic problems, food problems, resource problems, problems of capital-goods distribution, energy problems.

The effects of the problems just mentioned on social, economic, political, and cultural change.

2. *Importance of Studies of the Future on Policy Formation*

What is futuristics? Advances in the sciences that will completely alter the profiles of human development. Individuals and agencies concerned with studies of the future.

Typical problems: the sociology of the future;[11] methods of future forecasting; achievements and errors; future studies and policy formation in government, internationally and in industry; waste as a problem in futuristics; the "system break" and its effects on society; "future shock" and its effects on human adaptability and stress.

D. "Psychology and the Social Order"

The quest for personal identity in modern mass society, the problems of mass culture and mass education, the problems of alienation and anomie in the twentieth century, psychological factors in political and industrial conflict, man versus the machine in modern life.

The contributions of humanistic psychology, existential psychology, phenomenological psychology, and ethnomethodology. Critiques of monolithic behaviorism, sensitivity training, "scientism" in psychology, clinical appoaches that demand adaptation to one's milieu, social criticism and community mental health, the problems of the intellectually marginal in mass society, adaptation problems of the gifted, brainwashing and its cryptic forms in mass society, social conditioning via advertising, etc.

The work of Maslow, Allport, Erikson, Berne, Fromm, Rollo May, Meerloo, Vance Packard, Garfinkel, Goffman, etc.

The preceding four descriptions are to be taken as a sample only of the content of the convergence-type course. Materials and/or bibliographies for the remaining SSI courses are usually furnished to students enrolled in them.

How, in fact, is the content of a convergence-type course handled? This can best be understood, I believe, if I present the outline or synopsis of the actual themes covered in the presentation of one of these courses. For this purpose I shall choose the course entitled "The City of Man" (SSI-415).

Topical Outline of the Themes Taken Up in the Course Entitled "The City of Man"

1. *What Is Meant by the Term* Community?

(a) Tönnies' distinctions between a *gesellschaft* and a *gemeinschaft*, dwelling-group atmosphere.

(b) extensions of the meaning of the concept of community for a complex, technological milieu whose bureaucratic structures intrinsically promote alienation.

(c) ideas concerning authentic community from Utopians, from Prince Kropotkin (*Mutual Aid*), from Wilhelm Röpke and other decentralists, etc.

2. *The Pathologies of the Modern Community*

(a) *Social Pathologies*

Alienation, anomie, bureaupathosis, permanent identity crises, the sense of powerlessness, institutional and group fragmentation, group conflict based upon misunderstandings, the breakdowns, frustrations, and tragedies that accompany the social and economic complexities of the modern community, the blasé attitude (Simmel), decadence (Joad et al.), sensate pathology (Sorokin), etc.

(b) *Physical Pathologies*

i noise, congestion, stress, dirt

ii experimental and scientific evidence for the effects of urban stress, noise, congestion, etc.

iii air pollution

iv water pollution

v physical pathologies peculiar to an urban civilization: nutritional morbidities, esthetic blights, destruction of the environment, land mismanagement, soil misuse, transportation errors, agricultural tragedies, etc.

vi physical misdesign of the modern urban center, misuse of technology in relation to community health and needs, etc.

3. *Some Examples of Authentic Communities*

i medieval and nineteenth-century examples of authentic communities (Kropotkin's *Mutual Aid*)

ii the Hutterites

iii some classical utopian concepts of community

4. *The Spectrum of Community Formation*

i the homestead

ii the village or hamlet which is a satellite to a central governing unit

iii the communitarian colony

iv the intentional community

v the small decentralized community

vi the specialized community (the ideas of E. A. Gutkind, Julius Stulman, etc.)

vii the modern commune (youth communes, agricultural communes, Skinner's ideas and Twin Oaks, etc.)

viii the new European cities and new towns (Great Britain, Sweden, Finland, Germany, etc.)

ix urban renewal

x metropolitan and urban planning: philosophies, objectives, and results

xi aquatic communities: the sampan communities, Marinopolis, Hydropolis, the designs for aquatic communities developed by Buckminster Fuller, the Armstrong seadrome

xii the proposed, underwater cities, early experiments with Conshelf and Habitat, etc.

xiii new technologies for new terrestrial, urban communities: the proposed mid-Manhattan Geodesic Dome; the New Jersey Peneplain Megastructure; the Platform City; Swedish and Red Chinese mountain cities; the imagined Arctic city of Alert; new cities in deserts (Israel); developmental economic and social planning for the small-scale, industrial community (Staley, Richard Meier, etc.); Paul Goodman's ideas on community (*Communitas*); etc.

xiv Auroville—The World's First Planetary City

Auroville, near Pondicherry, India. Its philosophy (Sri Aurobindo), detailed description of its physical aspects and proposed institutions, planning by Roger Angier and French architects, its achievements to date, etc.

xv The Megalopolis and the Urban Region

xvi Ekistics, Ribbon Urbanism and Ecumenopolis: The City That Covers the Globe (Constantinos Doxiadis)

xvii The Scientific, Intentional Microcommunity (SIMC)

5. *Modes of Planning Relevant to Community Innovation and Redesign*

i aggregative, intersectoral, and input-output types of planning: values and defects

ii the Leontief Input-Output Model

iii Sadhana: the self-sufficient, decentralized community

iv for what do we plan?

6. *Paideia, Community, Technology, and Self-Development*

i authentic community and the promise of technology

ii reduction of social complexity, elimination of social pathology, maintenance of the credits of an urban civilization, and SIMC.

From the material presented in this section we can then see what types of themes are likely to be drawn upon for classroom discussion and treatment in an interdisciplinary social course of the convergence type. They are also, of course, the types of themes that generally reflect directly the kinds of problems for whose solution individual experts, governmental commissions, and research groups formulate proposals, policies, and plans. At the same time, the themes taken up serve to show that information, concepts, and quantitative procedures of analysis—where these are customarily regarded as being peculiar to different, traditional fields—may have to be drawn upon, if the theme is to receive adequate treatment.

Finally, from the synopsis or outline of the convergence-type course entitled "The City of Man"—a course that is currently devoted to (1) an examination of the undesirable features of the modern large-scale urban center and (2) an examination of the spectrum of proposals for community redesign—we can obtain a somewhat fuller notion of the convergence-type approach in action. The phrase "community redesign" in the present context refers to town or community planning. It also refers to a selection of those technologies that will guarantee the provision of those amenities, proprieties, and cultural advantages provided by the big city, while eliminating many of the physical and social disadvantages of everyday life in our metropolises, conurbations, and megalopolises. Finally—and this is the most important of all considerations concerned with social and community reconstruction—the phrase "community redesign" refers to the life styles desired by groups which seek more humane and more socially just modes of living together. This, in turn, implies that community redesign, in the physical sense, will have little importance unless those who are cooperating in the quest for community can provide clear answers reflecting a consensus on the question "What is the good life?"

VII. Blending Literature and Social Science into Convergence-Type Courses

The preceding section has concentrated on the convergence approach when the channel for viewing our problems and themes is almost wholly lodged within the social sciences proper. However, the potentiality of the convergence approach in higher education, for certain types of problems and themes, is greater within the realm of literature than it is within the confines of the social sciences themselves. One of the problems which, I believe, can be handled better within literature than within the social sciences is that of alienation in our time. There are several reasons why I believe that the teaching of literature would be more conducive to a theme of this sort than the teaching of the social sciences.

First, the theme of alienation allows one to shuttle back and forth between the novel and nonfiction, the former presenting the feel of the conditions of alienation, the second the actual conditions of alienation. Second, the novel provides the powerful emotional impact for the reader that the factual minutiae and theories of the social sciences cannot. A third consideration is that the emotional impact of the novel (or play) may prompt the reader to want to learn something of the genesis of alienation, the forms of its expression, the conditions that maintain it, and some of the contemporary proposals for eliminating or reducing it. However, once the imagination has been aroused by the novel or play, that same imagination, playing upon the factual and theoretical aridities presented by the social sciences, will succeed in accomplishing something special. It tends to invest any context of alienation described in the literature of social science with a measure of the feelings which were aroused by the novel that was first read or the play that was first attended. Fourth and last, the reader who has made the transition from the novel or play to some familiarity with the sociological, psychological, economic, and cultural conditions of alienation is likely to become quite knowledgeable about the theme of alienation. Once this knowledgeability has been achieved, he is like to convey some of his newly acquired understanding and emotional involvement to others with whom he comes into contact.

Alienation—which has been considered by many to be the most serious social problem of the twentieth century, precisely because individual and group misunderstandings and conflict flow from it—lends itself rather well, as I have already said, to study by the convergence approach. At the same time alienation has been an increasingly central theme in twentieth-century literature. For these reasons, I believe it will be of considerable value if I present a table showing several of the forms of alienation in our time, some of the novels that have dealt with those forms of alienation, in whole or in part, and some popular nonfiction sources that disclose factually aspects of one or more of these same forms of alienation. The teacher can then make use of the convergence approach by organizing his own reading and the reading assignments of his students in such nonfiction sources. By doing so he can facilitate the achievement of the fourth objective of the convergence approach. At the same time, such a teaching procedure will help to bring out the relationship of prevalent social values both to the forms of alienation in our time and to the solutions currently being proposed to dissipate some of these forms of alienation.

The choice of methods for achieving convergence-analysis treatment of alienation in the classroom will be one that the teacher will have to work out for himself. There are no courses in this sort of thing. But the individuality, insight, and innovative gifts of the teacher come to the fore at this point. If he is effective, dedicated, and insightful and, at the same time, truly and deeply concerned with the havoc alienation has wrought in the twentieth century, the convergence procedures he employs will set many of his students on fire, both intellectually and spiritually. I am using the term *spiritually* in the sense of the *felt* values toward which an individual may be drawn. If the teacher approaches the convergence task without real personal involvement or understanding or in some wooden routinized fashion, the results will be feeble, uninspiring, and irrelevant to the needs of American society. Such an aborted approach will simply provide new forms of boredom to which the student is exposed.

Some Forms of the Problem of Alienation and Some Novels and Nonfiction Sources Dealing with These Same Forms

Problem	*Illustrative Fiction*	*Popular Nonfictional Sources for Information on the Problem*
Political Alienation: in the form of corruption in our cities	*The Last Hurrah* by Edwin O'Connor	1. *The Shame of the Cities* by Lincoln Steffens 2. *Boss: Richard J. Daley of Chicago* by Mike Royko
Political Alienation: in the functioning of the democratic process	*The 480* by Eugene Burdick	*The Case against Congress: A Compelling Indictment of Corruption on Capital Hill* by Drew Pearson and Jack Anderson
Alienation in Education: in the form of the alleged irrelevance of modern education	*Up the Down Staircase* by Bel Kaufman	*Crisis in the Classroom* by Charles E. Silberman
Alienation of Man from Man: in the form of breakdowns in social responsibility in business	1. *I Can Get It for You Wholesale* by Jerome Weidman 2. *What Makes Sammy Run* by Budd Shulberg	1. *The Organization Man* by William H. Whyte, Jr. 2. *Life in the Crystal Palace* by Alan Harrington
Ethnic Alienation: in the form of indifference to genocide	*Exodus* by Leon Uris	*While 6 Million Died* by Arthur D. Morse

In the above table five forms of alienation are set forth, together with some novels that, in whole or in part, express these forms and some nonfiction sources that deal with these same forms of alienation. By extended reading of nonfiction materials, both popular material and work done by specialists, the teacher puts himself in a position to deal with any particuliar form of alienation through the convergence approach. The novel used can be the text in a course in literature, and the nonfiction material becomes the expanded reading assignment the teacher provides the students. It is natural for the teacher to be the guide in dealing with alienation because his wider experience and more extensive background facilitate the task of providing greater illumination for the theme of the novel. In this way the convergence approach lends itself to the actual classroom treatment of the interdisciplinary relationships between literature, on the one hand, and various social-science disciplines, on the other.

From the entries in the table, I think it will be clear that the convergence approach to interdisciplinary analysis will help make the theme and problems of alienation come alive—for both the teacher and the student. If one extrapolates to other themes which are dealt with in the American novel, it should be equally clear that the same illumination and enrichment are possible for other important social problems and issues and for many of the current needs of American society. Finally, it should be abundantly clear, I believe, that the desire of participants in the ADE interdisciplinary conferences to work out innovative relationships between the concerns of traditional departments and that of departments of English can be most cogently facilitated by interdisciplinary course offerings of the convergence type.

VIII. The Role of Values in the Social Sciences

In an earlier portion of this paper, I made the point that when dealing either with descriptions of social problems or solutions proposed for them, it is essential to recognize that certain values or goals are often implicit in the measures we take. For a good many social problems, because of ends that power groups seek to attain, the values entailed are often made perfectly explicit. The presence of value considerations in the contexts of study and research for that group of disciplines that seek to be value-free in inquiry is something of an embarrassment. However, to be troubled by the difficulty involved in dealing with the relation of fact or theory to value issues and to value judgments is not to deny that values are involved in describing or trying to solve a social problem. The issue, as it has been put traditionally, is that theory, methodology, and fact should not be interlarded with value considerations, sentiments, or unexpressed biases, since such adulteration would be the death blow to science, particularly social science. This research posture is very well taken and this professional fear is completely justified.

But these attitudes often pass over into either or both of two irrational and obstructive points of view. One irrational point of view is to eschew any intellectual concern over the relationship between facts and values and to refuse to recognize the role played by values in some of the social sciences. If this happens we find ourselves dealing with a position that refuses to traffic with value questions because of the deeply held conviction that they will adulterate the scientific enterprise. In short, we have to throw out the baby of value judgments and the roles they play in the social sciences, with the bathwater of potentially covert but illegitimate adulteration of fact by sentiments and biases of various sorts. The second irrational point of view the desire to achieve a value-free social science sometimes takes is the failure to recognize that we are making value choices even when we think we are not. We make them in some of the presuppositions of a given social science, whether pure or applied. We make them in the methods by which we attack a given research objective. And we make them in the interpretations we spin from the findings of the social sciences themselves. For reasons such as these, it is important to recognize that questions of fact and value are related, particularly in applied social research and in the formulation of a public philosophy. The only caveat we need consider is the very legitimate demand that cannot be reiterated too often: not to confuse the two types of consideration—facts and values—in our ongoing research.

In the convergence approach to interdisciplinary social science—and this approach is only one possible authentic meaning of interdisciplinary social science—we consciously direct our research, our conceptualizations and hypotheses, and our proposals for the solution of real problems toward a value-laden pole. But to do so need not generate a confusion between what are facts and what are values. There is simply no meaning to the request that we solve a social problem but exclude considerations of value. This is to ask not only for a logical absurdity but also for a practical one. A convergence approach, being substantially related to the policy and planning sciences, can hardly eschew values without becoming ridiculous and sacrificing its *raison d'être*. If we wish to meet the needs of American society and our schools and to restructure curriculum to meet both these objectives, the recognition of the value content of the social issues with which we are struggling is imperative.

Many distinguished social scientists have recognized this fact, among them the sociologist and economist, Myrdal; the chemist, philosopher, and professor of social studies, Polanyi; the sociologist, Alvin Gouldner; and many others. The contemporary British educator, M. V. C. Jeffreys, in his book *Personal Values in the Modern World,* has tried to show how important it is to face up to the role of values, both in the social sciences and in the broad canvas of public administration.[12] Sir Geoffrey Vickers, the British industrialist and management expert, corporation lawyer, and specialist in economic intelligence, has done likewise in *Value Systems and Social Process.*[13] Vickers has stressed particularly the role of values in ecological administration, in the planning and policy sciences, in governmental and institutional administration, and in many other areas. He has emphasized the folly of believing that we can exclude questions of value from such activities as choosing, planning, controlling, revaluing, appreciating, learning, and surviving—activities which enter into hundreds of problem-solving situations. In the senses stressed by the personalities I have mentioned, the convergence approach to interdisciplinary social science has a respectable background and it is the most natural approach for building bridges between applied social science on the one hand and literature and the humanities on the other.

The most fruitful recognition, however, of the importance of the convergence approach to an understanding of our social problems lies in the juxtaposition of two concepts mentioned previously in this paper: the concept of an "envelope of problems" and the concept of what Seligman has referred to in *Most Victorious Victory* as "normative criteria." This concept involves the recognition that if we seriously intend to deal with our social problems and issues, the solutions proposed for them must be immersed in given outlooks of social value, must reflect a clearly describable public philosophy, and must express a personal morality. The task of pushing forward the frontiers of knowledge and research in the social sciences—a task quite different from that of dealing with our social problems—must be value free. The task, however, of applying that knowledge to the solutions of our social ills must be value-saturated. There is no escape from this necessity.

Recent scholarly efforts along the lines of intellectual integration, accompanied by an attempt to apply the fruits of these efforts at integration to the solution of our social problems—which are now recognized as transnational—have resulted in putting an official stamp of approval on the convergence approach. Two of these recent developments are focal in the convergence approach. One is the establishment of a consensus concerning our interrelated problems. The set of such interrelated problems is called "The Maze of Continuous Critical Problems" (CCP's). This maze proves to be what I have earlier called an envelope of problems. The second focus on which a consensus has been reached is the conviction that if world society is not to experience breakdown and decline, then a planetary type of democratic guidance and control must be inaugurated. This guidance and control is referred to as normative planning. It is, of course, the expression of precisely those constraints of value-expectancy that Seligman had in mind when he spoke of invoking "normative criteria."

There are several scholarly and administrative groups throughout the world that have reached consensus on what the component problems are in "The Maze of Continuous Critical Problems." Among these component problems, as suggested by the scientist Hasan Obzekhan, we find the following:

hunger and malnutrition; large-scale underdevelopment; large-scale poverty; uncontrolled population growth and size; unbalanced population distribution; inadequate education; insufficient medical care; obsolete welfare practices; growing environmental pollution; spoilage of nature; wastage of natural resources; generalized underemployment; obsolete system of world trade; urban sprawl; decay of inner cities; inadequate transportation and communication; inadequate shelter; inadequate law enforcement; inadequate crime control; obsolete correctional practices; inadequate recreational facilities; discrimination vs. minorities; discrimination vs. the aged; increasing social discontent; crystallizing of youth alienation; growing participation crisis; growing administrative illegitimacy; inadequate conception of world order; insufficient authority of international agencies; polarization of military power, continued nuclear escalation and inadequate understanding of CCP's.[14]

A variety of methods are being developed and tried out for solutions to these nests or envelopes of problems. Most of the efforts at solution are coming from a group of the world's leading thinkers and informed administrators who have formed an organization called The Club of Rome.

An account of the envelope of transnational problems which the entire world now faces has been given by Aurelio Peccei.[15] Peccei is managing director of Italconsult, an Italian think tank, is vice president of Olivetti & Company, is president of FIAT Concord of Buenos Aires and Cordoba, is the most active leader of The Club of Rome, and is the author of several publications. In the work of The Club of Rome we see (1) a widespread recognition of the intellectual and social value of the convergence approach and (2) an unashamed demand that the solution to our problems be linked to questions of social value. In addition, the members of The Club of Rome reflect an outlook which insists that technology and the law be made to serve human purposes. At present, our values bend the energies and spirits of men to the imperatives of technology, to the anachronisms of the law, and to the ongoing but insightless behavior of many of our institutions. Above all, in the work of the members of The Club of Rome, the humanistic and humanitarian values of literature are regarded as the purpose of all human activity, with science and technology serving as handmaidens to the fulfillment of the humanist tradition.

The one sad note that must be emphasized for teachers in literature and the humanities is this: Although there is increasing recognition that our social difficulties and ills constitute a maze of interrelated problems, there is not a single novel that has yet been written—good or bad—to bring this situation to public consciousness and with some emotional impact. This interrelatedness has been emphasized to some extent in science fiction and for imagined nests of future problems. But, to the best of my knowledge, no flesh-and-blood novel has been written about the maze of our continuous, critical problems—the ones we are actually facing today. What a neglected opportunity a genre of this sort would be for contemporary literature! If modern literature continues to neglect this vein of social concern and if modern writers continue to turn their backs on the social responsibility to make this feature of our existence come to life for those who love literature, that would constitute a cultural tragedy of some sort. It is only through a literary treatment of this theme—probably demanding a trilogy—that the average reader can be given an emotional contact with the critical complexity of twentieth-century society and the tragedy and frustration that complexity is producing for individuals and groups. It is not too late for Western literature, particularly American literature, to develop a school and a genre to meet this crisis and this need.

The convergence approach offers one avenue interdisciplinary efforts may take to enrich the relationships among traditional academic disciplines. The survey approach is useful, but it is likely to be restricted to the presentation of a plurality of viewpoints rather than their unification. Of one thing we can be sure: we are not going to serve American society and American schools best solely through specialization. Specialization we must have, of course, and its major, professional importance in pushing forward the frontiers of knowledge does not require justification. But inasmuch as most modern social problems cut across our traditional specialties, being embedded in a matrix where different causative conditions are the province of different academic specialties, the interdisciplinary approach is basic. Cooperation is of the essence here. Since our tasks have to be problem oriented, let us not argue over the relative merits of generalists and specialists. Instead, let us ask how a full grasp of our current difficulties can be most easily expedited. In my father's house there are many mansions, and what takes place inside that house cannot be ascribed to the characteristic activity in only one of these mansions. We are here to work together, not to stake out claims of intellectual squatter sovereignty for different specialties.

Notes

1 The regional ADE Seminar, which took place under the auspices of the University of South Florida, was intended to focus on the important contributions that research in related fields can make to the improvement of interdisciplinary programs. The workshops in Florida concerned themselves with ways by which related departments can restructure curriculum to be responsive to the needs of American society and our schools.

2 The type of approach to interdisciplinary study emphasized here is found in a number of academic locations in the United States. One finds it, for instance, in the Department of Social Relations at Harvard, in some of the programs encouraged by The New School for Social Research and by Emory University, and, in the past, by some of Columbia University's programs in general education. One also finds many new colleges introducing interdisciplinary programs linking facts and values, but concentrating on environmental studies. One of these is Huxley College in the state of Washington. Each institution provides a variation in the way it proposes to link questions of fact with questions of value. I have chosen to make use of the curriculum in the Department of Interdisciplinary Social Sciences of the University of South Florida only because it is the one with which I am most familiar.

3 The Department also offers a fascinating bloc of interdisciplinary, area studies courses that are just as important as those to be described in this paper.

4 John Gillin, ed., *For a Science of Social Man* (New York: Macmillan, 1954).

5 *Psychological Analysis of Economic Behavior* (New York: McGraw-Hill, 1951).

6 Roy R. Grinker, *Toward a Unified Theory of Human Behavior* (New York: Basic Books, 1956).

7 *Ventures in Social Interpretation* (New York: Appleton-Century-Crofts, 1968).

8 An example of one explicit method of relating such materials was provided by John Fischer of *Harper's*. See "Survival U: Prospectus for a Really Relevant University," *Harper's*, Sept. 1969, pp. 12–22, esp. pp. 20–22.

9 "In the Public Interest: Student Activists," *The New Republic*, 19 Feb. 1972, pp. 10–11.

10 Ben B. Seligman, *Most Notorious Victory* (New York: The Free Press, 1966), pp. xi, xii.

11 For a general discussion of some of the typical problems in futuristics, see Henry Winthrop, *Vistas of the Future: Prospects and Problems* (Tampa: Univ. Of South Florida, 1971). The author has discussed some of the problems in the relatively new field of the sociology of the future. See Henry Winthrop, "Utopia Construction and Future Forecasting: Problems, Limitations, and Relevance," in *The Sociology of the Future*, ed. Wendell Bell and James A. Mau (New York: Russell Sage Foundation, 1971), pp. 78–105.

12 *Personal Values in the Modern World* (Baltimore: Penguin Books, 1962).

13 *Value Systems and Social Process* (Baltimore: Penguin Books, 1968).

14 "Toward a General Theory of Planning," in *Perspectives of Planning* (Paris: Organization for Economic Cooperation and Development [OECD], 1969).

15 "Where Are We? Where Are We Going?," *Successo*, Feb. 1970, pp. 119–26; "The Predicament of Mankind," *Successo*, June 1970, pp. 149–56; "How to Survive on the Planet Earth," *Successo*, Feb. 1971, pp. 129–36.

Appendix

THE resolutions and workshop reports which emerged from the ADE interdisciplinary seminars of 1971–72 make up the following appendix. The speeches printed in the text of this volume and the numerous position papers prepared for each seminar provided much of the material for the debate which led to the numerous recommendations for action. However, these ideas themselves evolved from a number of different sources.

Change in English

Report of the Grove Park Institute English Group*

In June 1969, the Consortium of Professional Associations for Study of Teacher Improvement Programs (an organization now defunct) sponsored a seminar in Asheville, North Carolina, at the Grove Park Inn. Representatives of twelve disciplines met to discuss the involvement of their professional associations in teacher preparation programs and to make recommendations to their colleagues and their associations. The group from English wrote a statement about the teaching and learning of English and made a series of recommendations. The Grove Park Statement follows:

I

For a decade most serious discussion of English as a school activity or subject—whether of the ways of teaching and learning that are appropriate in the English classroom, or of reform in the English curriculum, or of the training or retraining of English teachers—has been carried on within the assumptions held and the conclusions advanced by the members of the Basic Issues Conference (1958). But in recent years, for a number of reasons, the prevailing view of English has been seriously challenged; a new view has been demanded and has been slowly emerging.

Ten years ago it seemed to members of the Basic Issues Conference that the most important matter was to clarify the real nature of English, to rescue teachers from the confusion of materials and ends within which they were forced to operate, to reestablish English as a discipline fully as intellectual and systematic as, say, algebra or biology. English, it was then said, is language, literature, and composition—a tripod of sorts, though some may have felt that language in fact subsumed the other two members. Correspondingly, language was defined as the study of grammar(s); literature as the close critical analysis of literary texts, and composition as a combination study, including, first, the theory of effective writing as set down in rhetoric (generally of a new rather than old sort) and, second, the practice of writing or of rhetorical principles in the form of exercise themes. This clarification, it was thought, would make possible a curricular reform that would produce better-prepared students for the colleges, and, incidentally, improve also the school life even of the "non-college-bound."

This "content" curriculum, with its tripartite division into language, litera-

---

* Reprinted from *ADE Bulletin*, No. 22 (Sept. 1969), pp. 71–74.

ture, and composition; its residual but continuing concern for developing the skills of reading, writing, speaking, and listening; and its focus upon the academically able student provided the impetus for curriculum development in the 1960's. It is now fully challenged.

It has been challenged by the social revolution in American education during the latter half of the 1960's and by such important events as the Dartmouth Seminar of 1966, to name but two of the catalytic forces now operative. Now needed and now emerging is a new curriculum, a new sense of the relation of student and teacher in English. In this new view, the first concern is with the child's ability to use language comfortably and freely. English is less a subject for study than it is an activity, or a set of activities, more or less directed, more or less purposeful—activities that allow children to explore, to try out their various uses of language, from the everyday to the artistic, and to grow in and through such explorings, such tryings. Here English is a child reading, writing, talking; responding, expressing, explaining, sorting out; communicating, making contact, thinking. Here English is a new curriculum responsive to children as children, not as incomplete adults, which will be directed to the imagination as well as the intellect, which will provide occasion for comfortable, free use of the child's own language as the medium of learning (though not necessarily of instruction), and which will treat literary works as sources of pleasure as well as for exploration of human experiences. Here English is a new teacher aware of the social implications of English as a national language made up of many dialects, aware of and able to cope with the complex teaching of English in all aspects: listening, talking, writing, and reading.

English, in this view, is work organized toward truly humane ends: first, achieving the fullest possible growth in the individual child's expressive and responsive, as well as his intellectual, system; second, developing in children the ability and willingness to organize themselves for working together, for carrying on learning cooperatively rather than in rivalry.

Such a view has tremendous implications for all those in English from pre-K through Ph.D. It has immediate and urgent relevance to those planning school programs and those preparing English teachers. Such a view demands a sophisticated and careful response to the dilemma of schools and whole school systems which are under the impression that many of their children cannot read or write. Such a view demands a thoroughly conscious awareness of the social implications of English. Perhaps the profoundest implication stems from the deep involvement of a national language in social change and conflict. Such a view implies a new and serious commitment to seeking useful combinations and relationships with other disciplines and areas of learning activity. Such a view demands a sophisticated determination to explore a variety of ways to achieve change.

II

As an immediate step to demonstrate the commitment of the professional associations in English to the improvement of teacher-preparation programs, the Association of Departments of English, MLA, and NCTE are urged to sponsor a two-day fall conference of the chairmen of English departments and appropriate representatives of the colleges of education in the ten universities preparing the largest number of English teachers for the American public-school system. The goals of the conference will be:

1. To give national professional visibility to the urgent need for the improvement of teacher preparation programs in English.

2. To discuss with a limited number of consultants the substance and implications of theoretical statements of

key issues in the teaching and learning of English commissioned by the associations.

3. To develop specific strategies for involving community representatives in teacher-preparation programs.

4. To recommend specific program changes which can be studied by other departments training substantial numbers of English teachers for the schools.

5. To commit a small number of key professional leaders to the continuing examination and improvement of teacher-preparation programs in their own departments.

6. To provide a cadre of professional leaders who can conduct similar action-oriented conferences throughout the United States in cooperation with the associations.

III

If the English profession is to respond effectively to the current crisis in education, it must do more than simply call a conference. Fundamental change in the teaching of English, from kindergarten to Ph.D., is needed, is inevitable, and is already under way. This change is frequently radical, often takes place in an isolated segment of the curriculum, and has profound effects on other levels of the curriculum—sometimes rendering them irrelevant. The only question for the English profession is whether to resist change doggedly, to observe distantly, or to become involved in order to shape the change as intelligently as possible.

It is therefore recommended that the concerned associations—MLA, NCTE, IRA, and others—sponsor and support a joint Commission on Critical Issues in the Teaching of English, pre-K through Ph.D., made up of distinguished and committed English scholars, teachers, and education specialists. The director of this commission should be appointed and supported jointly by the various organizations, should be given a title such as Secretary for Teacher Education and should devote full time to critical matters of education. This commission should be given the charge of determining the critical areas where change is most rapidly occurring or most urgently needed, and, where appropriate, of persuading the profession to change. Such a commission might well begin its work with a series of small group meetings devoted individually to some of the most pressing issues (such as racism in the English curriculum, or the failures of an articulated curriculum, or the problems in teaching reading, or the irrelevance of Ph.D. programs).

But the Commission should look forward, after careful preparation, to a comprehensive Conference on Critical Issues in the Teaching of English. This Conference should take as its task a redefinition of the basic issues identified in the 1950's, a reconsideration of the answers, solutions, and programs developed in the 1960's, and recommendations for action and change for the English profession in the 1970's.

After the Conference, the Commission on Critical Issues in the Teaching of English, pre-K through Ph.D., should exploit every means at its command to spread and intensify the impact of its findings and recommendations on the profession, using the resources and conventions of the professional societies; spreading the word through speeches, discussions, debates; and sponsoring one or more publications carefully designed to interest and persuade readers within and without the profession.

IV

The professional associations, in cooperation with a major university committed to teacher education, should seek funding for the establishment of a Teacher Preparation Resource Center in English, which would:

1. Provide expert assistance to departments considering program changes.

2. Coordinate efforts to inform English departments about model programs, new directions in the teaching of English, etc.

3. Undertake research into the improvement of teacher-preparation programs and coordinate efforts to disseminate the results of such research.

4. Provide fellowship (pre- and post-doctoral) for research into the teaching and learning of English, for experiences in teaching English at various levels, and for curriculum development.

5. Conduct workshops, seminars, etc., for college, university, and school teachers of English.

6. Provide avenues for the involvement of community representatives, textbook representatives, student representatives, representatives of other disciplines and of educators at local, state, and national levels in the development of innovative teacher-preparation programs in English.

> James E. Miller, Chairman
> Sister Mary Edward Dolan
> Wallace Douglas
> Leo Fay
> Robert Hogan
> Alan Hollingsworth
> Paul Olson
> Michael Shugrue
> Sharon Morrison, Rapporteur

The Gull Lake Conference*

6–8 November 1969

Follow-up funds granted by the USOE after the Grove Park meeting of June 1969 permitted ADE and the Department of English at Michigan State University to call a two-day conference on teacher education from 6-8 November 1969 for thirteen chairmen of English departments preparing substantial numbers of secondary-school English teachers. Under the direction of Alan Hollingsworth, chairman of the department at Michigan State, these chairmen, aided by five Michigan State students and nine resource persons from the schools and professional associations, met at the Kellogg Foundation Conference Center at Gull Lake. The participants not only undertook a revision of the preliminary Grove Park Statement on English but prepared a second statement of their own. The new Report on the Relationship of School and College Departments of English emanating from Gull Lake and signed by the department chairmen who attended begins as a mea culpa but contains many strong recommendations.

* Reprinted from *ADE Bulletin*, No. 30 (Sept. 1971), pp. 12–13.

A Revision of the Grove Park Statement in English

For a decade most serious discussion of English as a school activity or subject—whether of the ways of teaching and learning that are appropriate in the English classroom, or of reform in the English curriculum, or of the training or retraining of English teachers—has been carried on within the assumptions held and the conclusions advanced by the members of the Basic Issues Conferences (1958). But in recent years, for a number of reasons, the prevailing view of English has been seriously challenged; a new view has been demanded and has been slowly emerging.

Ten years ago it seemed to members of the Basic Issues Conferences that the most important matter was to clarify the real nature of English, to rescue teachers from the confusion of materials and ends within which they were forced to operate, to re-establish English as a discipline fully as intellectual and systematic as, say, algebra or biology. English, it was then said, is language, literature, and composition—a tripod of sorts, though some may have felt that language in fact subsumed the other two members. Correspondingly, language was defined as the study of grammar(s); literature as the close critical analysis of literary texts; and composition as a combination study, including, first, the theory of effective writing as set down in rhetoric (generally of a new rather than old sort), and, second, the practice of writing or of rhetorical principles in the form of exercise themes. This clarification, it was thought, would make possible a curricular reform that would produce better-prepared students for the colleges, and, incidentally, improve also the school life even of the "non-college-bound."

This definition of English envisioned a curriculum divided into language, literature, and composition. It maintained a residual concern for developing the skills of reading, writing, speaking, and listening. And it focused on the academically able student.

It has now been challenged by the social revolution in American education during the latter half of the 1960's and by such important events as the Dartmouth Seminar of 1966, to name but two of the catalytic forces now operative. Now needed and now emerging is a curriculum in elementary and secondary schools based on a new conception of English. In this new view, the first concern is with the child's ability to use language comfortably and freely. English is not only a subject for study but also an activity, or a set of activities. Here English is a student reading, writing, talking; responding, expressing, explaining, sorting out; communicating, making contact, thinking. Here English is directed to the imagination as well as the intellect; provides occasion for comfortable, free use of the student's own language as the medium of learning (though not necessarily of instruction); and treats literary works as sources of pleasure as well as occasions for exploration of human experience. Here English is a teacher aware that the national language is made up of many dialects, aware of and able to cope with the complex teaching of English in all aspects: listening, talking, writing, and reading. This new view derives from a growing recognition that the United States is a multifaceted society rather than a single, well-integrated culture. English, in this view, is work organized by truly humane ends.

Such a view has important implications for all those in the field of English from pre-K through Ph.D. Such a view demands a sophisticated and careful response to the dilemma of schools and whole school systems which are under the impression that many of their children cannot read or write. Such a view demands a thoroughly conscious awareness that English is a national language deeply involved in social change and conflict. Such a view implies a new and serious commitment to seeking useful combinations and relations with other disciplines and areas of learning activity. For university and college departments of English especially, such a view requires that members of their faculties recognize many of their students as prospective teachers of English. If their students are to teach English differently, they must themselves be educated in new or revised undergraduate and graduate curricula which emphasize writing and the study of language as well as the study of literature and literary history; which encourage and enact new ways of teaching; and which permit prospective teachers to use language and to respond to literature freely, pleasurably, and with their own sense of discovery.

Vivian Robinson
Howard W. Webb
Maynard Mack
Donald Gray
Alan M. Hollingsworth
Charles Hagelman
Harry Finestone
George Worth
Sister Sheila Houle
S. K. Heninger, Jr.
Margaret I. Pfau
David F. Sadler

Gull Lake Report on the Relationship of School and College Departments of English

Departments of English have wide responsibilities and multiple roles. Some of these have been managed well, some less well. Some we have tended to ignore altogether. We have been gratifyingly successful in developing the research skills of our Ph.D. students. But we have not been as successful in equipping them to engage the interest and respond to the concerns of their students while conveying the content of our discipline.

In addition, most of us have ignored the problem of public education and the role of the department of English in the preparation of teachers. We have allowed to develop—have even encouraged—a gulf between ourselves and the teachers of English in primary and secondary schools and in community and junior colleges. When we find ourselves condemning the students who come to us unprepared, we must ask ourselves how *we* have prepared their teachers. Similarly, we have not put our wits to the problems of continuing education, although we insist on the truism that education does not and should not end with the B.A., M.A., or Ph.D. degrees or with teacher certification.

There are, of course, reasons for these failures: the inadequacies of financing, the lack of time and energy. Spreading oneself too thin and doing nothing well is a real danger. Nevertheless, we have set up and perpetuated a system in which the rewards of prestige, promotion, and money have gone almost exclusively to those engaged in research and graduate-school teaching. In an age of rapid change, this system becomes increasingly difficult to justify as we try to educate on higher and higher levels groups which we have previously neglected. As members of the profession we must accept our responsibility for the manner in which English is taught and learned from kindergarten through the Ph.D.

Although the English teacher today is charged with teaching the broad range of skills that deal with communication, these skills are, on the whole, quite different from those generally included in the preparation program of English teachers. As the Grove Park Statement implies, the so-called "new English" requires teachers whose knowledge and abilities go beyond subject-matter skills to embrace an understanding of children and their needs, interests, and concerns. Under these circumstances school and college English departments cannot continue to remain isolated from each other as if their goals were mutually exclusive. The needs and aims of our profession, the teaching of English, can best be met through increased cooperation among universities, community and junior colleges, and the public schools.

Many universities, of course, pride themselves on having "good relations" with the schools; such self-approbation is no longer sufficient. It is time for the universities and colleges to commit themselves, so far as their resources permit, to the successful development of cooperative relationships and programs with the public schools and with community and junior colleges. Such programs can provide important experiences for three groups:

—pre-service teachers, by supplying them with opportunities to observe and experience the problems of public-school teaching, and by allowing them, early in their undergraduate careers, to meet, enjoy, and learn to know children;

—university faculty, by giving them the understanding of public-school teaching problems that is essential if their goals as teacher trainers are to be consonant with those of the schools;

—experienced teachers, by making the concept of "continuing education" something more than the acquisition of extension-division credits, thereby acknowledging that the university responsibility to its students does not end with the granting of a degree.

Cooperation among public schools, universities, and community and junior colleges may be encouraged, without cost to departmental budgets, in any or all the following ways:

1. Arrangements for members of the department to visit local high-school English classrooms, make observations, and discuss common problems with high-school teachers.

2. Invitations for interested high-school teachers to attend college department meetings when teacher preparation is discussed; selected teachers might be asked to become permanent members of committees charged with designing programs for teacher preparation.

3. Conferences with recent graduates who are teaching in local public schools to share experiences and pool ideas about needed changes in the preparation of teachers.

4. Use of public-school teachers and supervisors and community- and junior-college teachers to teach or help to teach courses for undergraduates or for graduates seeking in-service credit.

5. Reciprocal use of English department members in community and junior colleges and in primary and secondary schools.

6. Acceptance of joint responsibility with schools of education for the supervision of student teachers.

7. Frequent invitations to supervisors and directors of instruction in neighboring districts to report on the department's program, the success of its graduates in public-school positions, problems of preparation, and so forth.

8. Establishment of local organizations among universities, junior and community colleges, and public schools to facilitate discussion of common problems and goals.

9. Encouragement of effective consultation with the community.

10. The use of selected undergraduates for tutoring in local schools.

Vivian Robinson
Howard W. Webb
Maynard Mack
Donald Gray
Alan M. Hollingsworth
Charles Hagelman
Harry Finestone
George Worth
Sister Sheila Houle
S. K. Heninger, Jr.
Margaret I. Pfau
David F. Sadler

The Bellwether Conference on Graduate Education*

In October of the following year, ADE and the University of Massachusetts sponsored the Bellwether Conference at Amherst to discuss the impact of the academic job market in the 1970's on graduate training in English. The agenda of this brief meeting included a paper by Edmond Volpe of the City University of New York entitled "The Failure of the Ph.D." (See ADE Bulletin, No. 27, Nov. 1970, pp. 4–10) and a report by Carl Woodring of Columbia University on the recommendations of the MLA Manpower Commission.

Professor Volpe's paper dealt with the need of the major universities to produce scholarly educators rather than research specialists. He argued that in the major cities, the education of ghetto minorities cannot be relegated solely to the community colleges; that the multiplicity of teaching responsibilities in most colleges and universities has made the traditional training in Ph.D. programs unsuitable for future teachers; that while academic scholarship must be preserved, it must be placed in a proper relationship to education in general; that graduate education must be aware of the needs of community-college students, since community colleges will in the immediate future be the major employers of Ph.D. candidates.

After discussing the Report of the MLA Manpower Commission (see PMLA, November 1970 and the Chronicle of Higher Education, *12 October 1970), and current statistics on the job market, the group passed the following recommendations:*

Recommendations

We recognize the collective responsibility of graduate English departments to train college teachers for all segments of higher education, and to this end, we urge:

1. That departments of English which now offer doctoral degrees undertake to reduce the number of students admitted to these programs.

2. That variations of standard graduate programs be developed.

* Reprinted from *ADE Bulletin*, No. 27 (Nov. 1970), pp. 2–3.

3. That institutions which plan to establish new programs leading to graduate degrees in the study and teaching of literature reconsider the necessity of these programs.

4. That a national conference followed by regional conferences be held between graduate departments and departments of four- and two-year colleges to determine requirements for undergraduate teachers of English.

Other Recommendations

1. That ADE issue about four times annually a job information booklet to which all departments of, or including, English will be invited to list specific vacancies or to describe the needs and situations in their institutions in not more than 150 words.

2. That regional MLA's be requested to hold conferences in the spring with attention to new Ph.D.'s seeking positions.

3. That no chairman require from an applicant before January 15 a final answer to an offer of a position without tenure for the following academic year; and that between January 1 and March 15, a final answer should be required no sooner than two weeks from the time of the offer.

In addition, twenty-five chairman pledged up to $100 to assist ADE in gathering and publishing information about the job market. The first national report on recruitment in English will be published late in February.

Participants

Adams, Richard	Tulane University
Allen, Jeremiah	Dean, College of Arts & Sciences, University of Massachusetts at Amherst
Altenbernd, A. Lynn	University of Illinois at Urbana
Appley, Mortimer	Dean of the Graduate School, University of Massachusetts at Amherst
Bartel, Roland	University of Oregon
Bryant, Joseph	Syracuse University
Eastman, Arthur	Carnegie-Mellon University
Finestone, Harry	Dean of Academic Planning, San Fernando Valley State College
Frank, Joseph	University of Massachusetts at Amherst
Freedman, Morris	University of Maryland
Gerber, John	University of Iowa
Gray, Donald	Indiana University
Gross, Theodore	City College of the City University of New York
Hollis, Carroll	University of North Carolina, Chapel Hill
Johnson, Dudley	Princeton University
Jordan, John	University of California at Berkeley
Kiely, Robert	Harvard University
Knotts, Walter	State University of New York at Albany
Kolb, Gwin	University of Chicago
Megaw, Neill	University of Texas at Austin
Morris, Alton	University of Florida, Gainesville
Moynihan, William	University of Connecticut, Storrs
Nash, Ralph	Wayne State University

Poirier, Richard   Rutgers University, New Brunswick
Price, Martin   Yale University
Rothwell, Kenneth   University of Vermont, Burlington
Ruland, Richard   Washington University, St. Louis
Schaefer, William   University of California at Los Angeles
Shrodes, Caroline   San Francisco State College
Shugrue, Michael   Association of Departments of English
Spengemann, William   Claremont Graduate School
Stewart, David   Idaho State University
Volpe, Edmond   City College of the City University of New York
Watt, Ian   Stanford University
Woodring, Carl   Columbia University

MLA-ADE Manpower Survey*

Nearly eleven hundred of the twenty-three hundred English departments in the United States and Canada completed the MLA-ADE Manpower Questionnaire, a return of more than 46%. The data which have been collected are being carefully analyzed by the MLA Manpower Commission over the summer and will be published for the profession early in the fall. That 56% of all four-year departments and 33% of all two-year colleges supplied statistics suggests the general awareness of a tightening job market and the need to obtain reliable information about the supply of and demand for faculty over the next five years.

The 23% decline in new full-time positions from academic 1969–70 to 1970–71 heralds a five-year decline in available new positions, one which will affect departments offering graduate work in English more seriously than departments in junior and community colleges and in four-year colleges offering the undergraduate major. While the need for full and associate professors in many areas will grow and opportunities will open for specialists in composition, linguistics, and the teaching of reading, the new Ph.D. graduating from one of approximately 150 institutions will find obtaining a position difficult, particularly if he is committed to a literary specialty and to an academic position in an institution offering the M.A. or the Ph.D. Previous teaching experience, an interest in teaching and developing introductory courses, and a willingness to teach a wide range of courses rather than a special field will distinctly increase his opportunities for employment.

As the candidate for a faculty appointment talks with department chairmen, he should also be aware that only 59% of all departments have begun recruiting by the end of December and that nearly 40% have not completed their hiring until after the end of April. Indeed, almost 60% of all departments complete the recruiting process between 1 April and 30 June. He should also know that only 52% of departments regularly schedule interviews at the MLA Annual Meeting.

While the Ph.D. is preferred by 57% of all departments, junior and community colleges prefer the qualified M.A. (44%) or a doctorate in teaching (32%) rather than the Ph.D. (11%). In fact, only 31% of all junior-college departments indicate that they are willing to hire the traditional, research-oriented Ph.D. About one-third of all departments give great weight to the field of specialization of the candidate for a position, but 52% consider the area of specialization less important than their need for qualified undergraduate teachers.

Asked to name those specialties which are most likely to be in great demand, departments indicated their need for persons qualified in freshman composition,

* Reprinted from *ADE Bulletin*, No. 26 (Sept. 1970), p. 25.

comparative or world literature, linguistics, and as generalists most frequently. In four-year colleges as well as junior and community colleges, English departments will be hiring faculty members interested in these areas and in Black Studies and Contemporary American Literature. Black Studies and Linguistics also turn up among the five greatest needs in departments awarding graduate degrees in English. The greatest needs in traditional areas of scholarship appear to be Contemporary American Literature, Renaissance Literature, the Literature of the Restoration and Eighteenth Century, and Contemporary British Literature.

Obiter Dicta on the Bellwether Conference*

Joseph Frank

University of Massachusetts at Amherst

WHAT many of us liked to call the Bellwether Conference took place at the University of Massachusetts at Amherst in late October of 1970. It was here that thirty chairmen, most of them representing highly respected and prolific Ph.D-granting English departments, passed a series of resolutions based on the current facts of academic life. They boil down to three recommendations: that we not increase the number of English teachers we are unleashing on the higher-education marketplace, that we modify their training to prepare them more realistically to teach in community and state colleges, and that the establishment—us guys—be more understanding and effective in helping them to get jobs. That such unanimous and presumably prestigious advice was both obvious and overdue has certain implications, and since I was chairman of the conference, I feel relatively qualified to suggest their import.

This two-day meeting was hard-working and serious, though not solemn (the conviviality fully lived up to the ADE norm). Part of this seriousness was, it seemed and seems to me, based on guilt: we had made it, and had it made, but maybe our potential successors were not even being allowed to set foot on the academic escalator. To what extent was our success and our empire-building of the 1960's responsible for this bind? Certainly our share of the blame was not large. We could all plead good private intentions and bad public advice. Yet I did detect a sense of personal guilt in most of the conference participants: hence our seriousness—and our incipient aggressiveness. For the first time in any such meeting I heard, if informally, realistic threats to bring into line those English departments which did not cooperate in mitigating the problems of academia. Guilty or not, we seemed ready to punish any putative offenders.

Second, I sensed a marked shift away from the view that teachers of college English are individual professionals, toward the view that they are members of a vocational group. One can argue whether white-collar unionism is good or bad, but most of the conferees—an employer group *par excellence*—seemed ready, if not to promote this trend, at least not to fight it.

Third, more than ever before I got the impression that our in-group—generally middle-aged, scholarly, liberal—was not only willing to get rid of much of its inherited professional baggage, but that we felt a sense of relief, even of expiation, in doing so. We were self-consciously moving away from "culture" toward "service," away from "elitism" toward—if only slightly toward—"participatory democracy"—and the quotation marks can suggest our discomfort with the nomenclature, not with the direction. We did not want to find ourselves in the position of the Classicists of a half-century ago, and we were anxious to Do Something.

---

* Reprinted from *ADE Bulletin*, No. 28 (Feb. 1971), pp. 9–10.

These obiter dicta are admittedly impressionistic and apparently cynical. We all love good books, colleagues, students, and we were exerting our conscientious and collective best to help all three. The Bellwether Conference was thus a proper and potentially functional gesture. But maybe it was too little and too late.

Maybe. And yet I don't think so. Somehow working with thirty English department chairmen who were sufficiently concerned about other people's future to alter their own present was exhilarating. Such exhilaration was, in itself, condescending and even smug, but it was not standpat. Guilt is usually immobilizing and destructive; exhilaration is usually kinetic and affirmative. I therefore look back on the Bellwether Conference not as another straw on a swaybacked camel but rather as a hopeful straw in the wind. That this is written on the eve of a new year may account for such possibly sentimental optimism. Even so, the October session at the University of Massachusetts indicated that 1971 might see a great deal more hard-headed concern for English and its practitioners, less soft-shouldered shrugging, than did our years of grace.

Resolutions Adopted by the 1971 San Fernando Valley State College—ADE Seminar*

Although the workshop reports and the recommendations of the June 1970 ADE Seminar did not reflect any specific move toward interdisciplinary study, it was clear to the planners of the 1971 Seminar that substantial interest in this field had been created, particularly by the remarks of Harold Tayor on English as creative expression and by Alan M. Hollingsworth's warnings, which he called "Last Chance for English." Consequently, interdisciplinary studies played a large role in the 1971 seminar, primarily centered on Professor Hollingsworth's paper "Beyond Literacy" and the workshop in interdisciplinary studies which he led.

The resolutions of the 1971 Seminar follow:

1. The participants and consultants of the ADE Seminar in Los Angeles, June 1971, unanimously support the efforts of William Schaefer, Executive Secretary Elect of MLA, to bring order to the Faculty Exchange by a new system of seasonal listings, not only of the positions available in colleges and universities but of actual prevailing job conditions.

2. The 1971 ADE Seminar urges that the Association of Departments of English seek funding for a pilot project on the evaluation of the teaching of English, which project would aim to produce: (1) a redefinition of our professional goals in the period of crisis facing us in the 1970's; and (2) the discovery of more sensitive and useful means of determining the relative success of our teaching in achieving these goals.

3. The current and projected expansion of two-year and four-year colleges and the need to provide a new kind of teacher for English and interdisciplinary programs justify the growing commitment to the principle of the D.A. degree as an important alternative to the Ph.D. for the preparation of teachers, and we recommend: (1) that the Executive Committee of ADE and the Executive Council of MLA urge the United States Office of Education and

* Reprinted from *ADE Bulletin*, No. 30 (Sept. 1971), pp. 3–4.

various private foundations to increase support for D.A. fellowships; (2) that MLA and various professional organizations, perhaps in cooperation with the Carnegie Corporation of New York, sponsor national seminars on the role and configuration of D.A. programs for preparing teachers in new modes of English and interdisciplinary studies; that participants in such seminars be drawn from two- as well as four-year colleges; and (3) that organizers of D.A. programs be urged to coordinate their efforts, to seek more nearly uniform models for the D.A. degree in accordance with the "guidelines" for teacher-training programs adopted by CCCC and NCTE.

Northwestern ADE Seminar: Toward a Definition of Literacy for the Seventies*

The impulse toward interdisciplinary studies comes from a variety of sources. Do our instructors need to be more closely attuned to the interests and needs of students? Should our graduate-degree programs be more cognizant of the demands of new job markets, such as the community colleges? Is English study to become responsible for the teaching of basic reading to students who simply can't? Must English departments teach teachers how to teach reading? Must literacy—one of our primary concerns—deal with media other than the printed page? Should English become concerned with the Third World and with popular culture? If the answer to most of these questions is in the affirmative, then interdisciplinary studies are called for. Where there has been general dissatisfaction with overspecialization in undergraduate programs, uncritically accepted conventional requirements, and rigid departmentalization, the move toward the interdisciplinary concept has seemed an answer. More positively, interdisciplinary work has been revived as a response to new intellectual interests of faculty and students in philosophy, psychology, and the social and physical environment, as well as non-Western and non-traditional cultures. It has its basis in a regard for breadth in education. However, the attendant dangers of superficiality and generality possible in interdisciplinary study have been much in everyone's mind.

These concerns are clearly reflected in the workshop reports and resolutions presented on the final afternoon of the Northwestern Seminar in November 1971:

Summary

Those who attended the Northwestern seminar heard Paul Olson of the University of Nebraska set forth "the kind of tragic burden of lack of perception which all of us bear." In his speech (reprinted on pp. 46–60 of this volume) Olson noted, "If the English department is predicated on the notion that the schools can provide abundance, freedom, accessibility, then the classroom formats, the tests, the exams, etc., have to be set up precisely to encourage abundance, freedom, accessibility. If the notion is that literature holds the mirror up to nature, then literature must be brought home to nature." Professor Olson continued, "If the study of literature is to be genuinely democratic, then I think it has to be the study of the total fantasy life of the people, that is, of their games, their rituals, their myths, their daydreams, their nightdreams."

Professor Olson touched on concerns expressed by many participants in

---

* Reprinted from *ADE Bulletin*, No. 32 (Feb. 1972), pp. 3–5.

working papers prepared for the seminar. Alan C. Purves, Director of Unit I, the experimental living-learning unit at the University of Illinois at Urbana, wrote:

The need we sensed could be summed up as a need to break away from the pre-doctoral studies curriculum that permeated all of the university humanities (and social sciences). Students were being trained only to lead academic lives; they were not trained to use skills other than those of the scholar critic in their treatment of humanistic studies. For example, no connection existed between literary study and such modes of perception and action as cinematography, computer science, information retrieval, systems planning, urban planning, graphic design, or theater. By encouraging students to make such connections, the group believed that they could better prepare the students to operate in a rapidly changing world. The primary means of such encouragement was to take the form of apprenticeship training, on-the-job training in real situations—work in film studies, urban planning centers, publishing houses, and the like. This work was to replace course work in those skill areas and hopefully to provide entry skills so the student could gain employment. But the oil of courses in the humanities and the water of apprenticeship training needed a catalyst. There were to be a series of reflexive seminars, in which the student, a professor in the humanities, and a mentor from the apprenticeship area were to explore the *language* of the area, to reflect upon the work experience and to examine how the humanities and the skill area could interpenetrate each other.

And Warren French of Indiana-Purdue University at Indianapolis wrote, "During our planning we have found ourselves repeatedly considering two kinds of interdisciplinary projects—one organized around a quite specialized, often academically unorthodox type of material; the other, around a historical period. Proposals for the latter kind of study have tended to emphasize a classroom-oriented, scholarly approach to materials of established value; proposals of the former kind, on the other hand, have tended to emphasize individual evaluations of material for which there are no standard criteria of evaluation."

Workshops identified a number of common concerns.

Workshop A on "The *Inter* in Interdisciplinary," directed by Wallace Douglas of Northwestern, presented the following points to the final general session:

1. Interest in interdisciplinary approaches to "English" ought to be taken for reasons other than the current condition of the job market.

2. Members of the workshop expressed some suspicion of departmental structures. There was a suggestion that "English" ought rather to be part of a division of language, communication, and associated arts.

3. There was somewhat strong rejection of required courses, of a set curriculum in English.

4. Members of English departments should, for purposes of curriculum planning, work from a broader concept of their material. They should consider other linguistic forms, other media of expression and communication than the verbal and (even narrower) the written.

5. Indeed, it is also necessary for them to receive into college English a somewhat broader range of communication situations than they do at present. In addition to ordinary academic writing and talk, often in the nature of practice or testing activities, students might be allowed to become involved in various kinds of off-campus situations and with people whose lives may not be directed by the experiences and values presumably shared by the majority of college students.

6. Members of the workshop seemed willing at least to entertain the notion that English, insofar as it involves, or can be made to involve, the students' use of their lan-

guages, is somehow connected with general growth and maturing.

7. It was suggested that in the seventies "literacy" will come to be thought of as more than being lettered in the English classics; indeed, as more than being lettered. It will have some connotations of having the means to cope with the real world. This will obviously, it was agreed, put considerable pressure on English departments.

It should be noted that there was some feeling that the workshop had not given enough time to the problem of the functionally illiterate student now being admitted at least to urban universities.

8. Finally, toward the end of the last session of the workshop, there began to be expressed a feeling that a new model of "English" is necessary, a model which would make the subject and those who profess it a resource to work with (not against) people.

For such a model to be realized, it was agreed by some, English teachers will have to adopt a fairly open conception of or attitude toward learning, realizing, for example, that they may need to expand their notions of what they may need to learn so as to take in the anthropological, the sociological, the psychological, and perhaps even all the riches of cultures other than the literary. Much self-education was foreseen to be a necessity.

Workshop C, "Planning an Interdisciplinary Program," directed by Daniel Bernd, made the following recommendations:

1. The *ADE Bulletin* should continue to print articles describing operating interdisciplinary programs. Such articles should be subsequently collected and published in some form.

2. The *ADE Bulletin* should select and publish articles on the strategy and tactics of engaging faculties and administrations and administrators in interdisciplinary programs.

3. Sessions like these should involve a broad spectrum of disciplines. New relationships with other disciplines should be encouraged.

4. A committee or committees should be set up to make available consultants to colleges or groups, or groups within colleges, who wish to embark on interdisciplinary endeavors.

5. The graduate schools should be encouraged to take a flexible stance for those undergraduates who have pursued a course of interdisciplinary studies.

Workshop E on "The Responsibilities of English in Higher Education," directed by Harry Finestone, presented the following report:

The workshop found agreement on two fundamental issues regarding the study of English: (1) cultural pluralism, not only native but international, and (2) media pluralism, which includes film, television, theater, and so forth.

To include both considerations in the study of English leads us clearly to interdisciplinary study, since English *departments* are not equipped to teach all that is implied in the concerns of English described above.

Furthermore, knowledge of the above will lead to a new kind of literacy, as students must become literate in more than the printed page.

However, Workshop E did not believe it feasible or wise to abolish the current English curriculum—it merely considered it wise to enlarge it in a number of ways.

The horizontal-interdisciplinary curriculum will exist alongside the vertical-specialized curriculum. Current departmental rewards go to those who work in the vertical curriculum. Until proper rewards in terms of tenure and promotion are given to those who teach in the horizontal curriculum (rewards for teaching with other faculty members and for taking instruction in other areas, as well as rewards for writing articles), no true development in that area will take place.

Workshop Notes

1. There is no need to rely on federal funds. We can plan interdisciplinary programs by giving up part of what we have been doing.

2. What we do in colleges and universities has implications beyond the four-year colleges.

3. Interdisciplinary studies can help to integrate free electives in a meaningful fashion through cores of relationships.

4. We urge the dissemination, by brief descriptions, of all new types of programs so that the profession can begin to share its knowledge.

5. There is need to stress rhetorically the following: interdisciplinary studies are not meant to replace English. The horizontal curriculum exists alongside of and because of the vertical curriculum.

6. The concerns of English stretch beyond ordinary departmental boundaries. We have no wish for English departments to be imperialistic and take over other departments. We need to reach out to other departments for help in organizing interdisciplinary programs.

7. Departmental structures make interdisciplinary efforts difficult.

Tampa Workshop Reports*

The participants at all the seminars were interested in practical as well as theoretical problems: How are interdisciplinary courses financed? How are they administered? Who should direct them? How are faculty recruited. What problems of commitment to traditional departments are encountered by professors teaching interdisciplinary courses? No uniform answers exist for these questions, but the seminars did attempt to deal with them directly.

In February 1972, the Seminar at the University of South Florida heard reports from five workshops.

Report of Workshop I

Chaired by George M. Harper
Florida State University
Reported by Donald E. Morse
Oakland University

The unstated assumption underlying most curricula is that the student will at some time and in some place make the connections between the discrete courses

* Reprinted from *ADE Bulletin*, No. 33 (May 1972), pp. 70–74.

he takes. Interdisciplinary studies assumes that such connections are not necessarily self-evident, but need to be discovered and explored.

Discussion about interdisciplinary studies should recognize both the changing nature of the discipline of English and the great variety of institutions, institutional settings, faculties, and students which the discipline seeks to serve. There is no one program that will answer the needs of all students; nor is there one that will be appropriate for every two- and four-year school. Institutions are not monolithic, but various, and so our programs must also be various.

English seeks to serve an almost bewildering array of constituencies, including undergraduate English majors, who then follow one of the professions of law, medicine, or business (see Linwood E. Orange's revealing article, "English: The Pre-Professional Major," *ADE Bulletin*, Feb. 1972); English majors who then teach in high school or go on to graduate work (only a small percentage of our students, however); nonmajors who elect English courses while majoring in another subject or enrolling in non–liberal-arts programs; those in the familiar service courses within the university, such as technical writing, communication skills, composition, and reading; those in the newly emerging service courses for business, industry, television, and correspondents; and the community beyond the university. As the needs of our students change, so must our programs. Interdisciplinary studies may provide part of the answer to our question of how best to meet these new and old needs; but part of the answer must also lie in our recognizing the clear and pressing need for pluralism in undergraduate, graduate, and professional programs. It is ironic that our pluralistic discipline often leads to repetitive programming across the country rather than to variety.

At the graduate level, we should insist that no program penalize a student who takes all or part of his undergraduates work in interdisciplinary studies. Within the existing graduate programs, interdisciplinary studies provides a means of broadening the student's academic and teaching experience. Special courses could be offered in "The Teaching of Interdisciplinary Studies" for future teachers in high school, two-year and four-year colleges, and universities. These courses could be synchronized with programs in apprentice teaching and stress the relationships between the academic disciplines and today's society and its educational needs. While it is often presumptuous of us to ask colleagues in other disciplines to give of their time and energy so that our courses may become interdisciplinary, we might strike an attractive bargain with them to exchange graduate students. Such a program of "Inside Internships" could lead to real gains in teaching and research when English graduate students spend a term or two working with professors in psychology, anthropology, or history in exchange for graduate students in those departments assisting in English. In addition, there are fully interdisciplinary graduate programs, such as the new Stanford Ph.D. in "Modern Thought and Literature," and the older graduate programs in the humanities, such as Florida State University's; some of their features could be adopted by or adapted to other programs.

Interdisciplinary studies can also find a place in many undergraduate programs under the familiar Humanities or Comparative Literature rubric or the newer Popular Culture. There are also new opportunities for teaching English within interdisciplinary studies to older students within and without degree programs, to community groups, and to others of the new constituencies we seek to serve. Within the traditional English offerings, experimental interdisciplinary courses may be introduced under umbrella or topics courses without benefit of catalog copy; and most departments recognize the problem-centered course, which is often interdisciplinary, as a legitimate and necessary means for broadening the English department's offerings. New interdisciplinary programs that constitute the total offering of a college or university may also evolve—but most likely at new institutions, such as the University of Wisconsin at Green Bay, whose undergraduate program focuses on ecology and is organized without traditional departments or colleges.

Whether on the undergraduate or graduate level, we recognize that the English is particularly well suited for interdisciplinary work because of the multidisciplinary nature of its subject matter.

Some Observations on Interdisciplinary Studies (George M. Harper)

A. Since the completely integrated interdisciplinary program (such as, for example, the one at Green Bay, Wisconsin, focused on ecology) is perhaps impossible for institutions structured along traditional lines, the most satisfactory and usual adjustments may be one or more of the following:

1. Institutes focused on unified subject matter which cuts across disciplines and even languages: for example, medieval studies, linguistics, and so forth.

2. Collections of courses for programs or degrees focused upon a single theme or goal: for example, urban studies, comparative literature, and so forth.

3. Unions of departments for advanced degrees focusing upon a theme, a historical period, a critical problem, or a social revolt: for example, the Ph.D. in Modern Thought and Literature at Stanford (which includes interdisciplinary core courses in the Modern Tradition).

4. Team-teaching courses on such subjects as literature and the film, popular culture, urban civilization, and the like.

5. Humanities courses, which may be interdisciplinary, or programs, which may be mere collections without theme or thesis (the cafeteria approach).

6. Individualized reading based upon the student's interests or goals and the supervisor's capacity.

B. Neither the faculty nor the structures of most institutions of higher learning are readily adjustable to interdisciplinary studies, especially in the humanities, which are less adaptable than the social sciences or the natural sciences. As a result, in our search for a cure for all our ills, we may rush into unsatisfactory experiments such as:

1. Generalized courses which attempt to embrace all learning in a few packages.

2. Team-teaching courses: although many of these can be exciting, their success is likely to be dependent upon the teachers rather than the concept, and the courses frequently remain on the books long after their usefulness has been served.

3. Institutes or centers: although they may sometimes break down restraining walls, especially in the physical sciences, institutes tend to overgeneralization, as some humanities and comparative literature programs do; and once established they tend to resist change, especially when research funds are involved.

4. Collections of courses (for a program or degree) which do not constitute an organic whole.

5. Graduate programs which do not have adequate

markets for their products: American Studies is a case in point.

6. Courses which attempt to approach one discipline from the viewpoint of another. Although many of these are valid, few of our faculty are adequately trained to present the subject matter of another discipline properly.

Report of Workshop II

Chaired by Edward Martin
University of South Florida
Reported by Sister Lora Ann Quinonez
Our Lady of the Lake College

The chairman established, as a basic assumption underlying the discussion, that interdisciplinary studies are never a goal in themselves; they are always a means to other ends.

I. The following items were introduced and discussed in the group.
   A. The nature of interdisciplinary studies:
      1. How can other disciplines illumine the study of literature, e.g., philosophy, psychology, cultural anthropology?
      2. Can the isolation of a problem arising from the human condition bring together disciplines which have something to contribute to its exploration and/or solution?
      3. An interdisciplinary course perhaps ought to be defined as "a course that involves somebody else." Concern was expressed over the tendency to have "interdisciplinary" courses which remain wholly within the English department. Such a practice may lead to dilettantism. It was pointed out, however, that, especially in some younger scholars, there is increasing evidence of interdisciplinary training and interest secured both in formal course work and through self-education.
      4. The word *discipline* suggests a pattern of thinking, a set of agreed-upon premises for inquiry. Interdisciplinary courses should, then, provide the student with experiences of different modes of thinking around a common subject, with methods of exploration by which he can relate to that subject.
   B. Curricular and instructional issues:
      1. The use of large lecture classes for interdisciplinary work was discussed. There seemed to be differences of opinion regarding their effectiveness, especially for the younger student. Several thought lectures should be used in conjunction with small group discussions.
      2. Special topics labels are a good means to use in experimenting with courses, especially if there is some doubt about the feasibility and/or reception of new courses. Some departments use very general course titles and descriptions in the catalog which permit great flexibility in making changes without requiring approval by formal curriculum committees.
      3. There should be provision for internships in career alternatives to teaching for the English major. Departments should consider giving credit for employment in off-campus work situations, e.g., insurance companies, advertising agencies, newspapers, museums. The practice would permit a student to experience, while still in college, circumstances which would assist him in deciding on his course of studies.
      4. The importance of identifying student needs and desires in the development of interdisciplinary courses was emphasized. Faculty should be aware of the tendency to decide for themselves what students want. Observation of increased or decreased enrollments in certain types of courses, the use of course evaluation forms, the practice of including students on

curriculum committees—all these are valuable in determining student attitudes.

5. The "piecemeal" approach was reaffirmed. It is perhaps unrealistic to expect a college curriculum to be changed as a whole. Those members who are interested in developing interdisciplinary courses should be encouraged to do so.

6. It was noted that the traditional alliance of English with other humanities and arts disciplines seems to be shifting in the direction of the social and behavioral sciences.

C. Administrative and budgetary problems:

1. Shifts in institutional and/or departmental purposes pose problems in the best use of tenured faculty members, some of whom are left literally with nothing to do. Under these circumstances, interdisciplinary work might be seen as a threat to job security.

2. Courses staffed by people from several departments may cause problems in the allocation of FTE credit and in the subsequent allocation of funds.

3. It is sometimes difficult for institutions and departments to introduce significant innovations because of the intransigence of other institutions and agencies in the system. Thus, for example, junior colleges are concerned about the transfer of credits to four-year institutions; senior colleges worry about the attitude of graduate schools toward nonconventional courses listed on a transcript; professional and accrediting agencies of all sorts impose requirements—and, therefore, limitations—on persons who wish to be certified practitioners in a specific field. It was pointed out that, despite our legitimate desire to move in new directions, it is unjust to the students to equip them with nonmarketable skills and knowledge. Change is essential, then, not only in the curricular and instructional practices of colleges and universities but in the framework which the system demands.

4. English departments sometimes find themselves in jurisdictional conflicts with other areas, e.g., theater, film, mass communication, foreign literature in translation.

II. The members of Workshop II who formulated but did not vote upon a draft of the following resolutions presented them for approval at the final general session. They were adopted with some editorial revisions.

A. The English department conceives its function too narrowly when it defines itself as centered exclusively—or even primarily—on the study of literature. Its legitimate province embraces the study of language in all its uses. In their search for staff, therefore, English departments should include candidates possessing greater versatility in the skills required for work in language.

B. English departments—in both undergraduate and graduate programs—should adopt as a conscious stance for the seventies the principle that curricular flexibility and diversity are both necessary and valuable. No single model can—or should—dictate curricular and instructional design.

C. English departments having graduate programs are urged to consider restructuring such programs according to the principle enunciated in B, in order to offer—within the American system of graduate education—significant options appropriate to the variety of activities engaged in by English departments.

Report of Workshop IV

Chaired by Calhoun Winton
University of South Carolina

The workshop on interdisciplinary studies involving the other language departments (Workshop IV) held interesting discussions on the practical and theoretical aspects of interdisciplinary programs. These came to center around two questions: *Why* institute such programs (i.e., goals) and *how* do so? (i.e., methods). The committee also affirmed two general propositions: (1) That a knowledge of the nature of language is or should be fundamental to the English curriculum and (2) that fostering an appreciation of literature in foreign languages (ancient and modern, Western and non-Western) is a legitimate concern of English departments, in cooperation with other departments whenever possible.

Several goals were discussed, including the possibility of effecting some administrative economies by avoiding duplication of courses and faculty positions. Such programs, it was felt, would (1) make the undergraduate curriculum less narrow and generally richer; (2) would produce a more cosmopolitan outlook in a world of shrinking distances and mass communication; and (3) would encourage a sensitivity to the social, regional, and functional varieties of English.

Means or methods considered ranged widely. On one edge of the spectrum was the institute separate from or independent of the departmental structural system which would cooperate with departments as appropriate. The possibility of programs which would involve interdepartmental cooperation was set forth as being next on the spectrum. Beyond this is the possibility of actual interdepartmental sharing (joint appointments, cross-listed courses, and so forth). It was also felt that departments of English have a legitimate concern for teacher preparation in all areas relating to English language and literature.

The workshop expressed the feeling that there was or should be a natural affinity among departments of languages, linguistics, and English (as well as other departments interested in the uses and acquisition of language such as education, psychology, sociology, and anthropology) and that interdisciplinary programs involving these departments should be encouraged by the individual teacher and the department.

Participating: James Alatis, Frederick Conner, Marion Folsom, William Free, Richard Ruland, Stanley Wanat.

Report of Workshop V

Chaired by Stanton Millet
University of West Florida

In a series of workshop discussions concerning possibilities for development of a Doctor of Arts degree and the relationship of such a degree to interdisciplinary study, participants agreed on the necessity for new patterns of training in English at the graduate level. In part, this agreement springs from recognition of the great diversity in emphases and goals at all levels of English instruction. At the junior-college level, provision is now made in English courses for vocationally-oriented students as well as for those in traditional academic programs. In both junior colleges and four-year institutions, varied courses and programs have been developed for students enrolled in teacher-education curricula in English, for students in other disciplines who are taking elective work in English, and for students pursuing the conventional baccalaureate in English. Each of these constituencies is likely to require competencies of a different kind than those ordinarily thought to be provided for prospective teachers as part of the Ph.D. program. In addition, however, workshop participants judge that in the years immediately ahead, English teachers will be called upon to teach a great variety of interdisciplinary courses. Because interdisciplinary study is in some sense an attempt to integrate knowledge from a variety of disciplines, students and educators alike will view it as an effective means of dealing with the "knowledge explosion." As the traditional general-education requirements of course work in a variety of disciplines decline in importance, interdisciplinary study may replace the customary freshman- and sophomore-level courses in composition, genre study, and survey courses. Courses that cut across traditional departmental lines will be particularly appropriate for continuing education, which will certainly grow in importance, and they will be important, too, because they appear to provide a means of dealing with the affective as well as the exclusively cognitive aspects of literary education.

In order to meet the varied needs of students at all levels, and to participate effectively in interdisciplinary study, the college English teacher will need training in six areas: teaching methods, language and writing, literature, interdisciplinary study, media, and literary scholarship. Training in teaching method may be accomplished by internships, by graduate-level seminars and colloquia, by supervised teaching of limited duration, and by combinations of these approaches. In the area of language and writing, college teachers will need preparation in rhetoric and oral communication, theories of language learning, and theories of language development as well as the traditional preparation directed to teaching students to achieve acceptable levels of competence in writing. In the area of literary training, workshop participants agreed that the ideal prospective college teacher would be something of a generalist, with a broad overview of English and American literature, not a specialist in a particular period. Specifically, his preparation should include some work in theories of literature, in the nature of literary response, and in critical analysis. In order to participate effectively in interdisciplinary teaching, the prospective teacher should have some graduate-level study in two or more areas of knowledge other than his own field, the intent being that he learn the vocabulary and basic approaches of selected disciplines so that he would be able to work effectively with experts from those disciplines, in team teaching or other cooperative ventures.

There was general agreement that the prospective teacher would need training in use of nonprint media. Such training would include both practical instruction in the use of videotape and other devices and work in mass communication theory, the latter looking both toward effective teaching in interdisciplinary areas and toward new kinds of approaches to conventional courses in literature and writing. Finally, defining scholarship rather generally as "scholarly activity" rather than as the preparation of a traditional dissertation, workshop participants suggested that the research requirement for a doctoral degree might well be revised in order to provide several alternatives to the thesis: wide reading in a variety of fields, whether or not such reading leads to publication; intensive study in some special topic or literary period; or participation with another faculty member—perhaps from a different discipline—in the development of a new course.

Members of the workshop agreed that the degree structure appropriate to provide the training outlined above would vary from institution to institution. At some, the Doctor of Arts degree would be the most appropriate means of preparing college teachers. At others, the Ph.D. itself might be appropriately revised. Members of the workshop questioned the assumption that the Ph.D. is in fact exclusively oriented toward research. They noted that the majority of Ph.D.'s in English have had some teaching experience as graduate assistants, and that many have had some form of instruction in college teaching methods. Further, they noted that the Ph.D. program in English used to be considerably broader than it is now, providing for work in one or more areas and study of two or more foreign languages. They saw no reason why the Ph.D. should necessarily exclude the kinds of training regarded as important for the college teacher.

As a corollary to the main line of the discussion, participants in the workshop noted that, at present, viable interdisciplinary programs are most likely to exist in large institutions as a result of accidental combinations of expertise and interest. Where this is so, they strongly recommend that arrangements be made to support faculty members in developing these interests. Too often, the development of interdisciplinary courses must be carried on without released time from other duties, and without financial support from the departments concerned.

Interdisciplinary Studies—The View from Texas: A Report on the Texas ADE Meeting, 10 March 1972*

Jeff H. Campbell

Southwestern University

In March 1972 the Texas ADE, with impetus from the national seminars, sponsored a meeting on interdisciplinary studies.

AT its 1971 meeting, the Texas ADE sought to identify and face some of the challenges departments of English face in the fluid academic situation of the 1970's. Although no one claimed to have identified all the challenges or to have formulated successful plans to meet those challenges, there did seem to be a consensus that departments of English could no longer rest secure in the comfortable position of being the guardians of and revealers of a cultural heritage eagerly sought after by all who pretend to the claim of being educated. It seemed clear to most of us that we could not be satisfied with seeking to preserve the status quo of yesteryear. The *ADE Bulletin* has kept us well informed of the many factors which seem to dictate the necessity of change if we are to follow Robert Frost's example and viably offer the continuing richness of our literary tradition as a "momentary stay against confusion." In other words, to draw on Frost in a slightly different context, we agreed in 1971 that we must somehow learn in the midst of changed circumstances "what to make of a diminished thing."

Therefore, the 1972 meeting was devoted to a discussion of interdisciplinary studies as one device or approach which seems to offer promise of meeting current challenges while at the same time preserving hard-won strengths. We sought to probe ways in which departments of English can face the problems of developing interdisciplinary courses to broaden and enrich their offerings without seeming imperialistically to co-opt the territory of other disciplines, thus finding new vitality and escaping the charge of moss-backed irrelevance.

The discussion began with a panel presentation. The first panelist was Nicholas Franks of South Texas Junior College in Houston. Mr. Franks cited the great problems faced by junior colleges in introducing interdisciplinary studies. Junior colleges seem to be more and more dominated by vocational-technical programs, with federal support going there rather than to the broader humanities area. Further, junior college students are very much concerned about the transferability of their courses and are hesitant to enroll in experimental work which may not be accepted by a senior college. Nevertheless, at South Texas interdisciplinary courses have been tried, such as a course involving the government, history, anthropology, and English departments. In two years, however, a total of only twenty-four students had enrolled for the course, and it was dropped because it was too expensive for the school to continue. A more feasible experiment involved sharing instructors between the philosophy and psychology departments when two classes were studying Skinner and Freud. Mr. Franks believes that the teaching of literature must be interdisciplinary, but that specific interdisciplinary courses will

* Reprinted from *ADE Bulletin*, No. 33 (May 1972), pp. 74–76.

probably have to begin on the graduate level, then work down to the senior college before they can be effectively instituted at the junior-college level.

Bernard O'Halloran of Incarnate Word College in San Antonio spoke on the problems and prospects of interdisciplinary work at a liberal-arts college. He suggested that English teachers have always taken pride in their ability to integrate knowledge from various fields, and he agreed with Mr. Franks that the teaching of literature must be interdisciplinary by its very nature. He cited some interesting experiments at Incarnate Word involving the creative use of the January "mini-mester." One course involved eight different departments in a study of Romantic literature. The freedom of the January term solved scheduling problems, and students could register for credit in English, French, or history. No quizzes were given, but tutorials, conferences, and a paper were used instead, with an examination at the end. Student enthusiasm was great. The second course was similar, but with only five departments involved. It was called "The Age of the Enlightenment." The third course was entitled "The Celtic Rebels" and dealt with Joyce, Yeats, and Shaw; this time only the English and drama departments were involved. All three courses were highly successful, but they proved to be about twenty percent more expensive than an ordinary departmental course. The demise of the January "mini-mester" at Incarnate Word seems to doom such courses, since ways cannot be found to solve the scheduling problems of the fifteen-week term. World literature, however, has been turned into an interdisciplinary course, no longer the property of the department of English but now involving teachers from other departments as well.

The problems of interdisciplinary courses at a large state university were discussed by Harrison Hierth of Texas A & M University at College Station. He cited five major problems: the difficulty at such an institution of establishing new courses; the service function of departments of English, whereby they are forced to serve needs and requirements set by other departments; the fact that most freshman-sophomore courses are taught by teaching assistants who are usually willing to experiment but need careful guidance and supervision; the fact that state universities are research-oriented so that faculty members are pressured to write rather than experiment with curricular possibilities; and the fact that state universities have expensive graduate programs which tend to promote a narrow focus. Despite these problems, Mr. Hierth cited much interest in interdisciplinary work on his campus at all levels and expressed hope for a new course, "Language and Communication," sponsored by the departments of anthropology, linguistics, mass communications, modern languages, and psychology. This course *has* been established, and it hopes to attract uncommitted students to help them make up their minds what they might like to do. Mr. Hierth cited three compelling needs for pursuing the development of interdisciplinary work: the crying need for less stodgy and more relevant curricula in English; the need of the student to know more about himself as a person; and the need of the student to have more options in developing his course of study from the vast array offered by a large university.

Developments at the graduate level were discussed by Edwin Gaston of Stephen F. Austin State University at Nacogdoches. Stephen F. Austin is one of four emerging state universities in Texas seeking to develop a Doctor of Arts degree. The coordinating Board this spring denied the authorization of the degree, but prospects for future approval seem good. The D.A. would seek to be a teaching degree rather than a research degree like the Ph.D. and would also allow some desirable interdisciplinary work. English teachers, Gaston agreed, must be interdisciplinary in their teaching, but too often they are not qualified to dip into psychology, sociology, or history as they do. The D.A. could make possible a broadened background so that teachers might be more competent in areas beyond literature itself. He also suggested that while we wait for graduate programs to train better interdisciplinary teachers we might more effectively utilize the talent we have by promoting reciprocal exchanges among faculty members. They could thus enrich each other's classes and help teach each other at the same time.

Thomas Perry of East Texas State University at Commerce reiterated that English teachers are and always have been interdisciplinary, but stressed that we should examine our reasons for being interdisciplinary and thus avoid the errors of superficiality and egotism. At East Texas State good use is made of the "umbrella" course-listing that allows experimental courses to be offered under a general title. Two particularly successful courses Mr. Perry cited were "Science and Literature," taught by two English professors and one each from science and psychology; and a course entitled "Historical Fiction," taught jointly by the English and history departments. At East Texas State the Department of English will be superseded next year by the Department of Literature, Language, and Philosophy, its very title giving it the opportunity for broadening the scope of possibilities for its majors.

Bruce Coad of Tarrant County Junior College in Fort Worth took issue with the assertion that vocational-technical training dominates the junior-college scene. On the contrary, he said, his experience indicates that junior-college students are eager for courses which show connections; they are tired of fragmentation and artificial barriers. He also took issue with the suggestion that interdisciplinary courses must begin at the graduate level. If one waits for the graduate schools, he suggested, he may wait forever. Mr. Coad suggested that perhaps the most effective way to produce needed change is for colleges—junior and senior—to implement new interdisciplinary courses; then the graduate schools will tool up to train people to teach the courses. Tarrant County is undertaking a significant experiment in offering its remedial English in an interdisciplinary way, involving the speech and reading departments as well as English. Tarrant Country also has the "umbrella" course, making possible various experimental undertakings. Despite his belief in the necessity of interdisciplinary work and its possibilities at the junior-college level, Mr. Coad sees problems involved in solving the problem of teaching-load division. Furthermore, he finds few junior-college teachers truly capable of interdisciplinary work.

A vigorous floor discussion followed the presentations of the panel members. Although this year, as last, we left the meeting without a sense of having neat, easy answers to the problems facing us, we did have a renewed sense of exciting possibilities available to us. Interdisciplinary courses are clearly no panacea, but they may provide us a way to expand the "diminished thing" of English into greater things than our previous philosophies dreamed of.

Reports from the National Conference on the Future of Graduate Education in English, Knoxville, Tennessee, 22–24 April 1971*

One of the immediate results of the Bellwether Conference was the Conference on the Future of Graduate Education in English. The proceedings of that meeting are worth examining in the context of the interdisciplinary seminars.

Foreword

The Conference was jointly sponsored by the Association of Departments of English and the English Department of the University of Tennessee. Major support was provided by the John C. Hodges Better English Fund. Additional support is gratefully acknowledged from the College of Liberal Arts and the Graduate School

---

* Reprinted from *ADE Bulletin*, No. 30 (Sept. 1971), pp. 12–13.

of the University of Tennessee and from the ADE–San Fernando Valley State College 1970–71 EPDA Seminar.

Planners of the Conference hoped that four things, besides the usual side benefits of such meetings, would happen: (1) ways would be found to reduce the manpower crisis; (2) two-year colleges would be convinced that by hiring Ph.D.'s they would improve the quality of their programs and at the same time contribute significantly to changing a crisis into a benefit to American higher education; (3) the rationale of the ACE ratings of graduate programs would be examined in depth to determine whether such ratings have a beneficent, a neutral, or a harmful effect; (4) the intricacies of tenure provisions and promotion practices would be given a hard review.

The Conference was attended by more than 120 participants from approximately 100 colleges and universities. The Resolutions adopted at the final session hint at what was accomplished. (See page 245.)

The manpower crisis was not solved, although all participants showed a keen awareness of their responsibility and, through them as department heads, the responsibility of their institutions for contributing to a solution.

Two-year colleges were sparsely represented, but some progress was made in displaying the advantages to such institutions of employing Ph.D.'s interested in working with lower-division students.

The ACE ratings were examined with care, with some acerbity tempered by wit and urbanity. The fundamental purpose of the ratings—the improvement of quality in graduate work—was only glanced at. If the ratings do not serve this purpose, then the huge enterprise needs to be revamped (as one of the resolutions emphasizes) or abandoned.

Discussion of tenure and promotion revealed, as did all other topics considered by the Conference, the diversity of politics and practices in these areas. The surplus of college teachers will tempt administrations to be critical of the tenure system and of the rigid prescriptions of the A.A.U.P.

Kenneth L. Knickerbocker
University of Tennessee

Opening General Session

After greetings from K. L. Knickerbocker, head of the Department of English at the University of Tennessee, John H. Fisher, Executive Secretary of the Modern Language Association, set the backdrop for the conference by suggesting that recent changes in higher education have created problems for English departments in the 1970's. The democratization of higher education has led to the realization that the teaching of English is a political act; and the change in our biological inheritance (from ninety-five percent British in 1776 to forty-five percent British in 1940) has cast the English professor in the role of defender of British culture, as expressed in language, against a growing tendency to reject that culture in favor of American literature, bilingual education, and, most recently, black English. As a result of these developments, the English requirement is being curtailed in our colleges, English literature is becoming less important in our high schools and two-year colleges, and dissatisfaction with our present Ph.D. training is growing. For English literature a permanent, respected place will remain in secondary and higher education, but the day of English literature as a cultural phenomenon (a ritual of initiation) is over. How flexible should our graduate education be under these new conditions?

Presiding: Kenneth L. Knickerbocker

In Defense of the Ph.D.

I am cast in the role of defender of the faith.

I call it a role, not because I do not in fact adhere to the faith, but because my accustomed attitude in these matters is rather critical than encomiastic. Having devotedly found fault with English studies for the past however-many years, I must now gravely inform you that they are "sound at bottom."

My situation is not eased by the nature of this audience. History provided no occasion for Martin Luther to convert John Calvin to Christianity, or vice versa. If the occasion had occurred, I wonder whether even they would have been so brash as to undertake it. The most impracticable of all audiences, Aristotle tells us, is one already persuaded, and in its own terms.

I am aware that our community of loyalties does not mean that we are in agreement. Wherever two or more of this faith are gathered together, prayer is less likely than argument. For this reason it may be well for me to specify some items of the general problem that I have no wish to defend. These items are of two kinds: those on the one hand in which the prevailing criticism is spurious and defense ought to be supererogatory, and on the other hand, those for which there is no adequate defense—at least, none that I know.

To the first class belongs the asseveration that the young men and women who have gone out of the universities with Ph.D.'s during the past decade or so are not effective in their classrooms. I don't know where this curious bit of misinformation comes from. It must be from somewhere off campus. Beyond the elementary levels English courses are elective. Yet they have grown prodigiously. I suggest that anyone who has misgivings on this point consult enrollment statistics, both the absolute increase in numbers of students and the increase relative to other disciplines and to university and college enrollments over all. Ineffective teachers don't get large volunteer audiences.

To the same class belongs the characterization of these learned young people as having been trained into a scholarship so remote and esoteric that it alienates them from genuinely humane concerns. Whoever thinks that English faculties are too scholarly surely hasn't been to the handball courts lately, or the taverns, or the library. Nor has he listened to their conversations among themselves and with their students.

More sound, generous, humane teaching is being done during this present year by people who either have the Ph.D. in English or who seek it than by any other category of persons working at the collegiate level. This has been true for some time. This being true, the oversupply of these teachers that we read about in the papers seems to me something for the economists and demographers and HEW to worry about—not because Ph.D.'s are too many, but because society doesn't know how to use them. I worry about the population explosion. I am in favor of birth control. I worry, too, about individuals who for one reason or another have not yet found appropriate opportunity to use their talents. But when I lie awake at night it is not because twelve hundred English Ph.D.'s are emerging from the universities this year. From what I have seen of them, fourteen hundred wouldn't be too many, and I believe that even the economy will more or less agree when it gets a closer look at them.

I mentioned a second class of objections that I do not contest, the indefensible objections. Here I would place the charge that want of the degree can be used to exclude persons of proved ability from college faculties, just as laws of accreditation exclude such people, including Ph.D.'s, from high-school faculties. The conception of the Ph.D. as a permit to work, excluding all others, is an obnoxious conception. Many departments of English have proved by exceptional appointments that they do not accept it. But we are likely to take more comfort than we should in the exceptions that any of us could cite. The fact is that it is much easier to find a candidate with a Ph.D. for a college position than to find an equally or better qualified person who has followed another route to knowledge. In this connection, I don't construe my assignment as public defender to entail responsibility for attacking any alternative mode of operation, whether it be individual or institutional. I should rather have studied with Kenneth Burke than with most other people, and he not only omitted the Ph.D. but vigorously eschewed it. The doctorate in arts or the doctorate in language and literature may prove to be more effective in our current society than the English Ph.D. If so, more power to it. Defense of the Ph.D. in English requires no sallies against other responsible educational undertakings.

Perhaps I ought to say what in my opinion the Ph.D. in English is. I make students define whatever it is they are talking about. It is no more than fair that I do the same.

The Ph.D. in English marks successful completion of a disciplinary program of studies. The program is the best that students of English language and literature at the universities can devise, working together both locally in their departments and nationally through published criticism and discussion in such organizations as the Association of Departments of English and the Modern Language Association. Faculties stake their reputations on it. Its vitality is apparent in its demonstrated capacity for change, for assimilating new knowledge and new modes of thought, for attention to new and different voices, and for the surrender of outworn pieties. No valuable scheme of humane endeavor yields its rewards for mere conformity. Its strength is apparent in its stability, its memory of the experience of men over many centuries and of the subtle art by which experience is given permanence and importance for successive generations. Every valuable scheme of humane endeavor requires recognizable character, identity, which remains the same even as it changes. There can be only one such thing in a culture at any given time. It is the product of a widely shared devotion. When men decided that they no longer believe in it or want it, it will disappear, and the long process by which men through generations have built it will begin again, just as it does begin, again and again, whenever an attentive student glimpses for the first time the richness, the delight, and the power that accrue with genuine literary understanding, and undertakes to construct in his imagination a sodality in which such understanding can furnish the values governing the relationship of men.

If the Ph.D. in English be so defined, who can be its enemies? Against whom need it be defended?

I know a master builder, a businessman, who has triple-alpha intelligence according to almost any set of criteria you might care to name. He is, as we say, "outspoken," especially in his strictures on our profession. He concedes the utility of training in English composition, but on the question of what Shakespeare means at any given point, he says, "My guess is as good as yours."

He is wrong, in my opinion, but he isn't the enemy. Neither he nor any of the other thousands of good men who manage to live without literature as we define it are enemies. They can cause embarrassment, especially when they hold some academic title such as Dean or President, but every time one of them asks me with either real or pretended concern how I am getting along on the problem of who wrote Shakespeare, I just say, "OK," and shrug it off. They can tighten the budget, too, when times get hard, but as I suggested before, the economy is one thing and English studies another. Nothing essential is involved. There may be people who are in English studies for the money. If so, they have made a mistake.

I refer here only to the general class of a-literary persons, not to the exceptional hard-working, politico-economic antirationalists one finds in important offices—gubernatorial and up. A few new members of this species have been reported lately. I have heard a liberal California politician quoted in a warning that he issued to the academies of his state: the purpose of these men, he said in effect, is not to embarrass the university, as some of you (that is, us) may suppose, but to dismantle it. I believe that what he said is true. The concentrations of intellectual and scientific power of which some of our finest universities consist can only be frightening to certain forms of megalomania. These enemies constitute a real and present danger. But their kind is not new to the scene. We have had them around for quite a while. And on the record, they don't seem too hard to beat. English has no special exposure on this front. Every man of learning is equally threatened. I don't suggest that it be ignored, only that there is no occasion for panic.

The most effective attacks on English come from its friends—a situation not unknown in governmental, religious, and even familial circles. Such attacks may be dangerous and yet not be destructive. They may in fact be the means by which new energy and health flow into an undertaking whose endemic vulnerabilities are to habituate pedantry or esthetic elitism. I want to talk now about some of the attacks that I expect are coming from this quarter during the years ahead. My gifts as prophet enjoy no special privilege, except, of course, the privilege of this rostrum. You probably have your own lists of approaching conflicts, and your own appraisals of what they offer us by way of difficulty and by way of possible gain. We shall probably all turn out to be wrong at least in part.

The first of the big engagements that are coming requires no prophetic office, for it is on us now. Those who are in the large, public, urban situations can see it most clearly, but it will reach us all. Enclaves of immunity may be set up here and there, or may be inherited, but whether they can endure seems to me very much in doubt. The change is not so recent as we sometimes suppose. For a long time, at least since the beginning of this century, students, serious students, have come year by year from an ever-widening band of the societal spectrum. In recent years whole new populations have come in—have, with some notable perturbations, been welcomed in. We wanted it to happen this way, it has happened, and it will keep right on happening.

It is a mistake to suppose that this sweeping, revolutionary change in the population of higher education affects only the beginnings, the elementary work of English. Every apogee stands on its own base. Ph.D. courses in English reflect societal change just as freshman English does, and in the same ways. We used to use the phrase "standard American English" with confidence. Recently the phrase has become bad manners, and the thing itself is moot. If English changes, how can the Ph.D. in English remain the same? The *CBEL* is not a complete or terminal enumeration.

It would be comfortable if somebody could just tell all this turmoil to go away. It would be comfortable, but it would be wrong. The problem is not how to avoid conflict. The problem is how to emerge from it with a richer understanding of language and literature, and to make that new understanding as valuable within its new culture as the old one was in its own. And it is a problem. I know of no guarantees of success that we can count on. History provides some exemplary failures, and some exemplary successes, though none that quite fits our situation either in complexity or in stark magnitude.

One danger is that the situation seems to invite solution by bureaucratization. A hypothetical Department of Human Resources with a sufficiently categorical set of behavioral objectives and a billion dollars could organize higher education in this country into an almost totally sterile system. It is hard to imagine alliance with a creature of as foul a mien, but we may tolerate more of this sort of thing than we ought to. Perhaps we already have. All large institutions are vulnerable to it, and, for some reason, whether they be public or private appears to make little if any difference.

At another level, there are pressures to organize each academic department on the model of American industry into a rationalized set of "jobs." Insofar as this succeeds, English studies can only deteriorate. In saying this I challenge the unionized graduate assistant. I also challenge the flaccid senior professor, serving out his years to retirement in tenured indolence. The two of them and the Department of Human Resources are all playing the same game: organize the whole affair into a cage of rules, and then sit safe inside and gibber.

Most interesting are the challenges that will come from people who share the spirit of free and responsible scholarship, whose first concern is to understand and to disseminate understanding. The men who made the English Ph.D. in this country, and who gave it dignity, didn't like cages. They were rebels. Their heirs, I should hope, have not lost all cantankerousness. Their heirs more than anyone else are aware of the danger of time-serving, atrophy, mindless repetition to every humane enterprise, and especially to their own. These inheritors of the tradition are the ones whose challenge seems to me most to the point. They have a distinct advantage: they know what they are talking about.

Such men will determine important issues, among them whether the Ph.D. in English continues as one of the anchor points of higher education in the United States. There are a number of ways in which the decisions that they must make can be defined. To me the most satisfactory way is in terms of an old problem in criticism. It is an old problem, almost bromidic in its familiarity, but it continues unresolved, and it has been exacerbated in very recent years by the urgencies of young men and women, and some not so young, whose political frustrations prompt them to emphatic speech and action. In this sense the problem has a political aspect—which is unfortunate, for it is by nature a dialectical problem, incapable of categorical resolution. We can only hope to live with it in equilibrium, as we hope to do, for example, with justice and mercy. We have recently seen what unfortunate things can happen when the thrust for political power intrudes into matters of justice and mercy.

The old problem to which I refer arises from conflict between the technical and the moralistic aspects of literary study. I can illustrate what I mean: In March 1910 at Columbia University Joel Spingarn delivered a lecture entitled "The New Criticism," definite article and all. He proposed an alliance between genius and taste, between the poet and the critic. In his usage *criticism* is an honorific word. Benedetto Croce was his prophet. One of the peculiarities of Croce's esthetic is its inhibition of judgment. Having decided that a work belongs to the class of things which is called "art"—and the class may simultaneously include the *Divine Comedy* and a child's crayon drawing—the Crocean has no dependable procedure for preferring Dante to the child. The work of art is an absolute, without dependency on moral or logical premises, just as a text is an absolute to a philologically hygienic editor. This was Spingarn's position in 1910, the aspect of the problem that I have called, for lack of a better word, "technical."

The moralistic aspect is easier. Its advocate was Irving Babbitt, who responded to Spingarn through Paul Elmer More's *Nation* (7 Feb. 1918) as follows:

It is not enough, as Mr. Spingarn would have us believe, that the critic should ask what the creator aimed to do and whether he has fulfilled his aim; he must also ask whether the aim is intrinsically worth while. He must . . . rate creation with reference to some standard set both above his own temperament and that of the creator.

I shan't elaborate Professor Babbitt's famous position. I should like to remark, however, that not all of those who favored it were of Babbitt's stature. An old teacher of mine once said that the Ph.D. in English was invented in order to replace with something better a faculty composed chiefly of superannuated Methodist divines. The moralistic professor of English, who accepted the function of lay reader to the classrooms of the country, and who told over and over the lives of the literary saints, yielded in time, or so it seems to me, to another man better attuned to critical ideas of the sort Spingarn recommended and to philological standards that had been learned in Germany. The chronology of this process corresponds roughly with that of the elaboration of the English Ph.D. into a large institutional program. The two developments are probably related in other ways also.

I caricature all these attitudes. Croce wrote books about Shakespeare and Goethe, but none that I know of about kindergarten art. Joel Spingarn wrote a tough, antiquarian treatise on criticism in the Renaissance. Nevertheless, some elements of my caricature seem to function in reality. Some members of the very recent generations of students perceive the discipline of English as incapable of rendering a responsible judgment of any kind. In public affairs they equate liberalism with spinelessness. In literature they equate concern for the integrity of text with pedantry.

I haven't heard these students invoke Babbitt. In fact, they appear not to have read him. But he is their natural ally. Like him they are equipped with standards which transcend both their authors' and their own temperaments. We have circled back to old, familiar country, the only country in which objective literary study appears to revolution and to reaction alike in the same sad image.

This urgent rediscovery of ethical responsibility forces an issue. Most of us, I suspect, never proposed to abandon ethical responsibility. Insofar as. we are thought to have done so we have either been misconstrued or have by some error of omission or commission inadvertently misrepresented ourselves. Possibly, on a rainy day, or in the enthusiasm of an intrinsic analysis or of a textural emendation, we may for a moment and on a trivial point have been guilty as charged. To this degree, I, at least for myself, confess. Nevertheless, I feel no disposition to put on makeup, like Thomas Mann's old writer, and join the vehement young people. The reason for my indisposition is not that doctrines are being taken up, but that other doctrines are being forgotten. The heart of English scholarship is itself a doctrine. Both Joel Spingarn and Irving Babbitt exemplified it in their work. Generously learned over a spacious range of languages, cultures, and centuries, they knew that "to be young is not enough." The doctrine of scholarship is simply that of responsibility to truth. I know no other way to say it. Its opposite is not racism, anti-feminism, or war, but mindlessness—of which racism, anti-feminism, and war are three of many, many examples.

Understanding versus mindlessness, responsible action versus passionate advocacy—these are the crucial opposites. I believe that the severest trials of our profession during the next decade, as during the last, lie somewhere in this zone. The central doctrine of scholarship has become obscured. It requires reaffirmation, preferably by example rather than by fiat. I hope that as the decade passes we shall see once more that exact attention to the stuff of literature and language is a great civilizing force in the world, that it is indispensable to the dignity and peace of nations, as well as of private souls.

Henry Sams
Pennsylvania State University

Workshop I: Doctoral Programs in English

Opening Remarks

After several weeks of haphazard reading and thinking about "Doctoral Programs in English," I must confess to considerable frustration: can we say anything that has not already been said, and, if not, what virtue is there in restatement? I assume, of course, that many of you have not read all or even many of the various essays, statements, and so forth, that I have discovered in the past few weeks. I assume also that most of you gathered here believe that some, perhaps many changes are long overdue. I assume further that the humanities in general, English in particular, have a greater "dread of change" than the natural sciences and the social sciences. "In many universities," to cite a recent report written by Professor Albert J. Guerard, "Ph.D. programs [in the humanities] have scarcely changed at all, all innovations have been hard won." As a rule, Professor Guerard charges, professors of literature are less willing to experiment than our colleagues in the natural and behavioral sciences, including education.[1] Although that report was written in 1965 and much has happened since, I wonder if, as a profession, we aren't still "dragging our heels."

I am not here to argue change for the sake of change, or even to argue that we are less virtuous than our friends in other disciplines. Indeed, I readily admit that a very good argument—in the abstract at least—can be made that traditional values must be supported and that the humanities are the last bastion. However, because it is clear, in the words of Professor Thomas R. Edwards, "that the impulse to reform academic study is best seen as an aspect of a larger dissatisfaction with our social, political and cultural condition,"[2] we must make fundamental changes in the presentation of our discipline at both graduate and undergraduate levels, or we must defend our actions more vigorously than we have been forced to in the recent past, or some compromise combination of both. If we opt for defense alone, we are, in my opinion, almost certain to lose. And I have some basis for my judgment. When Professor Shugrue asked me some time in January to write a summary report for the state of Florida on the "growing tendency" of state legislatures "to mandate policies on such college and university matters as teaching loads, sabbatical and research leaves, tenure decisions, and faculty salaries," I bravely determined to find out first hand what the people in power really thought about our activities. I don't propose to bore you with the vicissitudes of my quest or to summarize the several prefiled bills in Florida. Many of you could recite comparable tales of woe. But I will say that the experience left me a chastened and sad if not wiser man. Although I did not achieve all I had expected, I talked with many people, including a former governor, the Commissioner of Education, and the Chancellor of the State University System; and I scanned several newspapers with more than usual care. One brief paragraph from an editorial in the St. Petersburg *Times* will illustrate my point: "Of course the universities themselves must change. They must make better use of their resources and staff. They must earn the respect of the state's leaders. And the leaders must acknowledge that in an enlightened society the centers of learning are agents of progress, not defenders of the status quo."[3]

There obviously aren't any easy answers. Most of this assembled body will, I'm sure, deny being "defenders of the status quo." Our very presence here is a recognition of the seriousness of our problem and an indication of a willingness to change. We agree, I imagine, though we may deplore the fact, that we are certain to receive the kind of supervision given to other units of the body politic as the university becomes less the community of scholars and more the instrument of social and political reform. We are in truth being forced to defend our actions by the values of the market place, in terms that are effectually a denial of what the discipline of English traditionally represents.[4]

So you say that I'm talking from both sides of my mouth, selling out to the money changers, falling into the traps set by the social sciences on our campuses. Maybe so. But I have convinced myself that the time has come for change—not just a grudging step-by-step withdrawal, but a fundamental change in the kind of training we offer many of our graduate students.

We ought to begin with an honest self-appraisal. As we know by now, thanks to Don Cameron Allen, only one in five doctorates from even our most prestigious institutions ever publishes the results of any significant research beyond the findings in his dissertation.[5] Which is not to say that the research degree has value only for those who publish, but rather that four out of five might have been less frustrated and better able to perform significant social service with different training. At least three conclusions are suggested: (1) that we have encouraged far too many people to pursue unfortunate goals; (2) that we have encouraged inadequately prepared institutions to offer the Ph.D. (originally NDEA Fellowships were used primarily to stimulate new programs); (3) that we have encouraged the waste (or misuse) of human and fiscal resources: (a) by attempting to build research libraries which are not needed (an institution not yet open in my state has a larger library appropriation than either Florida State or the University of Florida); (b) by forcing (through our tenure and promotion policies) many temperamentally unfitted people into directing graduate research and repeating the clichés which the values of the marketplace and academic social status have urged upon us. We can answer, of course, that many successful coaches never played the game, that fancy equipment doesn't make a team. There is little doubt, surely, that American higher education, in the afflatus and competitive zeal of the post-Sputnik years, has misdirected considerable sums of money and many man-hours of effort upon inadequate or unneeded Ph.D. programs. It is entirely possible, I think, that in most states (and the boundary lines are unfortunate here) one distinguished program per discipline supported by adequate faculty and physical facilities (whether library or laboratory) could better train at less expense all the research degrees demanded or needed. I am not, of course, suggesting that we turn the clock back or that we concentrate all our resources in fifty institutions or that we can determine at the B.A. level which people most certainly should pursue the research degree rather than some other degree. But I am suggesting that no state can or will adequately support several research facilities and libraries (by September 1972 Florida will have nine state and three private universities); I suggest also that the equation we are now following in most states is a search for the least common denominator.

Moreover, I am not arguing against the concept or the fact of the drive-in or regional university, but I do deplore the establishment of doctoral programs by political demand rather than social supply. Almost certainly the insistence (by academic people as well as legislators) upon a kind of lock-step duplication of all but the excessively expensive programs will result inevitably in mediocrity and uniformity. In our enthusiasm for copying the oldest and best programs (but usually with stiffer requirements), we have helped to foster a social and political climate which much of our training and experience denies. And the widespread current political partisanship insisting that every new institution must be called a university and must strive to be one surely leads to leveling. Let me suggest the obvious anticipated result in words I have used before: One degree will mean as much as another; one university will be as good as another; one Ph.D. will deserve as much as another; all funds will be allocated by mathematical formula. The strong will be starved, the weak will be force-fed. Ultimately, all "universities" in a given system will have the same quality (excellence if you're optimistic, mediocrity if you watch the legislatures and read the newspapers). In a word, as applied to higher education, democracy must mean absolute equality: virtue can be measured, and it can be legislated.[6]

Which is not to say that we must resign ourselves in quiet desperation, think to serve by standing and waiting. But what can we as a body do? Although I have no panaceas to offer, I will reiterate some suggestions most of you have no doubt already considered. We must here highly resolve to restrict the traditional Ph.D. to those who are in fact capable of significant research (it is too late, I fear, to restrict the institutions also). In our human (if not humane) eagerness to build empires, we have admitted many candidates who should have been enrolled in other programs. If these remarks take on a "holier-than-thou" tone, I ask forgiveness. I intend them rather as a confessional. In the past eleven years I have evaluated five to six thousand graduate applications; I have had some part in studying (evaluating in most instances) more than a hundred Ph.D. programs; and recently at Florida State, as Chairman of a "Special Committee on Graduate Assistantships," I have had the opportunity to consider the admissions policies of most disciplines on our campus. Moreover, I am frank to confess that I have been slow to learn: "you never miss the water till the well runs dry."

I am not, of course, arguing that we have been training too many teachers of English. Though we appear to be at the moment, we might in fact not be training enough if the nation were not suffering from a dread disease—economic dystrophy. But we have surely deceived ourselves and many of our students by offering the wrong training and encouraging false goals. Many of us have thought this for several years at least. As long ago as 1966, in a meeting at Johns Hopkins sponsored by the MLA, I was convinced by Don Allen and Charles Muscatine, among others, that some new degree or track was needed. My impressions were corroborated the following spring by the results of a questionnaire I addressed to the chairman of all the two-year colleges in Florida. In essence they said that the traditional M.A. was inadequate for their purpose. Some of them went further, telling me politely but despondently that the universities had paid no attention to their needs and were in effect behind the times—"antiquarian," to use Professor Guerard's term. I was thoroughly convinced but more than a little uncertain: how could we best satisfy their needs and our students' ultimate goals? Like many another, I was somewhat bewildered by the sheer variety and number of burgeoning intermediate degrees: M.A.C.T., M. Phil., Education Specialist, Licentiate, Candidate, Doctor of Arts, and so on. There was no general agreement, and no degree seemed quite right. If in 1966 the MLA had appointed a blue-chip committee charged with making detailed recommendations for a title, the extent of study, and the indispensable ingredients of a teaching degree, it might have been accepted; and we might now be talking about other things. What can we do in 1971? Since the problem is relevant to many other disciplines, we might be able to enlist the aid of some more comprehensive and powerful agency or organization. I suggested last spring to the four people I knew best in the U.S. Office of Education, those concerned with NDEA Fellowships, that a national committee be formed and at least token fellowships be offered to replace the phased-out NDEA's. Although I received a sympathetic response, nothing has happened. It strikes me still as a good idea, however, and I hope that this group will consider urging the MLA to recommend some such study to Professor J. Wayne Reitz and his colleagues in the Division of University Programs, USOE. If they are not receptive, we might persuade the American Council on Education to undertake the project. At any rate, it seems clear that we need help from some such comprehensive agency if we are to achieve consensus.

Although the two-year colleges, in particular, may not yet be certain of their needs, we should not wait for pat answers, or so I have thought. This spring again I decided to ask for advice, this time through a somewhat more sophisticated questionnaire addressed to far more people. Again the response, especially from the two-year colleges, was beyond expectations, and there surely is a lesson in that. The chairmen told me once more than we are out of step. Although I do not want to suggest that their answers will guide us to an instant resolution of our problem of overproduction, they can help us to solve the problem of malproduction—and in time perhaps the overproduction of research degrees at both graduate levels. Since we have not and probably cannot reach a consensus about an intermediate degree without assistance from some agency like the Office of Education, I am convinced that we should make adjustments in what we have. Assuming that the traditional M.A. and Ph.D. are still valid (my antique bias shows), I suggest that we should consider alternate tracks which will incorporate many of the features urged by my respondents. Most of you know these already, and you are probably sympathetic or you wouldn't be here. I will cite the most important and hope for your suggestions about additions and modifications. Using a scale of one through five ("undesirable" to "essential"), we measured the 44 responses (27 from two-year colleges, 17 from four-year colleges). There was in general far more agreement about needs in the responses from two-year colleges than those from four-year colleges. In a ratio of 3 to 1, the four-year colleges have less interest in the internship and very little interest in the special preparation, but they too want their people without the doctorate to return for further study. As we might expect, the two-year colleges place a high priority on such courses as "The Teaching of Writing," "The Teaching of Literature," "Advanced Composition and Rhetoric," "Contemporary Literature," "World Literature," and "Literary Genres"; the four-year colleges are less certain of priorities. The two-year colleges also place a high priority on courses in educational multimedia, educational psychology, logic, teaching oral communication, educational testing, and mass communication, most of which the four-year colleges are opposed to or consider of limited usefulness. In short, finding the right formula for an intermediate degree or different doctoral degree is complicated by the disparity between the needs and desires of the two-year colleges and the four-year colleges.

It is obvious, I suppose, that some of the old questions remain, especially about the Ph.D. How can we convince students that one track is not better than the other (the marketplace is on the side of the new track, of course)? What kind of meaningful exercise, if any, can we substitute for the dissertation? What part of the traditional requirements will we drop for the new ones? Would almost all our students be well advised to choose the new track? Or should it be a matter of free choice, and, if so, will the wrong students opt for one or the other track? Will the image of the department and the university suffer if a large percentage choose the teaching option? Should we attempt to offer some or all the pedagogical courses in the English department or ask our colleagues in education for more assistance than we now receive?

If many of these questions seem difficult, I can only reply that none of them seem irresolvable at the moment, and they seem relatively unimportant in the context of what we should be doing for the profession of English. We cannot make more jobs. We cannot satisfy all our critics. We must not turn our institutions into academic service stations. But serve we must, and change we must, and surely the time has come. I only hope it hasn't gone.[7]

George M. Harper
Florida State University

Notes

[1] I am indebted to Professor Guerard for permission to quote from his report, "Graduate Education in the Humanities," which was written at the request of John Mays, former Program Director, Science Curriculum Improvement, National Science Foundation.

[2] See n. 7.

[3] From an editorial of 11 March 1971.

[4] See my report "The Legislative Weather in Florida," *ADE Bulletin*, No. 29 (May 1971), pp. 24–27.

[5] Don Cameron Allen, *The Ph.D. in English and American Literature* (New York: Holt, 1968), passim. See also "The Muscatine Report," published as *Education at Berkeley* (Berkeley, Calif.: Univ. of California Press, 1968). In a recommendation for the Doctor of Arts, this report concludes, "The actual number of true research scholars produced is probably only a fraction of the total number of successful doctoral candidates" (p. 169).

[6] Harper, "The Legislative Weather in Florida," p. 25.

[7] In recent months many suggestions for changes in the traditional Ph.D. have been

made. One program at the MLA Meeting last December was devoted entirely to appeals for reforms in the Ph.D. Under the general topic "Need Graduate Education be Obsolete?" three papers were read: (1) Albert J. Guerard, "A Ph.D. Program in 'Modern Thought and Literature' "; Thomas R. Edwards, " 'Relevance' for Mandarins: The Paradoxes of Graduate Literary Study"; Richard M. Ohmann, "Academic Literary Study and the General Culture." I am indebted to Professors Edwards and Guerard for copies of their papers and other materials, and I hope very much that all three papers will soon be published.

Discussion

The discussion concentrated upon three topics: (1) the acceptability of the doctorate to the two-year colleges; (2) the validity of the belief ("myth"?) that the Ph.D. is a research degree and therefore inappropriate for the training of college teachers; (3) the problem of rewarding excellent teaching, especially in graduate institutions, which traditionally reward research rather than teaching. On all of these topics there was a wide range of opinion, and no substantial agreements were reached; however, the discussion established problems and positions for consideration at future meetings.

Workshop II: M.A. and M.A.C.T. Programs in English

In opening this session, Moderator Jack Reese observed that while most universities continue to regard the M.A. degree with varying attitudes of indifference, recent statistics indicate that junior and community colleges, with increasing enrollments, prefer teachers with M.A.'s rather than Ph.D.'s, and that despite efforts by a number of universities to design an intermediate degree specifically to meet this need (M.A.C.T. and others), results are unclear and give little indication of concerted direction. Participants responded to suggest a number of failures with the present programs. M.A. degrees are apt to vary widely from university to university. They seldom require supervised teaching. And the idea of an M.A. rarely attracts the better students, who may follow the subsidized, special course, but more as a means of getting the Ph.D. than out of any interest in junior-college teaching. What exactly inspires the "calling" to such careers is unclear, and few seem genuinely interested. The chief obstacle to designing a satisfactory program, all seem to agree, results largely from a lack of communication between these colleges and the universities. (As if to dramatize the point, of the fifty participants in the workshop only one was associated with a junior college.) Junior colleges serve widely divergent purposes difficult to bring together, and frequently respond more to local and political rather than generally educative instincts, such as the humanities or the respectable degree. Their teachers might thus best be trained, it was suggested, in Departments of Education or Communication. Some hope was urged that the "social commitment" of the current generation might well be turned to such careers, and that the local college might provide the cohesive force once supplied by other institutions (church, and so forth). Such goals were lauded. But the general tone of the workshop seemed more in keeping with John Fisher's concluding observation that, as the private schools of the past century were radically different from the public schools of this, so today's junior colleges, which are of the people and for the people, are eternally separated from the universities, and that in thus attempting to decide upon a course we are simply talking to each other.

Moderator: Jack E. Reese
University of Tennessee

Workshop III: Teachers for the Junior and Community Colleges

In many respects Workshop III continued the discussion of Workshop II. Moderator Bergen opened with a list of the "twenty-one competencies" recently endorsed by the Conference on College Composition and Communication as general guidelines for Junior College English Teacher Training Programs. Unable to manage the number and diversity of these, participants readily accepted Professor Altenbernd's suggestion that they be broken down into three categories:

1. Those now found in all training programs;
2. Those which ought to be included in all programs;
3. Those, incorporated already or new, which are *distinctive* to the needs of junior, community, or "two-year" colleges.

Discussion concentrated on the third category. A number of participants seemed to feel that the attitudes implied by this category were in fact basic to "sensitive, humane teaching anywhere" and need not be stressed in a special program, or else that they could be cultivated more effectively through "intern" programs which would give direct exposure to the peculiar problems involved. Some thought the stress on writing skills was misdirected—or at least exaggerated —in these times. Others observed that while some "competencies" may now be distinct, the necessity for these will pass away as institutions naturally shift from two- to four-year colleges, and we ought thus to anticipate the future by concentrating on a degree with a broader appeal, such as the D.A. The consensus of the participants, however, seemed to acknowledge something special about junior-college teaching, and to desire direction from programs. Professor Bergen described a number of experimental efforts under way at Miami-Dade to meet the "new" students' demand for "a different kind of learning." Professors Ferrell of Arizona State and Morris of the University of Florida outlined plans at their universities, following up studies underscoring the problem, to invite selected successful junior-college teachers to join their faculties and others to their campuses periodically to demonstrate methods which are effective.

Moderator: George T. Bergen
Miami-Dade Junior College

Workshop IV: Teachers for the Liberal-Arts Colleges

Opening Remarks

According to the rhetoric we hold dear, a good liberal-arts college is the true bastion of genuine education, a bulwark against premature specialization, a place where students learn the tools of knowledge and are given the challenge to use them, an Olympus where wisdom is prized above data-mongering, an academy to fund the intelligence with understanding and to develop it through strenuous exercise.

Sometimes, in fact, it actually works out that way. In spite of us. For I suggest that there is little coincidence between what we profess and what we do, and even less between what we do and what we ought to do. Specifically, I want to consider some of these discrepancies in terms of the way we select staff for our departments.

Having sifted through many hundreds of applications and spent long hours at MLA and on campus interviewing, we fill a vacancy by hiring a young Ph.D. who has written a thesis on the letters of an aunt of John Keats and thus is demonstrably a specialist in Romantic poetry. (Did Keats have an aunt? Does it matter?) This done, we've "covered" the period—"John here is our new Romantic man"—we don't have any embarrassing gaps. No academic gossip can whisper that we haven't had somebody "in Romantic" since old Crumrine drowned during a walking trip through the Lake Country. We can hold up our head. ("We've got this young man from Harvard"—or wherever is in vogue this year. "Needs a bit of seasoning, of course, but looks very sound.")

Let's examine ourselves this far. We assume that we need somebody "in the

Romantic period." One of the ways to have an "articulated" program is unquestionably to articulate by periods. But there are numberless other structures of articulation, and they, or a combination of them, may do much more for the student than articulation by historical segment. Granted, it might seem a bit grotesque to have a staff of twelve, none of whom knew anything but the Victorian period. But would it really be any less limited than a distribution by periods in which everyone approached literature with the same thin wash of literary history over an S. Klein's-closeout version of the New Criticism? And isn't that mix pretty much the current orthodoxy? Wouldn't, to push this to extremes, twelve versions of the Victorian period be just as valid as the same version of a dozen different periods?

Do we have to teach every period? Or teach every period through the agency of a "specialist" in the *period*? Does it really serve the student better to put him through a class in the eighteenth century, for example, than to require him to read in the period on his own, after he knows something about the range of ways one can deal with a work, with a literature, and with its relation to other literatures, to history, to culture, and to other arts, and so on?

If the student can't do such a job on his own, once he knows some methodologies, doesn't that provide a good deal of evidence that we are screamingly incompetent? Of course we can disguise our failures, as we do, by demonstrating that the student who takes our course in Shakespeare can pass a final exam in our course better than one who doesn't. But the fakery in that is obvious. And if we'd taught the student properly when he studied Chaucer and Dickens—or prosody and development of the drama—he might just do better on someone else's final in Shakespeare than our students can.

If, by the way, we can expect a properly taught student to do competent work on his own, why can't we expect it of a colleague? Why can't we say to Bill, who does Chaucer, "How about taking some time to work up a course in contemporary poetry?" The one thing we know absolutely about Bill is that he has demonstrated some ability to learn. That much, at least, is guaranteed by the Ph.D. Miles Hanley, the authority on James Joyce's language, was a Chaucer scholar. A number of studies indicate that significant contributions to any area of knowledge are much more likely to be made by people who have come into the field latterly than by those originally trained in it. No classroom educated Einstein in mathematics, much less in theoretical physics. Wittgenstein had no degrees in philosophy. Michael Polanyi moved from medicine to physics to chemistry to social sciences to philosophy, held university appointments in the last three, and did progressively important work with each change of field. John Crowe Ransom has recorded that he was intellectually becalmed for years before a class of bright young men asking new questions propelled him into a new criticism and into *Kenyon Review*.

It's just possible that Harry, who is getting a bit seedy after twenty years of Anglo-Saxon, might be rejuvenated if he were invited to turn his perceptions about language into courses that studied the language of literature from *Beowulf* to Burroughs. His Anglo-Saxon classes might also become a little snappier. I don't think that good minds die. I think they are killed by apathy, routine, and, finally, by fear. ("Take a shot at it, Harry. I know you can do it, and you may find it's fun.") When we're threatened, when we're conscious that we're a little less successful than once we were, we all tend to retreat to something we think is safe and secure. If you recall Kafka's story "The Burrow," you may remember that such a retreat has rather illusory guarantees.

When we have a small staff, of course, we double-up on fields (of necessity). In the present economic crunch, that sort of necessity is known to more and more of us. Unfortunate as reductions in staff are, they may remind us that some of our dogmas are supported more by catechetical (and Pavlovian) iteration than by any demonstration of validity. When we can rebuild, let us redesign rather than merely restore.

Now, consider again our "new Romantic man." If we are a liberal-arts college of medium size, we have (at most) three or four courses in which John's knowledge of the Romantic period is directly useful, and not all of these may be offered every year. Rarely will as much as half his time be devoted to teaching what we want to regard as "his field." John, obviously, has to be kept busy at something else, and so we load him up with, for example, freshman English. When we do that, we've got a teacher of freshman English who occasionally does courses in Romantic literature. His real job, that is to say, is to teach freshman English, and he has not been trained for that job. If he had been, we wouldn't even have interviewed him! (In my own school we don't have freshman English, although we offer a number of sections of literature-cum-writing, and provide a limited tutorial service for any student who wants counsel on his writing.)

However, let's say we hire John (or Jane) and we luck out. He happens to have unusual interests and knowledge in cinema or esthetics or structuralism. He can work effectively in interdisciplinary programs, and is quickly snapped up to work in the college's general-education program for which we provide several FTE's. He is successful in the classroom, and soon picks up all the teaching awards the campus offers. What's more, he publishes—perhaps on cinema and film history and criticism—and reads papers at MLA.

Within a few years, John is a showcase asset of the college, a glory of the department (in the view of the rest of the school). But odds are we'll refuse to promote him. Why? All his publication is outside of what, in the teeth of the facts, we continue to insist is "his field." We hired him as a Romantic scholar, and he damn well better behave as a Romantic scholar.

We pretend we're universities (the universities of our graduate experience long ago), and we're not. We're primarily engaged in the business of comprehensive liberal education, and our profile of an ideal faculty member in an ideal department ought to accord with our primary function.

We have a role and a responsibility and a claim, but we scarcely justify ourselves if we try to validate our curriculum or our personnel by saying "this has been orthodox" or "this is the pattern down the pike at the university." As money and students transfer to American Institutions or Urban Studies or The Third World, we can react by donning the robes of martyrs of the true faith, but the one certainty about martyrs is that they die, and historically the "true faiths" of academic life, in defense of which fine men have fallen, tend to seem, in retrospect, merely eccentric or antiquarian. The survivors write the histories, after all. Consider such true faiths as "Latin and Greek are the true discipline of the educated man" or "Philology is the only valid and responsible approach to literature." Across the country, departmental enrollments are falling. We will not reverse the trend by continuing to suppose that there is only one road to Mecca and that we own the toll booths. The fact is that no immutable law requires that we survive at all. If we intend to, we had better define some educational objectives which will make sense to students and colleagues and administrators, and then consider whether any of our traditional methods and assumptions are really optimum today. What should a liberal-arts student get out of studying literature? What can we best do to help him get it? How? Those are the questions, and if we get the wrong answers, the students (first of all) will grade our failure by continuing to change their majors.

And another question. How can we make the process as exciting for the student as (I trust) it has been for us? Will the means that served for us serve for him? I had always thought that they would, but most of the present evidence seems negative. We tend to look backward rather than forward. Worse, in a tour de force of muddy logic, we confuse our vital concern with previous literature and our devotion to some definition of the discipline with which we have been comfortable (forgetting that our academic orthodoxies are at most a few score years old, and somewhat less dependable than Dante or Shakespeare). We think we are defending literature when we are defending curricular habit fairly recently acquired.

When we seek staff, or plan programs, why not think in terms of a Marxist's approach and a Thomist's and an esthetician's, or of the relation between the structure of a language at a given time and place and the possibilities and limits that offers for a literature, or of a phenomenological approach (if I read the signs correctly, phenomenology is going to be the key term in the next great wave in literary studies), or of a mix of methodological, period, genre, and theoretical courses? Or a contractual approach to the major in which each student works out his own pattern of responsibilities in agreement with a supervisor? Or a pattern of lecture series (not lecture *courses*), of lengths appropriate to the subject matter, which are open to all and ancillary to a tutorial relationship between student and teacher? Or any of numberless other possibilities already defined in seminal works, or of others which, as an old man in the field, I am myself too hidebound to recognize or envisage?

And something else. By what right do we enter a classroom assuming that a student has an educational obligation to take our course and accept our approach to literature and put up with our notions of teaching? We can be smug and superior no longer. The future of the liberal-arts curriculum is up for grabs, and we are not going to be around long if we can offer nothing more persuasive than arguments from a tradition and authority as arbitrary and recent and uncompromising as most of those we have been using.

And it will not be enough for us to confront the reality of our situation today; we are going to have to get a head start on tomorrow. Apart from retooling present personnel, is there anywhere we can look for faculty who can do the jobs we need to do?

Well, once upon a time in Camelot there was a Ph.D. program dedicated to the education of graduate students to teach in liberal-arts colleges. It had an image of the liberal-arts professor as a man educated to an understanding of the methods and uses of disciplines beyond his own (how many of us do?), a man who could communicate with his colleagues in other fields, a man who had some sense of the possibilities and limitations of the role of his discipline in the liberal education of students. It also had the curious notion that a Ph.D. ought to demonstrate some capacity as a teacher before he was turned loose on the academic world. And the stranger notion that a dissertation ought to be written on a subject, and from an angle of interest, which could be expected to come directly into use in some ordinary undergraduate course during the early years of the candidate's first appointment to a teaching post.

Except for these provisions, this Ph.D. program had a fairly conventional definition of relatively concentrated graduate study. It mixed "standard" with interdisciplinary seminars—interdisciplinary as distinct from merely inter-subject. It introduced college-teaching internships. It invited critical and analytical and comparative theses. It used qualifying examinations which put a premium on being able to view a subject area from the top, see its topography in broad lines as well as in particulars, to work comparatively and intensely without losing perspective. It was a daring program for its time, if not daring enough. And it produced some very good teachers, and it was detested by some professors of considerable reputation and by some students who would have been successful in other Ph.D. programs. Curiously, liberal-arts colleges weren't interested in its graduates. Nearly all of them entered universities or state colleges, from Manitoba to Rutgers to San Diego. And it was expensive. And foundation support faded. And since it was the joint venture of a group of liberal-arts colleges, it fell into the difficulties of joint ventures. And it died in time to save it from most of the present embarrassment of Cambridge and Berkeley in being unable to place graduates. It was called the Intercollegiate Program of Graduate Studies (IPGS), and I served on its executive council for about ten years, some of them as chairman. I mention it here only because in some ways IPGS parallelled (although I think ours was better) Ed Volpe's blueprint for a doctoral program in a recent *ADE Bulletin* (which I think is essential reading for any chairman).

However, Ed wants to separate teaching and research, and call the "relevant" degree a Doctor of Arts: D.A. (As you know, the Carnegie people are sponsoring Doctor of Arts programs, and a number of them are already in production or about to get under way.) I disagree. I think scholarship is thinking hard after you've done your homework, and that vital research is not limited to highly specialized work within long-traditional patterns. I would think that new approaches to literature, new methods, new perceptions ought to be demanded of anyone who is teaching in a liberal-arts college. That demand is, in part, a demand for research, but it will not consist in doing to Fletcher what someone else has done to Beaumont, and it seems to me a corruption to argue that the only respectable scholarship is devoted to questions which cannot possibly concern more than half a dozen persons on the globe. Professor Volpe would restrict the Ph.D. to persons who want to devote their lives to esoterica.

Some of us are "heads" of departments and some are "chairmen." (The difference, of course, as we chairmen know, is that a chairman's maximum power extends to deciding which of the junk mail that comes in every day should be posted on the departmental bulletin board.) But whether we make decisions, or have just one vote in making them, I suspect that if we had two candidates for a position, of whom one was exactly what we needed and held the D.A. and the other was a mediocrity with the Ph.D., we would unhesitatingly support the latter. And perhaps we should, if only as a vote against the denigrating of appropriate education with a second-class degree.

The D.A., I think, is an example of the failure I have been talking about, the failure to accord respect to the vital and valid work we need to do, the failure that perpetuates the discrepancy between the dogmas we regard as holy-of-holies and our real obligation to literature itself and to the education of students. Perhaps today we need to concentrate on ways to speed more students into the delights of literature. Scholarship and criticism—have we forgotten?—are ancillary to that.

In short, we can scarcely blame the graduate schools if we continue to accept their products uncritically and if we are content to do nothing more than "prep" candidates for graduate-school admission.

Enough. Given the spectrum of liberal-arts colleges, and of their programs and orientations in literature, I have of necessity been arbitrary in picking as an example one type of situation in some of what are called "good liberal-arts colleges," by which is meant, perhaps, no more than that they are still rather hard for students to get into: "competitive," as the college guides say.

I hope that my remarks have also suggested a sort of movable scale. All of us need to have a new look at our definition of what we ought to do, and of what sort of teacher is needed to do the job. We can get the teachers we'll need in just two ways, by retooling present faculty and by hiring people who can do what we ought to be doing. What we ought to be doing today, and, even more, tomorrow.

Assuming, of course, that in our present practices all of us are not just working out the fulfillment of a collective death wish!

Basil Busacca
Occidental College

Discussion

Mr. Busacca's attack on the Doctor of Arts degree, in the course of his arguing for reform within the Ph.D., prompted most of the discussion that followed. The main argument concerned whether to reform the Ph.D. program to meet the challenge of teaching diverse undergraduate populations or to split the functions of graduate and undergraduate teaching between the Ph.D. and the D.A. Support for broadening the Ph.D., one participant argued, exists among both graduate students and department chairmen searching for candidates. Accrediting teams and college-wide promotion-and-tenure committees may present barriers to such changes, however, particularly in universities with new graduate programs. Those objecting to the D.A. acknowledged snobbism as a barrier to its acceptance, defended scholarship as not necessarily remote from undergraduate teaching, and feared that such a degree would further narrow the Ph.D. program rather than broaden it. Arthur Collins defended the D.A. because of the diversity of graduate students and of teaching situations.

Mrs. Vivian Robinson offered "Remarks" on teaching in black liberal-arts colleges, exploring the effect of desegregation on those colleges and then describing the problems facing their black teachers. As previously all-white schools began to integrate after 1954, they drained both good faculty and good students from the black colleges, which were unable to compete financially. Federal money given to public institutions to encourage them to integrate led to a "two-price system," in which state schools could charge far lower tuition than private black colleges. Also, although government Equal Opportunity Program grants, work-study programs, and abundant loan funds are available to students of the private black colleges, these financial arrangements cannot easily compete with obligation-free scholarships offered by largely white private colleges wanting to integrate. As wider opportunities for study elsewhere have led to declines in enrollment at most black colleges, financial difficulties have increased still further. At the same time, however, white teachers flooded into the black colleges, prompting some resentment from black students who felt they were being viewed as objects either of charity or of research.

Mrs. Robinson emphasized the black teacher's responsibility to two groups: the whole society and the black community. Difficulties in meeting this responsibility come from extremely heavy teaching loads, low salaries, and the need for remedial courses. As possible solutions she suggested increasing specialization of individual colleges and forming a consortium of adjoining colleges to offer students sufficient range of courses. She also recommended increased emphasis on black studies. In concluding, however, she spoke of her satisfaction in knowing students well, witnessing their success in struggling against odds, and seeing the progress of a race.

Workshop V: Meeting Junior- and Community-College Needs

Casting aside her prepared notes, Moderator Elizabeth H. Wooten opened this workshop session by reacting, and urging the participants to react, to two aspects of the problem covered in the opening sessions. First, she directed the participants' attention toward the twenty-one characteristics of the junior-college teacher presented in "Guidelines for Junior College English Teacher Training Programs," and it was agreed that the discussion would assume and build upon this base. Secondly, Mrs. Wooten was concerned about the effectiveness of the Ph.D. for the kind of work demanded by the junior colleges. She opened the workshop to a general discussion of these two points.

Many participants felt that a definition of the junior college and its needs is necessary prior to any debate. The term is a vague one which refers to many different approaches and qualities of education, and consequently it cannot be viewed as one entity. There is one characteristic, however, that is true of all junior colleges. This is the distinction between the terminal and the transfer programs, although the percentage of students in each program would differ greatly for each school.

This problem of defining the junior-college role and its responsibility to cover basics, and basics only, for those students who either will or will not continue their educations naturally led the discussants into the specific needs of this environment. The first emphasis, all agreed, had to be on reading. However, there was some discussion about the definition of the second aim—the idea of communication skills. Some participants held that junior-college teachers deal with large masses who cannot or will not respond. The role of the teacher is to bring them to life in any way and to count any response as successful. Others disagreed and felt that the English department's role is to contribute a general awareness of language and its uses on various levels.

Regardless of the lack of consensus in this area, the participants addressed themselves to the second point outlined by the moderator: How can the traditional Ph.D. student be better equipped to handle this situation? This discussion focused on two aspects: the inculcation of a better attitude toward the junior colleges and the implementation of reforms. The consensus was that an attitude change should occur and that the universities do indeed foster the discrimination which takes place. There was no agreement on how to accomplish change. Many felt that attitudes cannot be taught in such courses as psychology or sociology and that somehow the graduate faculty is responsible for changing the perspective. The discussion concerning implementation was more specific: applied linguistics, a longer internship, and greater interaction between graduate students and happy, successful junior-college teachers are needed.

Mrs. Wooten closed the workshop and formal discussion of the needs of the junior colleges by asking the participants what this conference had generated for them in the way of useful applications. The following summarizes the points made from the floor:

1. The emphasis in the future should be on regional as opposed to national meetings, which are not useful because of the great differences in the needs of various geographical areas.
2. Recent Ph.D's should be solicited for their attitudes about what their graduate schools had done and/or failed to do in preparing them.
3. Successful junior-college teachers should be included on the staff, and the graduate programs must have an internship which incorporates a liaison with the junior colleges. The meeting concluded with the general feeling that junior colleges need and will utilize the services of the Ph.D.'s but that certain revisions in attitudes and training are needed.

Moderator: Elizabeth H. Wooten
Cleveland State Community College

Workshop VI: Meeting Liberal-Arts-College Needs

Opening Remarks

In preparation for this workshop I have tried to find out what English chairmen in independent liberal-arts colleges think their needs are with respect to the graduate training of faculty members and the way candidates present themselves. I want to report what I have learned and then briefly get in my own innings.

I sent a letter to a number of chairmen asking about their needs and raising some other questions about departments in liberal-arts colleges on which we need to be informed. The number of responses I have received is not large, but they are careful and explicit. Their range is wide enough so that where a consensus appears, or a clear dichotomy, it is probably significant. Geographically they range from coastal Maine to southern California, from Michigan and Minnesota to Alabama and Texas. Among them are Catholic colleges, Protestant colleges, and independent colleges. In affluence and the degree to which they are well established academically they range from the Ivy League and the Seven Sisters to a southern black institution and Boondocks College in the Middle West.

It will not surprise you to learn, first, that the chairmen are unanimous in saying they are encountering no difficulty whatever finding qualified candidates for openings. One says, "We have never had the slightest difficulty finding good people to teach at X." Another says, "We received about five hundred applications, mostly from well qualified Ph.D.'s or A.B.D.'s, for a position that did not exist." Still another, writing in March, says, "I have had over 1,000 unsolicited applicants for positions since September 1970." An interesting note sounds in one response, suggesting that English *is* a cult: "We had abundant WASP applicants who are qualified as we would like them to be." The writer goes on to say that much more should be done to attract blacks and Chicanos into the humanities instead of letting them flow almost automatically into the social sciences.

Second, there is a strong consensus among these chairmen that they want people who have or are headed for the Ph.D. Only one response indicates that a chairman finds any promise in the D.A. All the others reject it as preparation for teaching in their departments, most of them very firmly. One who is expansive on the matter says this: "I see no promise whatsoever in Doctor of Arts programs: the very label implies a second-class degree, and any college concerned with its reputation is going to be reluctant to hire persons carrying such a label. I think the answer is, instead, increased flexibility within Ph.D. programs, so that a doctoral candidate may tailor his program to fit his professional objectives without being given a second-class label." It seems quite clear, for better or for worse, that liberal-arts colleges will not contribute significantly to a market for holders of the Doctor of Arts, especially when the Ph.D.'s they prefer are available in such numbers.

But, third, it is also clear that this preference is not an unqualified endorsement of present Ph.D. programs. On this point my correspondents divide between the satisfied and the troubled, and in this division there is a detectable correlation with the degree to which a college is well established academically. One of the satisfied writes, "Although many members of the department express individual misgivings about M.A. and Ph.D. programs, in fact it must be confessed that we look with the greatest favor on Ph.D.'s from manifestly distinguished institutions." Similarly, another writes, "I do not have misgivings about the M.A. and Ph.D. programs, as offered at first-class universities." On the other hand, one of the troubled puts the case this way: "I do have misgivings about Ph.D. programs, however, and they are—and have been—the same ones I, like others, have had for years: namely, an over-emphasis on research leading toward publication; the assumption that most young Ph.D.'s will be teaching largely in their area of specialization, at a university rather than a college, and that chairmen are principally interested in a candidate's publishing potential; continual (incredible) neglect of training in teaching techniques generally and in the teaching of composition particularly."

One chairman who expresses approval of present Ph.D. programs adds, "but I do have some concern about what they are led to believe by their graduate advisors concerning liberal-arts colleges." This note sounds, almost like a ground bass, through many of the letters: the attitudes and expectations picked up during Ph.D. study are not suited to gratifying and effective work in a small college; graduate students and their graduate-school professors fail to recognize differences between the university and college settings. Two chairmen can represent all who emphasize the point. One says: "Too much specialization at too early an age is sometimes destructive to degree candidates and it sometimes makes young teachers feel insecure about attempting things outside their specialty. It tends to make them too self-protective and insufficiently daring." Another says: ". . . the

Ph.D. programs become so very limited and so very specialized that frequently the instructor cannot adjust himself to the kind of task that I expect him to be able to do. . . . I would appreciate it if the candidates themselves would tell me a little more about what their interests are in the first letter but without telling me about all the advanced courses they may want to teach. I think that I might take a long and thoughtful look at any letter I received in which the candidate said he really was interested in teaching and that he would not mind teaching those fundamental English courses which we are all so familiar with. . . . I am very likely to give more favorable consideration to a person whose undergraduate work was taken in the 'small' liberal-arts college and who then has gone on for graduate work at one of the larger universities."

From all this I conclude, in summary, these things: the Ph.D. has rather firm support in independent liberal-arts colleges; the D.A. and other new degrees will have very little support there; the skills, attitudes, and expectations that Ph.D. students acquire are often not well suited to fruitful work in liberal-arts colleges, and hence they stir up some discontent among chairmen.

To this point I have been trying simply to report the state of affairs as word of it reaches me. I now want to supplement the report with some related ideas of my own.

I think it should first be asked whether graduate departments ought to be expected to listen attentively to liberal-arts colleges and, if so, why. The proportion of American undergraduates we teach and the proportion of Ph.D.'s we absorb into our faculties have declined and will almost inevitably continue to decline. As money pressures increase in the coming decade, many colleges will cease to exist—in their present form or at all. Surely there is abroad some temptation to think that the liberal-arts college represents a fading elitist past and the two-year college represents a blooming democratic future. And to some extent this is true. It cannot be countered merely by the widespread nostalgia humanists feel for the small college as a pastoral retreat. But the independent colleges do have solid value. They do foster personal relationships between undergraduates and faculty and thus enrich both learning and teaching. They have sent large numbers of very talented students on to graduate schools for advanced work. They have a resilient, adaptable tradition that may enable them to survive present challenges with their academic strength intact—at least those that have substantial financial strength as well. It is important that they do survive, for liberal education carried on without the direct professional pressures from an interpenetrating graduate program has value as a norm and an influence. So the independent colleges should be listened to.

With respect to graduate training, I feel that some of my colleagues at other colleges are too confident that their world will continue to turn as it has turned in the past. That is, I am one of the troubled, not one of the satisfied. I believe they should be willing to consider teachers holding the D.A. (I say this from a special perspective, for I have taught graduate students at Carnegie-Mellon and know their quality; indeed I had a hand in designing the D.A. program there as it now is.) But I believe, further, that they will need teachers holding Ph.D.'s who are prepared to work widely within the traditional subject matter of the Ph.D. in English and also well beyond that subject matter. I do not see how the Ph.D. in English can long survive in a more flourishing state than the Ph.D. in Greek unless it is willing to enlarge its scope. On such an adaptive enlargement depends, in my view, not only the future of graduate study in English but of undergraduate English as a liberal art.

Let me explore this briefly, though what I say will in part have a familiar ring. When René Wellek and Austin Warren looked at "The Study of Literature in the Graduate School" (published in 1947 in essay form in the *Sewanee Review*; later included in the 1949 edition of *Theory of Literature*), they felt that the traditional literary specialist was no longer the teacher most needed in departments of English:

. . . we should seek to make our professors of English into professors of Literature. (*Theory of Literature*, 1949, p. 290)

Universities should appoint to their vacant chairs only men of general intellectual and literary distinction, the best they can find. (p. 291)

It is the present presumption that a man teaches only after he has published a book or article on the author to whom the course is devoted. We might better argue, however, that he should teach the course only till he has published his book. After his view has been developed and committed to print, it is a waste of time to have it repeated and diluted in lectures. (p. 291)

A professor of literature should be able, with proper *ad hoc* preparation, to teach and to write on any author or period within his linguistic compass. . . . Research of a "factual" sort is not necessary to the production of sound criticism. But, what the teacher-critics does need, of course, is the grasp his training in the methods of literary scholarship should give him—the ability to judge the general reliability of published research, the ability to analyze the assumptions and logic of other literary scholars, the ability to analyze a poem, novel, or play. (p. 291)

Preface to Second Edition, 1955:

We have . . . decided to drop the last chapter of the first edition ("The Study of Literature in the Graduate School") which ten years after its publication (1946) seems out of date, partly because some of the reforms suggested there have been accomplished in many places. (p. ix)

In 1955 Wellek and Warren dropped that chapter from the second edition of *Theory of Literature* "partly because some of the reforms suggested there have been accomplished in many places." That judgment seems to me to have been a wild flight of euphoria. Every graduate student who inquires after a job to this date pigeonholes himself as a specialist in some field.

We ought, I think, to be able in a Ph.D. program to give students a sound grounding in language, in methodologies of literary study, in esthetics and literary theory, and in practical criticism. We ought to be able, further, to give them greater scope than our traditional subject matter on which to exercise their growing skill.

Chaucer should be there, but why not place him beside Cervantes or Fielding instead of the Pearl Poet and Langland? Pedagogic interests should be acceptable. A student interested in Tolstoi or Proust or Grass should have some chance to work with them in graduate school instead of reading them afterward. Literature of the Third World should be included, as should film.

I do not mean to suggest diluting the Ph.D. (though some will think I am doing so), or to suggest distorting it into relevance. I do mean to suggest extending sound work with literature over a broader range. I do mean to suggest addition, restructuring, realignment of emphases—not subtraction.

Ed Volpe suggested this morning that there is futility in these ideas, that at the present time value structures will not allow them to be considered seriously. Mike Shugrue has said the same. I don't believe, however, that those who think as I do can afford to stop saying so. Paradoxically perhaps, the future of English as an undergraduate liberal art seems to me closely tied to the graduate professional programs that train undergraduate teachers of English. They will gain or lose ground together.

I want to see the Ph.D. degree flourish. I agree that scholarship is responsibility to truth. But I would align myself with both Henry Sams and John Fisher, between whom I see no irreconcilable differences whatever. Scholarship must survive; to survive it must be exercised professionally from the start in diverse ways and on a greater range of material.

Neal Woodruff
Coe College

Discussion

The discussion session saw great need for active programs of teacher placement in graduate schools using extensive briefings and personal interviews to acquaint each student with the different qualities sought in university, junior-college, and liberal-arts-college teaching. One graduate school has typed out a list of its professors and the different schools where they have connections. This "old boy" method of hiring was seen as undemocratic but necessary because of the percentage of unspecific, dishonest recommendations in students' dossiers. One member suggested a national file of dossiers with standardized kinds and sources of information. Another pleaded for honesty in giving the relative completeness of the student's dissertation. Most agreed that the lists of students and their specialties sent out by graduate schools were a crude and useless sales device. Some disagreement arose about the overall quality of the flood of application letters received by all schools this year. Some felt that by claiming too many skills, some applicants buried their individual personalities. Many noted an increased eagerness to teach freshman composition. Others felt that many letters, in sticking to the "MLA format," emphasized the student's specialty and so inadvertently snubbed the more general needs of the liberal-arts college. Some felt this attitude is implanted by the graduate schools; others saw it as the fault of the hypocritical evaluation and interviewing procedures of the colleges themselves. Most agreed that the ideals of a liberal education—breadth of interest, flexibility of approach, eagerness to work up courses in new areas—should not be stifled by the graduate schools and should be encouraged in college faculties by sharing advanced courses and developing newer, more experimental ones. One participant pointed out the difficulty of publishing while carrying the broad, heavy liberal-arts teaching load. The moderator said the applicant should ask each school's publishing policy at his interview. None of the eight liberal-arts schools represented claimed to require publishing for promotion or tenure. Some members, however, saw the danger of overspecialization in doctoral programs as a myth. They pointed to the close connection between research and teaching, the relatively small portion of the program taken up by the dissertation itself, and the variety of techniques and approaches that could be employed in preparing it. One participant asked whether any of the schools represented had had trouble finding well-suited candidates for all their openings. When no one denied it, he questioned the value of even discussing hiring criteria, since no amount of suitable preparation could lessen the percentage of applicants unable to obtain one of the small number of positions available.

Workshop VII: Supply and Demand for M.A.'s, M.A.C.T.'s, Ph.D.'s

Moderator Webb opened this workshop session with personal remarks about how the present state of affairs in Illinois has resulted in the following conditions at SIU: a freeze on hiring, a reduction in assistantships, and a reduction in the required courses in freshman English. He stressed that although he was near panic, as was the profession, we must work not only on reducing the number of graduate students, but also on extending their usefulness and promoting society's need for them. He suggested that we might do this by fighting the reduction in general-education requirements, opening vistas toward professions other than teaching, restructuring the graduate program, and vitalizing attitudes and training in traditional programs.

The ensuing general discussion concerned itself with three major points. The first related to the moderator's comment about the effect of a general reduction of requirements as one of the immediate causes of the lack of openings. Most respondents stated that they either had to reduce the number of staff positions or could not increase them; the feeling was mixed, however, about the efficacy of fighting the reduction of requirements. Some felt that it was inevitable in the future of education and that the schools would have to adjust accordingly. Others agreed with the moderator in holding the line against allowing either external or internal decisions to affect this. For those so affected, the alternative proposal was the creation of courses on the freshman and sophomore level which attracted the students and combined reading and writing, for example, under a thematically structured course.

The second aspect of the discussion was oriented toward the problem of the Ph.D.'s. What were the short-term plans for handling these problems? Several solutions were advanced. The first involved the department's taking care of its own graduates for a year until a job could be found. Eight department heads were doing this. The other plan was for the creation of a term position, called either an instructorship or assistant professorship, whereby the Ph.D.'s were hired for a year's nonrenewable contract to teach basic courses. Some members objected to this latter plan because it re-created a second-class society, where the people in this position would be second-class citizens. The consensus was that, unfortunately, this aura would be attached but that this was better than having no jobs at all. The third solution was to filter Ph.D.'s into the secondary-school system in order to improve the overall quality of education. In some states there are stringent certification requirements, but these could be overcome by modifying the training. In other states there are no requirements, but there are not enough jobs open for all who want them.

With these rather gloomy comments about the stopgap measures that are now being used and a general awareness of their nonavailability, the participants turned their attention to long-term solutions. Everyone agreed that a greater and more specific dissemination of information was vital. The ADE should recommend that each school make a statement for publication about the situation at that school. This information should include such facts as the total number of available jobs, the supply, the financial situation, and so forth. Certain problems were raised about the fact that much of this kind of information is not known until the end of the school year. However, it was felt that several reports could overcome this problem. The more important resolution, which not everyone agreed to, was that there should be an across-the-board reduction of graduate students. It was suggested that, once the information had been assembled, all participating members reduce across-the-board by X percent, the X to be worked out by the ADE. The workshop ended with several participants gathering to formulate a more specific resolution to present.

Moderator: Howard Webb
Southern Illinois University

Workshop VIII: Open Admissions and Graduate Education

Edmond Volpe's opening statement claimed that the recent rapid growth of junior colleges made open admissions a fact rather than a question. This fact could be justified by the number of students now eligible for college whose intelligence had not been adequately measured by standardized tests. Reaching these students, however, demanded a revamping of graduate education to teach the development of intellectual skills rather than scholarly control of certain areas. Mr. Volpe felt that if this preparation were relegated to education departments or teacher's colleges, they might usurp the role and the status of the Ph.D. program.

As Mr. Volpe had predicted, his proposals set off a lively series of questions: Was not "the development of intellectual skills" already the purpose of most freshman composition courses? Could such an approach be made to include the whole curriculum? Should a work of literature, for instance, be presented as something to know about, or should it rather become an exemplar on which a student might test ideas from different fields or from life itself? Should the graduate schools be using this approach, or should the new teacher work it up in his own undergraduate classroom? Could this reform of higher education level off the tremendous cultural gap between the students destined for the Ivy League and those able to enter college only under open admission? Finally, did the latter students really want the intellectual sophistication offered by this new approach or only the social and economic status offered by vocational training?

Some participants applauded this drive for status; others saw it threatened either by cultural barriers or by the economic impossibility of having "all chiefs and no Indians." Some blamed the campus protests on the disappointment of these disadvantaged students; some blamed them on the questioning encouraged by Mr. Volpe's brand of curriculum reform; others, who saw these students as victims of society, felt that their protests might help change this society. To the charge that these protests were undermining America's faith in and support for higher education, these same members countered that America had faith only in the specialists produced by this education—that it was the current oversupply of such "products" which caused the corresponding decline in financial support.

One member suggested that the tight labor market could be eased and the experience, maturity, and motivation of all college students increased by initiating a two-year national service program for high-school graduates. Others suggested combining junior college with the last year of high school to offer remedial help for those now entering under open admissions. All agreed that the different backgrounds and attitudes of these students were forcing them to reappraise the methods and goals of higher education.

Moderator: Edmond L. Volpe
City College, CUNY

Workshop IX: Promotion and Tenure

In her introductory remarks Moderator Shrodes expressed the danger of projecting upon a discussion of tenure and promotion the extreme views which are peculiar to California and a few of its colleges. Although one's view of such policies will be in large part a function of the character and constituents of one's own institution, she suggested that it is possible to define a number of problems common to all institutions. The more common threats to tenure and promotion appear to be the elimination of positions by economy-minded state governments or trustees and subtle forms of political repression that may be exercised by some college administrators. Internally, departmental or college-wide policies may limit the dispensation of tenure and promotion to those scholars whose publications reflect a special kind of scholarship. She suggested that the context of a discussion of tenure and promotion is the forces outside and within the profession which militate against a faculty member's legitimate expectations and his rights to due process.

The discussion which followed suggested that the debate over tenure and promotion is being organized around several well-defined issues. First, there is an increasing awareness that distinguished teaching should play a larger role than it now does. Many universities are now using visitation to the classroom; more perhaps require the results of student evaluations. Connected with this trend is the increasing demand by administrators that measurable objective data (such as that provided by student evaluation) be provided in tenure recommendations. Perhaps the most dramatic development is the increasing discussion of five-year tenure review as a substitute for the traditional concept of tenure. Many college presidents seem to feel that the time is ripe for such a change. The more frequent use of visitation to the classroom and student evaluation has also brought new problems. Students, for example, may defend a teacher because they know his position is threatened, yet privately confide that he is not effective. The granting of tenure may, in fact, become a public issue to be fought out between students and administrators. Many younger faculty object to the double-faced nature of visitation: that is, even though the procedure is presented as an aid to effective teaching, it may represent a threat to the young teacher's career. Following the discussion, two conflicting conclusions were expressed. One view is that each state university that comes under public pressure is going to have to fight its own battles over promotion and tenure because each case is unique. The other view suggests that the profession must come to some agreement over standards for promotion and tenure. Otherwise, tenure problems will become unmanageable.

Moderator: Caroline Shrodes
San Francisco State College

General Session: ACE Ratings of Graduate Programs and Faculties

In his opening remarks, Moderator Carl Woodring suggested that four questions should be considered in regard to the ACE ratings: (1) Is a rating program worth doing? (2) Does anyone know how to do it? (3) Is the ACE rating program well done? (4) What do we do now that we have the report?

Responding, Charles Anderson of the American Council on Education attempted to provide a rationale for the ACE ratings. Since the current rating is, in effect, a redoing of the 1963 Cartter report, Mr. Anderson suggested that one good reason for attempting a new rating was to avoid freezing the reputations of graduate programs. He then outlined the methodology used in preparing the ratings. The results were obtained from a questionnaire survey sent to knowledgeable scholars identified by graduate deans. The respondents were asked to score graduate programs of which they had knowledge in three areas—the graduate faculty, the effectiveness of the graduate program, and changes made in the past five years. Of the eight thousand questionnaires sent out, six thousand were returned, from which the final results were compiled. Mr. Anderson felt that three principal needs could be met by the ratings. Although they are probably least helpful to the academician, since he already has some idea of the relative positions of graduate schools, he can use the survey to advise students as well as in his own career, and academic administrators need guidelines in future planning. Secondly, the ratings are of value to students planning for graduate training. And, finally, planners outside of higher education need such information for decisions affecting the universities. Mr. Anderson stated that if the ACE ratings were not available, these planners would use other, less reliable information.

David Bevington's response to the ACE ratings centered on the effect such ratings might have in discouraging new approaches in graduate education. Prestige graduate schools need change rather than congratulations, and the ACE report could adversely affect change, since graduate deans using the ratings might well ask their institutions to follow the leaders. The ratings assume a certain set of standards by which excellence in graduate training is measured—primarily publication and scholarship. Publication eminence is a suitable criterion for certain kinds of institutions, but should such criteria apply to all graduate schools? The ACE ratings have the effect of reinforcing such criteria. Mr. Bevington indicated that the prestige institutions have a responsibility in leading graduate education. They should retain the teaching of scholarship for those prepared to do it, but they should also offer a diversity of approaches to bridge the gap between scholarship and teaching. The ACE ratings have not done enough to encourage new programs.

Richard Beale Davis questioned the reliability of a questionnaire survey. For example, how much do or can the University of Nebraska respondents to the questionnaire know about Massachusetts or South Carolina? He also observed certain tendencies, such as that of the "old guard" AAU schools to retain high ratings and the tendency of private institutions to outrank state universities. He concluded by stating that he doubted the value of such ratings, but if they are to continue, (1) they should be done regionally; (2) a committee of people who are experts should weight the findings of the regional evaluators and then arrange and order ratings only after thorough investigation, including, possibly, visits to the institutions; and (3) the evaluators should ask the smaller college or undergraduate college staffed by the rated institutions its opinion of the graduate preparation at each institution.

Claude W. Faulkner stated that such a report as the ACE ratings can measure only scholarship, not teaching, and thus it is a carryover of a reward system for publication from the individual level to the departmental level. In addition, the terms used in rating departments are so vague as to be almost meaningless. Since, he suggested, there is no consensus on what we should be doing in graduate education, it's hard to say who's doing it well.

George J. Worth also questioned the reliability of the report, since it is obviously very difficult to know what goes on in other departments, especially in regard to such matters as curriculum and advising. Therefore, the report is making judgments on very sketchy information. He stated that if there were sufficient time and resources, there might be ways of finding out which were the good graduate programs. Such a method would include on-site inspections of institutions by experts who would conduct interviews and give evaluations, although he would not recommend that, since the whole matter of ratings is of questionable value, even to students considering graduate study. Mr. Worth noted that all the prestige institutions were now in serious trouble with their students and suggested that in the process of getting good ratings they were doing things which produced these troubles. A distinguished faculty which provides high ratings may not, in fact, be accessible to students. He concluded that the choice of a graduate school is a serious matter—too serious to be left to graphs and reports. The ratings are open to abuses which can cause people to make serious mistakes.

Replying to the criticism of the ratings, Mr. Anderson noted, in regard to Mr. Davis' point about the lack of knowledge on the part of the respondents, that a majority of the answerers checked the "I don't know" category, which would indicate that the respondents were not attempting to make judgments when they had no information. He also noted that there was a correlation between the number of people who rated an institution and the high score that institution received, suggesting that the ratings were primarily a visibility index or a reputation index. Mr. Anderson admitted that the report is only one of many tools available to students selecting a graduate school, but one thing it can do is to point out many good schools in addition to the most prestigious ones. Mr. Anderson stated further that Mr. Davis' recommendation of selecting respondents from small liberal-arts colleges was considered, but lack of time and resources prohibited this. He stated that there was no obligation for another report, but said he felt that it very well may be done again for the simple reason that people will look at *some* rating, and if a current rating is not available, they will use an old one. He did suggest, however, that the rating will probably never be done again in the same way. The present rating measures reputations, but there is a need to go further to see how reputation has been gained. He concluded that it is an imperfect instrument, but its benefit is greater than its harm.

The meeting was then opened for questions from the floor. Gordon O'Brien, University of Minnesota, asked why there was no mention of library holdings. Mr. Anderson answered that the limitations of time and money prohibited this. John Guilds, University of South Carolina, asked: Were the only people to rate English departments English professors? (Answer: Yes.) Were they allowed to rank their own departments? (Answer: Yes.) Does this not produce a vested interest? (Answer: This does not significantly affect the score. There is only one-tenth of one point's difference in the score when these answers are removed.) Would regional ratings affect the rankings significantly? (Answer: There is no more than three-tenths of one point's difference between national and regional ratings.)

Arthur Collins, State University of New York, Albany, asked: Has anything happened with the recommendation that graduate study be limited to fifty institutions? Mr. Anderson answered: No. But this recommendation does not mean that only fifty should have graduate programs, rather that only fifty should produce research-oriented Ph.D.'s. Mr. Collins asked if Mr. Anderson had been persuaded by Mr. Worth's statement that this would be an unwise thing to do. Mr. Anderson answered that he did not think it would happen.

Kenneth Knickerbocker, University of Tennessee, noted that when the 1963 Cartter report came out his department was not rated, yet all his faculty came from the prestigious institutions. He had pointed out this irony to Cartter, whose reply was that he should take the report to his president in an effort to buy two prestigious professors. Mr. Knickerbocker asked: What happens to the prestige institution which is raided? If your reputation goes up, does its reputation go down? Mr. Anderson answered, Yes, if you get a really good man.

Mr. Anderson concluded by posing this question: What happens if we do not have this type of rating? People want something to measure graduate programs. The report represents a compendium of expert opinion. If it were not available, people would find other data.

Moderator: Carl Woodring
Columbia University

Speaker: Charles Anderson
American Council on Education
"The Rationale of ACE Ratings"

Discussants:
David M. Bevington
University of Chicago

Richard B. Davis
University of Tennessee

Claude W. Faulkner
University of Arkansas

George J. Worth
University of Kansas

Concluding General Sessions

Resolutions

1. *Moved*: That the conference extend its appreciation to Kenneth L. Knickerbocker and the English Department of the University of Tennessee for hospitality and charm extended during the conference.
Unanimously approved.

2. *Moved*: That this conference disavow that any practical use is to be gained from the current ACE Ratings of Graduate English Departments, and encourage ACE to investigate more effective methods of evaluation.
Approved.

3. *Moved*: That this conference call upon the ADE

membership to protest the development of any policy that would restrict federal support of graduate education to a limited number of the most prestigious institutions as identified in the recent ACE report.

Unanimously approved.

4. *Moved*: That English departments and college and university administrations be urged to consider their "reward" system so as to give significant attention to qualifications other than published research in determining salaries, promotions, and tenures, and that among those other qualifications be systematically evaluated success in teaching and important professional and administrative service.

Unanimously approved.

5. *Moved*: That this conference reassert the enduring value of the Ph.D. degree, with its emphasis on scholarship, as a highly effective vehicle for the training of college teachers, while at the same time it encourage continued experimentation with other programs of graduate study designed to meet the expanding and varying needs of students and teachers in our discipline.

Approved.

6. *Moved*: That this conference urge MLA, ADE, and NCTE to extend their efforts to provide full and accurate information concerning the number and kinds of positions available in the English departments of institutions of higher education.

Unanimously approved.

7. *Moved*: That this conference urge MLA, ADE, and NCTE to investigate means of maintaining and increasing the demands for the services of holders of degrees in English.

Unanimously approved.

8. *Moved*: That this conference urge MLA and ADE to consider equitable means of adjusting the supply of various kinds of degree holders to the demand for their services.

Unanimously approved.

9. *Moved*: That graduate English departments be (1) urged to employ a community-college "specialist" to assist in liaison between nearby community colleges and the graduate English department; (2) urged to place in their curricula some courses, other than literature and linguistics, determined to be needed by prospective or practicing teachers of the first year of college English; and (3) asked to consider a teaching internship, at least elective, for every advanced degree.

Unanimously approved.

10. *Moved*: That this conference instruct the ADE Executive Council to explore the possibility of the MLA or the ADE sponsoring every six or eight years a rating of graduate English departments.

Approved.

Presiding: Martin Price
Yale University

ADE-CCNY Seminar, April 1972*

The workshops at the seminar in New York in April dealt primarily with the relation of open admissions to interdisciplinary study.

Resolutions of the Open Admissions Workshop

Passed at ADE-CCNY Seminar, April 1972

With the shift in admissions standards that has taken place in many colleges throughout the country, it is urgent that programs of study be designed that will provide a positive climate for the personal and academic development of students.

We therefore recommend that colleges develop a positive approach to language learning that will remove the stigma of remedial instruction and broaden the base of responsibility for each student's development through interdisciplinary approaches to language study.

We further recommend increased resources for:

1. Supportive services such as writing labs and learning centers.

2. Planning and development of curriculum and materials.

3. The organization of agencies within colleges for creating staff understanding, from top administrative posts on down, of the new college student.

4. An ADE clearinghouse for the circulation of information on open-admissions programs and problems.

Finally, we affirm that the grades we traditionally use are not sensitive measures of the total progress of all students, and we urge the development of more accurate methods of describing this progress.

Workshop on Curricular Tactics**

The workshop on Curricular Tactics met for three sessions during the April CCNY-ADE Seminar an Interdisciplinary Education.

Prior to the opening of the workshop, participants received the following agenda from Professor Joseph Frank (U. Mass., Amherst), the workshop leader:

I would like to keep my workshop informal and open-ended. I am assuming that the participants are interested in curricular reform and innovation. Therefore I would like to use a very short and simplified outline—something like the following:

(1) How to manipulate administrators.
(2) How to cajole colleagues.
(3) How to utilize students.

Though the above suggests Machiavelli's *The Prince* for advanced reading, I don't think any homework is necessary.

In the workshop which followed, no specific set of topics was universally adopted and discussed. Participants did, indeed, address themselves to questions one and three proposed above; nevertheless, they also discussed several other major questions. Discussion was informal, unstructured, and open-ended in nature and scope. No attempt was made to confine discussion to any particular, systematic progression, though there were occasional attempts to limit discussion to the subject at hand, i.e., the means rather than the ends of interdisciplinary

---

* Reprinted from *ADE Bulletin*, No. 34 (Sept. 1972), p. 53.
** Reprinted from *ADE Bulletin*, No. 35 (Dec. 1972), pp. 36–38.

education. The workshop arrived at no specific resolutions for the seminar at large, yet amid the workshop's broad exchange of experience and ideas some degree of unexpressed unanimity was probably arrived at.

Professor Frank opened the first session of the workshop with the following statement:

Two components of change are at work today within English curriculums: the first is a broadening and redefinition of the concept of "English," a process through which the discipline is being made more inclusive; the second is a quantitatve and qualitative democratization of college education in general, through which curriculums are tending to become both more expansive and more relevant. The implication, of course, is that interdisciplinary studies suggest both a means and an end for such changes.

Four major questions were thereafter discussed by participants in the three sessions of the workshop. For the sake of clarity I shall outline these questions topically—though not necessarily in the order in which they were discussed (since they were discussed in no particular order). Answers provided are not necessarily definitive or exclusive. Not all questions were answered.

I. What is the purpose of interdisciplinary studies?

Q. Are teachers bored?

Q. Are we appeasing students?

Q. Are interdisciplinary studies helping to engender better courses and educational experiences?

Q. Have not the problems encountered in teaching language courses to minority students become interdisciplinary as a result of necessity?

Q. Are not ethnic studies hazardous which center more on problems of identity than on specific skills?

Q. Is there not a certain inherent difficulty in agreeing on basic assumptions when a white teaches a course in black studies?

A. We can teach literature of all kinds as literature; we cannot, however, all teach certain experiences (e.g., the black ghetto experience). (M. Shinagel, Union Coll.)

A. Fisk College in Nashville offers an extended seminar in the methodology of teaching black studies. (R. Purnell, Fisk Univ.)

Q. What reasons can be given for the crises which English departments face today?

A. The New Critical approach, once secure in its methodology of attacking works of art as autonomous organisms, is today under attack from sociologists, psychologists, economists, and others.

A. English departments in large universities may offer the entering student the only small classes he will encounter in his freshman year. Beyond the skills he is teaching, the English teacher also fulfills a certain humanizing role of leadership, a role which will have great bearing on the success or lack thereof which a student may have in the subsequent three years of his college education. (J. Frank, Univ. of Massachusetts, Amherst)

A. The large body of students enrolled in English courses is made up of a very diverse assortment of specialties and interests—not just of English majors. We must first recognize just who our constituents are. (P. Stein, SUNY, Genesee)

II. What is the role of faculty in interdisciplinary studies? What standards should be adopted in the recruitment of young faculty?

Q. Does our graduate training allow us to teach general courses well? Have we been taught any methodology?

A. A professor is no longer a teacher (in the conventional sense of the term) when he is teaching an interdisciplinary course; he is a resource to the class rather than an authority figure. (A. Bierman, CCNY)

A. It is incumbent on us to be scholars in Chaucer and his background—as well as in contemporary black literature and its backgrounds. But we must also learn what is universally human in all literature. (M. Konick, Lock Haven State Coll.)

Q. How do we recruit well-trained teachers who will be qualified to participate in interdisciplinary education?

A. Perhaps we should be encouraged to hire people with broad backgrounds and not just narrow labels. We need people who are able to teach and administrate interdisciplinary studies. Too many of the people we hire have little actual teaching experience. (M. Shinagel, Union Coll.)

A. One tactic for recruiting specialists in black studies is to sponsor one of your black undergraduates, send him to graduate school with aid from your own administration, and then bring him back when he receives his degree. This has proved successful at Houghton College. (J. Barcus, Houghton Coll.)

III. How can students be attracted?

A. Perhaps students should be involved in the construction of topics and the selection of materials.

Ex. In the sciences at CCNY there are several "double" seminars restricted to twenty students and requiring readings and a research project. Two faculty members, each from a different discipline, teach the course. A reading list and syllabus are prepared for the first few weeks; thereafter, the program and reading list grow out of the course. The weakness of such courses may lie in a loss of focus and continuity, while the strength lies in the sharing of work load and of planning by students and faculty. (A. Bierman, CCNY)

Ex. Three types of freshman seminar were experimented with at Trinity:

1. a seminar with a topic and a stated reading list
2. a seminar with a topic but no reading list
3. a seminar with no topic and no reading list

Results: students did not like the first; professors did not like the third; the second was most successful, but five weeks were generally lost in a fourteen-week term. (R. Foulke, Skidmore Coll.)

A. Perhaps students should be involved in administration.

Ex. At San Francisco State students were persuasive in demanding that an alternative experience be set up in conjunction with community colleges in the area. Students also are effective on the general policy advisory board. (C. Shrodes, San Francisco State Coll.)

Ex. In 1963 students at CCNY met with the English department to restructure the curriculum and the department. Students were very helpful. Most departments at CCNY have some sort of student caucus that acts with it on curriculum matters.

Ex. Since the inception of Paine College, students have been represented on all committees. (V. Robinson, Paine Coll.)

IV. How can administrators be manipulated?

A. "Innovation" as a label for a course having the support of at least two students may be a very strong persuasive tool for generating courses with an administration. (J. Frank, Univ. of Massachusetts, Amherst)

Q. How can faculty senates be circumvented?

A. Experiment for a year! Not even the most conservative administrator will say no to an experimental course which you promise faithfully to evaluate regularly.

You may even find it no problem to get a second year's support from the administration.

Q. How do you handle interdisciplinary courses financially? From where do the funds derive?

A. Certain departments are more interested in such experiments and will be willing to release a professor to teach the course. It results in an interchange.

A. It all depends on the will of human beings involved in the situation. It does not depend on beautiful plans. Paper plans are worthless. Put your emphasis on humans. It is a cop-out to say it is the system. You can still accomplish an awful lot if you are determined. (W. Birenbaum, Staten Island Community Coll.)

Q. How do you circumvent the FTE (Full Teacher Equivalent) so as to permit professors to teach outside their departments?

A. At the moment, chaos in some schools is so great that you can get away with quite a bit. (W. Birenbaum, Staten Island Community Coll.)

Q. How are tactics modified and controlled by the existence of a new type of English chairman, the chairman appointed not for a tenured period but for a three-year term?

President Birenbaum of Staten Island Community College concluded the final session of the workshop by pointing out three major obstacles that stand in the way of productive interdisciplinary studies:

1. Not enough people truly understand the meaning of freedom. Freedom requires discipline.

2. Courage is at total war with the security instinct; the latter overcomes ideology, conviction, and freedom.

3. There is a danger that high-strung goals will overshadow the absolute necessity of conveying weaponry systems to students (i.e., mathematics and English). There is a dangerous tendency to substitute identity courses for weaponry courses. English and mathematics skills have tremendous political and economic importance.

Michael J. Rose
Alma College

ADE San Francisco Seminar, June 1972

Finally, the San Francisco Seminar in June 1972 voted approval of one written workshop report and passed resolutions which summarized the work of the year.

Workshop Report on Interdisciplinary Studies*

Preface

The workshop on the design of an interdisciplinary program resembled at different moments an encounter group, a seance, a team-teaching unit in search of a classroom, and the most voluble floating crap game in this man's town. There were seven or eight faithful participants, a dozen occasional contributors, and a half-dozen other critical voyeurs—and there were many problems, obstacles, disadvantages. In the interests of concentration and simplification, the group talked largely in terms of a single situation—an introductory program for first-year

---

* Presented in San Francisco on 30 June 1972. Reprinted from *ADE Bulletin*, No. 34 (Sept. 1972), pp. 62–64.

students suitable, with modifications, for use in any existing American academic institution, elitist or community-oriented. Despite this effort to limit or contain the subject, the members of the core group were not of one mind about which kind of interdisciplinary work—which model or style—is "best." Furthermore, there's been no time to circulate the present document among the members for amendment and criticism. What follows, in other words, is one man's perception of a continuing group discussion that appeared to produce a number of important points of agreement, but that couldn't by any means be said to have "closed the subject" or "finished the conversation."

Points of Consensus

We believe that the development and implementation of effective interdisciplinary programs involving imaginative literature is a matter of urgent priority for the nation's college and university language and literature departments. One reason for this urgency is, of course, our interest in self-preservation. There has been a steady erosion in the viability—as measured by students, younger faculty and the general public—of the curricular patterns of most contemporary, "orthodox" English departments. What is more, there is evidence—witness the language of the recently enacted legislation creating the National Institute of Education— evidence that present patterns for the study of reading and writing are perceived as utterly remote from contemporary need by those who will wield substantive power in the field of educational research in the decades ahead. Speaking bluntly, there is ground for believing that the new "educational Establishment" in process of creation intends to bypass the traditional study of "English" entirely.

But these considerations of self-preservation are trivial, as we see them, compared with the consequences for the national life as a whole of the waste of the great intellectual resource called "imaginative literature," imaginative creation in the verbal arts. America's present agonies—the rents in its social fabric, the country's cruelty and clumsiness abroad and at home—are exacerbated by the obliviousness of men of power to the uses and functions of the personal imagination, and by the lack of training in sympathetic penetration of the inner psychological realities of lives different from one's own. The primary urgency, in short, for the reconstitution of "English" isn't self-preservation for self-preservation's sake; it is, instead, the national need for command of those invaluable intellectual resources which are, in some sense, in our custodianship.

Calling for change and reconstitution is one thing, however—breathes there a person in the whole landscape of contemporary education who doesn't proclaim himself or herself as a supporter of change? It's one thing to call for change, and quite another to develop and evaluate new models of performance, and to proceed from these to the assessment of the kinds of structural modification essential for the nourishment of new forms. The members of this workshop recognize and value a variety of interdisciplinary forms, while at the same time believing with some passion that mere patchings-together of existing disciplines—mere collections of "various points of view" without purposeful interaction among them—is no advance over the past. We are convinced that success in reinvigorating awareness of the uses of imaginative power can be achieved by work shaped by a governing concept—as, for example, by the concept of culture that serves as a center for the American Studies and English programs at UC (Davis). Success can also be achieved by interdisciplinary work that is thematically ordered—as, for example, through a focus on "Freedom and Anarchy," or "The Search for Human Values." And there is a third focus—it can be called situational, and aims at the reconstruction of human experience from the perspective of its innerness— that appears promising to us.

We are in agreement, further, that success *cannot* be achieved except if the interdisciplinary ventures are understood from the start as requiring transformations of structure, significant realignments of relations between teacher and students, administration and faculty, college and community. Commitment by the student to a view of himself as passive "recipient," commitment by administrations to inflexible modes of assessing teaching loads, self-conceptions by teachers that imply all-knowingness or the notion that the act of teaching doesn't necessitate *continual* self-transformation—all these are major obstacles to effective work of the sort vital now.

Our central belief, however, is that initial preoccupation either with structural change or with debate about which model is "best" would be a mistake. The essential for us is a fresh address to the real authority of our subject: its witness to the power and complexity of individual human feeling, its capacity to classify "details of feeling" (in Tolstoi's great phrase), its challenge to the myth of "mass men." Our "field" involves centrally the question, What is the human creature like in his particularity? What goes on inside other people? What, in common or uncommon situations, is the inner truth of experience as shown by individuals? No adequate answers to those questions can be given without consideration of public, historical, economic, "objective" environmental forces. But neither can an adequate answer be developed without consideration of the inner, grainy, first-hand, personal response—the stuff of imaginative literature. In our view it is this complementarity of the forms of knowledge that provides the basis—the ultimate rationale—of interdisciplinary study. Only when departments of English commit themselves to act in full accordance with it can we justify ourselves and begin to play the kind of role in the national life that our "materials"—Shakespeare or Conrad or Keats—summon us to play, and that we have too long dodged or fudged. In sum, we are saying that interdisciplinary work is vital to the future both of English departments and of "community" in the large; and we are saying that, for such work to have genuine meaning, it must be founded on a rediscovery and reconstruction of the substantive realities of our subject.

Benjamin DeMott
Amherst College

San Francisco Resolutions

The San Francisco ADE Seminar passed the following resolutions:

1. With a USOE grant, the Association of Departments of English has sponsored four regional Seminars on English and Interdisciplinary Studies during the academic year 1971–72. These Seminars have made evident the interest of English departments in interdisciplinary programs. Such interest exists, as well, in other departments in most colleges and universities. Most chairmen have come to see that departmental and student concerns lie in creating educational programs which will create bridges among departments and form meaningful patterns for integrating knowledge for students. In no area are such programs more needed than in teacher preparation in which language study, reading, writing, and the study of literature all intertwine and in which cooperation among departments of English, film, drama, speech, linguistics, for example, seems inevitable.

Accordingly, the chairmen of the San Francisco ADE resolve that it is the responsibility of English departments and especially of chairmen to foster responsible, responsive teacher-education programs which incorporate the best curriculum research and the best of interdisciplinary study.

2. Be it resolved that the ADE Seminar participants urge the ADE to collaborate with Alan Hollingsworth in the preparation and presentation of a Reading/Writing Seminar session at the 1972 Modern Language Association National Convention. The purpose of the Seminar would be to make available to the Modern Language Association constituency at large a methodology and related reading materials and information suited to the ongoing concerns of writing, reading, and English department teacher-training at the college level. We particularly urge that the proposed seminar at the MLA National Convention give further explication of the Chomsky/Goodman methodology.

3. English chairmen should take the initiative on their respective campuses to establish committees consisting of representatives from foreign languages, English, linguistics, speech, theater, communications, and comparative literature departments for the purpose of strengthening and improving the teaching of language and literature and of reassessing the role of language and literature in the institutional curriculum.

4. A joint ADE-ADFL Forum should be scheduled as a part of the program of the 1972 MLA Annual Convention in New York on the topic of interdepartmental cooperation in the teaching of language and literature; the Forum should be followed by workshops on such special problems as (1) interdepartmental courses and programs in general education, (2) interdepartmental cooperation in the preparation of majors, (3) interdepartmental cooperation in the development of new programs and curricula, and (4) interdepartmental cooperation in graduate programs.

5. Joint ADE-ADFL seminars on interdepartmental cooperation in the teaching of language and literature should be scheduled in 1972–73.

6. Increasingly, institutions of higher education are granting credit for courses in writing through the College Level Examination Program. Since serious doubt exists as to the suitability of substituting CLEP for courses in composition, the participants at the San Francisco ADE Seminar urge the executive committee of MLA to evaluate CLEP in a special seminar at the New York MLA Convention in 1972. The participants further urge that NCTE and CCCC also engage in a similar study.